378
f 267a

DATE DUE

DEC 10 1993			
NOV 24 1994			
DEC 1 1 2009			

DEMCO

APPROACHES TO
EDUCATION FOR CHARACTER

STRATEGIES FOR CHANGE

IN HIGHER EDUCATION

THE PAPERS included in this volume were prepared for and discussed at the seventeenth meeting of the Conference on Science, Philosophy and Religion in Their Relation to the Democratic Way of Life, which was held at Loyola University Center in Chicago, Illinois, on August 29, 30, and 31, 1966. The Conference theme was "Education for Character: Strategies for Change in Higher Education." Each paper represents only the opinion of the individual writer. The authors of papers are listed on pages 403–405.

Symposia of the Conference on Science, Philosophy and Religion are listed on pages 407–409. A report on the Conference as a whole is given in the Appendix.

This is a Jacob Ziskind Memorial publication.

Approaches to
Education for Character

STRATEGIES FOR CHANGE IN
HIGHER EDUCATION

Edited by
CLARENCE H. FAUST *and* JESSICA FEINGOLD

Published for the
CONFERENCE ON SCIENCE, PHILOSOPHY AND
RELIGION *by* COLUMBIA UNIVERSITY PRESS
NEW YORK AND LONDON 1969

Clarence H. Faust (retired) was formerly Vice-President of
the Ford Foundation and President of the Fund for the
Advancement of Education. Jessica Feingold is Director
of The Institute for Religious and Social Studies, The
Jewish Theological Seminary of America.

Library of Congress Catalog Card Number: 70-83386
Copyright © 1969
by the Conference on Science, Philosophy and Religion
in Their Relation to the Democratic Way of Life, Inc.
3080 Broadway, New York City
Printed in the United States of America

PREFACE

by Louis Finkelstein

FOR TWENTY-EIGHT YEARS participation in the Conference on Science, Philosophy and Religion has provided me with vital education for which I cannot express adequate thanks. There is no way to describe the stimulation received from association with Conference members, or to list their important contributions to its striving for collective wisdom.

However, in grateful and affectionate memorial to Lyman Bryson, for many fruitful years Honorary President and Chairman of The Conference Executive Committee, The Conference on Science, Philosophy and Religion Lecture was renamed for him, The First Lyman Bryson Lecture being presented by Richard McKeon on August 30, 1960. Fellow officers of the organization share my satisfaction that The Second Lyman Bryson Lecture was given by Clarence H. Faust on August 30, 1966, and insisted that this notable paper, "Some Reflections on Education and the Formation of Character," be printed in this volume.

Beyond that, we deeply appreciate his willingness to serve as editor of this eighteenth Conference symposium, with the assistance of Jessica Feingold, whose help has again been indispensable in every phase of the Conference activity.

Distinguished intellectual and religious centers, such as the American Philosophical Society, Columbia University, Harvard University, and The University of Chicago, have been hosts to the Conference. In 1966 we were particularly fortunate to meet at Loyola University Center, Chicago. That is reason for gratitude, not only to Loyola University but to the officers of the Charles Weinfeld Memorial Foundation, especially its President, Melvan M. Jacobs, who made possible the return of the Conference to Chicago after twenty years.

Although an independent institution, chartered by the State of

New York, since its preliminary discussions in 1939 the Conference has been supported by The Institute for Religious and Social Studies of The Jewish Theological Seminary of America which continues to house and maintain the Conference administration and to underwrite its publications.

To quote Alan M. Stroock, then Chairman of the Seminary's Board of Directors:

> If the search for truth is a valid goal for the Seminary—and it is; if Judaism (like other religions) with its respect for the sanctity of the individual and his right to approach God in his own way, has been a catalyst, bringing men and women together in this important venture—and it has; then the goals of the Seminary are in no small part fulfilled by its relationship to the Conference on Science, Philosophy and Religion.

> Other members of the Seminary Board and of the Faculty share my hope that we may be privileged to help so the work and influence of the Conference will be deepened, yet expanded, to focus on fundamental philosophic and spiritual issues the wisdom of Africa, the Middle East, and the Far East, as well as Europe and both Americas.

May, 1967

INTRODUCTION

by the Editors

I.

OPENING the Seventeenth Conference on Science, Philosophy and Religion, source of this compendium, Harold D. Lasswell, Chairman of the Executive Committee, said:

To speak briefly in very broad outlines of the purposes and the history of the Conference, the initiative was taken in 1939 by Chancellor Louis Finkelstein, who was concerned with creating a continuing vehicle which would make it possible for men and women of diverse specialized backgrounds and varied constituencies to come together for the discovery and consideration of common problems. Hence, the extraordinary range in terms of identifications with faith, identifications with intellectual concerns, and science, biology, physics, social sciences, scholars, in the sense of theologians, specialists in philosophy, and the humanities.

What has happened during these years since 1939? It would not be possible to present any very well-documented appraisal of what the impact of the Conference has been. We can, however, assert that one of the major purposes has been to influence the frame of mind and approach of those who directly participate. Consequently, if one were attempting to assess the impact of a conference such as this, it would have to be sought in whatever indications there are of whether this kind of experience and interchange has in any way contributed to the discovery of common problems by the specialists who are involved.

Of course, after a Conference experience everyone returns to his special obligations and constituencies, and has all kinds of opportunities to make effective or ineffective use of whatever insights have been stimulated by this kind of exchange.

In addition to the immediate impacts on those who participate directly, there have been many indirect consequences which are to be attributed in part to the publications. These publications have met wide and varied reception and multiple use, and, once again, it is not easy to assess the direction of the effect. We can, however, indicate that there has been a rising use of materials that attempt to formulate common problems in the diversified frame of reference that characterizes an attempt of this kind.

If you will look over the history of Conference publications, you will see that there is quite a discernible shift in the type of emphasis. At the very beginning, everyone was impressed by the appearance in Europe of the danger and threat which was at that time formulated in the Nazis.

As the years have passed, the Conference has engaged itself in the discussion of pressing problems of public policy. It also engaged in discussions which were effected by these considerations, but which came as a byproduct of the efforts at common discussion and problemsolving under these circumstances.

There has been, in general, a movement in the direction of consideration of the more permanent and continuing issues that arise in undertaking to deal with a society of the kind and in the sort of world in which we are involved.

The present Conference does express this. It expresses not only a concern for a problem that is continuing, the problem of characterizing character and of formulating strategies for dealing with it, but the emphasis here is increasingly in the direction of discussing kinds of problems about which we, ourselves, can do something directly. Consequently, we are not gathered here simply to exchange generalized definitions of the term "character." We are not here entirely to formulate the wideranging questions that our common civilization allows us to propose.

We do have a somewhat selective frame of reference, and that is this. Our responsibility as educators, concerned especially for advanced education, is in the university and professional school world. The question, then, that is formulated for our consideration is in terms of our own understanding of what the opportunities and the agenda may be that is appropriate for the conduct of educational preparation and training in our society.

II.

Exploring so basic and universal a problem as education for character it would be unrealistic to expect study in depth or even superficial consideration of even the most serious aspects of the need and ways to approach the goal, were it possible to articulate the goal itself.

Therefore those who organized the Chicago meetings of the Conference saw them as a first step on a long, perhaps never-ending road, and the editors hope this book will open, rather than close, a study which demands the greatest possible involvement by the greatest possible diversity of talent and experience.

Analysis of the nature of responsibility (Albert Hofstadter), particularities of civil education in our technoscientific age (Harold D. Lasswell), character and the arts and disciplines (Richard McKeon) provide background. School and college in relation to social change (Daniel Bell), moral codes and teacher education (Arthur W. Foshay), inculcation of responsible behavior (Robert J. Havighurst), urban crises in the Northern United States (Bernard Mackler and Peter M. Elkin), are topics indicating the many complicated issues which require thought and action. Chapters on the ethical influence of specialized professional training for public service (Stephen K. Bailey), the law (Wagner P. Thielens, Jr.), business and management (Edgar H. Schein) open paths for further investigation into other areas of our postgraduate system. That for theologians and clergymen—regardless of denomination—is perhaps changing more rapidly than in many generations, according to the papers by Robert O. Johann, S.J., Robert W. Lynn, and Seymour Siegel.

The variety of approaches which might affect education for character is indicated by papers on language consciousness (Arthur J. Brodbeck), the mass media (Louis G. Cowan), a graduate seminar on personal growth (Willis W. Harman), LSD-25 (John C. Lilly), and the impact on psychiatric resident physicians of an effort to share power in the hospital community (Robert Rubenstein and Harold D. Lasswell). Moral training of police and of the growing Armed Forces should not be neglected, Michael J. Murphy and Ben M. Zeff show us. While the educational problem is both gigantic and complex at home, Daniel Lerner's article is important reminder of the international scene which must be investigated.

Papers on the effects of racial discrimination on character training had been expected from Horace R. Cayton and Joshua M. Morse, but they were prevented by illness from completing manuscripts for publication. Conference Chairmen are most appreciative of the excellent draft by Donald A. Bloch regarding family aspects of education for character, and that by Daniel A. Greenberg on the education of scientists, which stimulated discussion at the Chicago sessions, but have been omitted here because of the authors' dissatisfaction with their own material, contrary to the opinion of their readers. These themes require publication.

III.

On behalf of all Conference officers the editors express deep gratitude to all who participated in the program, to those who attended the sessions, to the original writers, to the officers and staff of Loyola University Center which extended gracious hospitality to the Conference gathering, and above all to Chancellor Louis Finkelstein of The Jewish Theological Seminary of America—the President of the Conference.

The 1966 oral proceedings were recorded; they are available at the Conference offices to qualified students.

The Seventeenth Conference and eighteenth symposium (two volumes were produced from the Sixteenth Conference) will have been well worth the effort invested by so many distinguished men, if it has lit a candle in the search for the character needed to create a better world.

May, 1967

CONTENTS

Contents   *xiii*

APPROACHES TO
EDUCATION FOR CHARACTER

STRATEGIES FOR CHANGE

IN HIGHER EDUCATION

I. SOME BACKGROUND
FOR DISCUSSION OF
EDUCATION FOR CHARACTER

Chapter 1. THE STRUCTURE AND GROUND OF RESPONSIBILITY

by Albert Hofstadter

I. Responsibility as Trustworthiness

THE ESSENTIAL problem regarding education and responsible behavior is that of education *for* responsible behavior. But behavior is not merely a single act and the problem of education does not merely concern the enabling of a single act of responsibility, as for instance the prompt repayment of a loan from a friend. If we think of education for behavior, we think of the cultivation of more or less permanent traits of the person. Education *for* responsible behavior is the educing *of* responsibility as a trait of personal character; a quality or disposition that manifests itself over a lifetime (or close to it) in a wide variety of responsible acts.

In this personal sense we can speak of responsibility as consisting in the trustworthiness or reliability of a person in regard to burdens, trusts, offices, obligations, duties, and other charges that are laid upon him. The problem of education for responsible behavior is at core the problem of the cultivation and development in the person of such trustworthiness or reliability as an enduring trait of his character.

It is more nearly accurate to speak here of trustworthiness than of reliability. Trustworthiness is eminently a characteristic of persons although we also attribute it to things like statements or accounts (or even to a personal instrument, like a sword); reliability is more closely a generic character of both persons and things. Accordingly, trustworthiness emphasizes the voluntary nature of the moral agent more than does reliability. A person can be *en*trusted with a trust, not so a thing; if the warrior regards his sword as trusty, it is because he animates it with a living metaphor. We rely on a thing such as an instrument—*e.g.,* the steering mechanism of an auto driven at high speed—because we believe in its intrinsic stability, its unchangingness as possessor of the feature in question. The inner stability that belongs to the trustworthy person, however, is a stability in the performance of freely willed action—a steadfastness of the free moral being.

In addition, trustworthiness has two aspects, one dependent on the other: that of fitness, ability, or suitability for being trusted, and that of worthiness to be trusted. Taking the second first, trustworthiness is worthiness of trust, reliance, dependence. The trustworthy person *merits* being entrusted with a trust. This aspect of the concept represents our valuation of the person on the ground of his dependability as a free moral agent, and it points to his possession of a value of the nature of personal worth and dignity which we intend in viewing him as meritorious. That is an essential part of our concept of responsibility, from the prospect of trustworthiness, as a merit.

Worthiness to be trusted, and hence entrusted with a trust, is itself grounded on the first aspect of trustworthiness, namely, fitness, ability, or suitability for being trusted. This is the aspect stressed by the concept of reliability—a reliable person is one who may be relied upon to do what he is supposed to do. If he tells us something, then it will be, to the best of his ability, true; for telling presupposes the purport of being true, and he may be depended upon to try to realize that purport. If he is given a rightful order, then he will try to execute it faithfully. And so on. Reliability in general, in persons as well as in things, suggests a certain stability or consistency. In the person, this consistency is the constancy of his endeavor to do what he is supposed to do. Where we find such constancy and consistency of character and behavior, we recognize that the person *can* be relied upon without our being disappointed, *i.e.,* he is *fit or suitable* for reliance; and accordingly he figures as being reliable in the context of responsibility—reliable as a person entrusted with a trust.

This is the basic feature in responsibility as a trait of character, this intrinsic moral constancy that manifests itself in the consistency of the person's behavioral endeavors to fulfil his obligations. It is the ground in being of the personal value or worth of responsibility as a virtue of the moral character. Now the question of education for responsibility is part of the general question, raised in Plato's *Protagoras* and *Meno,* of how virtue can be acquired and whether it can be taught. Our observation of the distinction between the aspects of worthiness and fitness to be trusted helps to give point to this question. What would have to be acquired and taught is not the merit or worthiness itself but the inner consistency of moral being by which the person directs himself freely and steadily toward the fulfilment of his obligations and which is the primary ground of our factual trust in him and of our valuation of him as being worthy of our trust.

Education for responsible behavior, then, has to do with the cultivation of this moral trait of character. The trait is complex. It is a unity that builds up in the joint process of differentiating and integrating two other essential features of responsibility. These two features are related to liability in regard to a charge and to capacity in regard to the discharge of the charge. Before naming and discussing these features it is necessary to note the strategic position of charge in the structure of responsibility. The word "charge" is the most useful general word we can find to convey this strategic position. It covers that *for* which a person is responsible, being the generic name for the objective content of our liability. We may be charged with the management of a trust, the custody of a person, the filling of an office, the satisfaction of an obligation, the performance of a duty, the execution of an order, the taking to heart of an exhortation, the making good of a violation. All these and many others are charges laid upon us, the fulfilment of which is the discharge of the charge. The charge is laid upon us as our burden. What we do when we act responsibly in regard to the charge is to discharge it—to unburden or free ourselves of the charge in an appropriate manner, not by throwing it off but by fulfilling it faithfully. Thus at the center of the concept of responsibility there lies the concept of the faithful discharge of charge, and responsibility itself as a personal trait may be defined as *the fitness, based on the constancy of his endeavor to discharge his charges faithfully, of the person to be entrusted with the discharge of charges.*

II. Two Basic Features of Responsibility: *Responsiveness and Readiness*

Because of its pivotal role in responsibility we must lay bare the structure of the faithful discharge of charge. Emphasis should be placed on the faithfulness of the discharge, for it is not just the action

of discharge but more decisively their underlying intention and motivation that make behavior and character responsible. Faithfulness of
discharge shows that the self is really being responsible and not merely
assuming the appearance of responsibility.

The essential character of faithfulness is that of constant, steady
devotion and loyalty to the given cause, which latter is here exactly the
basic trust entrusted to us, namely, the discharging of charges. How is
such faithfulness to one's trust shown? What are its fundamental features? They are the two basic features mentioned earlier, the one as
relating to liability in regard to a charge and the other to capacity in
regard to the discharging of the charge. They may be called responsiveness to liability and readiness to act in discharge, or more briefly,
responsiveness and readiness. It is through the steady interplay of his
responsiveness and readiness that a person functions as faithful, and
thus actualizes responsibility as a trait of his character and behavior.
Through responsiveness he harkens to the call of the world in so far as
the world is the context and source of the charge that is imposed upon
him. Through readiness he brings to bear his own capacities as a self-
determining and competent agent upon the task of discharging that
charge. Thus the interplay of responsiveness and readiness in the person is a process by which he brings the world and his own self into
reciprocal operation in the specific form of the faithful discharging of
charge. It is, in other words, a process in which the person realizes a
certain dimension of his own being (attaining to a certain level of
truth of his own being) in the very act of interrelating the world's
demand and the self's capacity.

III. The Structure of Responsiveness

Response is a general category of behavior. In the context of responsibility it refers to our responses to the charges or obligations that are
presented to us as ours and it includes our behavior not only in accepting, rejecting, or attempting to modify the charges but also in en-
deavoring to effect their discharge. Responsiveness, however, is not to
be identified with this general tendency of response. I use the word
"responsiveness" here in its specialized sense, according to which to be
responsive to something is to be sensitive, impressionable, and receptive

toward it, to be inclined to answer it and be amenable to it, to react to it in harmony and sympathy. It is a combination of perceptive capacity and openness—including flexibility, pliability, and adaptability as well —of heart, mind, and will. As regards responsibility this means the sensitive, receptive, understanding perception of charges and the adaptable, obedient reception of the liabilities they impose on the self.

Responsiveness in this sense is the self's willing and understanding disposition to harken to the demands made upon it by charges assigned to it. It is the heeding, or careful attention, that the self accords to those demands. Suppose that it is our moral obligation to be mindful of the welfare of others. Responsiveness in this case means that we do not merely grant this obligation grudgingly but that, in right order and right degree, we open our vision and our heart to the plight of others and willingly assume the charge of being mindful of their welfare as a personal liability of our own.

The important notion here is that of *the intelligent, sympathetic, and willing assumption of a charge as a personal liability*. It is this that constitutes the responsiveness in responsibility. What we respond to, in being responsible, is the charge that calls upon our mind, heart, and will with the voice of obligation. The charge—to be mindful of others' welfare, to repay one's debt, to be honest and efficacious in public office, to devote oneself sincerely to the education of one's pupils—calls upon us, claims our acceptance of it as being due to it, summons us to give ourselves over into accord with it. This call of the charge appears to us as the imposing of a liability. It tells us that we are liable in regard to the charge—not only susceptible to it, as being exposed to it as a subject, but bound to accept it as a burden that belongs to us as our own, and hence answerable and accountable in regard to it.

What we are responsive to—what we answer to in being responsible —is this call to us by the charge to assume liability for its discharge. It points to liability as to a moral role that we are requested (in a unity of solicitation and demand) to take upon ourselves. Liability is the decisive mediating factor between the charge and the personal self. It is how the self exists as being the subject of a charge. To be the subject of a charge, *e.g.,* to be a debtor, is not merely to have the charge as a neutral attribute or content, in the way in which a leaf is green or a bottle contains ink. It is to exist as being liable for the debt (charge), *i.e.,* as answerable and accountable for its repayment (discharge). Liability thus belongs to the sphere of finite personal being, the being of a personal self that is both competent and required to exist, in one direction of its being, as the subject of requirement, solicitation, command that come from beyond the self in the form of a call to self-commitment to answerability and accountability. It is by means of this kind of self-limitation through relationship to an other that the finite self is enabled to be, in one important dimension of its being.

The essential content of liability is answerability or accountability. In the end these two words signify the same thing—the susceptibility, by right, of being called to account. If as treasurer I am entrusted with the funds of an organization, I am answerable or accountable for what happens to them. I can rightfully be called upon by the proper authorities (whether the members, the officers, or the state government) to give a statement or explanation of what I have done with the funds and, in case of a violation of the trust, to lie open to retributive or other reactive treatment. In being requested to accept the office of treasurer I am being asked to take the charge upon myself in assuming (among other obligations) this liability to the call to answer, account for, undergo retribution, etc. And in assuming the responsibility I take this accountability upon myself as my own, at once exposing and limiting my being in this definite direction.

Applied to the concept of responsibility this implies that the responsiveness in responsibility is *the intelligent, sympathetic, and willing assumption of answerability and accountability for behavior that counts as the discharging of charges.* It is through this disposition to take upon myself the burden of answering or accounting for my behavior—including particularly the giving of justifying reasons, causes, or grounds and the accepting of just retribution or other reactive treatment and cost—that I am able to relate my personal self to the charges that emanate from that self's world. Responsiveness is the factor in me that bridges the gap between my self and the moral world beyond. It is how I *actively receive* the world as a world germane to my being as a moral personal self.

Such activeness of reception—a receiving which is an acting through and through—differentiates a living response from a nonliving one; and when what is received is a charge and the liability of being answerable and accountable for its proper discharge, the reception is of the peculiar nature of personal activity, intentionalistic with the full concrete intentionality of the person's mind, heart, and will. It is not a merely passive undergoing of compulsion from without. Our liabilities need not be in themselves fetters that restrain our spontaneous activity as personal beings, so long as they are chosen and willed by us in an independent and free acceptance of the charge with all the responsibilities that accompany it. Harkening to the call of a charge that we identify as ours is listening to it in order to heed and obey it. No liability can ever be merely forced upon me. The externalities of conforming with it can, indeed, be imposed, as by threat of condemnation, ostracism, a fine, a prison sentence, but not the heedful obedient harkening that constitutes the personal act of assumption of accountability.

Responsiveness, therefore, is the disposition toward and the power of free acceptance of liability for a charge, and hence of accountability for its discharge, that only the personal being can possess and that is his avenue of access to all the spheres of obligation that constitute in the widest sense the moral dimension of the world.

IV. The Structure of Readiness

By responsiveness, the personal subject relates himself through the assumption of liabilities to the charges that come to him from the moral world. By readiness, he relates himself through his fitness or competence to the discharging of charge that is required of him. Readiness is thus the counterpart of responsiveness as competence is the counterpart of liability. The word "readiness" appears here in the specialized sense of the person's preparedness to call on himself to exercise his competence faithfully in the discharge of obligations. In this sense readiness is the peculiar dispositional trend that relates the responsible subject to himself, as responsiveness is the peculiar dispositional trend that relates him to the world's spheres of obligation.

In a broad sense readiness includes the fitness or competency required for the assumption and fulfilment of a given charge. I am ready to carry out the duties of a citizen, a student, a lawyer, a physician, or a judge, only if I have developed the competence to do so. But in a narrower sense, which is the one chosen here, readiness refers exclusively to that state of preparation in mind, heart, and will to set oneself into action—that integral state of preparedness of intellectual, affective, and conative intention—that is necessary for the faithful discharge of charges. This means that the person must be prepared to call on his own powers of action (fitness, competence) with a demand that is adequate to his liability. As the world calls on him by way of its trust and accompanying liability, so he must call on himself by way of the readiness of his spirit to undertake its task.

One of the responsibilities of a father toward his son is that of serving as an ethical exemplar. Whether the son is to follow that example is a matter of the son's own responsibility. But the obligation of the father is clear: in his speech and behavior toward and in the eyes of his son, he ought to be authentically, and as well as he can be, a prototype of morally valid being. It is true that a like obligation falls upon all men in all concerns of life, not simply in fatherhood. Still, when a man becomes a father this obligation gets an access of stringency, and so far as a man becomes aware of his fatherhood so far is his awareness of a liability in this regard strengthened. So much is this the case that the word "father" attracts to itself transferred significances like "a distinguished example or teacher," "one who deserves filial reverence," "leading man," and "trusted leader."

The readiness of a man to discharge the responsibility of fatherhood therefore includes being prepared in mind, heart, and will to enact the role of ethical exemplar for his son. This is not a matter of taking on an imaginary role as in play acting. It is a matter of seriously being ethical and of enabling one's son to behold, in the one to whom he owes his coming into the world and to whom he looks and entrusts himself for guidance in life, a living model after whom he may shape his own moral being. Consequently the readiness is a readiness to be ethical in actuality and not merely in appearance, to function authentically in the role of example, teacher, friend, and trusted guide, and thus to be the worthy object of filial reverence and faith.

No one can call upon himself with a light mind to behave in this way. Even in this single aspect fatherhood is a demanding liability and confronts the father with stern requirements at least equal to its pleasures. Yet though the demand is serious, the father who is genuinely ready for his responsibility must be unhesitating, unreluctant, eagerly disposed, and prompt both to move into action here and to persevere. *Readiness is a willing and nerved determination to act resolutely in the requisite path of the discharge.* Obviously it includes also the preparedness to undergo willingly the costs as well as to enjoy the fruits of this action.

As determination to act, readiness presupposes capacity to act, especially in the sense of fitness, or competence and qualification, for the action in question. Every responsibility carries with it its own requirements as to the person's capacity to discharge the charge. If I contract to make a purchase I must have the means of delivering the selling price; if I assume a debt to be repaid at a certain time I must be able to hand over the amount at that time; if I set myself up as a clergyman I must have the competence to deal faithfully with the people of the parish entrusted to my care; if I wish to be a teacher I have the obligation to develop and use effective pedagogical methods. All the good intentions in the world are futile without the essential fitness of the agent of responsibility, and therefore no one is or can be responsible without adequate preparation in competency for his tasks. It is even true to say that the degree to which one can be responsible varies with the degree to which one has powers, qualifications, and talents that can be developed and used effectively for his task. Not everyone can be a responsible astronaut, philosopher, or mayor. No one but a son of God could validly assume the responsibility of being a ransom for man's guilt.

There would be no point in attempting to give a detailed discussion in this place of the forms and dimensions of fitness for the discharge of charges. We may however observe that this fitness has both a general and special component. Because responsibility, as we are examining it, is a generic character trait, it relates to a wide variety of actions required for the discharge of a wide variety of charges. It therefore has a universal aspect so far as it is the same trait that manifests itself in the different undertakings, and a particular aspect so far as the trait manifests itself in this or that particular variety of undertakings (leaving aside the question of the individuation of it in this or that individual situation). So far as I have developed responsibility as a genuine trait of my character, so far will I strive to be genuinely responsible in regard to my liabilities as a man, a citizen, a husband, a father, a worker, a friend. These different responsibilities are not logically derivative from my responsibility as a pervasive character trait. In them the character trait receives an evolution into definiteness. The general and particular stand here in an organic, dialectical relationship. They are necessary to the growth and persistence of each other. My responsibility of character grows with the attainment of responsibilities as man, citizen, husband, etc., and these particular responsibilities evolve with the evolution of my character.

For the general character of responsibility I require a certain general competence. I must be a free, self-determining moral agent, living and acting in and through those capacities and impulses of mind, heart, and will that qualify me to respond to my trusts and account for my conduct in discharging them. I must be able to understand all the different charges that devolve upon me in my varied social roles, and I must be able to envision and take the measure of the values affected by my commissions and omissions of acts in discharge. I must be able to be moved and to move toward the realization of positive values and deterred by the prevision of negative values and sanctions. On the other hand, for each special role and each particular charge I need to have also the particular qualities, positions, possessions, and powers that qualify me for proper discharge of the obligation. To pay my debts I must have a dependable source of income; to be a voter I must come of age; to be a student I must master adequate study methods; to be any kind of professional—economist, lawyer, dentist, engineer—I need special training in the vocation and perhaps even a license; to perform the marriage ceremony I must be authorized by the state.

In its relation to such fitness, readiness can be redefined as *the willing and nerved determination to summon the self, as the fit and competent agent of discharge, to a resolute response to its charge.* It is a being prepared to call upon the self as a personal moral agent to activate its resources for its life in the world. The self must emerge from the innocence of its privacy and enter into the experience of the historical world of persons—a world of obligations, possibilities, dangers, and opportunities. Its responsibility is the moral competence to exercise its being in that world in a manner that validates its own personal truth.

V. Responsibility as Moral Competence

Responsibility as a personal trait has been defined above as the person's fitness to be entrusted with the discharge of charges, based on the constancy of his endeavor to discharge his charges faithfully. This endeavor to discharge charges faithfully, which lies at the heart of responsibility, is a living interplay of responsiveness and readiness. Through his responsiveness the person reaches out toward the world, heedfully listening to its calls, and thereby opens a path of access of the world to himself in his being as a person, by the assumption of accountability for acting in the discharge of a given charge. Through his readiness he reaches down into himself, calling upon his own personal powers, and thereby opens a path of access of himself to himself and to the world in his action as a person, in the resolute execution of his trust. These two come together into their intrinsically intended interplay in the person's attempt to differentiate them and combine them into a single behavioral process: the faithful discharge of a charge sincerely assumed.

Such a behavioral process is an act of personal responsibility. Both the assumption of accountability and the resolute active endeavor are kept in force throughout the process, and their steady interrelation, playing into each other, keeping mutually in touch, constitutes the faithfulness in the act. *Responsibility as a character-trait is just this faithfulness made into a constant, abiding perseverance, a diligent and stable steadfastness in keeping both paths open for communication and thus keeping the self in an enduring symbiosis with both its world and itself in their rightful relation.* If we are to think of the trait of responsibility as the person's moral competence to exercise his being in relation to the world as source and context of obligations, then this competence must be identified as precisely the perseverance and steadfastness that give faithfulness its hold in existence.

What are the roots of this moral competence? They are threefold and one, as may be seen from the structure of responsiveness, readiness, and the interplay of the two. The capacities and impulses that form the foundation of our general moral competence, and that concretely pervade all our special competences, are not merely intellectual in nature.

No mere application of logical thinking and scientific method—or of what is sometimes called the "method of intelligence"—can suffice to determine the quality, quantity, or direction of my readiness to discharge a charge, any more than it can determine my responsiveness to the charge and its correlative liability in the first place. The intelligence that enters into both readiness to act and responsiveness to liability is a morally qualified intelligence at whose core there is a realized perception of the values and obligations in the situation. But in addition to intelligence, both feeling and will participate essentially in the structure; and, moreover, moral intelligence, feeling, and will interpenetrate each other. These are the roots of faithfulness and they intertwine into the upright stock that bears the whole of responsibility. They are grounded in the three basic dimensions of human being: cognitive, affective, and conative. This is a matter of decisive significance for the problem of education for responsibility, since it entails that education here has to direct itself toward the joint cultivation of all three roots.

One element in our general social obligation toward others is gratitude. To be suitably grateful for kindnesses proffered and benefits received is an essential constituent of the moral dimension of our sociality. Being suitably grateful would therefore be an instance of the exercise of responsibility. A responsible person displays his responsibility when, answering to a kindness proffered or a benefit received, he is responsive to the liability connected with the receipt of this favor and ready to discharge faithfully the charge bound up with that liability.

(People of independent or proud spirit find it uncomfortable to have to be grateful. They experience it as close to a fawning servility. Hence on principle they try to avoid being the recipient of a benefit and insist on paying immediately for everything they get. But the discomfort of gratitude in such persons does not prove it to be anything other than obligatory. It shows only that they find the obligation onerous and perhaps even threatening to their sense of human dignity.)

The exercise of gratitude, then, is the obligation or charge that falls upon us, and that we incur as a responsibility, as a result of being the object of benefaction. What is its structure? When we try to describe it we discover that it must be looked at from different angles just because it shows itself in different aspects. These aspects are not separate like the facets of a jewel; or if they are, then the jewel must be transparent so that the others may be seen through each of them. They are aspects in a more intense and intimate sense. Seeing one aspect does not hide the others from view. On the contrary, all are reflected in each, and only when all are seen as reflected in each and in all, do we begin to have a vision of the whole, the gratitude itself. This is due to the relatively high ontological level of gratitude as a form of personal actuality.

Gratitude is an integral whole of feeling, knowing, and willing. When we see it in the aspect of feeling we call it *thankfulness*. When we see it in the aspect of knowing we call it *appreciation*. And when we see it in the aspect of willing we call it *acknowledgment*. But each of these three aspects gives us the whole, namely, gratitude, in its full complexity, not just one separate side.

Thankfulness is feeling, but it is not just feeling. It is feeling, knowing, and willing all in one, but seen from the angle of feeling. It is thus a feeling that is at once, *qua* feeling, a knowing and a willing. It is identical with appreciation and acknowledgment when they are seen on their affective side. It is (affective aspect:) a warm feeling of (conative aspect:) good will toward (cognitive aspect:) one who is perceived as a benefactor. The good will and the perception are intrinsically essential features of the feeling; without them the feeling would collapse into a mere flutter.

It is the same with *appreciation*. The appreciation in gratitude is an appreciation of the benefit received and of the benefaction of the benefactor in granting it. As appreciative, gratitude is seen predominantly in its cognitive aspect. To be appreciative of a benefit one must be, in the first place, *sensitive* to it as that particular benefit. One must have an adequate awareness of it in its relevant aspects, as for instance the values and liabilities involved. Such sensitivity and awareness are the analogues in moral matters to sense-perception in the field of cognition of nature. Without moral apprehension of value, without sensitivity to and feeling for these essential objects of moral insight, no moral knowledge or authentic moral judgment is possible, because the material data necessary for them would be lacking. But there is secondly the element of *understanding* that also takes its place in appreciation and shows itself in the capacity to estimate the magnitude and importance of the values, obligations, sacrifices, benefits, consequences involved. The combination of sensitivity and estimative power gives rise to judgment, and it is especially as judgment, in which values are estimated and claims validated, that appreciation functions in gratitude.

But appreciation, although it is sensitivity, perception, estimation, and judgment, does not reduce to them alone. Its recognition of the benefit is a thankful one. Far from being a merely neutral perception of a merely intelligible value, it is a warm and, as we say, appreciative recognition of the benefit as a benefit and of the benefactor as a benefactor. Thus it is the concrete feeling of thankfulness, but seen on the side of the moral intelligence that is at work in the act of being thankful. And conversely, being thankful is precisely being appreciative of the benefaction just as what the benefaction is.

Finally, the *acknowledgment* in gratitude is an act and attitude of will, but it is not merely that. We acknowledge the benefaction in two essential and interconnected ways. We *admit* the fact of it and the validity of the correlative obligation that lies upon us and we *show* our appreciation by a suitable external form of acknowledgment. The admission of the benefaction as such is an expression of the attitude of our will, the will-to-acknowledge. The showing of appreciation occurs in the most typical way by means of an expression of thanks. The expression of thanks manifests our thankfulness (feeling). The showing of appreciation manifests our appreciation (cognition). And the expression and showing and admission all show our good will in the matter. Acknowledgment of benefit, *i.e.,* gratitude-as-volition, is thus a voluntary act, expressive of our conation in gratitude, which is at one and the same time thankfulness and appreciation, or gratitude-as-feeling and gratitude-as-knowing.

In order to be able to be grateful for a benefit a person has to be able to enact in his own existence such a triply threefold unity of moral intelligence, feeling, and will. He has to have developed sufficiently the capacity to be thankful, to appreciate, and to acknowledge, and all of them in the intertwined relationship that allows them to be one with one another in their very distinction.

Since each is essentially, not merely coincidentally, involved in the others, the cultivation of the capacity for gratitude cannot be separated out into three separate strands, as though in one room a child could be taught how to feel thankful without yet knowing how to appreciate and acknowledge a benefit, and in other rooms he could be taught appreciation and acknowledgment in equally separated ways. The capacity to feel thankful, to appreciate the values and obligations of a benefit, and to acknowledge its existence and the validity of one's own obligation—this is a *single* capacity, with a concretely spiritual unity, and can only be cultivated as such: as a single, wholly individual act of a living person.

The capacity to be grateful is one instance of responsibility understood as moral competence. Only a person who has this capacity is fit for gratitude and therefore competent in regard to the right reception of benefits. But what is true of gratitude is true of all other instances of the moral competence to be a responsible being. Study of any of the virtues connected with the faithful discharging of charges would lead to analogous conclusions. Think of the old Platonic cardinal virtues of justice, wisdom, courage, and temperance; or of such Aristotelian virtues as liberality, magnificence, pride, good temper, friendliness, truthfulness, ready wit, friendship; or of modern virtues such as brotherly love, truthfulness and uprightness, trustworthiness and fidelity, trust and faith, modesty, humility, and aloofness, and the values of social intercourse.[1] When its structure is adequately unfolded each of these turns out to be a capacity with the same type of concrete spiritual unity as that of gratitude—a triply threefold unity of moral intelligence, feeling, and will. Each has a subtly complex and differentiated unity of intention, with an intentionality that is at once emotional, insightful, and purposeful.

Aristotle points out that the name of moral virtue, *ethike,* is formed by a slight variation from the word for habit, *ethos.*[2] Habits are produced in us not by nature but by doing: "the virtues we get by first exercising them, as also happens in the case of the arts as well. For the things we have to learn before we can do them, we learn by doing them, *e.g.,* men become builders by building and lyre-players by playing the lyre; so, too, we become just by doing just acts, temperate by

[1] This latter list follows the discussion of the second group of special moral values by Nicolai Hartmann in volume II, section VI of his *Ethics,* translated by Stanton Coit, Macmillan, Co., New York, 1932.

[2] *Nichomachean Ethics,* Book II, chapter 1, translated by W. D. Ross, The Clarendon Press, Oxford, p. 1103a18.

doing temperate acts, brave by doing brave acts."[3] This concept of virtue as habit can interpose itself as a formidable obstruction to a correct view of the cultivation of responsibility, especially if we think of a habit as a matter of being accustomed to do a certain kind of thing, being wont to do it, doing it in a customary or usual way, as a result of frequent repetition. For understood in this way, which is the normal way, a habit is conceived as an act or practice that, because of its repeated performance, becomes inbred and thus fixed and automatic, a second nature. In the case of bad habits, like addiction to narcotic drugs, the fixation can be so profound that it is virtually impossible to undo again. But a mode of disposition of the soul which can be so fixed and automatic, which can remain perfect as a habit even when it has degenerated into a wholly perfunctory and unthinking performance, cannot constitute the category of such persistently vital and intelligent structures of character as the virtues. *Responsibility can never become a habit.* What becomes a habit is the dead outward form of responsible action, made into a fixed and inert shell that covers a life secretly remaining underneath.

It is, of course, the same with the arts. One does not become an artist simply as the result of forming habits. The architect who builds by habit or the poet who writes by habit (and even the shoemaker who makes shoes by habit) produces an inferior article, lacking the freshness, spontaneity, vitality, authenticity, and essential rightness that comes only of the combination of a living *tact* in operation with a living *spirit* inspiring the production and the product. Genius, even talent, can never be a habit. Not even skill can be a habit; for skill means constant aliveness to the relevant factors in the changing situation and the competence and power to turn them to one's ends. Skill is proficiency, dexterity, not usualness of performance. Skill makes use of habits but is not itself a habit. If, then, training in responsibility is like training in the arts—and in important respects it is—such training is not in habits but in the unity of feeling, insight, and endeavor, *i.e.,* in fitness and competency to be responsible. No man is an authentically creative artist who is not concerned in the depths of his person with issues that can only be resolved, or aims that can only be reached, in and through his art. No man who is not passionately concerned with

[3] *Ibid.,* pp. 1103a32–1103b2.

beauty or ugliness, tragedy or comedy, the sublime or the trivial, truth or illusion, or other comparable forms of artistic reality, can be a genuinely creative artist.

What does this imply regarding the cultivation of responsibility?

VI. The Ground of Responsibility in Care

It is with the moral competence of responsibility as it is with true artistic competence: authentic works of responsibility, having the rightness and vitality that belong to them as authentic, spring only from the tact and living spirit of genuine responsibility in the person. Only the person who is really concerned for and cares about the subjects and contents of his obligations is capable of acting responsively in regard to them. Responsiblity grows out of care as the ground of its origin. We could even say that responsibility is what care becomes actualized as, when care is unfolded into practice in the sphere of the discharge of charges. Care is the *potency* of responsibility and, conversely, responsibility is the actuality taken by care, *i.e.,* how care is differentiated into a concrete reality.

As responsibility can never be a mere automatism or habit, so care is no mere potentiality. As responsibility is feeling, intelligence, and will in a triply threefold unity of act, so care is a triply threefold unity. Indeed, care *is* the original threefold unity of human act and activity, of which responsibility is a differentiated form. If we are to think seriously about education for responsibility, we must think first and foremost about the cultivation of care itself—the cultivation, that is, of the primary ground of all genuine forms of human actuality.

Care is the basic human potency and, when itself cultivated, the fundamental human competence. It is human being in its ground, the primal unity of heart, mind, and will. Seen in the perspective of responsibility it is the ground of unity of responsiveness and readiness in trustworthiness or faithfulness. The faithful person is precisely the one who had made his care for an object into an abiding and competent inclination to take care of it. He is the one in whom the spirit of concern and solicitude has developed a vitalized and powerful tact for carrying itself out in the concrete forms of the assuming of liability and the discharging of charge. Only in the context of care does anything either matter or not matter. Only in this context is there importance or triviality, greatness or paltriness, essentiality or inessentiality, worth or worthlessness, eminence or baseness. The world is a human world only in so far as it attains to the level of participation in the categories to which these distinctions belong, categories that lie far above the ordinary subject-object distinction of the methodology of logic and scientific method, namely, the categories of life, purpose, personality, spirit, and truth.

Care can be understood in a narrow sense and in a comprehensive sense. In the narrow sense care is an unhappy state of mind in which we are oppressed, burdened, or disquieted, or undergo tension and suffering on account of fear, worry, anxiety, doubt, concern, grief, or sorrow about an object of our solicitude. Such a troubled mental state is one outstanding variety of care, an extreme and on that very account atypical variety. The supposition that care (concern, solicitude) in this narrow sense is the core of human being has led to distortions within existentialist thinking (in which, as in Heidegger's *Being and Time,* rather than being widened, this narrow sense was deepened and ontologized into a root anxiety about our nonbeing) as well as concerning the basic character of existential philosophy. Any theory that tries to make this narrow sense of care into a clue to human being falsifies itself from the very beginning—constitutes, one might say, an expressionistic distortion of the real actuality of human existence. Such a fallacy, however, does not belong to the essence of existential thinking, but only to some of its contingent historical forms.

In the comprehensive sense, care is concern or solicitude in whatever form it takes—troubled or untroubled, melancholy or gay, serious or frivolous, interested or disinterested, intense or torpid. Ordinarily we tend to stress the insistent forms. That is, we think of him who is troubled, melancholy, serious, interested, or intense as caring, and him who is untroubled, gay, frivolous, disinterested, or torpid as not caring. But these latter seemingly privative forms are as much and as purely forms of care as the seemingly positive ones. To be untroubled about something is to be in as genuine a state of solicitude as to be troubled about it. In both cases we are concerned regarding it. The difference between the two lies in quality, quantity, and direction, rather than in generic substance. The same holds for the other seemingly privative forms—gaiety, frivolity, disinterest, torpidity.

Understood in this comprehensive sense, care is the most concrete form of being that human being displays. It is consequently the supreme generic category of human existence. It is, indeed, precisely the triply threefold unity of feeling, intelligence, and will, generically and as such. If, then, we look to see how these three dimensions exist in this concrete essence of human being, we shall observe the ultimate subject for the education of the human individual as human.

In its feeling, care has the variable affective quality peculiar to the varying degrees of concern, interest, and solicitude. Hence its affective side discloses the changing pattern of *seriousness and unseriousness*. Because we are here confronted with affective phenomena, the factor of psychical distance, or degree of participation of the self in the object comes into play effectively. Differences noted above as subsisting between seemingly positive and seemingly privative forms of care are actually differences allied with differing psychical distances from the object of care. When we are psychically close to the object, as in dealing with matters of great moment, our emotional tone is one of seriousness and gravity. We find ourselves feeling sober and sedate, earnest, severe, perhaps even solemn. When the object strikes us as of lesser significance and importance, we recede from it psychically, our emotional tone eases in the direction of levity, and then we feel more light-minded, unburdened, and careless, even to the point of liveliness and gaiety, volatility and frivolity, humor and silliness; and it may also be that beyond a certain point all forms of mattering fade away entirely.

The understanding that belongs to care—and this means, consequently, the primal form of human understanding *qua* human—is best named when we first realize that it is the understanding that is native to the pattern of seriousness and unseriousness just noticed. Namely, it is the understanding of the important and the trivial as such. It is the understanding in which we comprehend and deal with what matters in all the degrees of mattering. In this form of understanding we know in terms that transcend the usual forms and categories of theoretical cognition, such as space and time, number and measure, cause and effect, systematic interrelation and statistical aggregation. This theoretical knowledge is itself embedded in (it would be more nearly accurate to say abstracted from) a more concrete context in which things show themselves to us in their possibilities of value, significance, and importance. In this concrete context a cause becomes a means and an effect an end; space becomes the arena of life and history, time the march of its drama; number and measure take the count of friends and enemies, joys and sorrows; system and chance become the order and disorder, the destiny, of a world building to a whole or falling apart. The understanding relevant to care is the understanding that grasps this world in all these features, and guides care along the course of its life within the world. It is the power to recognize values, meanings, importances in their qualities and degrees, and hence enables us to grasp actual beings in our world in their full actuality, to recognize possible ends and possible means, and to bring them together into life-paths realizable within the world's scope.

The standard name given in our language to such understanding is *wisdom*. No other name will serve as well. As a man's care is so is his wisdom, as is his wisdom so is his care: sapient or silly, profound or shallow, sober or giddy, acute or stupid, prudent or rash, judicious or eccentric, solid or fatuous. A man's wisdom—and every man in fact has his own wisdom, indeed *is* his own wisdom—is his basic intellectual competence as a man.

Finally the conative or volitional side of care presents itself in two related groups of phenomena, the phenomena of *caring-for,* which have to do with inclination and with charge. On the one hand, care is caring-for in the form of caring-about. To care for something is, on this side, to have a liking for it, to be fond of it, to find it suitable to one's taste. At deeper levels it is to esteem it, to have regard or respect for it, to love it, to revere and worship it. All these are modes of *inclination*. They determine the direction of our dispositions toward and wishes for the object of care. They fashion the shape of our preferences, show our partialities, and thus represent the subjectively qualified orientation of our will.

On the other hand, care is caring-for in the form of taking care of, supervising, managing, providing for, attending to needs, performing services. The doctor cares for his patient, the nurse for her infant charge, the lawyer for his client, the senator for his state, the policeman for his beat. The object cared for (better, *to be* cared for) is the charge. And care, as a conative phenomenon, is represented by our fundamental sense of *responsibility*—what Kant would have called our sense of duty as opposed to our inclination. It is at this point that we observe most distinctly the region of transition of care into responsibility. Care, seen here as potency for responsibility, is the so-called sense of responsibility which, as a phenomenon of will, is the conative impulse toward the object taken as a charge. It is the basic attitude toward things by virtue of which we let ourselves be in charge of them or take charge of them.

Since inclination and sense of responsibility exist in a dialectical relationship, tension arises between them. This is the area of the disagreements that occupy so much of traditional theoretical disputation in ethics, in issues such as egoism and altruism or hedonism and formalism. It is the area in which is developed the competence of the human individual to attain to his moral dignity. This includes on one side his freedom and on the other the binding of his freedom to the responsibility of discharging charges. Hence it is here that the human individual confronts the inescapable task of solving the dialectical problem of differentiating and integrating freedom and order as the two facets of his own being, his care. Here it is that he must face the challenge of the dialectical resolution of conflicts of obedience and revolt, law and crime, family and outer world, friendship, citizenship, love, and alienation.

But because care is a triply threefold unity of seriousness, wisdom, and caring-for, the latter cannot be determined without the former two being simultaneously determined, and conversely. Each of the three determines and is determined by the others, and therefore is also self-determined through determining the others. This is why responsibility cannot be a habit; for a habit could be developed by concentrating mainly on caring-for to the exclusion of wisdom and seriousness—with the consequent collapse of caring-for into routine formality and ritual, and the consequent decline of the individual into a humanoid shell.

Responsibility cannot even be an art. For an art can afford to stick mainly to the unserious side of seriousness, and be play this side of seriousness (I do not discuss here at all the question of life beyond both freedom and responsibility as a seriocomic form that could transcend the two). Responsibility is inevitably serious. Seriousness, distributed suitably to the degree of importance of the object, is the emotion that inspires responsibility and that demands a real actualization in the worldly works of responsibility.

Wisdom is the insight that goes beyond all merely artistic vision and that gazes into the true importance of things. It is the knowledge that informs caring-for and that *is* caring-for in its cognitive aspect. Responsibility is thus the practice of wisdom and the combined power and endeavor to *act* whose potentiality is given in care.

Education for responsibility is therefore first of all the cultivation of genuine seriousness (including its proper gaieties), the development of authentic wisdom, and the unfolding of uncorrupted caring-for, all together in the single process of the *educing of care*. To draw care out into the actual and concrete faithfulness of responsibility, with its steady interplay of responsiveness and readiness, is the same process. We learn to care only by learning to be faithful and we learn to be faithful only by learning to care. The process of education of care and trustworthiness is in part like artistic education—one learns only by doing. But—and this is the wondrous but also the tragic aspect of the subject—care and responsibility are serious, and education in them comes only through existential immersion in the serious matters of life themselves, in every form of practice, domestic, civil, and religious. Responsibility can be educed only by allowing and giving people responsibility and wisely caring for the growth of their seriousness, their wisdom, and their caring-for—only by seriously and wisely caring for their care. This is the charge given to the educator for responsibility: the caring for man as care.

Chapter 2. CIVIL EDUCATION IN THE TECHNOSCIENTIFIC AGE

by Harold D. Lasswell

I.

WITH THE INVENTION of civilization 7,000 or 8,000 years ago[1] the literary heritage of mankind began to include both contemplative and manipulative propositions about the incorporation of the young into the roles appropriate to adult members of the political sector of culture. The *Arthasastra* of India, concerned almost exclusively with the education of princes, have many penetrating things to say about the part that is expedient to allow the prince's classmates to take as adults in his counsels.[2] By far the most spectacular and influential innovation in the literature and practice of *paideia* was in classical Greece.[3] It is impossible to this day for any active and sensitive mind to fail to respond to the brilliant legacy of the world whose principal perspectives are identified with Plato and Aristotle. Though no democracy in the modern sense, the Athens of the Great Age was a dramatic and self-confident contrast to "oriental despotism." Operating in a broadened framework of powersharing, political education began to assume the shape appropriate to a polity where every voice is entitled to be heard.

Essential generalizations took shape in Greek political and social theory: The stability of the constitution depends on stability of personal character; the constitution can be undermined by failure to transmit the appropriate character; therefore the continuity of public

---

[1] Consult V. Gordon Childe, *What Happened in History,* Penguin Books, Inc., Baltimore, 1954.

[2] See especially Kautilya, *Arthasastra,* translated by H. R. Shamasastry with introductory note by J. F. Fleet, 4th edition, Sri Reghuveer Printing Press, Mysore, 1951.

[3] W. Jaeger, *Paideia, The Ideals of Greek Culture,* translated by H. G. Highet, 2nd edition, 3 volumes, Oxford University Press, New York, 1943.

order depends on political education. The classical writers did not draw sharp lines between political and total education. Nor shall we, save where distinctions contribute to science or policy.[4]

II. Civic Education in the Social Process

We must, however, be prepared to meet questions about the scope and strategy of civic education in societies, historical or present-day, that require relatively refined models of the social and political process. Let us therefore present such a model, even though most of its implications cannot be worked through in the present discussion.

By the social process we mean *man* striving to optimalize preferred outcomes (*values*) through *institutions* using *resources*.[5] The model utilizes eight value categories, of which the one with which we are most directly concerned is *power*. In the shaping and sharing of power the preferred outcomes are *decisions,* or the giving and receiving of support—as in votes and fights—in commitments that affect the most important values at stake in the context, and are sanctioned by the use of severe value deprivations against any challengers. We classify decisions as *law* when they are authoritative and controlling.[6] When they are controlling, though not perceived as authoritative, decisions are exercises of *naked power*. When they are alleged to be authoritative, though they do not control, it is an instance of *pretended power*. The institutions of government, law, and politics are the practices specialized to the pre-outcome, outcome, and post-outcome phases of decision. Some institutions are conventionally perceived in a given context as *officially* charged with authority and control. Functionally speaking, however, the actual government may include only some of these official structures and decisions. The term *public order* designates both the institutions of government and the institutions in the social context

---

[4] See discussion in Harold D. Lasswell, "Political Constitutions and Character," *Psychoanalysis and the Psychoanalytic Review,* volume 46, 1960, pp. 3–18; Harold D. Lasswell, "Person, Personality, Group, Culture," *Psychiatry,* volume 2, 1939, pp. 533–561.

[5] Harold D. Lasswell and A. Kaplan, *Power and Society: A Framework for Political Inquiry,* Yale University Press, New Haven, 1950.

[6] For an extended analysis of authority and control in a given field, consult M. S. McDougal and F. P. Feliciano, *Law and Minimum Public Order,* Yale University Press, New Haven, 1961.

that are protected by law. *Civic order* refers to the institutions protected by mild rather than severe sanctions. (Obviously the official and actual public orders can be distinguished from one another.)

In common usage "civic education" refers to the preparation of the inexperienced to play mature roles in government, law, and politics.

You will notice that the theoretical apparatus can be employed to refer to any social context whatever, regardless of scope, range, or domain. As a rule when we talk about government, law, and politics, the intended context is territorial, and the topic is a nation-state, a subnational body politic, or transnational government. Equivalent distinctions are useful when we consider any of the pluralized sectors of a community. Think, for example, of the wealth value and economic institutions; and consider the private market. Participants in production, distribution, investment, and consumption develop systems of public and civic order within the market. It is possible to discover how young people are prepared to participate in market activities, and how people at any age may be made ready to carry out a particular function. We could, in fact, complete the inventory of value institutions in society and make equivalent distinctions, identifying the socialization practices in each. Thus: well-being, or the institutions of safety, health, and comfort; enlightenment, or the institutions of information; skill or the institutions of education and specialized expression in the professions, vocations, and arts; affection, or the institutions of family, friendship, and larger loyalties; respect, or the institutions of social class and caste recognition and discrimination; rectitude, or the institutions of ethical and religious belief and conduct. The distinction between authority and control in the power process can be paralleled by similar differences in each sector. Hence public and civic orders can be identified for each value, and civic education is a feature of pluralized as well as territorial components of social process.

In summary:

Social process: man, values, institutions, resources

Values: power, enlightenment, wealth, well-being, affection, skill, respect, rectitude

Power: law (authority, control)
　　　　naked power (no authority, control)
　　　　pretended power (authority, no control)

    public order (official, actual)
    civic order (official, actual)
    territorial (national, subnational, transnational)
    pluralized (by value-institution)
    civic education (or public order and civic order education)
    territorial (national, subnational, transnational)
    pluralized (by value-institution)

III.

In the interest of concentration the present discussion will emphasize civic education for the territorial units referred to above. In bodies politic where the making of important communitywide decisions is widely shared, everyone is expected to play the citizen's role, whether he occupies a high or low official or unofficial position at any stage of his career. By contrast in bodies politic characterized by the privileged exercise of authority and control in the hands of a self-perpetuating few, a master and subject relation is supposed to prevail, implying that sharply contrasting modes of civic education are appropriate to a ruler or a ruling caste, and to the rank and file of the population.

The problems that arise in connection with civic education are presumably present in varying degrees of intensity in all bodies politic. The more we learn about primitive social systems, the less plausible is the image of the savage caked in custom who is unable to resist or innovate any component of the cake. Nonetheless, civic education became an object of literary awareness and systematic reflection only as a result of the self-awareness and self-observation cultivated in urban civilization.

Reflect for a moment on the profound consequences that followed from the changes in the pattern of life situations introduced in the city. Every new situation—whether in the sector of wealth, power, enlightenment, rectitude, or some other value—provides a somewhat novel focus for the attention of participants; in turn, this fosters novel perspectives. The new frame of attention relates to the somewhat novel operational routines in the new setting, which are sustained by relatively distinctive patterns of value indulgence and deprivation. Given the novel experiences generated in new situations, predispositions are mobilized to accept new ideological doctrines, formulas, and miranda. Changed predispositions, connected with the rise of new social groups shaped by the experiences obtained in the new configuration of life, may lead to revolutionary innovations in the established system of social order; and in turn, this brings into play both deliberate and unplanned reorientations of civic education as a means of economizing the cost of perpetuating the revolutionary elite, and their system.

Wherever they occur, changes in the prevailing differentiations and integrations of the social process carry important consequences for civic education; and in our age these changes are accelerated by the tendency toward universalizing technoscientific civilization. It would be acceptable to call our epoch an "age of dispersion" as a means of emphasizing the dispersion of ego-identities that result from the situation—changing impact of science and technology. To alter a relatively stable and slowly changing world situation, is to bring into the world social process an unstable and rapidly altering melange of perspectives, operational routines, and resource modifications.

In terms of perspectives, there occurs a great proliferation of identity symbols that are made available for incorporation along with primary ego symbols to renovate traditional patterns of self. At one extreme the primary ego—the "I", "me"—is integrated with symbols of reference to many other egos, ranging from the neighborhood to the province; the nation, the region, the globe; and, among pluralized groups, from family and school to organized and unorganized associations relatively specialized to wealth, rectitude, enlightenment, respect, and well-being. At the other extreme are the impoverished "selves," selves whose primary ego is utterly withdrawn or totally absorbed in parochial identifications.

The principal consequences affecting civic education are twofold, one relating most directly to world public order, the second to the public order of advanced technoscientific societies. The interactive effects of the two are of undeniable importance. They can, however, be conveniently separated for contemplative and manipulative purposes.

The impact on world public order of the trend toward universalizing the civilization of science and technology is to endanger man's security on a wholly unprecedented scale. So far as we know, mankind has always been divided into tribal, imperial, city, or national segments.

Sharing the expectation of violence these segments have engaged in chronic preparation for "the next war," no matter how unpalatable the idea of war may be to small or large elements in the population. The technoscientific innovation has thus far failed to overcome the traditional division of the world arena; the world arms race is accelerating, not diminishing. The question that rises in the context of civic education is whether it is possible to devise a strategy of education that will contribute to the bringing into existence, by agreement of a worldwide public order, of at least minimum security.

The second question—related to the internal evolution of advanced technoscientific societies—is of fundamental importance for civilization, assuming that mankind does not destroy itself in a nuclear catastrophe. A common feature of the age of dispersion is the expansion of pluralistic as well as territorial conflict. The multiplication of groups, generated by the differentiating impact of innovation, carries with it pressure-group associations of all kinds devoted to the propagation of particular interests. Traditional conceptions of the common interest are perpetually breaking down, leaving individuals and associations with an impoverished equipment of workable norms adapted to the compromise or integration of value demands.

A deeper consequence of changing life configurations is the phenomenon variously labelled "anomie," "loss of identity," or "alienation." What is meant is the spread of a farreaching sense of anonymity as a human being, or of thingness, of being an entity deprived of humanity.[7]

Let us bring the inner changes together by speaking of a crisis of responsibility. The hyperpressure of special *versus* commonly perceived interests, and the withdrawal of attachment to the decision structures and functions of the larger world are manifestations of the age of dispersion. Assume that we accept the challenge involved in attempt-

[7] A forthcoming study by Carlos Fortin on the concept of alienation in Marx (and subsequently) will help to differentiate the several meanings attached to the term and its near neighbors. See Karl Marx, "Economic and Philosophical Manuscripts," in *Early Writings,* translated and edited by T. B. Bottomore, McGraw-Hill Book Co., New York, 1964; Erich Fromm, *Marx's Concept of Man,* Frederick Ungar Publishing Co., New York, 1961; R. Garaudy, *Humanisme Marxiste,* Edition Sociales, Paris, 1957. More concretely, Robert Blauner, *Alienation and Freedom: The Factory Worker and His Industry,* University of Chicago Press, Chicago, 1964; Gwynn Nettler, "A Measure of Alienation," *American Sociological Review,* volume 22, 1957, pp. 670–677.

ing to realize the goal of human dignity—as partially formulated, for instance, in the Universal Declaration of Human Rights—on the widest possible scale, how can civic education be employed as an effective instrumentality for the purpose?

IV. Civic Education and World Public Order

Any recommended strategy of civic education depends on the orientation of the recommender toward the constitution of the political arena in question.

Let it be made explicit that the word "constitution" as employed here does *not* have as its primary referent the impressions left by pen or press on parchment or paper. The term refers to the configuration of expectations and of operational routines concerning the basic allocations of power in a system of public order. The startingpoint for the analysis of character and constitution among Greek thinkers was the constitution. Once adapted to a particular constitutional system the character might become a dynamic factor in change. If the character began to change to a significant extent, the way would be paved for bringing into power an elite committed to different value goals for the body politic, hence the political system would be altered as a consequence.

As indicated before, it is unthinkable that champions of the dignity of man can give unqualified support to the present constitution of the world arena. So long as the expectation of violence prevails, and the globe is divided into power units competing in an ever more ominous arms race, it will be intolerable to acquiesce in the present system of public order as a beneficiary of civic education. The challenge is whether we can reverse the traditional role of deliberate civic education, which has been conformist, and transform it into an instrument of fundamental change, hence preparing characters in advance that demand and in turn meet the demands of a world constitution that brings greater security from war, and does so without unacceptable consequences.

What does this imply? A unified world order, it is evident, can come by conquest or agreement, and either path may be followed rapidly or slowly. In the former case (conquest) a successful world conspiracy might undermine willingness to launch a surprise attack, or incapacitate resistance to a surprise attack, to a degree that would obviate nuclear warfare or confine it within "moderate" limits. It is realistic, I think, to dismiss this possibility as unlikely, given the parochialism of the environment of those who manage these weapons.[8]

The second case (agreement) could be realized *if the "principle of simultaneity" were successfully applied to the key decision spots in world politics*. According to this principle the most active elites of Washington, Moscow, and Peking, for example, must simultaneously consent to the introduction of an inclusive decision process in which authoritative control of the instruments of violence are concentrated in the hands of representatives of the world community as a whole. Furthermore, objectives must be understood in the same way and actively pursued. Hitherto in world history the many initiatives on behalf of global unity have failed, the principal difficulty being that *each innovation has been introduced at some local spot* (Paris or Moscow, for instance). Other elites of power, therefore, have perceived the change as a tangible threat to the perpetuation of their own authority and control. Such a threat is regarded as outweighing the advantages of unity, even assuming that unification would follow. Acting on this perception, established elites have prevented the proposed new program from achieving universality. Having this record in mind, we infer that unless the perception of expected net advantage is simultaneous, proposals of voluntary unity will continue to fail, and the elites of the world arena will continue to be divided.

The preceding analysis indicates that our proposed revolutionary stance toward the present world—which institutionalizes war—implies no simple program. We might, it is true, despite all hazards, train conspirators. However, I surmise that few of us will adopt this as our program of civic education. No doubt we would fear that a seizure of power by "Communist" or "capitalist" militants, in the unlikely event of success, would be more likely to launch a world prison managed by a self-perpetuating caste of guards than to inaugurate an era of global security.

---

[8] Some insight into the perspectives of the weapon specialists can be obtained from Morris Janowitz, *The Professional Soldier, A Social and Political Portrait* (Free Press), Macmillan Co., New York, 1960.

If nonconspiratorial, shall our revolutionary program of civic education attempt to indoctrinate the young with the view *that all national governments are inherently immoral,* hence entitled in no case to receive military service (that is, service as "butchers of men")? If we ask first about the chances that the propagation of such a view will be permitted in the "Communist" world, the answer is not in serious doubt. It is presumably true, of course, that Soviet political groups support pacifism in the "capitalist" world in the hope of undermining its capacity to resist conspiracy, surprise, or war, and that non-Soviet elites are willing to aid pacifism in Peking or Moscow.

Granted the controls exercised by totalitarian rulers, the possibility is to be considered that as Russia, China, and other such societies grow more prosperous (or, at least, as their elites enjoy more prosperity), their young people will behave like sons and daughters in rich capitalist economies. Is it "inevitable" (or at least "highly probable") that industrial societies will alienate the younger generation? For the moment it is enough to say that we cannot exclude the contingency of a "psychic epidemic," the possible occurrence of crowd seizures on a global scale and a general withdrawal of participation in military activity. (As of this moment let me say flatly that I see no convincing symptoms of the early stages of such a movement.)

If we reject conspiracy or pacifist indoctrination as promising programs, can we at least prevent civic education from contributing as much as in the past to the perpetuation of war and world division? I believe that we are justified in asserting that American civic education has already achieved a praiseworthy degree of success in this direction. Collective attachment to war has been modified. Recall that our ideological outlook reflects the conflicting themes imbedded in the myth system that Americans share with all legatees of the tradition of Western Europe. Consider the following doctrinal statements: "As a patriotic American citizen, I am in favor of maintaining national independence from external control. At the same time, I favor a foreign policy that settles differences by peaceful means, and accepts the equal claim of other nations to independence. Recognizing the danger of war under present conditions, I favor strengthening the United Nations, in the hope of establishing enough mutual trust in common purposes to bring about at least a minimum system of effective public security."

These statements are widely acceptable to Americans, although minorities associate themselves with such propositions as: "My country right or wrong"; "The U.N. is a Communist front lulling us into false security"; "War is still the test of fitness to survive:" "War is part of unchanging human nature."

It would be too much to assert that the effect of civic education in the United States, or in any other major power, is likely to prove an efficient means of changing the world's constitution. The obvious difficulty is that the established elites are able to absorb the focus of attention of the entire population to a degree that precludes the growth of identities, expectations, and demands that can be synchronized across national lines and guarantee the rise to power of mid-elite or dissident elite elements.

We must not, however, fail to attempt to seize every opportunity that is offered by the new technology to penetrate the self-absorption of young and old in the principal countries. I have in mind, especially, the unprecedented opportunity now only a few short years away that can eliminate the present dependence of TV broadcasting on stations that mediate between a communications satellite system and the individual viewer. Imagine that a communications commission devoted to world realism and understanding would provide millions of young people with receiving equipment capable of viewing Comsat programs originating with, or supervised by, the commission. If the United Nations cannot live up to this opportunity, it will be necessary for private associations to step in and to establish confidence in their integrity as genuine supporters of the common interests of mankind in security by agreement. This is the greatest opportunity for worldwide civic education that has ever existed.

V. Civic Education and Personal Responsibility

The second problem of civic education mentioned earlier appears in all modernized or modernizing societies. Is it possible to develop strategies of action that overcome the dispersive tendencies generated by the changing life situations inseparable from technoscientific civilization?

The most obvious challenges to the internal public order of advanced bodies politic are connected with the multiplication of particular and special interests at the expense of norms that clarify and guide the discovery and implementation of common interests. In societies like the United States where private capitalism has been a preferred institutional form, the evidence of conflicting interests has been visible to all. At the same time the situation has been confused by the complexities of ideology and the peculiarities of civic education. In one popularly sloganized form the ideology is extremely simple: "Whatever is good for business is good for America." The "invisible hand" is supposed to operate through the market mechanism to blend the pursuit of wealth into the achievement of human dignity. However, it cannot be said that this ideology of gain has gone unchallenged. It has been modified by a professional ideology—largely propagated by salaried clergymen, teachers, and officials—that criticizes the "corruption" and "selfishness" of the unrestrained pursuit of "the almighty dollar," and glorifies the superior morality of the direct service of God and man at the sacrifice of "material" advantage.

Our educational institutions have been caught in the confusions and conflicts inherent in this ideological situation. The schools have inculcated the pursuit of wealth rather indirectly. The educational system was originally in the hands of theologians, and the professional rather than the entrepreneurial stamp has continued to characterize much of its rhetoric. Presumably there is less direct admonition to pursue wealth and power than to live a moral or religious life. As rectitude values emphasize honesty and service, this carries a pejorative implication for business and politics, both of which are traditionally viewed with ambivalence. On the one hand, great respect goes to presidents, senators, representatives, governors, and mayors; and to corporation chairmen, presidents, and other business figures. On the other hand, "graft and corruption" is a standard complaint about politics; and business is pictured as rapacious ("dog eat dog"), and deceptive ("let the buyer beware").

Evidently the pursuit of wealth and power has been more encouraged in the home than in the school. The same teacher or clergyman who conveys a faint (or strident) tone of adverse judgment of businessmen and politicians may have a wife who is resentful of scraping and pinching on a professional man's fixed income; and the teacher or clergyman may himself kowtow to the demands of a school board or a board of elders composed of businessmen.

In an agricultural era the situation could be kept ambiguous, for the traditional farmer did not think of himself primarily as a profitseeking businessman. Business was a style of life connected in his mind with an urban environment, an environment often perceived as hostile. Farmers were obviously concerned with such material data as market prices. But the dependence of their operation on weather and other "natural" conditions, and the absence of rigorous bookkeeping procedures, combined to nourish an ideological coalition with theologians, "moralists," and other elements in society who refused to celebrate the pursuit of profit as the principal aim of man in this life and as a means of demonstrating his fitness for grace in the next. Even the pursuit of another 160 acres was not universally perceived in wealth terms. It was an enlarged commitment to nature (and God) and to the building of an enduring basis for a family way of life.

An urban style of living was bound to dissolve the respectgiving alliance of farmers with teachers and clergy (and physicians). Would the result be candid acceptance by the educational world of the profitseeking economy, and the adaptation of all educational institutions to turning out jobminded students? Would academic men themselves join in measuring themselves, not according to salary but in entrepreneurial terms, even if they remain partially involved in an academic career? If this has become the case, any recommended program of civic responsibility would seem to encounter very grave obstacles indeed. Undoubtedly the entrepreneurial trend has deeply permeated education. In recent times, for instance, the expansion of the physical and social sciences has multiplied the skills that can be adapted to the production of marketable goods and services. Engineering schools of many kinds have come into existence or vastly expanded the scope of their operations in teaching and research. We note that teachers and professors may increase their income by consultative practice; and in many cases it is feasible to engage in business by obtaining a stock interest in return for professional advice or an inventive idea.

It is easy to exaggerate the novelty of these developments. Professors of law and medicine, for example, have long been accustomed to supplement fixed by variable incomes obtained from consultation. Often they have learned of investment opportunities and moved into active business. The frequency with which law has been a steppingstone to politics is notorious. But perhaps it is worth recalling that for generations ambitious young men and women, entering new communities as teachers, have stepped into the business or political class by marriage, friendship, or exchange of technical knowhow. The interpenetration of academic, ecclesiastical, business, and political life has always been much closer than is generally acknowledged. Often the business tie is familial, with the professional member benefitting from the assets and connections of parents and siblings.

VI.

If we acknowledge the fractionalization of industrial society, it is important to search for the factors that keep alive a conception of common interest, or that hold some promise of having this effect. Has civic education been swallowed up in the profit-seeking, job-getting ideology of a business society? Are we to assume that lawyers, doctors, civil servants, teachers, and scientists are "in it for what they can get," measured in dollars?

Several factors hold such a development in check. First of all, economic opportunities are spread unevenly through the professional, and notably the academic, community. Hence other ideologies have a chance of survival; standards can be preserved, thanks to the zeal of jealous colleagues. Speaking broadly, scholars in the humanities have had relatively few chances to strike it rich. Until recently, for example, mathematicians were rather innocent of the dollar-providing world of practical affairs. Today this distinction goes to some fields of literature and history. However, we must not overlook the fact that all these ladies and gentlemen are not condemned to unheated towers of ivory, glass, or brick. They, too, may hit the jackpot with textbooks, or even as publishers. There is always the chance of writing a best-selling novel or play (perhaps depicting an alleged scandalous decline of morality in academia, thus converting an aggregate decline of rectitude into an economic asset of the skillful writer).

A second major factor counteracting the primacy of the dollar is the growth of the social sciences and of computer technology. The expansion of the social sciences beyond the field of economics is now proceeding on an explosion course. Thanks to the computer, it is practical to devise and keep up to date more and more comprehensive input-output models of the entire social process of any territorial or functional context. Postulated goal models can be evaluated in terms of probability and of comparative costs and benefits (not only in terms of wealth, but of power, respect, well-being, and other value criteria). Instruments are being rapidly improved that enable the scientist or the policymaker to arrive at creative and realistic judgments on aggregate policy.

For some time enconomists have been available to deal with aggregate problems, since they are accustomed to operate with theoretical models of wealth production, distribution, saving, investment, and consumption. Unlike the "practical businessman," they can provide intellectual guidance to collective alternatives of action. Specialists on public health have moved in the same direction, using empirically validated models of the factors that affect the rise or fall of mortality and morbidity. Specialists on the sociology of knowledge, especially of science, are devising parallel analyses of the factors that account for the rise and fall of enlightenment. In the same way political scientists are examining the shaping and sharing of power among national, transnational, and subnational units. Specialists on the rise and fall of caste or class, or of ecclesiastical or educational institutions, are adopting the same approach.

We are rapidly reaching the point at which alternative versions of the common interest can be programmed and the results compared. I foresee that one result of this intellectual innovation will be the growth of a clarified perspective about the places in the decision process where public service rather than ego-aggrandizing standards are needed. Instead of vague objectives of public service, it will be feasible to define relatively explicit specifications for notions of responsibility to public or civic order. One way to think about the problem is to consider the consequences of allowing voters to sell their votes to the highest bidder. Note that the primacy of the individual pursuit of economic gain is recognized—within limits—for stockholders; but it is not supposed to influence "representatives" or "delegates" on elected boards of directors. Delegates are expected to demand of themselves that they disregard "ego" advantage in wealth terms and identify with the constituent's advantage, thus acting on behalf of a "self" in which the primary ego adopts the standpoint of another ego.

No matter how complicated the computing technology, or how elaborate the simulations of past and future, some self-limitations will doubtless be regarded as advantageous to all. For instance: The machines must not be tampered with; programming and processing operations must be in the hands of trustworthy persons.[9]

It is not to be hastily assumed that it is impracticable to define complex and variable roles in the decision process. In everyday life we are well accustomed to recognize the strategies appropriate to an umpire, or the degree of deception allowed a player in delivering a pitched ball or attempting to steal a base. It will, I believe, be possible to draw lines between permissible and impermissible deception at the functional phases of decision.

As was indicated at any early stage of our discussion the responsibility-crisis connected with the diffusion of technoscientific civilization is deeper than the clash of special *versus* general interest demands. It is commonly phrased as a crisis of alienation, of withdrawal of a sense of ego-commitment to the conventional decision processes of the larger society. The trend is often phrased in terms of deferred responsibility, if indeed the responsibilities of a traditionally mature adult are ever undertaken. The point is usually made by recalling the labor contributions that were once exacted from the young when agriculture was the dominant mode of production. As production moved away from the home, and the acquisition of the skills required by industry devolved to an increasing extent on schools, demands were generated that continued to lengthen the period of formal exposure to instruction, often delaying the age of family formation. At the same time, strata of chronically unemployed were localized in rural and urban slums.

There is little doubt that the older industrial societies have been uneasy about the socialization of the young, which of course, includes their incorporation into the political process. To go no further back

9 See G. A. Almond and S. Verba, *The Civic Culture: Political Attitudes and Democracies in Five Nations,* Little, Brown & Co., Boston, 1965; F. J. Greenstein, *Children and Politics,* Yale University Press, New Haven, 1965; C. E. Merriam, *The Making of Citizens,* University of Chicago, Chicago, 1931.

than the last years of the nineteenth century, it is noteworthy how the youth movement, taking shape in the well-to-do suburb of Berlin— Steglitz—aroused apprehension and defensive efforts at nullification. One branch of the German movement managed to preserve its autonomy, though most young people were presently recruited into adult-managed departments of political parties and churches. The autonomous organizations suffered a fate that appears to be built into every such initiative: its leaders grew up; and instead of leaving their organizations, often stayed, and generated a managerial cadre distinguished by the length of its reminiscences and the consolidation of its pension claims. Youth movements have the seeds of self-destruction implanted in their biology; even the medieval universities were taken out of the hands of the students by aging exstudents who grew up to be professors and deans.

Disaffected youth sends occasional shudders through the established layers of the body politic by gestures of repudiation aimed at patriotic cults and military obligations. Of this the celebrated Oxford oath is symbolic. It was the last public expression of a generation that soon marched off to pay one of the highest blood taxes in modern times.

After the seizure of power in Moscow in 1917 in the name of the denationalized proletariat, concern was intensified for the loyalty of youth to the nation-state. The origin of modern political science—with a relatively heavy stress on psychocultural considerations—is not unconnected with these happenings. It took shape in the decade of the nineteen-twenties. It evolved in an industrial nation where some private philanthropists had the idea of gambling on the possibility that revolutionary turbulence might be avoided in the long run, if scientific modes of analysis and observation were extended beyond economics to all the disciplines concerned with human relations. Charles E. Merriam's Civic Training Series is an early evidence of the attempt by established students of government, law, and politics to work in this area. After the jolt of World War II, and the intervening expansion of the social and behavioral sciences, the theme of civic training (deliberate socialization) has been extended to the study of socialization in general (or both deliberate and unpremeditated incorporation of a rising generation into the "Constitution"). The transmission of "civic culture" (in the work of Almond and Verba, for instance) belongs to this new wave.

The connection of these themes with war and revolution is not at random. The occurrence of war reemphasizes a fundamental requirement of any political system in a divided world. Because great wars are intermittent, systems of civic incorporation must operate during inter-crisis periods to keep young people willing to take the risk of dying for the national unit. The predisposition to do and die must be inculcated and sustained on a standby basis as an expendable resource of the body politic.

VII.

In advanced industrial societies the inculcation of civic responsibility is complicated by the maladjustments fostered by the fantastically accelerated tempo of productive capability. It is increasingly obvious that the application of science to production has made it *possible* to provide for a rising level of income for consumption, while also cutting the hours of work (assuming that population increases are kept in bounds). One way to characterize the emerging situation is to say that we can subsidize consumption while reducing the manhours of individual toil; we can disconnect basic income from the demand to "work."

Evidently, then, we do not need to emphasize as much as before the responsibility of each individual to "work" (engaging in "productive" activities as a *quid pro quo* for obtaining income). Manhours devoted to commodity production are of diminishing importance. In this sense, not only the contribution of youth but of the other age groups is becoming superfluous.

Why does this remarkable evolution exaggerate the problem of civic training rather than ameliorate it? There is a discrepancy between new facts and old norms. The facts are not invisible. Excess capacity cannot be permanently concealed. Meanwhile, the traditional ideology of "work" complicates the lives of young and old, many of whom are confused by the rapid transition of which they are part. Whole categories of skilled or semiskilled personnel are thrown out of an economically productive, hence respected, place in society. In some areas the young people are accustomed to think of their careers as hopeless, and their place in society as redundant. Human dignity presumably implies basic respect for the identity of an individual simply because he is human, coupled with the provision of opportunity to cultivate potential talent in ways that contribute to culture without necessarily providing a "work" income in the market.

The inference is that complex industrial societies are undermining themselves by molding characters whose inner conflicts are destructively expressed.

Think first of the lower strata. Here we find abundant evidence of hostilities directed against the self and others. It is not simply a matter of pointing to the mobs and riots of Los Angeles or of some other metropolitan center. Destructiveness is shown in personal quarrelsomeness, and in cruelty, both physical and psychic. Nothing exceeds the brutality of lowerclass person *versus* lowerclass person, once a crisis has been allowed to develop and inhibited rage is discharged against a member of the same neighborhood or family. (Internalization also occurs: gratuitous physical damage is inflicted by an individual on his own body. Many "accidents" are in this category. Alcoholism or drug addiction may be carried to a point of psychic and physical disintegration. Psychosomatic illnesses belong in this inventory.)

In the light of contemporary knowledge it is not too baffling to account for the broad incidence of these destructive acts. The lower strata tend to incorporate the value specifications of the strata above them, especially when the ideology includes the allegation that anyone who strives can succeed, and institutions like the public schools nominally open their doors to all. But many who strive—or who strive a little—fail to advance, often from lack of support in home and neighborhood, often from unconscious discrimination on the part of teachers and administrators.

Most of the hostilities generated in modern industrial societies are not guided and integrated by a counterideology directed against the established myth. The scientific observer is impressed, however, with the scattered signs of opposition to what is often called the "Middle-Class Mentality."

The middle-class perspective, as depicted in the usual model, emphasizes the demand by the self on the self to demonstrate merit. As inhibition and postponement of gratification are chronically required, inner conflicts occur. These conflicts are partly resolved by emphasizing superior morality (rectitude) and respectability (respect-worthiness). If the demand for "achievement" is defined as the demand for the external demonstration of merit, we can think of the middle-class outlook as especially oriented toward encouraging achievement.

Most ideologies that profess to reject the middle-class model fail to do so; more specifically, they partially incorporate its leading features, and reject only unessential details. Political movements in the name of socialism, for instance, demand disciplined service of power, followed by devoted service to the state as the supposed temporary agent of transition to a stateless, classless world. Such an ideology rejects, not the fundamental demand to demonstrate merit by action, but particular institutional practices with which the middle-class outlook was associated in particular historical circumstances.

Are there any life-patterns that are genuinely rejective of the demand to demonstrate merit, rather than take it for granted without demonstration? It is possible to formulate a theoretical model of the aristocrat that conforms to this requirement. According to such a model the true aristocrat simply *is;* he does not perceive it necessary to *do.* At the other end of the social scale it is possible to discover a parallel development among, for instance, some members of the second or third generation of the unemployed. The perception of the ego has something in common with the aristocrat, in the sense that a comprehensive claim to human dignity is taken for granted. Unlike the aristocrat, who has acquired self-confidence by introjecting respect from his nursery circle, and the larger world, the rank-and-file person must disregard his deprivational status in the eyes of the larger community. *His outstanding demand is to enjoy life, which means to maintain a euphoric mood.* If the aristocrat demands that he treat himself with imperturbable respect, and the middle-class person seeks to maintain a fusion of the sense of striving with sentiments of self-respect, the rank-and-file person is intent on avoiding whatever interferes with a happy inner state.

How can euphoria be sustained? Partly by spontaneous expressive behavior toward and with others. Hence the congeniality of dancing and music; and especially of improvisation. Hence, too, the predisposition toward gambling as a means of sustaining sanguine expectations; or the use of alcohol and other chemicals, and of promiscuous and varied sexuality. Hence, also, the avoiding of conventional responsibilities in the family, on the job, or in civic and political institutions. Evidently the demand for euphoria gives expression to a demand to give and receive love without further obligation. When the immediate environment is unwilling or unable to assist in sustaining the euphoric state, the individual retires to a cave of private mood and fantasy. The enemies of euphoria are time and responsibility; therefore the rank-and-file person is careless of time and evasive of responsibility.

The preceding model has already been glorified (by authors who are sufficiently middle-class to publish books) in much the same way that Marx or Lenin purported to speak for the proletariat. Perhaps the most systematic justification is by Norman O. Brown, whose criticism of Freud is that by accepting genitality as a valued goal, he capitulated to the freedom-damaging steamrollers of conventionality.[10] Genitality is interpreted in ways that include more than physical capability. Implied also is the acceptance of "maturity," or responsibility, which traps the individual in the whole dragnet of obligations defined by a particular culture. Brown speaks of pre-genitality as the path to freedom. On the physical level this implies giving active expression to polymorphous perverse components; on the cultural level, it implies the rejection of conventional burdens.

VIII.

It would be a gross oversimplification to assert that a single factor or feature of the social process can be singled out to explain the farreaching pheonomena of nonresponsibility that emerges in technoscientific societies. However, it is not inappropriate to draw attention to at least two sets of factors that are closely linked with alienation and with overinsistence on special interests.

The manifestations of alienation—whether acts of destructiveness or

[10] Norman O. Brown, *Life Against Death: The Psychoanalytic Meaning of History,* Random House, Inc., New York, 1959.

withdrawal from participation—are in all probability connected with failures to share power. The growth of differentiation and interdependence at the technical level has not been paralleled by a corresponding set of institutions adapted to the effective sharing of power. The hypothesis of exclusion from power as a source of nonresponsible character formation is strongly indicated from the study of personality development. Fixation or regression are failures to move forward toward responsible participation in the public and civic order systems of family and other primary units. Exclusion from power in any institutional setting tends to re-activate in the personalities of the excluded all the rebellious or withdrawal tendencies of which they are capable.

Overinsistence on special interests is another response-formation that attests at once to a nonresponsible orientation toward the larger context and to insufficient opportunities to exercise a responsible role.

Closely tied with power exclusion is a continuing failure of enlightenment concerning the common interest, of the relation between part and whole. Ideologies of the established order, if they profess devotion to the common good, tend to be dismissed as ritualized verbiage or "machiavellian" guile. Few continuing procedures are acquired that aid in clarifying the interplay of individual, pluralistic, and territorial interconnections. The built-in institutions of self-appraisal are inadequate to the requirements of enlightened choice or decision.

Failures of civic training contribute to, and in turn reflect, failures in the sharing of power and in the performance of the self-appraisal function throughout the social process.

IX. Fundamental Strategies of Civic Education

The foregoing pages have focussed on two objectives of civic education in the technoscientific age, both of which are given new urgency, and often new instruments of attempted solution, by the accelerated growth of technology and science. We have considered, on the one hand, the possible cultivation of a world constitutional system of at least minimum public order, and on the other, the development of an effective sense of public responsibility that succeeds in overcoming the dispersive tendencies of modernizing and modernized societies.

The overriding goal postulated for this discussion is the achievement of human dignity on the widest possible scale. A detailed explication of this objective would require a provisional blueprint for a technoscientific world in which voluntarily achieved unity and multivalued norms would provide a stable public and civic order capable of eliciting the service of young and old.

I take it for granted that any recommended strategies of civic education are addressed to all who have official or unofficial opportunities to clarify policy or to put policy into effect. Hence our suggestions, though heavily weighted toward the problem of putting our national house in order, transcend national boundaries and address all who are willing to listen, deliberate, and act.

First of all, our discussion called attention to the fact that *an opportunity of unexcelled magnitude will soon be a technical reality. The reference is to systems of satellite communication* that will make it possible, in principle, to address every person in the world at the same time, without depending on the editorial interference hitherto exercised by intermediate stations. I need scarcely underline the point that a common channel provides a focus of attention that can expedite the process of achieving a world-inclusive outlook, an outlook that clarifies common goals, describes common trends, analyzes conditioning factors, formulates projections, and evaluates policy alternatives. Potential goals can be clarified in concrete and vivid terms for the use of our human and physical resources in a world of fantastically varied creativity. A common image of man's past can grow out of the comparison of the various parochial histories of biology and culture. A common understanding can be communicated of the scientific technique of explaining the multifactor constellations that account for the innovation, diffusion, and restriction of biological and cultural traits and configurations. Shared images of future possibilities can emerge from the presentation of competing projections of probable future events. In every policy sector, it will be within the grasp of man to invent and compare strategies for moving toward a more inclusive world order that harmonizes with the goal of human dignity.

Observe that the exceptional opportunity for civic education on a truly global scale may be defeated, perhaps by determined countermeasures adopted by elites of power, wealth, or other values, who expect to suffer an impaired value position if a genuinely effective world order comes into being. Perhaps, however, any defeat will be due to people of good will, like ourselves, who fail to act promptly to obtain access to the new technology, and to utilize it skillfully for the stimulation of a fundamental framework of world identity, expectation, and demand. Many channels are at hand through which to act: various branches of the United Nations; the University network; the network of teachers and mass communicators, many of whom can operate transnationally to further the basic aim.

Our discussion has directed attention to the conditioning factors that must be controlled, if civic education is to become a potent instrument in overcoming the dispersive tendencies of a technoscientific age. A fundamental strategic principle would appear to be that *civic education must be coordinated with genuine devolution of power in all territorial and pluralistic institutions.*[11]

The perspectives and operational routines essential to effective adult participation in a democratic body politic must be acquired in immediate experience. When we examine the difficulties that come to the surface in complex modern societies, it is evident that one of the principal facts is that professed norms of shared power are in fact violated. Hence the recommendation of deliberate, articulate, and actual power devolution in family and school environments. There must be no "phoniness" in these institutions. For example, it is self-defeating to proclaim "family democracy" or "student self-government," if the facts of the situation are otherwise, and parents or teachers retain a dominant position. Civic education requires candor about the limits, as well as the zones of authoritative and controlling decision. It should be explicit and outside the realm of change that parents or teachers retain a veto power, as well as certain powers of initiative, in order to fulfil their obligations to the larger community.

That limitations on power-sharing should be treated with complete openness, does not imply they are beyond criticism or exploratory change. On the contrary, challenges are entirely permissible; and much can be learned by enlarging the limits of sharing. The same approach applies, not only to pre-adult situations, but to activities that are part of the institutional framework of adult life. An exploratory point of view

[11] See Robert Rubenstein and Harold D. Lasswell, *The Sharing of Power in a Psychiatric Hospital,* Yale University Press, New Haven, 1966.

can be expected to contribute to the training of citizens who must participate in the permanent revolution of technoscience.

Parallel to the strategy of devolution is transmitting *familiarity with devices of continuing self-observation.* It is not enough to consider power-sharing by itself, divorced from the context of values and institutions in which it is embedded and with which it is in continual interaction. If power is to be disciplined to serve the overriding goal of human dignity, power must be appraised in reference to every value-institution sector. Civic education also requires continuous appraisal; further than that, it calls for the transmission of skill in self-observation. To some extent it is possible for every individual to adopt procedures that enable him to "see himself as others see him," and also to bring to the full focus of waking awareness relevant features of the self that aid or distort his judgment.

Our society is becoming increasingly alert to the *necessity of joining comprehensive conceptual systems with procedures that relate the systems to the immediate configuration of events.* As a means of rendering this conception more explicit, I shall refer to the *continuing seminar technique,* and propose its deliberate dissemination as a guide, and as a component of civic training in every social institution and in every significant recurring situation within each institution.[12] In a technoscientific age, it is out of the question to provide comprehensive guidance to the untold thousands of institutional situations whose impact on civic training is of some importance. The only defensible strategy is to spread the concern for civic training throughout the families, schools, and neighborhoods (plus all other pluralistic and territorial units in the social process).

A continuing seminar technique can be applied by a single individual to his goals and policy alternatives, enabling him to keep in disciplined relation to past trends, conditioning factors, and future developments. The technique can be used by small groups of educators at any level of the educational process, varying from adjoining classrooms, schools, to schools systems. Continuing seminars are appropriate for

---

[12] In more detail, see "Experimentation, Prototyping, Intervention," and "Micromodelling," chapters 5 and 6, in Harold D. Lasswell, *The Future of Political Science,* Atherton Press, New York, 1963; Harold D. Lasswell, "Decision Seminars: The Contextual Use of Audiovisual Means in Teaching, Research and Consultation," in R. E. Merritt and S. Rokkan, editors, *Comparing Nations: The Use of Quantitative Data in Cross-National Research,* Yale University Press, New Haven, 1966.

action committees of boards of education, legislative committees, planning or appraisal agencies, public or private. The device is adaptable to those responsible for training in the armed forces, the police, the personnel of establishments devoted to correction, mediation, conciliation, arbitration, or adjudication.

Continuing seminars are instruments for keeping in intellectual control of the explosively expanding machinery of information processing, storage, and retrieval. If the specific objectives of civic education are to be progressively defined and redefined through time, they must take into account the vast data banks now being formed in all advanced societies. Moreover, as users of data those who concern themselves with official or unofficial programs will need to evaluate the adequacy of existing information, and raise new questions whenever critical judgment indicates the need.

Furthermore, continuing seminars are the appropriate place for programs to be worked out that utilize a balanced arrangement of *experimentation, prototyping,* and *intervention* to meet the challenges of particular territorial or pluralistic situations. Prototyping, by the way, is especially adapted to the task of institution-building, since it refers to a social practice deliberately inaugurated to improve available knowledge of strategies appropriate to the ends in view.

The technique of continuing seminars is adaptable to the requirements of young people at almost every stage of growth; and may well prove to be the instrument that aids in maintaining a sense of direction through the years.

The essential agenda of any seminar of the kind is a deliberate exploration of all dimensions of problem-solving. It is possible to achieve precision, vividness, and continuity by employing audiovisual aids and computing devices; but these are to be understood for what they are—namely, as subordinate ways and means.

The general conclusion, then, is that the urgent challenges relating to civic education in the technoscientific age—concomitantly an age of dispersion—can be met by determined devotion to the goals of human dignity, and by skilled adaptation of problem-solving procedures to the synchronization of power-sharing with the requirements of value-realization in the public and civic order of every territorial and pluralistic context in the world community of man.

Chapter 3. CHARACTER AND THE ARTS AND DISCIPLINES

by Richard McKeon

CHARACTER is in part natural and modified by natural causes; it is in part acquired and developed. What a person is depends on antecedent abilities, sensitivities, and inclinations, and on the circumstances and associations, customs, laws, and institutions which have influenced his life and growth. Acquired character becomes second nature at each point of development; and the beginning point of the delineation or the determination of character may be set at any stage: for particular purposes of analysis it may be prenatal, or a turning point in early childhood, or one of the numerous ages taken to mark maturity, or the moment immediately proximate to the actions under consideration. Education in a broad sense includes all external influences on the formation of character. In a more restricted sense it is limited to deliberate devices used to influence attitudes, impulses, and skills relative to values and according to norms set by social opinion, political ideology, technical fashion, and religious belief, or by partial heterogeneous mergings among them.

More than 2,000 years ago Theophrastus prefaced his work, *The Characters,* with the explanation that he had often wondered why, although all Greece has the same climate and all Greeks had the same kind of education, nevertheless all Greeks did not have the same structure (*taxis*) of character-traits (*tropos*). To satisfy that curiosity, he started to study human nature (*physis*), and to distinguish and compare kinds of dispositions. From the beginning, the study of character has had a comparative and normative basis: and from the beginning, it has apparently been easier or more interesting to study frustrations, anxieties, and pretensions than achievements, sufficiencies, and virtues: Theophrastus planned to investigate good and bad dispositions, but his work as it has come to us analyzes thirty bad characters and we have no evidence that he had extended his investigation to good characters. The aspects of character which have presented themselves for study are well identified by the words chosen to designate them. "Character" means the impress or stamp, borrowed from the minting of coins, by which types are diffentiated and classified. "Ethos" refers to the structure of feelings, motives, and conceptualizations by which actions are caused and to which responsibility for their effects is imputed. "Tropism" has acquired a primarily biological meaning, but "tropos" also meant the turn of character formed by the influence of common opinion and received values in a community. "Person" is probably derived from drama and from the mask of the actor, since in life, as on the stage, characters are perceived or imaged in presentation to viewers and audiences.

There have been as many conceptions of education as there have been theories of character. The adjustments of personality theory to learning theory are confused and puzzling unless the two sets of theories are ordered by relating comparable and concordant concepts. When the aspects of character under consideration are conceived as natural, education may be viewed as therapy to remove alienations which impede natural functioning and to produce insight into one's nature and the causes of deviation from natural processes and needs. When the aspects of character under consideration are conceived as ethical, education may be viewed as the inculcation of moral and intellectual virtues suited to the circumstances and potentialities of the individual and productive of powers of adaptation, self-realization, and autonomy. When the aspects of character under consideration are conceived as social, education may be viewed as the adjustment of the individual to what is acceptable to the society or communities in which he lives and as one of the means used by communities to preserve and strengthen their values and to train members to perform the functions essential to their continuation and their resistance to external dangers. When the aspects of character under consideration are considered as roles assumed or as parts in a game, or when roles or "natures" are conceived as the means by which we become a functioning constituent in a transacting group, education may be viewed as the acquisition of powers to win the equivalent of a game or a controversy or to be accepted in the role we play by knowledge of the rules or stage directions which govern it and by understanding of the opinions, motives, and devices of opponents, competitors, and fellow actors.

Investigation of the problems of the relation of education to character does not depend on determining whether character is essentially or primarily natural, moral, social, or dramatic. Character has all these aspects, and each of them may be made basic in a theory of personality or of education which takes into account as secondary factors or problems the aspects made primary in other theories. The two basic problems are problems of means and of sequence: problems of means are problems of character and learning, that is, the determination of character by actions and the determination of actions by character; problems of sequence are problems of form and matter, that is, the succession of arts and disciplines used in education and acquired from education and the succession of potentialities, problems, and situations for which they are needed and on which they are used. There are problems of means in the interplay of character and action which relate the causes which produce character to the actions by which abilities and actions are judged at each stage of education, and there are problems of sequence in education and in the development of character which relate competences and skills-in-action to theories and norms at each transition from stage to stage. Problems of sequence arise from the need to determine what disciplines should be imparted early because a) they are accessible to and usable by the many, and b) they might serve as matter for later disciplines requisite to the few who continue in disciplinary education. Both problems must be faced and treated in any theory of character. The language and the distinctions proper to moral character will be used in the following analysis because they are well adapted to the problems faced in "liberal education" and "higher education," and the results of the analysis should be subject to restatement to adapt them to character considered as natural, as social, and as dramatic and sportive. The lines of inquiry of the different theories lead to results which may be considered as supplementary and mutually reinforcing rather than contradictory and mutually exclusive.

Liberal education or education in the liberal arts was thought to be humane as well as liberating, to advance humanity as well as to secure freedom. The Romans applied the term *"humanitas"* to the cycle of learning or sequence of the arts, and sought the meaning of humanity in the achievements of great artists. The liberal arts were enumerated as prerequisites to higher education in law, architecture, and natural history. With the coming of Christianity, the liberal arts were transformed into the three arts of words or the trivium and the four mathematical arts of things or the quadrivium; and when the first medieval universities were established higher education was in law, medicine, and theology. The transition from medieval to modern education in the Renaissance can be described as a transformation to arts and disciplines adapted to the matters on which they are employed, rather than defined by the forms of thought and statement required for their acquisition and use. In the Middle Ages, the disciplines were arts or skills applied to any subject matter. All seven liberal arts might be employed in interpreting a text, sacred or human, or in analyzing a political problem, in the City of God or in terrestrial cities. The disciplines of the late Middle Ages were criticized as verbal and abstract, and new disciplines were established adapted to the subject matters of literature, history, and the sciences. Devices were borrowed from the old disciplines, particularly from rhetoric, and put to new uses on the concrete facts of history, the humanities, and the sciences. Mathematics ceased to be the arts of things and became an inclusive science in the Cartesian universal mathematics or a physical science in the Newtonian universal mechanics or a special science with applications in other sciences; and philosophy ceased to be the art of arts and the science of sciences to become a special science by adaptation of methods from the other sciences. Disciplines, as fields, were multiplied in the quarrel of the ancients and the moderns, which affected both the humanities and the sciences, and in the specialization which separated the literatures of different languages and cultures and the fields of different sciences in which scientific methods were applied to different natural processes. The humanities were sharply separated from the sciences in this specialization: the humanities studied values by making them facts descriptive of different times and cultures, and the sciences investigated facts by making scientific methods and scientific explanations value-free. The social sciences used scientific methods to investigate values as national wealth, social customs, psychological preferences, and human modes of living and association. Higher education continued to be in law, medicine, and theology, until teacher-training, engineering, business, agriculture, nursing, social-service, and library-training were added to the professional schools, and the graduate schools extended education in the humanities, the natural sciences, and the social sciences, and adapted the professionalism of older higher education to the proliferating specialization of the new fields.

We have thought of the modern problems of civilization, character, and education as problems of fragmentation which has destroyed communication among people of different cultures, different occupations, and different educational formations. We have sought the remedy in interdisciplinary cooperation in research and teaching. Interdisciplinary research is the cooperation of experts from different fields in the investigation of common problems. Interdisciplinary education has, in the twentieth century, taken the form of general education to relate the disciplines; of courses in crucial issues—international, national, and local—to relate the disciplines to the problems, policies, and ideologies of our times; and of courses in other cultures than our own to relate the different traditions of arts, attitudes, and values. The relations established among the disciplines are relations among fields treated, rather than among arts used. It is only by accident that the student in general education acquires the arts by which to perceive and appreciate the values achieved in the natural sciences, the social sciences, and the humanities, or the arts by which to relate them to each other; crucial issues are usually approached by means of arts to secure agreement on a proposed resolution rather than by arts to arrive at and judge a solution; and area courses teach the language and customs of a particular culture and not the arts by which different cultures approach common problems. We have made professional schools interdisciplinary by introducing courses in the humanities and social sciences in engineering schools; courses in the social sciences and psychology in law schools; courses in psychology and religion in medical schools; and courses in social service, psychology, and pedagogy in theological seminaries. The press of specialization in graduate schools gives selected interdisciplinary work a status of specialization in research.

Interdisciplinary education and research cannot be achieved simply by juxtaposing, adding, or uniting disciplines conceived as fields or by elevating one of the fields to the office of queen of the sciences to produce knowledge conceived as unified information concerning the facts and analyses of different kinds of data and experiences. We need new disciplines to identify and transmit the arts by which men act and integrate their purposes and knowledge. Such discipline can be formed by relating them to a new conception of character as a product and source of responsibility and autonomy rather than as an image and object of common approbations and private interests. The problems of means are problems of the adjustment of education to character. All men do not have the same natural abilities. At each stage of education, natural abilities are developed by practice and are diversified in new acquired skills; and skills, in turn, are generalized and directed by insight concerning causes and objectives which is acquired in the formation of arts. A man of great natural ability may need little practice and no conscious art, but the geniuses of thought and action furnish the examples for the development, in education, of exercises to produce like abilities and of analyses to produce like deliberate awareness of possibilities and how they may be utilized. The problems of sequence are problems of the adjustment of character to education. Experience is the product of repeated sensations and feelings, and skills in making and virtues in doing are habituations formed by experiences; the man of virtue and skill may act and produce without intellectual awareness of the rule of reason or the norms of value which are subject to examination and formulation by prudence and art; and the rationality and purposiveness of prudence and art have foundations in scientific knowledge and moral and esthetic values which need not be mastered by the man of art or prudence.

The relation between reason and action is ambiguous and generates a series of basic philosophic distinctions which have dogged education even in its least philosophical modes and phases—distinctions of thoughts or statements or actions and things (what is believed or said to be the case and what in fact is the case, what is undertaken and what is done, what is conceived and what is known, what is asserted and what is meant, what causes action and what is sought in action) and distinctions of fact and values (what is and what ought to be, what is known and what is decided, what is approved and what is done). The same ambiguities are present in "right action" and "rational action." An action is right if it is well adapted to the circumstances, resources, needs, and purposes of the agent, that is, if it is well done; an action is right if it improves the circumstances, realizes the potentialities of available materials, orders needs, and develops the abilities and interests of the agent, that is, if the end achieved is good. All actions, even erratic and neurotic actions are reasonable, since they have discoverable causes, of which the agent is frequently explicitly conscious. An action is rational when it is well adjusted to the character of a person and his purposes under the circumstances; an action is rational when the reasons for the action and the values achieved by it have been examined and judged. Good skills and good habits may be badly used, but they have the rightness and rationality of actions well performed; and such actions are put to good uses when they conform to rules of reason and norms of rightness which need not be reviewed in each action or by each agent. Education for character is the formation of moral virtues and technical skills adapted to the rational and the right by prudence and art; it is also the formation of intellectual virtues to relate what passes for prudence and art to values and reality and to judge and justify their pertinence to what is the case and to what is desirable. The first treats problems of means which must be faced at all stages of education. The second treats problems of sequence in which general education to produce the virtues and skills needed by all men is distinguished from higher education to produce some men competent to apply science and wisdom to the judgment of what is accepted as true and valuable.

Arts and disciplines were at various times in the past closely related to the formation of character and to the judgment of character by virtues and abilities. We have made some advances in the formation of new disciplines to serve that purpose today, but the change is impeded by conceptions of character and of arts and disciplines which make it difficult to relate problems of personality to problems of learning. Experiments in general education have been based on a conception of the liberal arts which we have inherited from the Renaissance when the term "fine arts" or "beaux arts" was used to differentiate the subject matter of the humanities and when the study of literatures was provided with systematic methods in the "ars critica." The development of the natural sciences made liberal arts colleges schools of arts and sciences. Much of what passes for general education merely brings together fragments of the fields of the humanities, the physical sciences, the biological sciences, and the social sciences, and it preserves the distinction of science and art in a stultifying separation of knowledge of facts and knowledge of values. Some remnants of the medieval liberal arts are occasionally used to isolate the arts employed to unify each of the fragments and to relate them to each other, but they also serve to perpetuate the medieval distinction between the arts of words and the arts of things.

The arts which are used most effectively in examining contemporary problems and in making decisions about them are those which relate facts and values, words and things. The formation of disciplines to train men in those arts is hampered by two diremptions in our customary use of disciplines as fields and disciplines as arts. We continue to make the distinction between intellectual judgments and esthetic judgments into a sharp separation: the statement of facts depends on a cognitive use of language, the statement of values involves an emotive use. We continue to make the distinction between laws and facts, lawlike statements and factual descriptions, into a like separation of disparate realms: words have connotations and meanings as well as denotations and references, and universal statements are judged by examining the words or symbols in which they are expressed (frequently making their certainty the expression of a tautology), while particular statements are judged by their empirical warrant. We must forget the radical separation of verbalisms and pragmatisms in the Roman arts, which were continued in the separate spiritual verbalisms and pragmatisms of the medieval arts, in order to penetrate to the relations of words and things; and we must abandon the similar segregations of humanisms and scientisms in the Renaissance arts, in order to perceive and appreciate facts and values. The recognition of the most particular and least disputable fact depends on generalizations of experience and knowledge which make it possible for us to perceive and judge it as a fact; the most abstract and formal statement or symbolic arrangement has a factual character and derivation which makes it possible for us to appreciate it as a concrete structure and interpret it in possible definite meanings and particular applications. What is is not what ought to be, but any selection and statement of what is depends on value judgments concerning it as it is and contains indications of what it may become; and any preference and appreciation of values depends on facts of taste and judgment and on facts about what is or about the possibility of changing it.

The new disciplines should be arts by which acceptance or statement of facts is related to the structures of thought and statement by which they are known or discovered, and by which perception or judgment of values is related to actualities in which they inhere or to possibilities by which they may be made actual. Some indication of their character can be derived by considering them as connections among disciplines considered as fields and as extensions of disciplines considered as arts. If the arts of facts and values, of words and things are combined in interdisciplinary assimilation of what have traditionally been distinct fields and distinct arts, four arts may be distinguished.

General education should include the art of interpreting facts and statements. Known facts are recorded facts, and facts are recorded in all the disciplines. The art of recovering and interpreting known facts extends to the facts recorded in history, presented in literature, and established in science and, from them, to the facts encountered in experience and interpreted in the light of known historical, artistic, or scientific facts. The structure and meaning of facts is the structure and meaning of truth. To be able to explore what is known, is to be able to appreciate and judge tradition and to use it in knowledge, action, and esthetic judgment. Changing applications of factual statements and changing meanings of true statements transform statements and facts into questions and problems. The interpretation of fiction and drama depends on facts and raises questions: interpretation of facts about Hamlet makes possible the appreciation of a play and raises questions that extend to other forms of esthetic appreciation and to practical and theoretic inquiry; the facts which an audience recovers with Oedipus while following the plot of a tragedy raise questions which psychology examines with respect to all men; the device of the Wooden Horse and the adventures of Don Quixote raise questions of esthetics, political strategy, and social and individual morality. In like fashion the interpretation of men and peoples discloses facts and raises questions about the nature and interaction of individual and society, human consensus and natural law; and the interpretation of things and processes discloses facts and raises questions about parts and kinds, actions and reactions. The structure of facts is a structure of consistency and coherence; even random occurrences have an order of probability, and the surprises of a hazardous world are consequences of the expectations of an orderly world.

The study of known facts should yield insight into a rich diversity of facts and into the congruences and homogeneities of their multiplex interrelations. It is an art of interpretation and recovery not unrelated to what the art of grammar was when it was the art of interpreting texts and uncovering the meanings and values they express. The new liberal art is a study of *questions* raised in the interpretation not only of literary texts and scriptures but also of scientific texts, of statements of policy, law, and custom, and of historical records, and in the interpretation of the facts stated and meant as well as the significances of language and the connections of thought. It is acquired by practice of an art of recovering facts in experience as well as of an art of seeing the import of statements in narratives, expositions, or arguments. Its subject matter is any factual statement or stated fact. It is the art of *recovery*.

The art of knowing and interpreting facts and statements should be supplemented by an art of discovery and invention. The study of known facts remains within the founded region of what men have accomplished. Intimations of the existence and influence of unknown facts beyond the frontiers of knowledge are conveyed by problems and incoherences encountered in accepted facts and accepted modes of procedure. Interest in creativity has recently led to experiments in the arts of discovery and invention in education. Like the art of understanding and interpreting facts already attested, the art of discovering and creating new facts depends on constituting structures by means of which facts in turn are constituted. The structure of interpretation is a structure of coherent meanings and consistent facts in which lines of implication and sequence may be detected or constructed; the structure of invention is an interpreted structure in which incoherences and contradictions indicate the need for new facts or for reinterpretation of unquestioned meanings and undoubted facts. Facts and statements have internal as well as external structures, and new facts are constituted by modifying the elements of old facts or by introducing new elements in combination with familiar elements. The elements of facts and statements are terms and concepts. Basic ideas have undergone a long history of change in each of the disciplines considered as fields, and many of them have moved from one discipline to another, adapting old meanings to new applications in which they get new meanings. Motion, matter, and infinity, organism, function, and life, constitution, law, and freedom, beauty, imagination, and expression have changed their meanings again and again in innovations and discoveries. Reconstituted as new elements they have also contributed to innovations by making perception of new facts possible and communication about them intelligible.

The study of the elements of facts should yield insight into the nature of unknown facts and practice in the arts by which they are investigated and made known. It is an art of selection and discovery not unrelated to what rhetoric was when it included a basic art expounded in treatises called *De Inventione*. Concepts and terms have fixed meanings. Changing meanings transform concepts and terms into "places" or "topics." Ancient rhetoric used "common places" as "seats of invention or discovery"; Francis Bacon reoriented places from search for forms of statement to inquiry into matters stated: he criticized "common places" which yield words and arguments and used "proper places" for the discovery of things and arts and for the advancement of knowledge. The new liberal art is a study of *topics* or places which lead to innovations in each of the disciplines as subject matters and in the common matters which make possible the transition of concepts and terms from discipline to discipline; it is acquired by practice of arts of discovery which uncover new facts by the heterogeneous combination of concepts and terms. Its subject matter is any term which is ambiguous or subject to dispute in a statement of fact. It is the art of *discovery*.

The arts of known facts and of unknown facts make use of structures. It is impossible to state or recover a fact in isolation from other statements or facts, and it is impossible to invent or select a concept, term, or element without presenting it as a constituent part of a statement or a fact. The art of recognizing and of making structures is the art of using connections for action, art, and inquiry. There are sequences and consequences in each of the disciplines considered as fields, and there are sequences and consequences which relate fields to each other. Consequences and sequences have literal and fixed orders in any particular statement or concrete application of them, but the orders they state or establish are *themes* which take on fixed meanings adapted to the facts stated and ordered. The innumerable plots and heroes of drama and fiction are variations on a finite number of themes of human action and suffering; the innumerable associations formed by men and the innumerable men determined by actions and associations are variations on a finite number of themes explored in theories of the relation of individual and society; and the innumerable motions initiated, transmitted, and altered are variations on a finite number of themes of matter and motion elaborated in inquiries into laws of motion. The sequences and consequences examined by any of the disciplines as arts may be found in any field; and any document—a poem, a judicial decision, or a scientific treatise—may be read as an instance of connections revealed by literary, social, or scientific methods.

The study of connections should yield insight into sequences of thought, action, and process, and practice in the arts by which they are used in thinking, doing, and making. It is an art of method and presentation not unrelated to what was once called the art of discourse, *"ars disserendi."* It is a new liberal art when it is applied to *themes* to relate different discourses, *"discursus"* or "runnings about," in words, in thoughts, and in things to each other by examining their formulation in poetical, rhetorical, and logical sequences. Its subject matter is any sequential or compendent whole ordered by methods of arranging, doing, inquiring, or knowing. It is the art of *presentation*.

The art of forming structures is ordered not only to facts and to the arts used to interpret and discover facts but also to principles and to the arts used to give structures objective foundations and ideal values. Action, art, and knowledge are organized according to principles, as are the parts and processes of any encompassing and organic whole. The system of any discipline orders the subsystems proper to the field, and it may be used to organize other disciplines considered as fields and to orient other disciplines considered as arts. The art of judging and establishing the authority or warrant from which consequences are traced and on which their validity and value depend is an art of relating sequences of thought, statements, and things by connections of ideas, words, and facts disclosed and tested in narrative, exposition, or inquiry and proof. It is the art of finding principles in reality and in values for methodologized orderings of recovered and discovered facts. Warranty is never absolute; it is a structure of structures. In antiquity metaphysics was called an "architectonic science" because it treated and established the principles of all sciences, theoretic, practical, and productive. Politics was a like architectonic science because the institutions and customs of states determine the activities and the permissible modes and available materials of activity to be pursued by its members, including activities in the arts and sciences. Poetics or the science of production was likewise an architectonic science because sciences and social and political institutions, like art objects and instruments of production, are products of arts. Principles are used reflexively on each other and are transformed from principles to consequences by changing the science used as architectonic: the philosophy of science examines the organization of the sciences, including psychology and sociology; psychology accounts for attitudes and doctrines, including those of philosophers and sociologists; the sociology of knowledge sets forth the structures of experience and expectation which determine beliefs and conclusions, including those of philosophy and psychology.

The study of systems and of transformations of systems of knowledge, action, and art should yield insight into the nature and uses of principles and into the art of establishing principles, combining them into fruitful sets, transforming them under the influence of other principles, and detecting and stating them as *causes, consensus,* and *paradoxes.* It is the art by which interdisciplinary connections are established among the disciplines considered as subject matters and the art by which hierarchical connections are established among the disciplines considered as arts. It is an art of principles and systematization not unrelated to the arts of analytic, dialectic, and sophistic. It is a new liberal art when its subject matter is extended to all inclusive organizations of things, actions, and knowledge and to the principles on which they are established. It is the art of *systematization.*

The problems of means are the same at all stages of education. Higher education, like any other stage of education, should be liberal education, and it should affect character by inculcating arts of recovery, discovery, presentation, and systematization appropriate to the abilities and interests of the person and his prior formation and education. Problems of sequence distinguish higher education from general education. General education is a prerequisite to higher education in the sense that the arts acquired in general education are used in the more determinate fields and specialized arts of higher education. Higher education is the basis of general education in the sense that the arts of general education and the selections of elements, the interpretations of facts, the methods of connections, and the systematizations of principles are derived from the arts and from the fields of the specialized disciplines of higher education. The problems of education for character in higher education are different from those of general education. Nonetheless, many of the problems of the relation of the arts of general education to the formation of character result from unsolved problems of higher education.

General education should produce some acquaintance with and interest in all arts and subject matters to relate all men in diversified communities and to differentiate men by giving each man an integrated individual character. The arts and disciplines of general education, to be effective, must have objectivity and purposiveness. The grounds and ends of general education in secondary schools, colleges, and adult education are determined and justified by higher education which uncovers and establishes accepted principles of reality and value and produces the exemplars and teachers of general education. Reality and values tend to be separated from each other and to be assigned to narrow mutually exclusive fields and to special unrelated arts in higher education. The tendency in general education to repair the dichotomy of words and things by treating facts in structures and to deny the dichotomy of facts and values by treating possibilities in actualities is hindered by the separation of problems of character and learning in higher education. If higher education is designed to develop competence in particular fields, even if the fields of scientific inquiry and those of moral and esthetic judgment are conceived to be distinct, competence in every profession and in each field of science, social science, and the humanities is made to consist in mastery of the facts and of the methods of treating the problems of the field; and the problems of attitude and purpose, taste and morality, feeling and will, adjustment and autonomy are separated from the problems of cognition and objective knowledge. Education then is thought to have become primarily intellectual and in need of reform to provide interest and motivation and to take into account the whole man, and the rational processes developed in such education have no direct relation to action or appreciation, responsibility or taste.

Yet the relation of education to character is clearer in higher education than in general education. In general education comprehensive arts and inclusive disciplines are acquired for the formation of individual character. In higher education specialized arts and competence in particular fields are inseparable from character traits essential to mastery of the arts and use of the competences employed in them. The specialized arts and disciplines of higher education are not defined solely by the subject matters on which they are employed: they are arts and disciplines only if they arouse interest and purpose, judgment and insight. They are a development of the self in relation to others by means of knowledge adapted to circumstances. Higher education develops kinds of character adapted to disciplines considered as fields and formed by disciplines considered as arts. They are subject, like other species or kinds, to generic descriptions which are particularized by application to particular matters and by specification in particular functions. Acquisition of the art of recovery in a particular field produces a receptive man, sensitive to known facts and consistencies, and conservative of established knowledge and values; acquisition of the art of discovery produces a curious man, resistant to the pressures of acceptance and conformity, and tolerant of incongruities and inconsistencies which open up possibilities of spontaneous self-initiation and innovation; acquisition of the art of presentation produces an open-minded man, imaginative in perceiving and forming connections; acquisition of the art of systematization produces a purposive man, reflective concerning possible orders of knowledge, action, and judgment and concerning the transformations of organizing principles and of the hierarchies of their systematic consequences. Higher education should form men who have acquired all these arts and unite them in an integrated character which is dynamic and self-assured in applying them within a special field and in extending them to relate knowledge and progress in that field to other men and their formation and to other problems and their resolution. The arts relative to character are disciplines formative of character. They are distinct from the arts of science, when the latter are limited to applying laws and law-like statements to processes and occurrences; and they are distinct from the arts of semantics, when the latter are limited to analyzing the meanings and applications of words. The arts of character are oriented to the intentions and purposes, problems and aspirations of individual men: they are skeptical and resistant as well as responsive to established facts and new facts, and perceptive and productive of actual values and possible values.

Disciplined sensitivity is an acquired art which transforms undifferentiated immediate experience into awareness of certifiable and interpretable facts. Competence in any field depends on mastery of the relevant facts, but knowledge acquired as factual information tends to make facts fixed, hard, and irresistible, and to make interpretations frozen presentations of facts as pertinent or irrelevant or fictive. Facts are not encountered readymade in experience. They are made, as their name implies, and their making depends on structures of knowledge, action, and art from which they derive their being and interpretation. Facts are discredited or made credible by changes in the structures in which they are perceived and stated. It is easy to show that an alleged fact is imaginary or fictive by interpreting it in a structure of coherence different from the one in which it is stated. Discredited facts are either abandoned or reinterpreted. It is easy to extend a structure of interpreted facts to more like facts. Accredited facts are either static tabulations or dynamic steps to new interpretations in which the initial facts are modified or discredited. The most successful interdisciplinary research and teaching are based on relating the facts of one discipline to the facts of other disciplines. Interdisciplinary juxtaposition of fields needs to be supplemented by more attention to the art of interpretation by which those relations are established and given meaning.

The development of sensitivity in higher education in the professions and in the arts and sciences depends on breaking the tyranny of fixed accepted facts reified as independent entities. There is a vast multiplicity of facts in any field and a vast number of interpretations of them as facts. To know more facts is to practice the art of interpretation more broadly. It is to raise questions of fact and interpretation. The coherent facts of a discipline are not a catechism of truths to be learned and re-peated: they are products of a structure of tried hypotheses which open up factual relations in the context of other structures which yield facts which at first seem irrelevant or dubious. The art of interpretation is used to make some irrelevant facts relevant and some dubious facts divergent aspects of relevant facts. Disciplined sensitivity is acquired by knowledge of more facts and use of more interpretations. It extends without need of extraneous disciplines from the problems of a particu-lar field to the problems of communities and other people and to their facts and sensitivities.

Disciplined originality is an acquired art which abandons or modi-fies accepted certainties and interpretations when they become involved in inconsistencies and present problems. Contradictions may be re-moved by reinterpreting the facts, or they may be removed by aban-doning them and reexamining the structure of concepts by which they are constituted facts. Every discipline has its basic categories which are employed without question and which seem to be fixed in the nature of the subject matter and to be so immediately discernible that depar-tures from them are recognized to be category mistakes detected and corrected by inspection and intuition. Categories are multiplied into the numerous elementary terms and concepts which take their place when the priority of a finite set of categories is challenged. They yield to topics or places in the art of invention when the interpretation of inconsistencies in facts suggests the need for new facts and for the invention of new categories to constitute them. The discoveries which laid the foundations of modern mechanics depended on the transfor-mation of concepts and categories. "Motion," together with "rest," are categories in Plato's analysis of being and becoming; "motion" is a basic concept and a subject matter in Aristotle's physics, defined in terms of matter, form, and privation and classified into kinds by use of the categories of substance, quality, quantity, and place; the inconsis-tencies and problems found in the Aristotelian concept of motion by Greek commentators in the third to sixth centuries, by Latin commen-tators in the fourteenth century, and by Galileo in the seventeenth century led to discussion, not of a single concept, but of a "topic" which made transition possible from concept to concept; Galileo lim-ited his analysis to local motion which he defined in terms of time and space; similar topics made possible transitions in concepts from weight, to mass, to matter, and from power, to force, to energy. The structures of defined elements of facts and statements are themselves facts ordered coherently and consistently; undefined elements provide the continuity among changing facts and concepts, and their efficacy for innovation derives from their inconsistency and incongruity with established structures and expectations. The art of invention is used to discover new facts by selecting new elements or newly defined elements from which to construct them. Disciplined originality is acquired by knowledge of topics which are the source of new elements and new concepts in a given field, and by practice in the art of selection which makes possible the combination of elements in new meaningful facts and interpretations. Originality acquired in creative selection in a particular field emphasizes the intellectual aspect of character traits adapted to creative innovations in the contradictions of practical action and the inconsistencies of cultural values.

Disciplined coherency is an acquired art to follow or establish connections of things or of discourse. It explores and creates the structures within which disciplined sensitivity detects and interprets facts. Facts are encountered in sequences of occurrences and are understood and stated in consequences of thought and discourse. Disciplined sensitivity is an ability to interpret and present; disciplined coherency is an ability to trace paths across structures of fact and to relate presentations methodically. It is not limited to the ability to recognize the adequacy and validity of a particular sequence or account or proof; it includes the imaginative ability to place presentations in different sequences and to recognize the "themes" which are set forth in different accounts as different connections of the same or different facts. "Freedom," thus, is employed in the acquisition of knowledge, the performance of actions, and the creation of art; it is a fact of knowing, willing, and feeling; it is analyzed in relation to the nature of man, knowledge of the good, use of power, and deliberative choice. Disciplined coherency is used to trace the consequences of any thesis in narrative, description, inquiry, and proof; it is used to move from thesis to thesis and from method to method by treating different accounts as variations of a theme. Disciplined sensitivity answers questions by recognizing facts; disciplined coherency elaborates themes to account for facts by connections or reasons among facts. The art of presentation is used to set forth and analyze sequences and consequences. Disciplined coherency is acquired by knowledge of the themes which establish connections in a given field, and by practice in the art of presentation which uses methods to establish theses by definition and hypothesis and to build the variant connections which particularize a theme. Disciplined coherency acquired in treating the connections of a particular field makes use of methods which extend its technical themes to connections which involve other men and the problems of life and action.

Disciplined purposiveness is an acquired art to establish principles of order among the structures of interpretation, discovery, and presentation. It seeks criteria and norms for the accepted, the novel, and the connected in principles which provide warrant of their objectivity and justification of their values. It is not an art limited to the subjective purposes of man nor does it depend on hypostasizing purposes in a teleological universe. It does not make commitments to matter or mind, accident or design, since it is the art used in controversies about them. It is committed only to the conviction that the connections of subject matters can be stated accurately and adequately in connections of discourse, and that the connections established by methodological inquiry and well-grounded proof can be tested by sequences of events observed or experimentally controlled. Disciplined purposiveness seeks the causes of the sequences traced by disciplined coherency, and it transforms the structure of known sequences by relating them to causes which condition the operation of their proper causes. We do not think, or act, or judge according to principles ordered in a strictly determined set. The principles according to which we proceed when our thoughts, actions, and judgments are orderly can be detected and stated, but disciplined purposiveness is needed to disclose the effect of other principles on the principles we explicitly acknowledge and the transformations of principles which result when the diverse subject matters are "reduced" to that of one discipline in the organization of knowledge and when the arts of one discipline are used to hierarchize all arts in the sequential use of arts. The literal principles in particular fields are related to each other in paradoxes which state the principles of architectonic sciences. When the principles of the dynamics of point-particles were extended to other motions they yielded the paradoxical principles of thermodynamics, of electrodynamics, and of the dynamics of the motion of light, and in further extension they yielded the paradoxical principles of relativity physics and quantum mechanics which order the motion, energy, and matter of the cosmos and of its least particles. The art of systematization is used to give ordered sequences of facts objective foundations and intelligible values. Disciplined purposiveness is acquired by knowledge of the paradoxes from which the principles of knowledge, action, and art are derived in a given field (which in turn are instances of the paradox that knowing, doing, and making may each be used as a principle to account for the others), and by practice of the art of systematization by which principles are related to each other by more inclusive principles from which they derive their application to things and their pertinence to ends. Disciplined purposiveness is adapted to the extension to any principle, and it is adapted to the principles of a particular discipline only by systematizing that discipline in other architectonic sciences.

Teaching for character in higher education does not depend on the addition of new arts and disciplines to those proper to higher education. It does depend, however, on a fuller use of the arts of interpretation, discovery, presentation, and systematization, and an understanding of their bearing on the person who acquires them as well as their bearing on the subject matters on which they are practiced. The art of interpretation is concealed in the presentation of facts, and competent and comprehensive reporting of the state of knowledge in the field becomes a substitute for disciplined sensitivity. The tyranny of facts cuts short the interpretation of facts to preserve their definiteness as facts and limits the multiplication of facts to preserve their relevance and consistency. The art of discovery is denuded of structure, and assured or spontaneous departure from customary formulations becomes a substitute for disciplined originality. The tyranny of novelty cuts short patient analysis of topics and obscures the relevance of novelty in the statement of facts to the resolution of incongruities and inconsistencies encountered in facts. The art of presentation is limited to a fixed view of the connections in a subject matter and of the scientific, practical, or esthetic method by which they are treated in the discipline. The tyranny of precision cuts short exploration of themes and limits variation of methods in their treatment. The art of systematization is reduced to an art of explanation, and principles are seldom referred to except in a mathematical sense. The tyranny of randomness cuts short analysis of paradoxes and of the ordering principles they yield and limits systematic formulations and statements of the relations of disciplines to establishment of domains of inquiry and survey of their borders. If the arts practiced on subject matters were used in education in their bearing on character, the influence of arts and disciplines would be clear in the abilities acquired; and use of those abilities as arts on the subject matters taught would transform the contents of education and the problems and methods of the disciplines considered as fields. Since general education borrows its arts and disciplines from higher education, education for character in higher education would provide materials and methods for the improvement of general education, as well as for progress and revolution in the arts and sciences.

II. SOME APPROACHES
IN SCHOOLS AND COLLEGES
TO EDUCATION FOR CHARACTER

Chapter 4. SOCIAL CHANGE IN EDUCATION AND THE CHANGE IN EDUCATIONAL CONCEPTS

by Daniel Bell

I.

LET ME BEGIN with some statistics rather than an epigram or anecdote, for sometimes statistics are as compelling, in their own way, as any literary narrative. At the University of California at Berkeley, judged by its peers (circa 1964) as the foremost university, for the eminence of its faculty, in the United States there are 17,000 undergraduates, of whom 10,000 are upperclassmen (juniors and seniors) and 7,000 underclassmen. The vicissitudes of this student body are extraordinary. Students do not come to Berkeley for four years: of those who enter as freshmen, only about *half* graduate; the other half either drop out or transfer elsewhere. Of the total graduating class, on the other hand, forty percent are transfer students who had been at Berkeley only during their upper-class years.

Consider another set of statistics about Berkeley dealing with the character of classroom experience. Of the 1965 graduating class, only four percent had been in honors programs and only eight percent had received any individual instruction. Of courses taken during the freshman and sophomore years, over forty percent were taught by graduate teaching assistants; in the college as a whole, sixty-five percent of the classes with fewer than fifteen students, and sixty-three percent of the classes with sixteen to thirty students, were taught by graduate students.

Berkeley, then, is a college in which most of the teachers—if one separates teaching by discussion from lectures—are graduate students, who are themselves still working for their degrees. But the lot of the graduate student is little better than that of the undergraduates. For a total graduate student body of about 10,000, the Main Library at Berkeley has 415 individual study spaces assigned on a first-come basis. The seventeen graduate departments in the humanities, with about 1,600 graduate students, have reading rooms that seat 124. Students in the sciences or social sciences—at least the best of them—are better off; given the extensive number of research projects, they become attached, often in a kind of feudal servitude, to a professor, and they are thus able to learn on an apprentice basis.

Though the student body numbers 27,000, only a small minority live on campus. Most students commute to school as they would to any place of work. Given the broken continuity of educational experience, and the separation from campus, is it any wonder that Berkeley, in the sad words of its Muscatine Committee, is not "a college community"? In that clumsy but powerfully suggestive term of sociology, it is not a *Gemeinschaft,* a place where people are bound together by common emotional ties, but a *Gesellschaft,* where relations are mediated, impersonally, by bureaucracy and bureaucratic rules.

If all this were an aberration, a special hothouse circumstance created as the price for assembling a great productive research faculty, one could only weigh the rival utilities and, on the basis of one's values, accept or regret the situation. But the sad fact is that Berkeley is not an aberration, for the situation there—at least the broken nature of the educational experience, if not the teaching by graduate assistants—is repeated at dozens and dozens of other institutions, without the saving grace of a distinguished faculty to compensate for the sin.

The situation arises out of the implosion of mass higher education. Just before World War II, about 1,300,000 students (or about fourteen percent of the young people between eighteen and twenty-two) were attending 1,630 institutions of higher learning. By 1964, almost 5,000,000 students (forty percent of the age cohort) [1] were attending 2,100

---

[1] The eighteen to twenty-two "age cohort" is a convenient fiction. Conventionally, one takes the number of students in college, and computes this as a percentage of the college-age group. Actually, a large number of college students may be over twenty-two, having decided to return to school after working for a few years, or the like. For convenience and comparison, the assumption is made that all college students are of one age cohort.

institutions that granted degrees. While the number of colleges, particularly junior colleges, has increased, a sizable proportion of the swelling number of students has gone into the State universities. Today there are eighty-five institutions of higher learning with more than 10,000 undergraduates, each.

The point is that today we have virtually come to accept the idea that every student is not only entitled to but should have a college education, just as in the 1920s the society decided that all students should have at least a secondary school education. It is estimated that by 1970 there will be a college-student population of almost 7,000,000, or about half the age cohort.

But what are the consequences of such a state of affairs? Most of the large State universities today, by law, admit every student graduating from high school with a grade of C or better. But in these schools the quitting rate at the end of the second year is already about fifty percent. What shall we do when this percentage begins to rise further? Especially in a society which tries to hide its failures? We have been avoiding the issue.

II.

This is one "manifest" aspect of change in the educational scene. A second is less easy to document; one intuits it, and confirms it to the extent one can, only impressionistically: This is the collapse of an orderly and systematic curriculum in the liberal arts colleges.

The bone structure of the liberal arts college has been the idea of general education. This has not necessarily been a commitment to crossdisciplinary or integrative courses which unite a number of diverse subjects or problems, though often, as at Columbia, Chicago, and Harvard, that was indeed the case. It has been, as a minimum, some commitment to a coherent arrangement or statement of curriculum, which was intellectually defensible within the aims of a liberalizing education.

This has meant, in practice, that the college has stipulated some courses or sequences of courses which students have been required to take outside of any specializations. Such courses have been within fields broadly subsumed as humanities, social sciences, and sciences;

they have either been common courses taken by all students, or courses which even though differing in content, were presumed to be equivalent in their treatment of congruent intellectual problems.

What one senses today is the falling apart of general education and its replacement by a cafeteria system whereby any and every kind of course is admitted within the corpus, so long as a student takes some— or any—courses outside his specialization. In the place of general education we have a "distribution requirement" in which the student has to take any one science course, any one humanities course, and any one social science course, with little regard for logic, coherence, generalizability, or any other criterion except the three different labels.

This disintegration of curriculum arises, in part, out of intellectual reasons. The hopes of interdisciplinary integrations, which were so high twenty years ago, have not materialized, at least on the general education level. Disciplines have become more intensive and specialized, reaching each other, if at all, at the peripheries or frontiers of concepts and problems. The multiplication of new knowledge, particularly in the sciences and the social sciences, has made it difficult to teach the subject by organizing it around "problems" or by surveys, while the effort to define underlying unifying conceptual structures, to the extent that they could be utilized in general education, has been lacking.

But while intellectual failures are evident, they do not predominate. In the past, such intellectual challenges have been met by intellectual responses. Today the failures are due chiefly to institutional reasons: the growth in size of many State universities has made general education courses unmanageable; the expansion of departments has led to an intensification of specialized interest, at the expense of the liberal or general education; the new opportunities for research and graduate teaching have drawn many senior persons away from undergraduate and general education. Many of the large universities, particularly those "on the make," have gone along with the current, instead of swimming against it. Eager to attract "name" faculty, they have emphasized research opportunities rather than teaching. But if research is to be encouraged, as it must be (for I do not separate research from teaching), these universities have failed to commit other resources, intellectual and financial, to the needs of undergraduate general education.

To make this sweeping indictment is not to slight the significant educational experiments that are under way at Chicago, Santa Cruz, Oakland, Montieth, Columbia, and even at Berkeley, where an Experimental Collegiate Program, following the inspiration of the old Alexander Meikeljohn plan, was begun two years ago, although it has now fallen apart. In fact, to name these efforts is to note how few are the responses, when the challenges are so vast.

Together, these two dimensions constitute a sociological axis of change, a change in the structure of education arising out of changes in the structure of the society. There is, as well, a second set of coordinates deriving from a change in the intellectual content of educational concepts themselves. It might be called the revolution in the concept of concepts.

The traditional idea of general education, implicitly or otherwise, was based on two premises: one, that there were invariant truths about human behavior which could be established by human reason, and second, that there was a range of knowledge (or books) which every civilized man ought to know under pain of being judged uncultivated. Both notions constituted what can loosely be called a "classical" concept of education and both were derived from the humanities.

Today, both notions are called into question. The first idea, of a common fount of wisdom, or a common book of knowledge, is difficult to maintain not only because of the multiplication of subjects arising from the quantitative accretion of new knowledge, but because of the new horizons which define our world. In the eighteenth century it was relatively easy for men to find a common ground of discourse, and even Emerson, when he made his first trip abroad in the 1830s, could quickly establish a rapport with Coleridge and Carlyle in discussing religion or literature. But in the syncretism of the modern world—a syncretism far beyond the world of Constantine with its mingling of strange gods—one is called upon to know the Indian Vedas, the doctrines of Zen, the themes of Negritude, and dozens of other intellectual doctrines in order to converse with the world's milling intellectual throngs. Even in the humanities, where the Bible and the Greek and Roman tradition has long provided a center of intellectual gravity, the thrust into our consciousness of the non-Western worlds has set us adrift.

In the sciences we have found that the world is no longer conceived as a fixed, bounded universe but as a set of paradigms, each intellectually coherent and self-consistent, which seek to explain a range of phenomena. And these paradigms themselves are subject to revision as new angles of vision are introduced. The revolutions in physics in the twentieth century—quantum mechanics; the complementarity theory of light particles and waves; relativity with its emphasis on shifting standpoints to measure space and time; the uncertainty principle regarding the atom; and Hubble's constant about the universe—have shaken our fundamental conceptions of matter and energy far beyond any previous period of human history, though with less impact on the philosophies of the day than the theories of Ptolemy and Newton had on the metaphysics of their worlds, an intellectual fact that itself underscores a change in the unity, if not in the character, of knowledge. What is clear is that science proceeds by creating successive conceptual structures, and one task of education is to show how new modes of conceptualization are established and how these become reorganized, when necessary, as new structures of explanation.

III.

How is one to meet these challenges of change? I have posed a number of problems—the introduction of a truly massive higher education; the disintegration of the general education curriculum; and the intellectual revolution in the nature of concepts—but in this paper I can only deal with them briefly.

To take the first. Few persons, at least not I, will dispute the argument that every young person in the country should be educated to the highest capacity of his potential and that government aid should be made available when necessary to insure that objective. It is, however, less clear that all students who have completed high school should be encouraged to go on to a liberal arts college. One is struck forcibly by the fact that in 1965, of the 800,000 males taking the College Entrance Board examinations, only *ten* percent scored 550 or better—which itself is only a respectable score. (The median score for freshmen in the Ivy League schools is about 650.) Although I am aware of the artificiality of these examinations, and while I do not accept the idea of a fixed intelligence, it is obvious that intellectual talents are not evenly distributed among all persons.

In an egalitarian society, it is desirable as a social fact to put as many students into college as have the talent. But it is a cruel deception of others, and an invitation to failure, to throw all high-school graduates into college because of an ideology. The consequences of failure may in fact be worse for the boy than the initial effort. Beyond that, one simply invites the lowering of standards—as is apparent in many high schools —in order to graduate all the students.

What we must seek to do is to raise the attainments and capacity of the boy, rather than to lower standards; but this is necessarily a long-run process. There is a more immediate, or proximate "solution." It is to differentiate the meaning of the term "higher education." In the next dozen years, for example, there will be a great demand for technicians whose skills will be needed in the newer fields of computer technology and the like. But while the skills for such jobs require training beyond the high-school level, it is not necessary to confuse technical higher education with university learning. One should differentiate the institutions of higher learning so that boys can find places in accordance with their abilities and possibilities. This means the creation of more junior colleges and community colleges, of technical institutions and business schools. The focus need not be exclusively vocational; in fact it should not be. But neither should one confuse a broadly based technical education with a liberal arts degree.

IV.

In regard to general education, the collapse of a liberal arts curriculum, at a time when there has been greater societal pressure to specialize, has led to several paradoxical ideological reactions—none more curious, perhaps, than the cry of the New Left for "freedom" in curriculum. Freedom in curriculum, as the issue is raised, seems to mean "no requirements." Freedom here is equated with completely free choice and the rejection of any constraints. (When my book *The*

Reforming of General Education appeared, with a set of proposals for a new curriculum at Columbia College, a number of New Left students, in a characteristic response, said: "Who are you, to tell us what to take?")

So defined, freedom is not freedom but the search for an identity. Poignant as this may be for a youth, it should not be confused either with freedom or education. Freedom has never been the complete absence of restraints (can there ever be such a state of affairs?) but the self-conscious shaping of one's future as between constrained alternatives. Nor is the freedom to take a potpourri of courses an education. Education is a confrontation—a confrontation with a tradition, a confrontation with a discipline, a confrontation with a teacher. As John Henry Newman said in his *What Is a University?*, "You cannot fence without an antagonist, nor challenge all comers in disputation before you have supported a thesis; and in like manner, it stands to reason, you cannot learn to converse till you have the world to converse with."

Education is also a judgment. To the young men who demanded "Who are you, to tell us . . . ," I can only say that I have studied the problem and made a judgment. The issue then is not between a judgment and *no* judgment but between rival assessments. And to any student who wants "freedom," I can only say that whatever one chooses, there has to be some consistent structure of meaning. I do not, for instance, insist that there is one and only one orderly structure, a trivium and quadrivium, which all must follow. But whatever education one seeks, it is incumbent that the sequence one selects can be articulated into some coherent intellectual structure which is rationally defensible. Without that, it is not education.

The sad fact is that at present the universities, for mendacious institutional reasons, have let the curriculum go by intellectual default. And it is ironic that the New Left has raised this default into an ideology.

V.

The final question—the limits of conceptualization—is the most difficult to define, for conceptualization divorced from subject simply becomes arrant scientism. On the other hand, to define education by the contents of a hundred great books, or a hundred great ideas welded together by a syntopicon, is a fruitless effort that merely repeats the controversy between the "neo-medievalists" (*i.e.,* Hutchins and Van Doren) and the "pragmatists" (*i.e.,* Sidney Hook).[2]

One way of cutting through the tangle is to define the issue not in terms of *what* one is to know, but how one is to know "the *how* of knowing." In other words, if one accepts, as I do, the importance of emphasizing conceptual schemes, how does one define its limits? In seeking to answer that question, I can try to answer, as well, the issues of substance which an education must confront.

Jerome Bruner, in a number of essays, most succinctly in "The Perfectibility of Intellect" in the volume *Knowledge Among Men,* has distinguished three modes of knowing—the enactive, the iconic, and the symbolic.

The enactive is knowing by doing. One learns (as among the primitives) by imitation, by initiation, by acting. All instruction is in context—in the bush, on the hunt, etc. "Among the Kung, one virtually never sees an instance of 'teaching' taking place outside the situation where the behaviour to be learned is relevant."

But in complex societies, however, there develops necessarily an "economical" technique of instructing the young by *telling* out of context, rather than *demonstrating* in context. This can take the substitute form of pictures, the iconic, or of the abstract or symbolic method.

The virtue of the abstract method is that it reduces our dependency on immediate experience. To know by experience is to know something intimately; but such knowledge, by its concentration on detail, is constricting. Abstraction allows us to overcome the particular. In the most abstract of all subjects, mathematics, we can unleash the imagination by teaching the student to think of the idea of number itself rather than the concrete referent of the number of apples or pears. What abstraction allows us to do is to codify knowledge and make it translatable into many different and varied circumstances.

---

[2] For a reprise of that issue, see Mark Van Doren, *Liberal Education,* Holt, Rinehart & Winston, Inc., New York, 1943; Sidney Hook, *Education for Modern Man,* New York University Press, New York, 1957.

The risks of abstraction, however, are precisely the distance it establishes from experience. When Machiavelli wrote his famous manual on the *Art of War,* he was able to propose a new theoretical ordering of battalions (a rearrangement of pikemen and swordsmen) which was a great advance over the motley assembly of uncoordinated medieval army companies. And yet—the story may be apocryphal—when Francis I asked him to assemble a battalion in accordance with his plan, Machiavelli was at a loss. He simply lacked the experience to translate his theory into practice. (Or, as another apocryphal anecdote has it, when a young Israeli was asked by the Israeli Navy if he knew how to swim, he replied, "No, but I know the theory of it.")

Man is not, contrary to nineteenth century thought, primarily *Homo Faber.* Man creates theories before he creates tools, yet the use of tools is equally necessary if he is to work out what he has prefigured. The simple moral is that any education has to strike a balance between the modes of doing, of representing, and of symbolizing, if a person is to grasp what he knows.

In a different fashion, I have sought (in my *Reforming of General Education*) to form other balances. I have argued that there exists today, more than ever, a need to bring to the fore the study of history as a means of emphasizing the immediate, the varied, and the contingent as a redress to the abstract. I have argued that there should not be a divergence between general education and specialism, in that specialism requires the context of inquiry in order to free it from the narrow bounds of mere training, while general education needs to be grounded in the rigor of disciplines before relationships can be seen and applied. And, finally, I have argued that it is a mistake to see the acquisition of knowledge as a unitary mode, for just as there is the enactive, the iconic, and the symbolic, so, too, there are the sequential modes (in mathematics and the sciences), the linked modes (in the social sciences), and the concentric worlds of the humanities.

The fundamental truism, perhaps, is that knowledge is relational. There is not, as William James said (echoed a generation later by the phenomenologists), simply a *state* of a consciousness, but consciousness *of* something. If there is anything enduring in the purposes of education—defined as the creation of self-consciousness—it is to teach students how to understand those changing relationships, their necessary and contingent features. That is the changeless element within the perceptual and conceptual flux; *that* is the eye of the hurricane of knowledge.

Chapter 5. THE MORAL CODE OF CHILDREN AND TEACHER EDUCATION

by Arthur W. Foshay

THE POINT of this paper is that the inadequate moral code taught in American elementary classrooms is governed by custom and the chance of history, that little is being done to affect it, and that we need not, and dare not, continue to ignore the matter in these violent times.

The moral code taught in school grows directly, without let or hindrance, from the educational legacy of the eighteenth and nineteenth centuries. The fierce warnings of the *New England Primer* [1] were still heard in American classrooms as late as 1800. McGuffey's readers, which happened to span the reign of Victoria almost exactly, proclaimed a combination of chauvinism and simple, country virtues, as did the other famous texts of the day. Probably no textbooks ever had as much influence on public beliefs and taste as the *Primer* and McGuffey. The school textbooks that replaced them took flight from all of this to the world of Thornton W. Burgess and Howard R. Garis—a vacuous fantasy-land of fairies and animals, and seventeenth and eighteenth century folk tales. These were supplanted by the "scientific," skill-centered, intellectually and morally empty readers and arithmetics we still use in most elementary schools. The history of

---

[1] *The New England Primer,* with an introduction by Paul Leicester Ford, *Classics in Education,* number 13, Teachers College Press, Columbia University, New York, 1962. For example, note these excerpts from the famous alphabet-couplets:

In Adam's Fall / We sinnéd all
The idle Fool / Is Whipt at School
Time cuts down all / Both great and small

Or this, from the "Westminster Shorter Catechism," reproduced in the *Primer:*

No meer man since the Fall is abel in this Life perfectly to keep the Commandments of God, but daily doth break them in Thought, Word, and Deed. . . . Every sin deserveth God's Wrath and Curse, both in this Life and that which is to come.

textbooks in American elementary schools is, whatever their strengths, a story of a steady, steep decline in moral content.

During this same two-century period, the teacher's role and function have also changed. Common school education during the days of the *Primer* was (to paraphrase) elemental, brutal, and short. A child had only to memorize the *Primer* to gain all the book-learning needed for a useful life. The teacher had only to govern this process by rod and rule; he did not require an advanced education, and ordinarily he did not have one. As the nineteenth century wore on, the amount and quality of the teacher's education increased. Normal schools appeared; county examinations assured a minimal level of knowledge and literacy. The level of the teacher's education has continued to increase during this century—though of course not fast enough. The normal schools have almost disappeared, and most of the teachers colleges have become general institutions, but by 1960 only forty-one of the States required four years of college for elementary school teaching certificates.[2]

With the lengthening of the school year during the nineteenth century, school books became larger. The seventy-eight pages of the *Primer* became six volumes of McGuffey, plus sets of arithmetic texts and the first specialized text, the *Webster Speller*. The sheer bulk of reading provided in elementary school textbooks doubled between 1890 and 1920, and has probably doubled again since 1920.

However, the increase in the amount to be read was accompanied in the textbooks by a corresponding decrease in concern with the moral code. The old nineteenth century standards of hard work and probity, taught through stories and maxims, were replaced with nothing, nothing at all.

The reasons for this decline in official attention to moral standards in the texts are generally understood. They need only be mentioned here. First, there was the confusion of moral with religious beliefs. Since the

[2] The exceptions, according to the 1960 National Education Association, *Manual on Certification Requirements for School Personnel in the United States,* were North Dakota (one year of college required); Nebraska (one plus); Colorado, Missouri, Montana, South Dakota, and Wisconsin (two years); Alaska, and Maine (three years). Forty-three states required four years of college for secondary school teaching. Quoted in Arthur W. Foshay, editor, *Rand McNally Handbook of Education,* Rand McNally & Co., Chicago, 1963. The effects of this situation are found, of course, in the small rural schools, not in urban districts.

school was not to teach religious beliefs, some people argued that private morality was none of the school's affair—and the school became morally neutral—at least in its official textbooks and other publications. Second, the culture changed, in reaction against Puritanism and religious fundamentalism generally, toward a less elemental code of public behavior, and the old moral precepts became suspect of hypocrisy. Third, there was the evolution of popular theological discussion and the attendant sharp social-class distinction between the religious fundamentalists and the religious intellectuals (as represented, let us say, by the contrast between the camp meeting evangelists and the higher criticism). Fourth, there was the emergence of cultural pluralism. Fifth, there was the emergence into popular consciousness of the social and behavioral sciences. The simple, rural virtues of McGuffey, *et al.* survived all of this for a surprisingly long time, but disappear they did—at least from the books.

With the longer school day and the lengthened school year, and the emergence of elementary school teaching as an occupation for upward-mobile women, all of which took place during the nineteenth century, the teaching of the moral code became one of the teacher's preoccupations. This did not happen by plan, nor has it been noticed by the educationists, though it could be documented in part by a study of the various discussions of "discipline" and "classroom management" since the early nineteenth century.

The code is still taught. During the early fifties, several of us examined the moral code of a large number of elementary school children in a Bible Belt community then of about 50,000.[3] There we found a system of social values and aversions—a moral code—that should be recognizable to anyone who knows American middle-class life.

Any value, to be studied, has to be taken as an attitude (a "predisposition to act toward or away from some referent"). Any attitude thus has a valence (the referent either attracts or repels), and an intensity (the attitude is strong or weak; it exists in some degree).

[3] Arthur W. Foshay, Kenneth D. Wann, and others, *Children's Social Values, An Action Research Study,* Teachers College Press, Columbia University, New York, 1954. The material used here is drawn principally from chapters 2 and 6, also from some unpublished material. While this study was deliberately very informal (it was intended to illustrate the possibilities and problems of cooperative action research) the findings mentioned here seem to ring true, and I therefore dare cite them.

Attitudes with a positive valence are called values; those with a negative valence are called aversions. Attitudes are learned, presumably, through positive or negative reinforcement. The way they are learned was described by Gordon W. Allport in his classic essay [4] on attitudes. Positive or negative values are learned, he said, by accretion, by association, by precept, through vicarious experience, and through traumatic experience.

The system of reinforcement associated with the learning of social attitudes is worth brief comment. One might assume that positive attitudes (values) are learned through reward, or positive reinforcement, and that negative attitudes (aversions) are learned through punishment, or negative reinforcement. That is how a child learns to like candy and avoid the hot stove. It does not appear to be the way social attitudes are learned. As far as we could tell through lengthy observation, social attitudes are learned chiefly through punishment. While some of the attitudes we found were stated in positive terms, as values, they appeared to be taught as if they were aversions: *i.e.,* they were punished in the breach, but only very slightly rewarded in the observance.

H. B. Pepinsky, in an unpublished study done in 1955–1956 at the Ohio State University campus school, found that the children had two entirely different vocabularies: the one associated with prohibitions was subtle, direct, and rich; the one associated with being a "good citizen at University School"—*i.e.,* the things to do, not the things to avoid—was ambiguous, general, and sparse.

It is possible, therefore, that much of the behavior we took to be evidence of social values and aversions was actually avoidance. This ironic possibility seems quite real when children explain "helpful" behavior . . . , for example, by pointing out that others were watching, and they didn't want to be thought unkind.

The elements of the social code we observed among these elementary school children (ages six to twelve) are given below in order of decreasing intensity. The intensity was estimated from the severity of punishments associated with violation of the code. It should be ob-

---

[4] Carl Murchison, editor, *Handbook of Child Psychology,* Clark University Press, Worcester, Massachusetts, 1933. (Reprinted by Russell & Russell Publishing Co., New York, 1967.)

served that the punishments, too, were determined by the code. Teachers did not punish the children physically. They "talked to them": they asked reproachful questions, or denied them privileges, or (rarely) ridiculed them.

Here are the values and aversions (the elements of the moral code) we found, in decreasing order of intensity:

property honesty
vulgar or obscene language
irreverent language
cleanliness
obedience
violence or physical cruelty
respect for official authority
courteous speech to adults
generosity with possessions
forbearance
completion of undertakings

The drop of intensity in this list was, we thought, very steep. Some elements of the code were punished scarcely at all, or so privately that we never heard of them. These elements therefore do not appear on our list. Gossip, or character assassination, was one of these.

It was striking to us that the teachers enforced this code, intended to do so, were confident of its importance, and believed (with good reason, we thought) that the community expected them to enforce it.

It should be emphasized that this is a finding about children, not adolescents or young adults. It is immediately noticeable, for example, that there is nothing in this code that pertains directly to the assumption of sex roles. Abraham Tannenbaum's study of the social values of adolescents suggests one effect of the appearance of sex roles in high school.[5]

In two academically-oriented high schools, one in the Midwest and the other in New York, he found that "athleticism" was more highly valued by boys and girls than any other quality, including academic achievement (which functioned to reduce the popularity of boys).

[5] Abraham J. Tannenbaum, *Adolescent Attitudes toward Academic Brilliance*, Teachers College Press, Columbia University, New York, 1062.

Moreover, the "enforcers" of this aspect of the adolescent code were the girls. The least popular boy (the biggest "drip") was the bright, hardworking, non-athletic scholar.

The code, as we observed it, was taught informally for the greater part in elementary school—at all those times when the children were "free." Every time the classroom activity changes (as from "discussion" to "free reading," or from "group report" to arithmetic) there is a momentary disorganization while the children reorient themselves. These are times when the social code is often broken, and the teachers intervene. The same is true of recess periods, "free play" periods, the lunch hour—in fact, at any time during the school day when the normal classroom rituals are not in charge. The elementary teacher, therefore, has as many as twenty opportunities every day to teach the social code. In our study, the teachers were fully aware of these opportunities, if one is to accept as evidence their anecdotes, and their interpretations of the anecdotal records they kept.

Of course, there are some formal occasions when attempts are made to teach values and aversions. In one local social studies program I know of, for example, the value "interdependence" is sought. The basis for the teaching is vaguely anthropological, but when one examines the program closely, it appears that the term "interdependence" refers only to economic interdependence among nations, and the purpose is not moral, but political. The people who designed the curriculum were seeking to teach about the necessity for the United Nations without stirring up the local Right Wing.

In Junior High School Physical Education classes, as David McClelland pointed out (in conversation), a good deal of "character" is in fact taught. The values of teamwork, withstanding defeat, and magnanimity in triumph, together with a certain physical courage, are indeed engendered, he thinks. One must add, of course, that these values are theoretically offered to everyone, but that because of the notorious weaknesses of Physical Education programs, they are actually offered to only a few.

Let us consider some properties of these codes. First, they deal with interpersonal, not intergroup, behavior. Second, they are parochial—they pertain strictly to the American middle class. Third, they center on property, speech, the body, and conformity. Fourth, in the main they tell children what to avoid, not what to do.

I shall make an assumption: that the social code of childhood remains essentially unaltered for most people, though during later life other elements are added to it. This assumption is based, I confess, largely on my own experience of teachers and parents over a generation; it is based, too, on one of the implications of the heavy, subtle impact of early life experience. I shall not defend the assumption further here, however; I ask the reader to make it with me, in order to deal with an urgent public problem that arises from the inadequacy of the social code of childhood.

The problem is this: the inadequacy of the unexamined social code of childhood, carried into adult life, is crippling us in these violent times. The "nice boy" of our Bible Belt town is called on to understand Orientals and Africans and our urban poor now. His moral code is in the public domain, because he himself has become an instrument of national policy. In what terms can he understand a man to whom craftiness has more survival value than property honesty? How is he prepared to act and feel about the dirty, often vulgar, urban poor? They will interpret his forbearance as snobbery. What they want is involvement, not tolerance. But involvement is missing from his code. What our "nice boy" does, if one is to believe what one sees, is to insulate himself from such people as well as he can. If he is in Europe or in the Middle East, he forms an enclave that looks, and sounds and even smells, like East Texas. At home, he flees his work, if it is in the inner city, to watch a TV actor portraying a comfortable world where the childish values and aversions are all one needs to deal with problems.

It is a fragile, ambiguous, incomplete, self-centered code. Moreover, it is monolithic and self-perpetuating. It is, after all, administered in school by teachers. The teachers are, in the main, local people, educated locally in a college staffed principally by other local people. At college, the teachers have passively learned the smattering of subjects that still passes for a higher education, with a weakly taught major field, usually Literature or History, or (too often) Education. I do not mean here to denigrate these colleges. These days, almost all of them are self-critical, and are actively improving. However, it is probably still accurate to say that they do little or nothing that would challenge the adequacy of the childish social code their students bring with them. College activities, of course, add to the code—but they do not challenge it. They do not give the prospective teacher the means to liberate himself from it, to question it, or to deepen it. H. Gordon Hullfish, who for forty years taught a course in the Philosophy of Education for Ohio State seniors, liked to tell of the typical response he received to his first writing assignment, which was to "write a few pages on 'What I Really Believe.'" The response, year after year, was the same: "Nobody ever asked me before."

The teacher learns at home and in elementary school the moral code he enforces, just as his students do. Nothing happens later to lead him to question it with any sophistication. He remains the prisoner of his childhood. The cycle is complete. Nice young people attend nice, undemanding local colleges, and return home to teach other children how to be as nice as they are. They believe deeply that the code is open and democratic—and so it is, but only to those who will accept its provisions without serious question.

Given sufficient determination, it ought to be possible to break the cycle during a teacher's undergraduate years in college. To do so requires that some college reforms already in process be accelerated and disseminated to the colleges teachers actually attend, that some good old ideas be revived and extended, and that we have a clear sense of the purpose of undergraduate education for prospective teachers.

Teacher education has passed through two distinct phases since the twenties. At that time, when most teachers were still coming from normal schools, people like Samuel Evenden of Teachers College tried to deepen and extend the curriculum by "professionalizing the subject matter"—*i.e.,* giving special treatment to college subjects so that teachers could use more of what they had learned in the lower schools. In effect, this meant that the college subjects were to become somewhat less theoretically oriented, but broader. Teachers, it was thought, needed a greater scope of information than did other people. Evenden and the others had other ideas, of course; they also tried to reform professional education—that education dealing directly with the art of teaching—to make it more realistic, and they sought to obtain for prospective teachers a very broad experience with humankind, as found in the slums, in factories, and in rural areas.

The days of "professionalized subject matter" have passed. At present there is a widespread agreement concerning what a prospective teacher's education ought to include. The terms of the agreement are as follows:

1. The teacher needs a liberal education of good quality; the teacher must first of all be well educated; there is no difference in what constitutes a good education for teachers, and for others.

2. The prospective teacher should spend a year or more (programs differ) learning how to teach, and what is entailed in becoming a teacher. A very large proportion of this time should be spent practising the art; in addition, the teacher should study a little psychology, a little about teaching methods and materials, and a little about the history of education.

The terms of the agreement can be found in a number of places: in *New Horizons for Teaching,* a policy statement by an NEA commission in the late fifties, or in the programs leading to the Master of Arts in Teaching, or in any number of postgraduate programs leading to teaching credentials.

But such programs, like their predecessors, still leave the question of moral education untouched. Let us paraphrase the *mot* attributed to E. L. Thorndike: "anything that is known is known in some way, and can be taught."

If teachers are to rise above the parochial, fragile, incomplete social code we have been discussing, then they have to gain the means. They have to know how such codes are made, and how they may be analyzed and reconstructed. This can be done in college, if a serious, consistent attempt is made.

Perhaps the general education of prospective teachers requires special treatment, after all, if they are to be freed from childhood morality. Two things can be done to bring this about, while the teacher-to-be is still an undergraduate. First, he should be put in contact with the knowledge most directly relevant to the making of moral codes: philosophy, anthropology, literature, political science, sociology, and psychology (including an emphasis on studies of achievement motivation).[6] Second, a serious attempt should be made to carry every

[6] The reference here is, of course, to D. C. McClelland's studies of achievement motivation. See David C. McClelland, *Studies in Motivation,* Appleton-Century-Crofts, New York, 1955, for the most comprehensive account of these studies. Professor McClelland has continued his studies, however; his work, and that of his students, should be followed closely by those interested in the development and modification of moral codes.

subject a teacher studies to its humanistic depth—that point at which it becomes clear that the subject is a productive way of contemplating the nature of man and his experience. Perhaps, having been carried to such a depth, the student will not overlook the marvel I once saw in a third grade classroom in Orinda, California, where a child, studying one of the new Science programs, confronted for the first time the question "what, then, is truth?"

To do all of this might well require a redefinition of "liberal education"; the student would have to take advanced work in several fields, not only one or two, if the fields are to be studied to reveal their moral import—which is often to be found in their modes of inquiry more than in their findings. Probably, since learnings about moral behavior are to be learned through experience, the student will have to conduct more inquiry himself than is customary now—and some didactic courses will have to give way. Surely, the student will require more time; colleges are bound one day to give up the long summer holiday for this reason.

Reforms of this kind are, of course, already under way. New College acted on many of them thirty-five years ago. If, following an undergraduate education of this type, the teacher were to study the moral codes of children as part of his professional education, perhaps he could see the codes with the necessary perspective. If he did, he might be freed to examine his childhood beliefs.

Such changes in college seem more available now than they used to, given the ferment in education. Their promise for the improvement of moral education is real, if it is grasped. Certainly, the need has never seemed so urgent as now, in our "world village."

Chapter 6. *AN EDUCATOR LOOKS AT EDUCATION AND RESPONSIBLE BEHAVIOR*

by Robert J. Havighurst

I.

WHEN THE WRITER and his colleagues began to study responsibility in children twenty-five years ago, the notion of responsibility seemed simple enough. It included reliability, accountability, autonomy. Responsibility was seen to be a central trait of moral character. When a group of sixteen-year olds were studied, using their reputation as an index of their character, the correlation coefficient of responsbility with *honesty, moral courage,* and *loyalty* were all of the order of .8 (see Table 1). The correlation coefficient of *responsibility* with *friendliness* was only .55, which was not unexpected.

We used a scaled check-list of statements describing various degrees of responsible behavior in sixteen-year olds. To make this check-list, we asked about thirty people to judge the degrees of responsibility expressed by a number of descriptive statements of behavior, and with the Thurstone Method of Equal Appearing Intervals we obtained the following scores on a scale from 0 to 100 for the following descriptions of behavior, among others.

69 Keeps appointments.

24 Is usually late for appointments.

71 Takes good care of school property.

11 Always forgets to do assigned homework.

5 Can never be depended on to complete a job.

94 Takes the initiative in assuming responsibility.

70 Gets down to work without being prodded by others.

82 Finishes assigned work whether checked up on or not.

92 Sees jobs to be done and does them without waiting to be asked.

16 Never feels any need to care for his room or possessions at home.

18 Lets others do the work he has agreed to do for his class or club.

31 Quits work as soon as the "whistle blows," even in the middle of a job.

41 Finishes most assignments promptly but in a careless, slap-dash fashion.

76 Works steadily and does not bother other people while teacher is out of the room.

47 Will carry out a task entrusted to him if it does not interfere too much with something he would rather do.

14 Likely to drop or neglect a difficult responsibility without bothering to notify anyone or find a substitute.

All the sixteen-year olds in the community were rated by one to eight adults in the community. The sixteen-year olds were also rated by their age-mates, using sociometric instruments. Among others, a set of word-portraits were presented to the group of sixteen-year olds, and they were asked to name those of their classmates who fitted these portraits. The following is one of the portrait-pairs for the measurement of responsibility.

Suppose you were going to choose boys and girls to plan a party, or to organize a campaign to sell savings stamps. You want boys and girls who have some good ideas, who will work hard, and who will stick to the job until it is finished. They know how to plan and they do careful work. They try to do their very best.

Some boys and girls do not do their share. They are careless and do not take very good care of things. They do not do good work on a committee. They cannot be counted on to do what they say they will do. They let other people do all the hard work.

A more sophisticated definition of responsibility recognizes two complementary aspects—responsibility to oneself and responsibility to society. The first is necessary for good mental health, and the second is necessary for a successful society.

II. A Developmental Definition

A description of the development of responsibility in these two aspects may be a good way to define the concept. There are five phases.

1. *Responsibility for oneself as an independent organism.* This is the earliest form of responsibility. It consists of habits of self-control and self-direction, starting with toilet habits, and developing into habits of punctuality, becoming able to cross the street alone, care of one's body such as brushing one's teeth, becoming able to travel alone, to be away from one's parents for extended periods of time, etc.

2. *Responsibility for one's behavior toward others in the immediate environment.* This starts with the child's learning to take the wishes and the feelings of others into account in controlling his own actions. At first it is limited to behavior with respect to mother and father and brothers and sisters, then expands to include playmates and others with whom he comes into close contact. This is the beginning of social responsibility—responsibility for the welfare of society. It gradually extends out from the family circle, as the child becomes able to trace the consequences of his own acts in the lives and feelings of other people.

3. *Responsibility rooted in the conscience.* After the age of four or five, the child increasingly takes into himself the voice of conscience—the rules that have been taught to him by his parents. He learns to hold up to himself such rules as the following: be prompt; do the household tasks assigned to you; keep your room neat; do your homework; keep your promises. By the age of nine or ten, some children are over-conscientious. They are conscience-bound. But others are quite irresponsible. The difference between these two groups of children appears to result almost entirely from the parent-child relations and from the examples set by the parents.

4. *Responsibility becomes rational and humanistic.* After the age of ten or twelve, some children who have been responsible through the controlling and punishing force of a rigid conscience become more humane and flexible in their responsibility. They become able to reason with their conscience, as it were; they become able to count the consequences of alternative kinds of behavior and deliberately to choose the alternative which comes closer to achievement of a number of ethical ideals, of which responsibility is only one. Other ideals equally worthy of service, as they see it, are honesty, loyalty, respect for the integrity of others, and moral courage.

When a child reaches this stage, he is responsible to a set of ethical ideals rather than to the introjected voice of his parents. He asks himself how his behavior in a given situation will affect the welfare of other people, and he chooses the behavior which is the best combination of honesty, loyalty, etc., in its effects on other people.

5. *Societal responsibility; Fidelity to social values.* It is a further step along the same line to full social responsibility—a form of responsibility for which a young person is ready by the mid-teens. At this point he understands fairly well the ethical values of his society and he attempts to achieve these values through his own actions. He has a moral commitment to the values of a democratic society. He has faith in the values of a democratic society, and he acts on that faith.

Responsibility at this level is defined not only in terms of the effects of one's behavior on real people whom one knows or can imagine himself knowing. It is also a devotion to social values, such as are stated in the American Bill of Rights. It covers one's actions as a citizen as well as one's actions as a friend and neighbor.

III. How Is Responsibility Learned and Developed?

The stages in the development of responsibility depend upon the experience a person has in his family, school, and community. The earliest form is largely learned in response to reward and punishment. The child learns habits of personal responsibility through being rewarded for what his parents define as responsible behavior and through being punished for what they regard as irresponsible behavior.

The second state—that of responsibility for one's behavior toward others in the immediate social environment—may also be learned through reward and punishment. However, there is some evidence that another form of experience—empathy—may come into play here. It has been noted that by the second year of life children respond to the emotions shown by others. Thus, if another child bursts into tears, a child may show signs of discomfort; and if another child smiles and laughs, a child may show signs of pleasure. A child can also empathize with its parents. Mothers sometimes tease their young children by pretending to cry or to show distress; more often mothers delight their children by smiling and appearing to be happy.

This quality of empathy may be a basis for an effective kind of training in early and middle childhood—as has been suggested by Martin Hoffman.[1] This is done by systematically pointing out to a child the relations of his behavior to the feelings of others. This is useful because the child may not at first connect his behavior with the distress or pleasure shown by another. The mother should say, "See, Johnny is crying because you took his toy," or "See, Sally is crying because you hit her," and later, "Daddy will be happy because you can dress yourself," or "Mommy feels badly because you tore your dress."

A whole program of child rearing may be built on this principle of empathy. A child may be taught systematically to observe the effects of his behavior on other people. When he hurts other people he will feel badly and when he behaves well toward other people he will feel good toward himself. Thus very little punishment is used, and a positive, relatively guiltless character may be formed.

All the stages of responsibility may be learned through the mechanism of imitation or modeling, combined with identification. It is established that the young child, probably as early as the third year of his life, forms the habit of *unconscious imitation* of those who are close to him emotionally. This habit extends to people who seem to him to be people of authority, though we do not know very much about this extension of imitation. It appears, also, that the child imitates a wide variety of types of behavior, from physical forms such as gait and vocal expression to language and personal habits and value preferences.

Sometime around the fifth or sixth year of his life, the child forms an identification with his parent of the same sex, and this heightens the degree of his imitation of this person. Other identifications are also formed, with the other parent and with certain teachers and other adults, and the child tends to imitate those with whom he identifies.

There is much that we do not know about selective imitation, or modeling, and much that we do not know about identification. But it is generally accepted among students of child development that traits of character are learned to a large extent through these processes. Therefore, we often say that character is caught, not taught.

The fourth and fifth stages of responsibility are achieved much more

[1] Martin L. Hoffman, "Early Processes in Moral Development," working paper for Social Science Research Council Conference on Character Development, November, 1963.

consciously than the first three, and with more intellectual effort.

At this stage of his development the youth "reasons with his conscience." He considers alternative modes of action and asks himself which is better in the sense that it will have better consequences for himself and for others. He thinks about the values of his society and deliberately tries to act in accord with those values. Thus he takes personal responsibility for acting in a socially responsible way.

It is probable that young people acquire this tendency partly through unconscious imitation of parents and teachers, but it seems likely that there is a considerable element of conscious practice involved, also. In other words, these stages of responsibility can be taught and should be taught as part of the curriculum of the school, the church, and other character-building agencies.

The junior and senior high school years are probably the most important ones for learning social responsibility through conscious effort. The educational program should combine a positive service to society and an affirmative stance, on the one hand, with the experience of critical analysis of the performance of society and its leaders in the service of social values, on the other hand. It might contain the following elements:

1. *Opportunity for service to society.* A variety of projects during the school year and during the summer for improvement of the school, the local community, and the wider community. This will lead to a commitment to social welfare and a faith in the improvability of society.

2. *Positively oriented study of society.* Stress in courses in social studies on the achievement of modern society in solving problems of public health, poverty, educational and economic opportunity, and the building of an interdependent world.

3. *Use of adult models who demonstrate both self-esteem and social fidelity.* Choice of teachers who are socially optimistic, active, and oriented toward the improvement of society. There is a greater chance in the future for the selection of teachers with appropriate personalities for certain age groups, as the teacher shortage decreases and opportunity increases to select the better ones. The use of biography in literature and the social studies could stress heroes with these positive qualities. A new set of biographical films produced by Elizabeth Drews of Michigan State University centers around the lives of contemporary

people who are making positive contributions to the life of society, who have faith in the improvability of this society, and who lead personal lives that can serve as models for youth.

4. Critical analysis of men and of institutions in their service to social ideals. In courses in history, literature, and social studies, there should be serious and critical study of the moral consequences of the performance of men and of institutions. Was Napoleon a good man? In what respects was he a responsible leader for the values of modern democracy? Was Abraham Lincoln and was Franklin D. Roosevelt a good man in the social sense? To what extent has the Christian Church been a socially responsible institution during the twentieth century?

What is needed is a balance between analysis and affirmation in an educational program for the teaching of social responsibility. The individual should be taught the values of his society and taught to analyze his own behavior and that of others in the service of those values. This kind of educational program should maximize responsible behavior as it was defined by Daniel Lerner in his paper on "Education and Responsible Behavior in Modernizing Societies," namely, "Responsible behavior is the most effective enactment of shared values of which an individual is capable." (Prepared for the Conference, November 8, 1965)

IV. Major Forms of Lack of Responsibility

There are five forms of behavior which show lack of responsibility, each located at a certain period of life.

1. *The Unsocialized Person.* A small proportion of children grow up with little or no self-control. They act mainly upon impulse, sometimes controlling aggressive impulses because they fear immediate punishment. This is the amoral-impulsive type of person, according to the typology of Peck and Havighurst.[2] They get into trouble from the time when they are big enough to harm others with their outbursts of temper. However, even they usually pass through the first stage of responsibility—that of responsibility for their personal, physical self. But they have no conscience, no inner controls that help to govern their

[2] Robert F. Peck, Robert J. Havighurst, *et al.*, *The Psychology of Moral Character*, chapter 1, John Wiley & Sons, Inc., New York, 1960.

actions in relation to other people. This group cannot be sharply separated from others who have enough self-control and social responsibility to "get by" under normal circumstances. A reasonable estimate of the number of definitely unsocialized persons might be two or three percent.

2. *The Alienated*. A somewhat larger group of young people reach adolescence with a very limited degree of social responsibility. They have learned to be responsible for themselves and responsible to a limited social group of their peers and their family. But they have no moral commitment to a larger social group. Generally they have had an experience of failure and frustration in school. Generally their experience with surrogates of the wider society has been unsatisfactory to them; teachers, employers, policemen, and social workers appear to them to represent an alien and generally hostile society.

An example of this group is Ronald, who is eighteen and has dropped out of school. In the following interviews we get a picture of the social setting in which Ronald is living, and of his alienation from the wider society. A school visitor was studying a group of boys of which Ronald was one: these boys all being marginal to school and marginal to the labor force.

INTERVIEW WITH MRS. LEWIS, GRANDMOTHER OF RONALD LEWIS

I did not mean to have an interview with Mrs. Lewis. When I drove up to the house, her husband, an elderly gentleman, was just coming in apparently from the store. I introduced myself and told him that I would like very much to talk to Ronald Lewis. He looked at me for a moment and said, "Ronald is not here. I don't know where he is but I think he is over at a car wash where he is working." He paused for a moment and looked at me again and said, "but I would like for you to talk to my wife and I know she will want to talk to you." I said, "Well, sir, I really wanted to talk to Ronald as I am from the Board of Education and am interested in the educational future of all of our young men and young women." He said, "Well, I wish you would talk to her." "Very well, sir, I will talk to her." He opened the door to his home—it's a home right on the street—there were about five steps up to the porch and the porch was enclosed in glass. As I went in I noticed that the front door had a glass panel and it had been knocked out of the door. Mr. Lewis said, "Come in, please come in." I went in. He called to his wife who was in the rear of the house. This was a very neat home, very clean and there were pictures on the wall and very homey. The grandmother came and she had on a bathrobe and she said, "Excuse my appearance," and I said, "That's all right, ma'am, I'm not going to take any of your time, but your husband said you would like to speak to me." and I explained to her why I was there. "Yes, sit down, I do want to talk to you about Ronald because I just don't know what in the world I am going to do with this boy. He's not here." She pointed to the door and said, "Do you know what happened to that door?" "No." "Well, we had some words before and he just broke the window to that door and it scared me to death. I don't know what's happened to that boy, something is wrong. He is a son of my son and my son is partly responsible for this boy being the way he is because he didn't discipline him when he was growing up. I tried to help him. But it's a broken home you know and my son is married again and the girl he is married to now works at the Bank and my son is studying electronics. This boy of his, I want to talk to you about him. He joined the Job Corps and went out some place in New Jersey and took training out there and then they sent him back and he got on a job here. He was working out south here, making about $10 a day and do you know that boy wouldn't go to work. I just don't understand him. For three days I thought he was going to work and I was giving him carfare to go out there and you know where he was—right down here at the pool hall— and I didn't know about it. He didn't even call out there to tell the folks he wasn't coming to work and of course they had to let him go; you know they had to let him go. Then he got another job up here and you know he didn't stay on that job; and he was offered a job with the city, with the Park Department, but he thinks he is too good for that type of job and he wouldn't do it. All he wants to do is hang around the pool hall."

INTERVIEW WITH RONALD LEWIS

Last week I interviewed the grandmother of Ronald and as a result of that interview was determined to meet Ronald face to face. I went to the house again today and was met by a barking off-breed dog that almost made me want to change my mind, however before he was able to bite, which he would have done, the grandfather came to the front door and called him off. I asked Mr. Lewis if Ronald was at home and he said, "No, he is at work over at the car wash, the West End Car Wash." I asked him the directions to the car wash and he gave it to me. I drove over to the car wash and asked the people there if Ronald Lewis worked here. I was told that he did work some of the time, but was not working today and that they needed him, but that if I really wanted to see him I could find him at the poolroom over on Olive Street. I left my car to be washed and went over to the poolroom and there I found Ronald playing pool with another boy. There were four people in the poolroom and I introduced myself to the group and asked which individual was Ronald. He was dressed in an imitation leather jacket, tight-fitting trousers and pointed shoes, and a peaked black hat. He said, "I am Ron." I introduced myself again saying, "Ron, I would like to talk to you." I explained to him that I was from the Board of Education. He continued to play pool and I waited until the end of the game, then I said, "Ron, could I talk to you now or just when could I talk with you?" "You can talk to me at my house." "Fine, I'll be glad to come to your house. What time will you be home?" He hesitated for a moment then said, "I'll be there at five o'clock." I thanked him and told him that I would be there at five o'clock.

At five o'clock, I was at the home of Ronald and I knocked on the door and was again told by another gentleman I had not met that Ronald was at work. I explained that I had an appointment with him at five o'clock. I was told that he usually gets home from work around that time. I thanked him and said that I would just sit in the car and wait. I sat in the car until about ten minutes after five at which time a station wagon, an old blue station wagon, turned the corner and drove up to the house. Ronald was in the car with a friend and after a moment or two of conversation got out and I called to him. "Ronald, I'm here, will you come over and let me talk to you?" "Sure." He came over to the car.

I began the interview by asking Ronald where he worked and he said, "Well, I work sometimes at the car wash around the corner, but I don't make very much." I asked him if he had any additional jobs. "No, I do not. I'm not altogether taking care of myself now. I live here with my grandparents and they take care of me." "Ron, tell me about some of your other jobs. Have you had any other jobs?" "Yes, I've worked for Medical Center in the supply room, but I quit that job because I didn't like the hours. I had to work all night and I didn't like that. I worked for the Tractor Company out there doing some custodial work, but it cost me too much money to get to work so I quit that job." "Are you doing anything now other than working at the West Side Car Wash?" "I just work there sometimes but I don't take care of myself altogether because my grandparents are helping me."

Most of the young people in this group come from economically disadvantaged homes. Most of them drop out of school without finishing high school. However, the great majority of children from working-class homes and at least half of the school dropouts are fairly responsible persons. The "alienated" group make up about ten percent of an age group under present conditions.

3. *The Uncommitted.* A group of adolescent boys and girls who are causing a good deal of concern at present is one which comes largely from middle-class families and has average or above-average intellectual ability. This group lacks sufficient social fidelity to be willing to commit itself to a full and whole-hearted participation in the occupational and political life of contemporary society. Instead, they remain uncommitted, refusing to accept the adult world with positive feeling, and retreating to a world of private and personal satisfactions. Kenneth Keniston has studied this type of youth.[3] He calls their attitude *privatism*. Such a person declines to become involved with political and social problems, and prefers to spend his time with music and art. He feels powerless to affect the great society, and turns to the things closer home that he feels able to control. He may value family closeness above meaningful work because he can control things within his family, but not in his occupation. Leisure activities may be more important to him than work because he can control what he does in his free time. "Many young people expect to find in leisure a measure of stability, enjoyment, and control which they would otherwise lack. Hence their emphasis on assuring leisure time, or spending their leisure to good advantage, or getting jobs with long vacations, and on living in areas where leisure can be well enjoyed. Indeed, some anticipate working at their leisure with a dedication that will be totally lacking in their work itself." But Keniston does not believe this will be satisfactory. He thinks this will cause a fatal split in a person's life. "The man who spends his working day at a job whose primary meaning is merely to earn enough money to enable him to enjoy the rest of his time can seldom really enjoy his leisure, his family, or his avocations. Life is of a piece, and if work is empty or routine, the rest will inevitably become contaminated as well, becoming a compulsive escape or a driven effort to compensate for the absent satisfactions that should inhere in work. Similarly, to try to avoid social and political problems by cultivating one's garden can at best be only partly successful. . . . Putting work,

[3] Kenneth Keniston, in *Youth: Change and Challenge,* edited by Erik Erikson, Basic Books, Inc., New York, 1962.

society, and politics into one pigeonhole, and family, leisure and enjoyment into another creates a compartmentalization which is in continual danger of collapsing."

The mood of our society includes frankness in formerly taboo areas, self-criticism, and skepticism. Youth are exposed to this mood very directly through the mass media (television, cinema, paper back literature, etc.). They read such books as Salinger's *Catcher in the Rye* and Golding's *Lord of the Flies,* and they are encouraged to read such literature by high school teachers of literature who represent the mood of society. These books are true portrayals of a part of human nature—an unpleasant part, and not the whole truth, by any means. Perhaps these are more accurate than the literature adolescents read a generation or more ago—*Rebecca of Sunnybrook Farm, Strive and Succeed* (Horatio Alger). Furthermore, the sober and realistic writing about the dangers of nuclear war and the difficulties of international control of armaments give young people an ample picture of the immorality of national policies.

Boys and girls are shown the seamy side of personal and political life and then asked to commit themselves to social loyalty.

At the same time boys and girls are confronted with the tasks of making good in school, of choosing an occupation, of establishing themselves with the opposite sex, and these tasks are set for them a year or two earlier than they were a generation or two ago, due to the social forces making for social precocity in the middle-class part of society.

Under the circumstances it is not surprising that contemporary middle-class youth show a considerable degree of self-doubt and lack of confidence in the political and economic structure of modern society. It is not surprising that a *privatistic* life is preferred to one of greater social commitment. Boys find it difficult to make up their minds what occupation they will prepare for. Some of them engage in a kind of sit-down strike against the academic demands made on them by school or college. Their fathers wonder why sons are so in-grown and uncertain, as compared with the greater assurance and task-orientation they remember as normal for their generation. There is not so much concern about girls, since they are not expected to show the degree of *instrumental activism* expected of boys.

4. *The Middle-Aged Slough.* The period from age forty to age sixty

is one which sees major changes in the nature of the social responsibility that is normally assumed by men and women. By this age, responsibility for bearing and rearing children is pretty well past. Also, responsibility for mastering an occupation has been achieved. The average man or woman by age fifty can say that he has successfully met the major responsibilities of his life.

There are other roles of middle age related to responsibility which have a certain amount of social pressure behind them. The tasks of becoming an informed and responsible citizen and of being an active member of church and other social organizations tend to assume more importance for people as they move into this period of life, but these roles have less motivation behind them than the roles of worker and parent.

Thus the activities involving social responsibility are often reduced or sloughed off by a person in this phase of life. Studies of the interests and activities of people in middle age show that some decrease their devotion to citizenship and other forms of social responsibility while others increase their activity in these areas. Programs of adult education based on the assumed attractiveness to middle-aged people of civic responsibility may not be as successful as programs of a more nearly sociable kind, such as theater and play-reading groups, music groups and music appreciation courses, travel and travel-study groups.

In other words, it seems that there may be a "middle-aged slough" which affects some but not all people. We do not know enough about this phenomenon to be able to tell what earlier characteristics are associated with it. We do not know what kinds of educational and other experiences are associated with continued or increased social responsibility in middle life; and we do not know what educational and other experiences are associated with the middle-aged slough.

5. *Disengagement from Responsibility After Age Sixty.* The *feeling* of responsibility for the welfare of society in general and for the welfare of one's own immediate circle of friends and relatives is related in a complex way to the *activities* of such responsibility. When a person is retired from his work and from his professional or occupational associations, he loses actual responsibility. He may in this situation transfer his feelings of social responsibility into other areas where he can still act responsibly. For example, he may become more active as a citizen.

On the other hand, he may withdraw or disengage himself from responsibility all along the line.

It is now somewhat of a controversial question in the field of geron-
tology whether older people disengage themselves from social responsibility due to some intrinsic psychological process that is an essential
part of the life cycle, or whether they are forced to disengage due to
social pressures such as compulsory retirement and the tendency by
younger people to push them out of responsible roles.

Research on this question by the writer and his colleagues indicates
that there are a variety of "life styles" or patterns of social engagement-
disengagement which show themselves after age sixty. These patterns
seem to be related to personality structure. In other words, some people
are active, responsible people throughout their adult years and continue
with this pattern in their old age as far as they are physically able to do
it, while other people are passive, dependent people all their adult lives
and they disengage themselves readily and comfortably from responsibility for others as they get into the sixties and the seventies.

It is a reasonable supposition that the characteristic of responsibility
is established in the personality by the early adult years at a certain
level of strength and complexity. Experiences during subsequent life
affect the ways in which responsibility is shown, but do not affect the
basic quality. A person with an active sense of responsibility for family
and society will continue this in one acceptable way or another all his
life, depending on his circumstances.

This hypothesis has not been tested systematically, by longitudinal
studies of people from adolescence to old age.

There is a final responsibility that has been studied in an exploratory
manner—responsibility for preparing for one's death. A recent paper [4]
reported on the extent to which older retired persons living in public
housing projects had made provisions for their deaths—for financial
arrangements, cemetery lot, burial insurance, etc.

The sample of people ranged in age from sixty to ninety-two, with a
median age of seventy-five. Median income was $70 per month. Two-
thirds had made responsible arrangements, one-third had done nothing

---

[4] Aaron Lipman and Philip W. Marden, "Race, Education, and Preparation for
Death in Old Age," paper read at the meeting of the Gerontological Society in Los
Angeles, November, 1965.

about it. There was a reliable relationship between amount of education and responsibility. Also, those living on welfare payments had been less responsible than those not on welfare.

The researchers conclude that those who have been well treated by society in terms of education and opportunity reciprocate by preparing for their death in a responsible way. Whether this form of personal responsibility is related to social responsibility is not known.

Conclusion

We have seen that responsibility is learned during childhood and adolescence, and that it is learned through experience. We are left with some unanswered questions. To what extent are personal responsibility and social responsibility related? And to what extent does the characteristic of responsibility persist through the life cycle, once it has been acquired during childhood and adolescence?

TABLE I

CORRELATIONS OF RESPONSIBILITY
WITH OTHER CHARACTER TRAITS
Correlation Coefficient of Responsibility with:

Honesty	.82
Moral Courage	.78
Friendliness	.55
Loyalty	.80

Source: Table 28, p. 244 in *Adolescent Character and Personality* by Havighurst and Taba (Wiley, 1949). These are tetrachoric correlation coefficients, based on average scores of seventy-seven 16-year-olds on four instruments for measuring character reputation.

Chapter 7. URBAN EDUCATION IN THE NORTH: TOMORROW IS TOO LATE

by Bernard Mackler and Peter M. Elkin *

The deepest problems of modern life derive from the claim of the individual to preserve the autonomy and individuality of his existence in the face of overwhelming social forces, of historical heritage, of external culture, and of the technique of life.—GEORG SIMMEL, "The Metropolis and Mental Life," in Eric and May Josephson, *Man Alone: Alienation in Modern Society,* Dell Publishing Co., Inc., New York, 1962.

The large city today is not a homogeneous entity; its people do not share a body of common beliefs, aspirations and behavior patterns. It cannot be regarded by any stretch of the imagination, as a melting pot, in which the various races and subcultural groups which fill its boundaries and spill over into its suburbs, have become amalgamated. Rather, in many ways, the American city is a sprawling hodgepodge of humanity, in which subcultural and racial pockets exist, some in almost complete isolation. It is precisely within these islands, adrift in, but not actually part of the mainstream of American society that are found in increasing numbers Americans whose styles of living and opportunities for advancement up the social ladder are so different or so limited, that they must be regarded as culturally disadvantaged.—SAMUEL SHEPARD, "Working with Parents of Disadvantaged Children," in C. W. Hunnicutt, *Urban Education and Cultural Deprivation,* Syracuse University Press, Syracuse, 1964.

THE PHRASE, "urban education," though highly suggestive, has a distinctly illusive quality. We suspect that it is more a euphemism than a concept, and a grand euphemism at that. For in "urban education," the "culturally deprived" have found a home. Clearly such euphemisms have little heuristic value. Indeed, they serve to cloud our per-

* Preparation of this paper was facilitated by a grant, 200-4-102, from the Welfare Administration, United States Department of Health, Education, and Welfare.

spectives by encouraging the development of new stereotypes, updating old ones and generally contributing to the kind of rigid, categorical thinking which militates against change.[1]

In the early sixties, cultural deprivation was coined to define *the* problem. Now we have a new concept, equally degrading and equally erroneous—Negro family instability. There are many explanations for a poor man's plight, but quickly coined concepts and easy solutions yield resentment from the poor and intellectual harangues from the verbally equipped. Last year (1965), the debate was over the intellectual environment of the home; now it is the family and social environment. Intellectuals disagree, fighting verbally among themselves, and scholarly papers are written from the opposing points of view. Some include racist jibes, white or Negro, but they are not plans. Rather, there are disagreements about causes and symptoms of being poor or being black. As S. M. Miller puts it:

> The use of a term like "cultural deprivation" leads us away from looking at ourselves as practitioners. We begin to scapegoat those with whom we are having difficulty.[2]

The problems which we are trying to confront, problems associated with poverty, racial discrimination—the isolation and alienation of large numbers of Americans from what we call the mainstream of American life—cannot be legislated out of existence. Surely, the tragic gap between the Supreme Court decision of 1954 and its implementation over a period of twelve years, ought to make us suspicious of packaged deals to alleviate social problems. Social problems are, after all, human problems, they are part of a man as well as of his social environment. One understands why the so-called War on Poverty, has been called a "war against the poor."

The social scientist, the city planner, the educator, predisposed to engage in action and placing great faith in the Power of the Word, must also take time to play the fool; to stand on the periphery and attempt to see the realities of a situation beyond the limits of his own

[1] B. Mackler and M. Giddings, "Cultural Deprivation: A Study in Mythology," *Teachers College Record,* volume 66, number 7, April, 1965, pp. 608–613.

[2] S. M. Miller, "The Search for an Educational Revolution," in C. W. Hunnicutt, editor, *Urban Education and Cultural Deprivation,* Syracuse University Press, Syracuse, 1964, pp. 114–115.

involvement. Mythologies are created by kings, to be exposed by fools. We have seen in recent years the development of a new body of myths, called collectively, The Great Society. But having "discovered" poverty as an embarrassing social reality and a barrier to achieving the goals of The Great Society, the mythmakers have sought to eliminate it, as it were, by fiat. Federal legislation has been passed and funds allocated for so-called action programs, with the fanciful notion that poverty is merely a *condition*. Our conventional wisdom has proved to be false, or, at the very least, limited by a pervasive middle-class world view, insulated and unable to see beyond itself.

Here, we look at Education—the System and the School—which has its own tradition of mythmaking. Where the goals of education have always been integrative, in the general sense of the word, teaching children the cognitive and social skills basic to what Simmel calls "the technique of life," we are suddenly faced with the shocking fact that our schools are failing to make good their promise and are in fact creating a subculture of second-class citizens.

The problems of urban education, then, are the *problems of the poor,* the people who are without the resources necessary to change the nature of their existence. We, the successful Americans, have built many barriers, both formal and informal, between ourselves and those who, in our terms, are different. We have over many generations reinforced poverty as a way of life, allowed it to develop its own culture, and its own stereotyped view of those who have kept them in bondage. With each promise unfulfilled, the gap becomes wider, with consequences that are universal and farreaching. The sins of the fathers are visited upon all of the children. Let us understand our mistakes, know wherein we have failed, and now, at a time when there is great reason to believe in the possibilities of change and in fact to effect change, let us not be mesmerized by official rhetoric and illconceived programs which promise more than they can ever hope to accomplish.

I. Defining the Situation

The key problems are functions of the following conditions: 1) patterns of residential segregation; 2) overcentralization at the system level; and 3) climate at the school level.

1. *Segregation.* If there are indeed any "social facts" pertaining to the problems of urban education, they are the demographic realities; that the urban school population reflects the influx of poor Negroes, Puerto Ricans, and other minorities who, for economic and social reasons, are forced to settle in ghetto areas. And this population growth will increase. In fact, C. Glatt predicts that many Northern cities will see Negroes outnumbering whites by the beginning of the next century.[3] Grodzins states that "within 30 years Negroes will constitute from 25 to 50 per cent of the total population in at least 10 of the 14 largest central cities."[4]

As R. E. Taeuber and Alma P. Taeuber have observed:

Residential segregation occupies a key position in patterns of race relations in the United States. It not only inhibits the development of informal, neighborly relations between whites and Negroes, but insures the segregation of a variety of public and private facilities. The clientele of schools, hospitals, libraries, parks and stores is determined in large part by the racial composition of the neighborhood in which they are located.[5]

As a consequence of zoning regulations, the neighborhood school persists, and reflects the character of the neighborhood it serves. It follows that a predominantly Negro area will have a predominantly Negro school population. Is this segregation? Not according to law. Rather, it is segregation *de facto,* which is presumed to be different, but which, in principle, serves the same purposes—to keep black and white separate.

When the Supreme Court declared in 1954 that segregation in the public schools was a violation of the Fourteenth Amendment, and subsequently passed implementation legislation providing that desegregation should proceed ". . . with all deliberate speed," it was generally assumed that the South was the prime target, where segregation existed *de jure.* Northern States having no laws regarding the commingling of races, no history of segregation as an instrument of public

---

[3] C. Glatt, "Selected Demographic Factors that Affect School Planning: A Look at Four Northern Cities," *Urban Education,* volume 2, 1966, pp. 35–49.

[4] M. Grodzins, *The Metropolitan Area as a Racial Problem,* University of Pittsburgh Press, Pittsburgh, Pa., 1958, p. 3.

[5] R. E. Taeuber and Alma F. Taeuber, *Negroes in Cities,* Aldine Publishing Co., Chicago, 1965, p. 1.

policy, felt, with some smugness that they had once again won the Civil War.

T. F. Pettigrew has recently pointed out that the distinctions between *de facto* segregation, or "The Northern Plan," is merely a more subtle form of segregation by law. This is evidenced by the fact that Federal, State, and local monies have been used to finance so-called public housing for low-income families, which are virtually segregated, and that the new schools built to serve occupants of public housing developments are, as well, segregated. Similarly, government-supported programs for urban renewal have in many instances displaced vast numbers of poor people, replacing slums with high-rise and high-rent housing, thus driving the poor deeper into the existing ghettos, or in some cases, creating new ones. Clearly, this is not merely the result of poor planning or mere capriciousness.[6] One can make a case for "The Northern Plan" as an instrument of public policy. Pettigrew also notes that many avid segregationists in the urban South are looking Northward with great interest at Mayor Yorty of Los Angeles, Superintendent Willis of Chicago, and Mrs. Hicks of the Boston School Committee, to "find out how they do it." There is reason to fear that so-called *de facto* segregation will become more the rule than the exception, if city and school politics are controlled by people with strong vested interests in keeping the races separate.

Where educators and social scientists have agreed that integration is a precondition for quality education, the demographic realities of the Northern city act to eclipse such notions. Indeed, how do you achieve "racial balance" when there aren't enough whites to go around?

The *de facto* segregation bind has been furthered by Conant's suggestion[7] that integration is not as important as the quality of education itself. Therefore, he suggests that ghetto schools be upgraded, emphasizing curriculum, the more formal aspects of learning. He further suggests that at the high school level, children from low-income families (*i.e.,* Negroes) be encouraged to enter vocational programs, rather than try to compete with the brighter, more advanced middle-

[6] T. F. Pettigrew, "Twelve Years of School Desegregation. The Struggle to Advance," paper read at the National Association for the Advancement of Colored People Convention entitled "The Tragic Gap between Civil Rights and Its Enforcement," New York, May, 1966.

[7] J. B. Conant, *Slums and Suburbs,* McGraw-Hill Book Co., New York, 1961.

class youth who are more clearly college material. These suggestions have been used extensively by citizens' groups who favor the *status quo* and have further served to reinforce the image of the lower-class child, the "culturally deprived," the Negro child, as less educable, if not innately inferior.

So long as patterns of residential segregation persist, the neighborhood school, as a concept and as a reality, will continue to reinforce inequality and make a mockery of the democratic ideal. If solutions do not exist within the present framework, as is the case in the larger cities, then new approaches will have to be developed.

2. *Centralization*. As a system urban education is characterized by a high degree of centralization, inflexibility, and poor communication at every level. As G. Watson defines the situation:

The American public school is a curious hybrid: It is managed by a school board drawn largely from upper class circles; it is taught by teachers who come largely from middle class backgrounds; and it is attended mainly by children from working class backgrounds. These three groups do not talk the same language. They differ in their manners, power, and hierarchy of values.[8]

If this is a simplistic view, it is also a gross understatement. Social class differences are only part of the problem. More important are issues of power and authority; the politics of education. D. Rogers notes that:

They (school officials) are no different than professionals and politicians in other city agencies or in City Hall. There are very few "innovators" and fomentors of radical change in big city politics . . . and those that exist have not flocked to the Board of Education.[9]

Critics of school organization refer to a "leadership vacuum," arguing that the Board is merely a public relations agency for a system which is structurally unwieldy from the top down. The fact that policies are made at the top, the consequences of which affect the entire city, makes no provision for individual differences, among neighborhoods, school principals, teachers, and students.

[8] G. Watson, Foreword to F. Riessman, *The Culturally Deprived Child*, Harper & Row, New York, 1962, p. x.

[9] D. Rogers, "Public Education in New York City," unpublished manuscript, Center for Urban Education, New York, 1965, p. 13.

The dysfunctions of centralization are seen in the relationship of the school system to other big city agencies. According to Rogers:

There is no glue holding together the operations of city agencies; the parts are not coordinated; the system is at times hopelessly fragmented. Each agency zealously seeks to preserve its own autonomy and tries to prevent decisions in others from encroaching on its domain.[10]

Given these conditions, it is easy to see why school boards in general have been ineffectual with regard to school desegregation, which is after all a touchy issue, with vast political ramifications. Robert A. Dentler, who feels that the key figure in the desegregation controversy is the superintendent, says:

School desegregation in Northern cities will remain a subject of moot speculation until at least one such superintendent takes a strong positive position and allows others to observe the consequences. The policy recommendations of city school superintendents are more than influential. They are profoundly indicative of changes in school practice. . . .[11]

Furthermore, says Dentler:

There may be no change, then, because the ability of the city superintendent and his board to act on any question of general interest in the community is limited by the risks that the central political agency, usually the office of the mayor, is disposed to take.[12]

It is charactristic of politicians, and school officials are no exception, that risk-taking depends upon the anticipated payoff. As Dentler says, "They do not press for significant social change if the effects upon their own access to authority are not predictable and promising."[13]

Finally the lack of communication, of functional unity between and within both public and private bureaucracies, creates not merely a *status quo,* but a vast waste of time and money. Short-range plans for change are largely ineffectual, and the absence of a vision of the future needs of the city makes long-range planning impossible. A Great Society, or what Mayor John V. Lindsay of New York City

10 *Ibid.,* p. 15.
11 R. A. Dentler, "Barriers to Northern School Desegregation," *Daedalus,* volume 95, number 1, Winter, 1966, p. 57.
12 *Ibid.*   13 *Ibid.*

spoke of during his first weeks in office, The Proud City, cannot be accomplished by rhetoric alone, nor by protesting citizens' groups, and surely not within the present bureaucratic framework of the educational as well as other public institutions. Mayor Lindsay's notion of people-run local city halls as clearinghouses for information, as well as for the expression of grievances, might well be adopted in an attempt to decentralize the school system, to make it clear to the invisible leadership at headquarters what problems exist within each neighborhood. Creating local boards of education staffed by local community leaders, with autonomy and the authority to act on local issues, might serve to stimulate citizen participation in school affairs, raise the morale of teachers and principals within individual schools, and generally facilitate good inter- and intra-school communication. Looking beyond the present structural arrangements, Miller asks:

What are the problems within educational institutions today? We have to look increasingly toward the internal structure and operation of education. This is particularly important now, for many of the new technologies and new programs will require a kind of administrative structure which permits and facilitates these programs.[14]

3. *The Climate of the School.* The third problem area, the climate of the school, is a residual category, and intentionally so, for the school, as an institution, is the resultant of the other two forces: the system from above, and the community from below.

Let us say a few words about what is meant by "climate" as it relates to schools. We recognize that the school itself is a social system, a miniature bureaucracy. The principal, as chief executive, has the authority to run the school his way. Teachers have delegated to them the responsibility for carrying out the functions of the school, and are granted some authority to do so, within the limits prescribed by the principal. The pupils, who have no authority, have no control over school policy, curriculum, teaching methods, etc. As E. Z. Friedenberg has put it:

. . . The first thing the young learn in school is that there are certain sanctions and restrictions that apply only to them; that they do not partici-

14 Miller, *op. cit.*, p. 116.

pate fully in the freedoms guaranteed by the State, and that therefore these freedoms do not partake of the character of inalienable rights.[15]

They have, however, the power of numbers, in much the same way that prisoners have over their custodians. But in the school as in the prison, social controls are built into the system to prevent the likelihood of mutinous activity. The individual plays the game, institutional style, when he is aware of the personal risks involved in resistance.

Climate, in the sociopsychological sense, refers, literally, to atmospheric conditions, to the "feel" of the place, as seen in the way people go about the daily round of life. In schools, the quality of principal-teacher and teacher-student relations are good indices of the climate. To be more specific, let us examine a hypothetical school situation in which the student body is predominantly white and middle-class, where teachers and students share a common frame of reference. Here, the sensitive teacher can safely make assumptions about the students in her class, using her own value system as a model. She knows how important education is to middle-class parents; that children from middle-class homes are taught to be future-oriented, and more specifically, career or profession-oriented, and that they must do better than their parents, in terms of acquiring status and valued objects. The school reinforces these attitudes and introduces a new dimension, competition. Indeed, the traditional K-12 structure makes it abundantly clear to the middle-class child that he must move upward in the school hierarchy, and that the facility with which he is able to "make the grade," will not only determine his future success, but serve as a measure of his worth as a human being, to himself as well as to his peers, his teachers, and his parents. Those who balk, or otherwise manifest an unwillingness to cooperate (*i.e.,* to conform), are invariably diagnosed by the school psychologist as "maladjusted," and will usually respond to some form of psychological punishment, such as being humiliated by the teacher in front of his peers, "sent to the Office," or, worst of all, told that if he persists in being uncooperative, a notation will be made on his Permanent Record—that omnipresent, though unseen secret file, which follows a person throughout his life.

15 E. Z. Friedenberg, *The Dignity of Youth and Other Atavisms,* Beacon Press, Boston, 1965, p. 90.

Numerical or letter grades, measuring the pupil's intellectual competence, as well as grades in "social living," or simply, conduct, measuring the extent to which he has learned the rules, are also part of the
teacher's repertoire. It is the clever child who learns early how to play
the game to his own advantage, which includes learning how to
manipulate situations and people.

There are obvious parallels here to both the prison and mental hospital, which, although they are more custodial than either correctional or
therapeutic (*i.e.,* educational) institutions, communicate to their in-
mates, through formal and informal means, the rules of the game. The
inmate who "wants out" (the equivalent of "staying-in" for the student), must first learn the institution's definition of a good inmate.
Then by the force of one's own needs, or through the use of simulation
techniques, may, in time, change his situation. But while he is in, the
inmate, like the student, is committed to "a career," and must create
and maintain a good public image. Only in his private moments does
the inmate-student reveal the differences between role and self.

The notion of good behavior by simulation is quite interesting. E.
Goffman notes that mental patients will carefully observe the behavior
of a fellow patient who is known to be up for release and proceed to
imitate his movements, attitudes, speech patterns, etc. (*i.e.,* imitate the
mental hospital's conception of a good patient, or of psychological
health), and thus convince the hospital staff that they, too, are well,
that they have been, as it were, re-educated, and can therefore be
released.[16]

The effectiveness of role-playing, of "taking the role of the other," of
defense mechanisms and coping strategies, or to use Goffman's terms,
"ways of making-out," depend upon how nearly accurate the individual is in his efforts to define the situation in terms of "the other."
Certainly a prerequisite for success in an institutional career is an
acquired understanding of the lingo, the style, and the ideology of the
superordinate. In a school, where middle-class values and expectations
predominate at every level, the system is maintained in equilibrium, at
least in so far as public performances are concerned. That a sense of
order be maintained is essential, but by no means is it an indication
that teaching and learning are actually going on.

Consider a variation of the role-playing model: the same middle-

[16] E. Goffman, *Asylums,* Doubleday, Garden City, 1961.

class school, but with a lower class, predominantly Negro and Puerto Rican clientele. The obvious cultural differences will produce divergent definitions of the situation, thus preventing clients from evolving strategies for coping with their situation in terms that are acceptable to the teachers and to the administration. In the absence of a strong internal communication system and a common frame of reference in teacher-pupil relations, attempts at cognitive and social learning (which is presumably the purpose of the school and the basis for its structure) will likely become irrelevant. The teacher is thus re-cast in the role of custodian, and the school becomes more like the prison and the mental hospital, a "total institution." M. Deutsch, observing this process, says:

. . . teachers are unprepared psychologically and intellectually to cope with the needs of the slum child. The middle class teacher in the slum area of cities often faces the unusual demands of her teaching situation with two debatable assumptions—assumptions which prevent her from empathizing with her students, particularly those from Negro or other minority group backgrounds. She assumes that the class system in America is truly an open system for anyone "who has it in him to climb the ladder of success," and she assumes that the middle class values which determine both the organization of the classroom and the content of the curriculum represent a standard of perfection, deviation from which is a moral, not an educational problem.[17]

When pupils cannot make a clearcut, operational definition of the situation, where they lack what F. L. Strodbeck has so aptly called, "The hidden curriculum of the middle class home"—teachers are likely to call their pupils categorically as "you people," or in describing "them" to others, as "these kids," followed by a stream of accusative statements regarding innate intelligence, moral standards, broken homes. . . .[18] Here Deutsch says:

The teacher's second assumption, that middle class values are normative, often prevents her from appreciating the positive values which the slum child's environment may develop in him: greater responsibility toward

[17] M. Deutsch, "The Disadvantaged Child and the Learning Process," in Meyer Weinberg, editor, *Learning Together: A Book on Integrated Education*, Integrated Education Associates, Chicago, 1964, p. 38.

[18] F. L. Strodtbeck, "The Hidden Curriculum of the Middle Class Home," in C. W. Hunnicutt, editor, *Urban Education and Cultural Deprivation*, Syracuse University Press, Syracuse, 1964, pp. 15–31.

siblings, greater ability for self-care, greater independence in play activities. She may see these values as simply disruptive in the established routine of the classroom.[19]

When the children are treated collectively with contempt because they do not understand what is expected of them and enter the situation with few, if any expectations, they will quickly come to see school exclusively in negative terms; as a conspiracy to hurt, cripple, and intimidate them, exploit their weaknesses and confirm already growing feelings of low self-esteem and perceptions of limited opportunities for advancement and participation in the society, as reflected in the lives of their parents, and in other adults in the home and community environment.

In an atmosphere of mutual distrust, clearly nothing even approximating teaching and learning can go on. What is more tragic perhaps, is the negative reinforcement which such an environment provides. To recognize that one is poor, or that one is black, is the reality dimension. To be classified "incorrigible," "stupid" or as "culturally deprived," is to set into motion a chain of self-fulfilling prophecies.[20] With no other way of dealing with a rejecting environment, one *becomes* incorrigible, dumb, culturally deprived, perhaps feeling that a negative identity is better than none at all.

It is dangerous to make blanket statements about schools, teachers, and children, for there are many dedicated teachers, principals, and parents who are teaching their children in the Northern ghettoes. Despite these many gifted and effective persons, the burden of failure is still apparent, even in the classroom of the conscientious teacher.

II. Resolutions and Solutions: A Look at the Reality Dimension

It is widely assumed that "quality education" is impossible without integration. We shall leave aside the notion of "quality education," as it raises too many tangential questions, such as: What can a school system hope to accomplish?, and the still broader question, *Can* the schools educate? We have thus far looked at the problems of urban education, externally, as the resultant forces impinging upon the

[19] Deutsch, *op. cit.*, p. 38.
[20] Mackler and Giddings, *op. cit.*

school, and internally, in terms of the school as a social system to look at the prospects for school integration. F. Riessman reminds us that:

> The school culture rewards certain styles of learning, or ways of working, while there are many other forms of learning that the culture does not reward. Often the assumption is made that if you do not learn in a particular way, you are stupid. The IQ tests typify this . . . They come directly from the school culture and they are meant to measure ability that is useful in the school culture.
>
> . . . we must realize . . . that there are many ways of learning. Some people learn best by reading and writing, some people learn best from doing and acting, some from seeing. What emerges is that the school system must make available opportunities to learn in many ways, through many styles.[21]

What then are the prerequisites for integration, or in Deutsch's terms, "the antecedents required in order to produce a social basis for work toward a truly integrated experience for the child?"[22] The answers to this question rest with the system; with the degree to which the board of education and the superintendent of schools see integration as a prerequisite to "quality education," and to the degree that public opinion is mobilized to force the board to move in a particular direction. Holding matters of residential segregation and zoning in check, should the board undertake plans to integrate the schools, what provisions will be made at the school and community level to prepare teachers and parents for change? It is in this area that the board and the superintendent have a vital role to play as a public relations agency. It has already been demonstrated that legalistic arguments for integrating the schools are not effective. Deutsch appeals the case for integration in this way:

> Segregation is an aspect of experience in the growing-up of both Negro and white children, and this experience plays a crucial role in determining their developing attitudes toward the self and toward the human condition.

[21] F. Riessman, "The Cultural Styles of the Disadvantaged," in Meyer Weinberg, editor, *Learning Together: A Book on Integrated Education,* Integrated Education Associates, Chicago, 1964, p. 26.

[22] M. Deutsch, "Dimensions of the School's Role in the Problems of Integration," in Gordon J. Klopf and Israel A. Laster, editors, *Integrating the Urban School,* Teachers College, Columbia University Press, New York, 1963, pp. 29–44.

It must be obvious, further, that an essentially non-democratic experience does not foster the growth of a democratic value system.[23]

Deutsch's appeal for integration is cast in moral and ethical terms. K. Clark, whose research on the psychological effects of segregation upon white as well as Negro children played an important part in the 1954 Supreme Court decision, has said recently that no legislation can hope to bring about "significant and enduring change," in the condition of the Negro American.[24] Citing that segregation has increased markedly in Northern cities since 1954, Clark feels this has heightened our awareness of racism as a dominant factor in American life and one which we allow to persist by failing to implement legislation. Looking at the immediate situation, rather than with a long-range perspective, Clark sees no alternative but to upgrade the ghetto school much as Conant suggested in *Slums and Suburbs*. This is not "selling-out," but feeling that one has "been sold out." [25]

III. A Note on Legislation and Implementation

The failure of legislation in general, whether at the Federal or State level, has been in the provisions for its implementation. Segregation in the public schools was outlawed twelve years ago, but the promise of "all deliberate speed" has not been kept. The lag between legislation and implementation has had a number of effects: 1) it has given the opponents of desegregation, North and South, time to organize their forces, develop strong pressure groups, and exert political influence at local levels to prevent desegregation of the schools; 2) it has given birth to the civil rights movement, a *raison d'être* for the Negro American, but at the same time, has tragically undermined the confidence of Negroes in the Federal Government, in its apparent unwillingness to believe in its interpretations of the Constitution and to provide means for its enforcement. One suspects that the major thrust of civil rights groups in the North is for jobs and housing, that the

[23] *Ibid.*, p. 30.

[24] K. Clark, "Twelve Years of School Desegregation. The Struggle to Advance," paper read at the National Association for the Advancement of Colored People Convention entitled "The Tragic Gap between Civil Rights and Its Enforcement," New York, May, 1966.

[25] Conant, *op. cit.*

education situation will have to wait; 3) it has created an atmosphere of mistrust between Negro leadership and those white liberals who have supported the cause of the Negro by contributing funds, but not in terms of action within their own *de facto* segregated communities. Thus, in spite of contributions, the white liberal has not joined the civil rights movement. As the movement is still only a Negro movement, and an increasingly fragmented one at that, the fact that few Negroes hold positions of political power within State and Federal governments, seriously limits the magnitude of change. The riots in Philadelphia, Harlem, Rochester, and in Watts, suggest some of the consequences of the politics of gradualism.

The solutions to the urban school situation with respect to desegregation-integration may be divided into two categories: 1) technical—working with the existing situation; and 2) environmental—restructuring the environment and the relationship between schools and residential patterns.

The technical solutions are variously busing, rezoning, pairing (Princeton Plan), and open enrollment. They are attempts to create desegregation, given the neighborhood school pattern as it exists in Northern cities. In most cities, they have been voluntary, placing the burden on Negro parents to decide whether they want their children bused into white schools, and they have been unilateral. Given the inferior quality of the ghetto school in terms of facilities, faculty, and extremely negative climate, surely no white middle-class parent is about to bus his child into an all-Negro school. The limitation of all of the technical solutions, including the so-called Princeton Plan, is that subtle forms of segregation are maintained within the technically integrated school. Ability groupings, or tracks, which are based on the results of standardized I.Q. and achievement tests, clearly discriminate against the in-migrants from ghetto schools. Patterns created in the home and in the environment, which are supported by the school, leave Negro and Puerto Rican youngsters no better off in the long run than if they remained in neighborhood schools.

At the high-school level, children from poverty backgrounds will usually be guided into general and vocational programs, often preparing them with skills which by graduation will have been automated out of existence. A comparison of enrollment figures by race and social class at the school level and at the municipal or State college level would be a good indication of how children in technically integrated schools made out in proportion to their white classmates, and in proportion to those who remained in ghetto schools.

What is wrong with the technical approach is that it is *only* that; that it in effect accepts the general situation and tries to deal with one symptom. Technical solutions to the problem of school segregation do not necessarily make for quality education. Where a school system is failing its middle-class clientele, how can it hope to do better in creating an admixture? A poor teacher is not going to become a better one, merely because there are Negro pupils in her class. And an authoritarian school principal will not become more flexible, when his school is desegregated. It is likely that he will become even more rigid. It is a mistake to think that integration can be accomplished merely by moving bodies around, or that desegregation will create equality education. Americans are noted for technical advances, but integration calls for far more (perhaps for less) than technology; it calls for a "true" democracy. The roots of segregation are deep in the hearts and minds of Negro and white Americans, and it will take more than social engineering to resolve the situation.

The environmental approach is that of the educational park, a complex of school facilities, located in the center of a city. The educational park would eliminate the need for local, neighborhood schools, because all children of elementary-school age would attend the common facility. If a large city had a number of parks, each strategically located, children from *many* neighborhoods would attend a single park. For example, in Kansas City, the Southwest Region may have two parks. And the city may have a total of eight or nine parks. It would require everyone to travel to school, rather than merely the Negro children, as in the case of the busing strategy. By centralizing facilities into a park, a good deal of money would be saved in the long run, money which is now being spent unwisely to keep an inadequate system going.

The concept of the educational park is still in the developmental phase. One can easily see where it could solve the problems of "racial imbalance" in a city the size of New Rochelle or Glen Cove, New York. But how does this strategy apply to a major city, such as New York, Chicago, or Washington, where white children have become an ever-declining minority in the public schools? Here, one must adopt what is called a metropolitan approach—"that fully integrates children, taxes and the community." [26] This would involve, in the case of Boston, incorporating quasi-suburbs like Brookline and the Newtons into the city—*i.e.,* make the city larger, by eliminating the suburbs. It is clear, in the case of the New York metropolitan area, that towns like Mount Vernon and New Rochelle, which were once almost wholly residential, have in the past twenty years become increasingly commercial and industrial. Wooded areas, virtual forests, have become housing developments, shopping centers, and highways. The few residential areas which remain do not warrant considering these towns as significantly different from the city on which they border. With improved public transportation facilities, educational parks could be built to consolidate city and immediate suburb, and become coordinated with urban renewal and redevelopment efforts, air pollution control, and other needed public services.

But what does all of this suggest in terms of administration? Our initial contention was that the school system was already too centralized. How does the environmental approach deal with the need to decentralize administration? The answer would be for each education park to have its own, autonomous administration—its own board of education, superintendent, etc.

The educational park concept raises its own unique set of problems, particularly—how to finance it, how to run it, and whether the fact of its size in terms of area and population, in terms of faculty, staff, and students would not be too unwieldy; and whether, in fact, increased centralization of a metropolitan region can facilitate greater decentralization. But with the technical solutions revealing their obvious inadequacies, with compensatory education only serving to stigmatize those who require compensation, with half solutions and bandaid solutions, patching cracks here and there while the very foundations are crumbling, the need to adopt more radical and more comprehensive measures does not belong to the future, but must begin now, in order to assure all children an educational experience of equally high quality.

[26] P. Schrag, "Boston: Education's Last Hurrah," *Saturday Review,* May 21, 1966, p. 76.

Epilogue. Public Education: It's Time for a Change

We see that public education has problems in goals, purposes, curriculum, staffing, administration, and is obviously floundering conceptually, but stands, for the most part, firm on its commitment to change ever so slightly. To change a *status quo* situation, extreme and intense problems have to be brought forth. The segregated communities present problems that may provide the leverage for reforming the entire educational process. Segregated school systems provide Negroes, Puerto Ricans, Mexicans, Indians, Orientals, and other "out-group" minorities with less than optional educational opportunities. In the process of formulating desegregation plans, the goals for general education reveal their ineptness, obsolescence, and disutility for learning. Although goals are served—upward mobility, staying out of trouble, conformity—learning for learning's sake is played down or neglected. It is ironic that with desegregation, problems facing general education are exposed. The question of quality education becomes the educational planner's problem, and now what is needed is an evaluation of the education of all children, not just bringing Negroes up to whites in ability.

As stated repeatedly in the paper, the most pressing question is racial isolation not only in curricula materials but more significantly in avoiding a "true" pluralistic society. The United States' inability to provide intellectual leadership to the world is reflected in its inability to live side by side with its own Negro and minority group citizens. At issue then is the "American" way of life, and, specifically, how it is reflected in schools, especially public education.

The Question of Commitment

The state of affairs—the present and its historical antecedents—belie where we are headed. Therefore, a review of what has occurred needs to be noted, even if only briefly. Certainly if one is to plan for change, and to present policy implications, the point of what we have done (or have not done) forces the policymaker to see the lethargy of the past, and this intensifies the commitment to bolder steps and a followup of these steps—an enforcement.

To study the question of desegregation and quality-integrated education, a series of communities needs to be studied, ranging from big cities, smaller cities, suburbs, towns, to rural areas.[27] Comparisons can be made across communities as to kind and degree of desegregation, the process by which a community initiates desegregation, how new plans are acted upon, how they are followed up, and how a community becomes integrated.[28]

		Community		
Areas for Study *for each Community*	*Large Cities*	*Middle* *Sized Cities*	*Suburbs*	*Rural*
1. The process of desegregation	New York	Bridgeport	Hackensack	?
2. Curriculum	Buffalo	Albany	White Plains	
3. Services for problematic youngsters	Syracuse	Utica	Glen Cove	
	Yonkers	Niagara Falls		
	Rochester			

FIGURE I. COMMUNITIES TO BE STUDIED

The plans for change may, and probably will, differ for each community. However, there is a strong possibility that there are common features of plans for the various communities. The plans will emerge, obviously, from what present problems exist, but our past research has indicated that educational parks and consolidation present important approaches. These approaches have never been fully worked out, and needless to say, have not been adopted (save in East Orange).

We need to include how these communities have proceeded once plans are presented to them—White Plains, New York, Hackensack, Buffalo, etc.—and see what happened, which communities moved and which did not and why.

We need to study plans that include legislation—plans that call for reinforcing programs that are successfully launched. Bayard Rustin calls this "creative coercion." This may be confusing, but we are asking how to aid the implementation of a plan, and it might be by Federal

[27] The staff at the Center for Urban Education has studied, is studying, or will study all the communities listed in Figure 1.

[28] A. Buchheimer and Naomi Buchheimer, *Equality Through Integration, A Report on Greenburgh School District No. 8,* Anti-Defamation League of B'nai B'rith, New York, 1965.

funds to communities that initiate desegregation, or it might be by legislating monies for a model community—a region that encompasses a city and its suburbs, or by removing funds from school boards that resist desegregation.

How would one plan for improvement and change with resultant maximal growth? It would be helpful if the needs of the inner-city populace were understood; their needs as seen by them and as conveyed by them to the planners. This kind of planning calls for planning *with* the poor, and therefore *for* the poor, not *around* or *down,* or *to* the poor. Let us look at many services, educational, health, welfare, housing, and see how present programs function, how they meet their goals or fail to, and how future planning can offset present limitations.

In education, particularly in large urban areas, a board of education is elected or nominated by the Mayor or City Manager. This group of officials is responsible to the populace for the education of their offspring. It is obviously difficult to plan for over 1,000,000 youngsters, as is the case in New York City, and understand just what each child needs. This has its obvious dilemmas but the reverse of planning programs on the basis of minimal information of program-outcomes, for example: pre-school programs, after-school tutorial programs, parent and adult education, are indicative of plenty of planning with no sampling of what the real needs are. It could be that a large central organization, such as the Board of Education, cannot plan for local communities, it can only function under broad outlines and suggest programs and expect indigenous leadership to individualize programs to meet the educational needs of the local community.

Another tactic that Boards of Education employ, both in big cities and smaller suburban communities, is that they listen to the most verbal and persistent groups. The Boards do not go out to the community, but await grievance and lobbying groups to attend hearings, protesting what is wrong. Until recently, minority groups rarely protested. Thus the Board represented a compromising or, at best, an equilibrating force, for it tried to ride a program between various points of view—never representing their own professional opinion nor competence.

Why does a Board of Education function this way? To survive! The populace cannot accuse it of taking sides or trying to represent one view—it is truly democratic in representing the majority *and* the minority. But the real question is not how to please everyone, nor how to appease the pressure groups, nor how to remain in power, or to survive. The real question is how to educate—to teach all youngsters to the maximum of their capacity. To address this question, political strategies (as pragmatic as they are) become vestigial. The issue now becomes, how do we give children, irrespective of their family income, optimal learning sequences. How do we insure top-quality teaching, facilities, special services, materials for all, not just for the privileged, assuming that we want to? The primary question is, do we want to educate the poor. And, then secondly, how? And for this we need to understand the problems. If we truly understand, the how will become apparent. Both the planner and the planned-for will explore what is needed, and right now this exploratory process is avoided.

Similar paradigms occur in urban renewal, in transportation facilities, in police and fire protection, in sanitation, in hospitals, clinics, and in welfare. Minority group members are planned for, rarely with. They have not been asked how they like to live but are told what the requirements are for new housing projects. They either meet the requirements of income, family size, no relatives or pets, or they move out of their neighborhood, evicted to find a new life, and in a more congested area. In Los Angeles, the poor are not asked what transportation facilities they need to get to work. The poor in New York most severely affected economically by the paralysis of the municipal subway and bus systems were not protected when transportation employees struck. Nor were the poor asked how they might be protected in the future. The police, fire, sanitation, hospital services for the poorer neighborhoods are invariably inferior to those for the more affluent neighborhoods. And so the same message comes ringing home. The poor—and often they represent a sizable portion of a city's population —receive second class services from elected and appointed officialdom chosen to represent them. We talk about altering this situation, but when will this talk become transformed into action? Tomorrow is too late!

III. SUGGESTIONS ON CHARACTER EDUCATION FOR PUBLIC SERVICE, THE LAW, AND BUSINESS

Chapter 8. CHARACTER EDUCATION FOR THE PUBLIC SERVICE

by Stephen K. Bailey

WE, OF COURSE, are not the first to address ourselves to the issue of character education for the public service. The subject is a hardy perennial of both political and educational philosophy. Many nations, cultures, and empires of the past—notably China and Great Britain—have developed either formal or informal systems of education and training for those aspiring to certain kinds and degrees of public responsibility. At this writing, outside of the United States there are nearly eighty institutes of public administration concerned with the intellectual skills and presumably, with the character of present and future public servants. Within the United States, there are perhaps one hundred graduate programs in public administration, public affairs, foreign affairs, or international service. In addition, of course, there are scores of professional schools and hundreds of liberal arts colleges which continue year after year to turn out young people who will make some aspect of the public service their life's career.

Most of these institutions of higher education self-consciously eschew words like "character" in the content of their formal curriculum. Most would admit, however, that they cannot escape ethical considerations in the process of selecting candidates for admission or recommending them for public service jobs when they are through. Personnel assessment and evaluation forms for the public service, like similar forms in every profession and occupation, ask respondents to rate such items as honesty, reliability, ability to get along with others, leadership capacity, and so on. FBI agents, in conducting security clearances, invariably click their notebooks shut with the ultimate question, "From everything you know, then, is he completely loyal to the United States?"—a question which presumably involves considerations of character.

Even if there is a feeling on the part of most higher educators that character traits and attributes should be acquired, to paraphrase Dean Acheson, "at the mother's knee and other low joints," there is at least a residual concern that both liberal arts and graduate professional education should reinforce the ethical wisdom of the culture. College and university catalogs are still redolent with references to "the whole man"; to educating "future citizens and leaders"; and to promoting "religious, ethical, and esthetic sensitivity." Whether educators are clear about ways and means of achieving these objectives is another story. But the sentiments remain and the desires are unquestionably genuine.

Furthermore, in terms of routine attributes of character, like honesty and reliability, our educational system—reinforced by familial, prudential, and legal pressures in the society generally—seems to have done a good job. Compared to most countries in the world today and yesterday, public services in the United States are run without serious corruption, and with a fair degree of efficiency in the performance of administrative tasks. Passports are issued with dispatch (at least, if the applicant has not alienated Frances Knight's patriotic standards); garbage is collected on time (at least, if landlords provide adequate containers for putting garbage along the sidewalk instead of letting it accumulate in the back yards of tenements); few pieces of mail are stopped, lost, or delayed (unless, of course, someone or something violates the Postmaster General's canons of obscenity or treason); since the scandals of the early 1950s internal revenue agents have been models of honesty (leaving aside the equity and honor in the legislation they are asked to enforce); bribery is rare enough to be newsworthy (if by bribery we mean obvious payoffs and kickbacks rather than more subtle deferences to special pleading and special interests).

In short, character education for the public service seems to have produced a clear administrative ethic even if it has not produced a clear policy ethic. Administrative honesty, reliability, and efficiency are not to be discounted in the creation and preservation of good and great societies; but by themselves they are inadequate defenders of the public interest. The large public questions of our age involve, as they have always involved, issues of justice, peace, opportunity, order, and freedom. What is an appropriate character education for those who would view the public service in these larger terms—who would wish to make tangible these philosophical abstractions of justice, peace, opportunity, order and freedom?

Here, philosophy and history have some lessons—both positive and negative. Three examples warrant elucidation and comment: Plato's *Republic;* the examination system for Chinese Mandarins; and the recruitment system for the British Colonial Service.

I. The Platonic Model

It was Plato who first impressed upon Western society that the formation of the good state depends upon the proper education of its political leaders. If his *Republic* no longer provides a convincing solution to the puzzle of providing tempered intellect devoted to the public good, the questions he raised still plague us, and the system he developed provides a useful normative model.

The traits of mind that Plato thought essential in the ideal public servants were wisdom, spirit, and, of course, devotion to duty. On the one hand, he wanted his rulers to be philosophers who would utilize rationality in the cause of the state; at the same time he saw that the love of knowledge alone would not fit a man for leadership. Thought must be combined with action; courage and mental vigor must be developed, both for the military and, we may infer, for the more peaceful affairs of state. To achieve these ends he presented an education in "music," "gymnastics," "science," and "philosophy."

The education of his "guardians" was to start early, for "the beginning is the most important part of any work, especially in the case of a young and tender thing; for that is the time at which the character is being formed and the desired impression is more readily taken. . . ." Therefore, "it is important that the tales which the young first hear should be models of virtuous thoughts. . . .[1]" Art, music, and literature as prime reflectors of virtue were to be continued throughout the educational process. Then, at age thirty, the most able and worthy few would be introduced to advanced philosophical analysis: the dialectic.

So central to the state was the education of its guardians that an extensive censorship was to be required to preclude art forms that

[1] Plato, *The Republic,* translated by B. Jowett, Book II, Oxford University Press, London, 1924, pp. 377, 378.

might tend to corrupt the future rulers from effective devotion to the duty their station imposed upon them. Not only was lying and impiety not to be portrayed except to receive its just desserts, but excess of any sort was to be banned. Passion distracts from duty, so temperance in all things was required, even in love and laughter. Harmony and rhythm were to be simple and forthright, conducive to sobriety, courage, and constancy. Departure from these esthetic norms could only be in the direction of degeneration. Thus questioning and change were to be discouraged in all things.[2] In Plato's later work this stasis became embodied in impersonal law.

Besides character training by indoctrination, Plato prescribed a two- or three-year period of athletics at seventeen or eighteen. This was intended, not simply to develop the ability of the guardians as warriors, but further to develop their qualities of courage and mental hardi-hood.

Education in the arts and sciences was to proceed alongside that for character, except during the brief period when "gymnastics" was stressed. From the age of twenty to thirty a more advanced education in the arts and sciences was prescribed and only at its completion, and on the basis of both technical competence and demonstrated loyalty to society and to virtue, was the advanced philosophic dialectic to be undertaken. At age thirty-five, the final tempering of the moral fiber was to come with a fifteen-year trial in the holding of minor offices out amongst the hurly-burly of life, mixing with the artisans whose souls were of "brass and lead." At age fifty, the mature guardian was ready to rule the society.[3]

Plato saw clearly that an appropriate education for public leadership needed to be long, diversified, both theoretical and practical, and di-rectly as well as indirectly concerned with traits of character. These are lasting and valuable postulates. His notions of censorship, and of the relevance of gymnastics to the arts of governance, are as questionable as the virtues of his utopia.

II. Mandarin Examinations

It is perhaps ironic that Plato's prescriptions were first tested—at least in spirit—by a culture which presumably had never heard of him.

---

[2] *Ibid.*, Book II, p. 376 through Book III, p. 418.   [3] *Ibid.*, Book VII, pp. 521–542.

Although based upon *The Four Books* and *The Five Classics* of Confucianism rather than upon Platonic ethics, the Chinese system of examinations for the public service bore a strong resemblance to major aspects of Plato's educational model.

The crude beginnings of the Chinese examination system have been traced as far back as the former Han Dynasty, perhaps 165 B.C. But the foundation of the program, which lasted to 1905, was created by the first Emperor of the T'ang Dynasty in 630 A.D. At the time the examination system was made the chief means of recruitment for the civil service, and the subjects it tested required preparation not only in the classics of Confucian philosophy and literature, but in a well-rounded curriculum which included mathematics, law, and political affairs. From these beginnings the system underwent a definite change in character, until in the Ming Dynasty (1368-1644) it received the form and substance that lasted until the abolition of the examination at the start of the twentieh century. Its latter-day content was restricted to the Confucian classics and its methods to the construction of the eight-legged essay.[4]

The works studied by aspiring public officials were an undifferentiated composite of personal ethics and political philosophy. The personal ethics stressed a high consideration for the good of others, a demanding code of propriety, and a reliance upon the mean, as in Plato and Aristotle, in determining right conduct. The governmental philosophy was one which taught a familial relationship between ruler and ruled, requiring monarchs to treat their subjects with love and consideration. Although the king was said to have the mandate of heaven and was therefore entitled to loyal support, the mandate was not inalienable. Severe oppression or even drought or famine could lead to a widespread judgment that the king's virtue had waned, causing him to forfeit the mandate. Withdrawal of support by officials and revolution would confirm the judgment, and the heavenly mandate would be shifted elsewhere. In the *Works of Kwan Tze,* the following passage expresses the relationship:

The monarch takes the people for his heaven. Their support makes him safe, their help makes him strong, their dislike puts him in danger and their

[4] Paul M. A. Linebarger, Djang Chu, Ardath W. Burks, *Far Eastern Governments and Politics: China and Japan,* 2nd ed., D. Van Nostrand Co., Inc., Princeton, 1956, pp. 15, 16.

hatred dethrones him. Therefore, as a good rider to his horse or a good archer to his bow, the care of a monarch for his people should be exceedingly well.[5]

The power of example was given high place and moral superiority thus was considered an important political device for leaders: "Possession of virtue attracts the people, the people bring territory and territory produces wealth; therefore, virtue is the root and wealth the fruit," goes one section of Mencius' *Higher Learning*.[6]

The character of public officials was intended to be practical as well as elevated.[7]

The content of the examination made literal and consecutive memorization of the approved literature of Confucianism essential—a quantity of approximately 80,000 words.[8] Success required an early start, and it was not unusual for infants of two or three to begin to learn characters and at five to begin reading and memorizing, without comprehension, *The Four Books* and *The Five Classics*. So demanding was the task that youths destined to try their skill at the examinations could be allowed little time for other activities than their memorization,[9] and the result was reminiscent of the Platonic system which required that future guardians hear nothing but the required state philosophy.

[5] As quoted in Pao Chao Hsieh, *The Government of China (1644–1911)*, The Johns Hopkins Press, Baltimore, 1925, p. 28.

[6] *Ibid.*, p. 6.

[7] One of the lessons taught by Confucius illustrates this well: Tze Kung asked, "When the Duke of Chi inquired about government, you said that government should be economical; at a second time, when the Duke of Lu asked about government, you said that government depended on the understanding of the ministers by the ruler; at the third time, when the Duke of Yih sought advice on government, you said that the chief duty of government was to make those around you happy and those away from you willing to migrate to your domain. All three questions being identical, why should your answers be so totally different?" "I answered them according to their circumstances," replied the philosopher, "The Duke of Chi was luxurious, his people suffered from his unnecessary waste; therefore, I told him to be economical. The Duke of Lu was deceived by his ministers, their deception wrought miseries on the people; therefore, I wanted him to understand them. While the people of Yih were ready to desert their state, because they were not satisfied with the Duke's rule; therefore, I wanted him to make them happy." *Ibid.*, p. 13.

[8] Linebarger *et al., op. cit.*, p. 66.

[9] Gerald F. Winfield, *China: The Land and People*, William Sloane Associates, Inc., New York, in cooperation with the Institute of Pacific Relations, 1948, p. 149.

The examinations system was graduated, beginning at the district level, continuing for the successful at the provincial level, and culminating for the one out of hundreds who could survive the second stage, with the metropolitan examination. Those who passed the third stage were destined to fill the highest positions, and they were then examined by the Emperor himself to determine their assignment and rank within the bureaucracy.

This, then, was the most extensive system of character education for the public service adopted by any society in history. In theory, it provided a system of open competition; it rewarded hard work; it stressed highmindedness in style and philosophy. Yet it made a curriculum, largely ethical in content, so artificial that even in regard to personal morality itself the performance of the Chinese was poor. Corruption was widespread for much of Chinese history; jobs in the bureaucracy were sold according to an official price schedule—a schedule so high that not more than twenty-five percent to thirty percent of the price could be recouped through the official salary. Even the examination system itself appears to have been corrupted, although the degree of dishonest grading was probably low.[10]

Far more serious, the intellectual content and techniques encouraged were not those needed by public officials in the conduct of their professional assignments. In consequence, brilliant mandarins were frequently totally dependent upon the under-clerks (tested only for reading, writing, and arithmetic) for the operation of their offices. And the under-clerks, treated like inferiors and paid only a pittance, regularly made a handsome living taking their lucrative cut from the public for each of the normal functions of government. Their indispensability and the Mandarins' lack of practical knowledge about accountability systems usually protected the under-clerks from retribution.

Even the social mobility built into a system of open examinations operated far from ideally. The extreme difficulty of the course of study meant that families who could not afford private tutors and complete freedom for study for their children were left at an extreme disadvantage. Then, too, for some groups (bannermen and Imperial clansmen) there were separate examinations. At the regular examinations a required proportion of degrees was reserved for the privileged classes,

10 Hsieh, *op. cit.*, p. 112 and pp. 99–183, *passim*.

sons and daughters of high officials, so that for one reason or another, the ratio of diplomas awarded to commoners as opposed to those of the higher classes was only about one in eight. And entirely outside the examination system were the practices of sale of office, office given on the claim of family service to the nation, office given on recommendation of a high official.[11]

III. The British Colonial Service

In modern times, no nation has been more concerned with the character education of rulers than Great Britain. This was especially so during the years of the zenith of the British Empire. For the British Colonial Service, the character of its young officials was a central concern. Thousands of miles from London, often separated from their local supervisory officers by large distances and rugged terrain, the personal and professional conduct of Colonial officials was largely a matter of individual ethics and intellectual resourcefulness. Expected conduct had very definite overtones of restrained crusading; the bringing of civilization to benighted peoples.

The officials who selected men for administrative posts in the colonies had a clear idea of the type they wanted and where they could be found. Put quite simply, they sought to recruit the traditional British gentlemen who could be counted upon for honesty, loyalty, devotion to duty under difficult conditions, a willingness to accept responsibility, social propriety, and a reasonable measure of intelligence and industry. The training grounds for these virtues were the "public" (private) schools and the great universities, and of these two institutions, it was probably the former which were the more important in character formation. As Sir Ralph Furse, the Secretary principally responsible for Colonial Service selection for nearly forty years prior to 1950, put it: ". . . the public schools are vital: we could not have run the show without them. In England, universities train the mind; the public schools train character and teach leadership." [12]

The public schools performed their educational role much less by course content than by school organization, relationships encouraged,

---

[11] *Ibid.*, pp. 139–183.
[12] As quoted in Robert Heussler, *Yesterday's Rulers: The Making of the British Colonial Service*, Syracuse University Press, Syracuse, 1963, p. 82.

and the inculcation of spirit. Obvious in the arrangement of public school life was an authoritarianism which featured established roles for the masters and the students, the prefects and the rest of the students and the gradations within the student body. Roles were clear, discipline was firm, order was established from above. But the system was seldom vicious or arbitrary, and the ability of superiors was generally recognized.

To a large extent, the "superiors" who enforced order and administered discipline were one's fellows, for the institution of the "prefect" called for an astounding degree of responsibility and authority for the everyday affairs of school life to be left to the boys themselves. Entrusted with the supervision of dormitory life, school prefects and head perfects saw to the many details of rising and sleeping, eating and studying, meting out punishment to their fellows when necessary for the greater good of the school. Often the prefects would be scholastic leaders of their class, but always they would possess an air of authority, a quality of leadership. a peculiar ability that caused others to follow their direction. If an applicant for the Colonial Service could bring a notation on his record that he had served as school perfect—or better as head prefect—at his school, he was almost certain of appointment.

Noticeable also in the character produced by the "public" schools, was an intense group loyalty. The feeling of being a proud part of an on-going institution or a corporate body was one which made appeals to school spirit (and later to the spirit of the service) an important wellspring of devotion to duty and the willingness to carry on.

Suited also to the needs of the colonial service was the quality of living under fairly severe conditions in a womanless society. Again, a toughening of character was encouraged which would serve well many a District Officer on tours of duty which required him to leave his family at home while he spent months at a time at a remote and comfortless outpost.

If the public schools fostered a kind of snobbery, they also encouraged a feeling of distinction and impartial aloofness. In later life this cast of mind would aid the colonial servant to retain the necessary impartiality of magistracy as well as a feeling of *noblesse oblige* and of the importance of adhering to the best traditions of the English gentry at all times, under all conditions.

The use of the public schools as a training institution for public service was not left to chance by the Colonial Office. Sir Ralph Furse and his aides maintained constant communication by letter and by visit with many of the schools, and encouraged an awareness on the part of the schools of the characteristics sought by the Service. At the same time, Colonial Service officials developed their own sense of the qualities and characteristics of the individual schools and of the habits and judgments of their masters. Officers on home leave were encouraged to visit their old schools and talk with the masters and the boys, and many a future public official formed a decision to devote his career to the overseas service through these encounters.[13] These encounters were frequently reinforced at the University level of "Oxbridge." Among the dons and the professors at Oxford and Cambridge were many who were passionately men of this world, men whose concern for academe was equalled by their passion for the forum, men who inspired generations of their students with the excitement of public service. Some cared more for the policymaking of parliament; others for the administrative role of the civil or colonial service, but whatever their particular enthusiasm, they often transferred it to their charges.

R.H.S. Crossman gives us a taste of their influence in a picture from his undergraduate days. He writes of H.A.L. Fisher, Warden of New College, Oxford:

Back in his study in the Warden's lodging, in the company of Gilbert Murray or Hilaire Belloc, of Graham Wallas or General Smuts, and surrounded by awed undergraduates, he would recapture the ecstasy which he had too briefly and too tardily tasted. The chilly effigy melted into life; the hooded, pale-blue eyes glistened with ironic tolerance of his elderly colleagues and with real affection for his young men, while he talked of politics and lived himself back to his seat at the Cabinet table in Downing Street or the League Council at Geneva or the Smoking Room of the House of Commons.[14]

Oxford, particularly, had many tutors over the years who saw their mission not simply as the construction of personal works of eminent scholarship, but as inspiring others to public service. Harold Laski,

---

[13] *Ibid.*, pp. 82–106, *passim* for material on public schools and the Colonial Service.
[14] R. H. S. Crossman, *The Charm of Politics and Other Essays in Political Criticism*, Harper & Brothers, New York, 1958, p. 8.

G.D.H. Cole, and, of course, Benjamin Jowett, Master of Balliol, were men of this stamp. Of the latter, his biographer writes:

> By temperament and inclination he was a philosopher. . . . But he was never a philosopher of the closet. He was a thinker after Plato's kind, seeking to share with others what he had found for himself and to use it for the practical ends of society. These ends he served through his pupils and his friends, and not by any attempt to play the part of public sage. His influence upon English higher administration in the later decades of the nineteenth century, and by natural consequence in the opening decades of the twentieth century, was very great indeed; much greater than has been generally understood, since it was an indirect influence, discoverable only by studying the life-stories of the men to whom he communicated it through his gospel of hard and unselfish work.[15]

For the Colonial Service specifically, W.T.S. Stallybrass, Principal of Brasenose College, served for decades as prime recruiter and recommender of scores of able men. As with the public schools, the links between the universities and the public service were fostered by government personnel officers. Through both informal communications and visits, and more formally organized faculty committees, the Colonial Service sought to maintain the flow from Oxford and Cambridge of well-tempered young officials.[16]

The record of the colonial servants trained under the "public" school-Oxbridge regimen need hardly be rehearsed. Men of order and culture, men of duty and fairness, the overseas Britons maintained the best traditions of their nation and class in the most unlikely places and under the most trying conditions.

The defects of the British approach to character education are easy to spot in retrospect. They are largely summed up in the word "elitism"—which sometimes led to a lack of understanding of, and empathy for, the aspirations of dependent peoples. But in terms of the culture in which he was reared and the needs of order and justice across the extended face of empire, the British colonial officer was by and large an extraordinary success story. Even today, British expatriates working in developing nations under programs of bilateral and multilateral tech-

---

[15] Geoffrey Faber, *Jowett: A Portrait with Background,* Faber & Faber, London, 1957, p. 24.
[16] Heussler, *op. cit.,* pp. 107–139, *passim.*

nical assistance are less handicapped by defects in character education than they are by the thinness of their educational exposure to applied social and physical science.

IV. The Lessons

Where have these brief allusions to Plato, to the Mandarin examinations, and to the British Colonial Service brought us? If we were consciously to borrow from these three systems, what notions would be worth borrowing? What aspects of the three systems should be avoided?

Taking the last question first, there is obviously little room in the modern world for rulers who are self-consciously a part of an educated elite. In modern democratic government, at least, mediation has eclipsed magistracy; negotiating skills are more useful than skills of command. Furthermore, the academic inflexibility and ethical prescription in the curricular or examination content in all three systems could unnerve a modern public servant for the sympathies, empathies, compromises, and conflict resolutions which are the stuff of his working life in a democratic ethos.

But the positive lessons of the three systems are far more impressive than the negative lessons. If modern institutions of higher education would take these positive lessons seriously, they could produce a dramatic improvement in the quality of public leadership in a single generation.

The first lesson is the desirability of postulating that the character of public officials is a basic and an ultimate concern of the educational system. Granted that character is molded by familial and cultural forces outside of the formal educational structure, this admission simply pushes the educational system's responsibility more broadly into the fabric of the whole society. With the general weakening of religious sanctions, secular education bears an increasing burden of articulating and refining the value premises of civilized behavior. If parents have not been educated to be concerned with the end and means of statecraft, with the pursuit of the common good, how can offspring be inspired to develop such concerns or to undertake careers in the service of the general community?

A second lesson of the three systems is that character for the public service is formed by a combination of practical academic, non-academic, and creative pursuits. So Plato supplements formal learning with apprenticeships in lower and middle management. So British "public" schools encourage qualities of leadership on "the playing fields of Eton" and in the systems of prefectures. So the examinations of the future Mandarin call for the creation of original poetry in ancient, often stilted art forms.

A third lesson of the three systems is to be found in their emphasis upon moderation: the capacity to subject passion and emotion to the disciplines of prudence and reason. Few attributes of governance are more fundamental, for these are the attributes which lead to constructive compromise. Modern, large-scale, democratic government is composed of myriad interest groups which organize and counter-organize to affect the course of governmental action. Located at the center of these forces, the public official finds that his actions and dreams must always take into account conflicting demands. Some attention must be paid to the opponents, as well as to the proponents, of change, if forces of opposition are to be kept at a tolerable level.

As Plato's great student, Aristotle, once put it:

Those who think all virtue is to be found in their own party principles, push matters to extremes; they do not consider that disproportion destroys a state . . . for when by laws carried to excess one or the other element in the state is ruined, the constitution is ruined.[17]

Bernard Shaw put the same issue in a more modern idiom when he wrote of Joseph Burgess, a Labor candidate who lost in a general election because he refused to compromise on an issue.

When I think of my own unfortunate character, smirched with compromise, rotted with opportunism, mildewed by expediency . . . dragged through the mud of borough councils and Battersea elections, stretched out of shape with wire-pulling, putrified by permeation, worn out by 25 years pushing to gain an inch here or straining to stem a backrush, I do think Joe might have put up with just a speck or two on those white robes of his for the sake of the millions of poor devils who cannot afford any char-

[17] Aristotle, *Politics,* translated by B. Jowett, Dial Press, Inc., New York, 1954, pp. 1309b 20, 1310a 1.

acter at all because they have no friend in Parliament. Oh, these moral dandies, these spiritual toffs, these superior persons! Who is Joe anyhow that he should not risk his soul occasionally like the rest of us? [18]

A healthy and continuing passion for the great ends of justice, peace, opportunity, order, and freedom must ever be subjected to prudence and to the humility of adjustment to others in consideration of appropriate means toward these ends.

The final lesson of the three systems is the importance of personal example—either the example of the public officials themselves, or the example of teachers or mentors in motivating their charges toward the public service. Fundamental to each system was the notion that exemplary behavior and the humane philosophies of individual mentors were the major guarantors of a civilized and ever-renewing polity.

These, then, constitute basic, viable, perhaps universal postulates for character education for the public service. Taken seriously by those responsible for the structure and policies of higher education and by those responsible for the career patterns and midcareer training of public officials, these postulates could stimulate educational reforms of considerable moment. They should at least stimulate a healthy introspection on the part of American colleges and universities. Put in the form of questions, is character education for the public service a conscious goal? Do courses in the relevant social science disciplines or even specially-detailed collegiate and university courses and programs in Citizenship, Public Affairs, American Civilization, Great Issues, International Relations, Public Administration, and Political Theory give adequate attention to the concept of public service and to the overarching public interest values of justice, peace, opportunity, order, and freedom? Do curricular, extracurricular, and job experience activities promote the kinds of practical problemsolving, creative opportunities and internships of special value to the prospective public official and the constructive citizen? Are students consciously exposed to conflicting pressures and to the arts and skills of achieving high goals while adjusting differences through compromise? Are students exposed to the excitement of the public service, and to the pride of a noble profession, by the concern and example of dedicated faculty?

[18] Hesketh Pearson, *GBS*, Harper & Brothers, New York, 1942, p. 156.

In one sense, of course, a diverse, complex, pluralistic society precludes by definition a single, formal curriculum for public service education. Instead, one must hope that each subject matter field, each discipline, each professional school will attempt to make students conscious of the great policy issues of our age and the role which each segment of the university's program can play in meeting and resolving these issues. The basic tools of communications and of modern scientific analysis are still the fundamental responsibilities of formal education. The discipline needed to master these tools necessarily involves attributes of character. Beyond the mastery of these tools, however, there remain aspects of character education which have been the traditional concern of political philosophy and of selected nations and empires to which this paper has specifically alluded. The future quality of civilized living on this globe will depend on the capacity of higher education to reaffirm the importance of these larger aspects of character education, and to refine in terms of present and future necessity the answers given by those in the past who have seen this issue to be at the center of civilized advance.

Chapter 9. THE INFLUENCE OF THE LAW SCHOOL EXPERIENCE ON THE PROFESSIONAL ETHICS OF LAW STUDENTS

by Wagner P. Thielens, Jr.

I.

MOST COMMONLY, when ethical education for the professions is discussed, the language employed is moral: It is stated that a professional school *should* teach the ethics of the profession to its students. Most debate is likely to focus on how this is best to be accomplished. But an important question is less often raised: what *is* the student taught? And this leads to another: what *can* he be taught that he does not already know? Perhaps these issues are left open or passed over because they call for facts, and the facts are not simple to obtain.[1] This paper will offer data from a sociological study of four American law schools that begin to provide some of the facts.

There are several assumptions hidden in the assertion that "a professional school should teach professional ethics." It presumes that the students do not adhere fully to ethical precepts when they enter the school; the precepts could hardly be taught to those who already know and believe in them. Also, such an initial lack could occur only if one of two conditions were true. Either the professional standards are at least in part different from the ethical standards of the entrant's lay

---

[1] In 1950, Elliott Cheatham carried out a survey of the views held by eighty-five law school deans. Concerning what law schools *should* do, he wrote, "The law schools are in general agreement on the importance of a strong sense of professional responsibility, and on the duty of the schools to aid in the development of it in their students." Concerning what the schools *do* do, the deans were more often uncertain, and in disagreement. Elliott E. Cheatham, "The inculcation of professional standards and the functions of the lawyer," *Tennessee Law Review*, volume 21, June, 1951, pp. 812–820.

world, and in addition not previously acquired as part of his preparation for professional school, or they are similar to lay standards, but the entrant is young and to some degree ethically unformed even in lay terms.

We, too, had better add a prior question of our own: What *is* the ethical condition of the entrant to professional school? By good fortune, we can put the data in perspective, for at least limited information is available on how the student compares with members of the practicing profession in adherence to certain ethical precepts.

Beginning in about 1950, the Bureau of Applied Social Research at Columbia University has been engaged in a program of research on the professions, including medicine, law, engineering, college teaching, and music. Focusing particularly on professional education, the program has included two studies of law schools. The first of these was made at Columbia Law School in 1952–1956. Following up some of the results, the second study traced the experiences of the law school class of 1964 at four Eastern institutions. With one exception, more than ninety percent of all currently registered members of this class at these schools completed lengthy questionnaires just before their entrance, midway through school, and at their graduation. In the law school studies, and in Bureau research at other professional schools, a principal focus of the research was students' adherence to professional ethics and values, including any patterns of change and development in these matters that occurred over the three-year school span.

We will offer here a small number of results from the Class of 1964 study, and discuss some of their implications. The data represent student replies to five queries, selected because they convey well and in comparatively brief form the principal outcomes found in our much larger body of ethics data. They are also verbatim replicas of five questions concerning ethical behavior that were presented to a cross-section of New York City lawyers in 1961, just before the Class of 1964 entered law school, as part of a study of ethics in the metropolitan bar.[2]

The five situations were chosen from thirteen used in the bar study. At the outset, a large number of ethical conflict situations was assembled from texts on legal ethics, published opinions of bar association

2 Jerome E. Carlin, *Lawyers' Ethics,* Russell Sage Foundation, New York, 1966.

committees on professional ethics, and informal interviews with selected lawyers. A special preliminary study was then made to find the most useful items. Those selected all depicted conflict situations in which lawyers who had been confidentially judged as unethical by colleagues would actually report taking the unethical action, and those considered ethical had taken the ethical action. In determining which responsive courses of action in a situation were to be considered ethical and which unethical, the official canons of ethics and detailed opinions of the New York bar association were consulted and closely followed. What is labeled ethical here thus reflects the formal pronouncements of the organized legal profession, and may disagree with going majority practice.

In each query a conflict situation is outlined in some detail, and a lawyer is called upon to select the action he would then take. Some of the alternative resolutions involve an ethically approved act, others describe an unethical one. In the bar study, attorneys were asked if such a situation had arisen in their practice, and then what they had done if it had, or would have done if not. The law school versions asked students to consider "some hypothetical situations which you might face as a lawyer." One of the student queries, in full, read as follows:

Lawyer A's client, without A's knowledge, failed to report a sizable amount of income on his tax return. The client was subsequently contacted by an agent of the Bureau of Internal Revenue who offered to overlook the matter for a sum of money. The client tells A that he (the client) is determined to make the payment.
(a) Do you—understand the situation pretty well, or
        —find some of the legal terminology unfamiliar?
(b) Would you (as A)
   —tell the client that it would be very risky to make the payment, but that if he wants to that's his business (U)
   —tell the client that if he pays off the Revenue agent you will no longer be able to represent him (U)
   —strongly urge the client not to make the payment, but continue to represent him on other matters (E)
   —tell the client that if he wants to make the payment that is his business, but not to tell you anything about it (U)

(c) How sure are you about what you would do:
   —Quite sure
   —Somewhat unsure
   —Not at all sure

The paragraph describing the situation and the alternatives in (b) were taken verbatim from the bar study questionnaire, but parts (a) and (c) were asked only of students. The labels "E" and "U" have been added, here, to show the ethical and unethical responses. In the remaining four situations (reproduced in full in the Appendix to this paper), the lawyer is sent a fifteen percent commission from the title company that has written a title insurance policy for his client, and decides whether to accept it as additional income from the case; he has negotiated the sale for property in receivership to a corporation and been offered an opportunity to purchase stock in the newly-formed corporation, and decides whether and how to make the purchase; he considers whether he should represent one of two business partners, both of whom he has formerly represented on both business and personal matters, who are now embroiled in a controversy; he sends a client to a colleague who is a specialist, takes no further part in the matter, and then decides whether to accept a referral fee of one-third the colleague's fee to the client.[3]

Using these data, comparisons may be made to show how the beginning law students differed from the practitioners, how the students changed in law school from entrance to graduation, and how they differed at graduation from the practitioners they were about to join.

II. The Entrants and Practising Lawyers

First, how did the ethical views of beginning students compare with the stance of attorneys? At one extreme, were the entrants a naive and untutored assemblage, or at the other, a group of well-informed idealists who far outshone the practitioners?

It should be said at once that the responses obtained from both attorneys and students to any of the five queries might well have been

---

[3] The lawyers were presented pre-constructed response options only for the revenue agent payoff situation and the title company situation. In the others, they were simply asked what they would do. For these three matters, lawyers' replies were recorded by interviewers and categorized by the researchers. The categories were closely followed in constructing the options presented to law students.

somewhat different if the situation depicted had been modified, or if the pre-structured resolutions (when offered) had been altered. For instance, different proportions might record "ethical" and "unethical" resolutions to the revenue agent situation if the client were described as less determined to pay the bribe, or if he had already paid it, or if the alternatives given as open to the lawyer were clustered more closely about a borderline between ethical and unethical conduct. The fact that, as the percentages of Table 1 show, seventy-four percent of the metropolitan attorneys reported an ethical response to this situation, could be perfectly compatible with another result, obtained from the same lawyers consistently adhering to a set of ethical practices, showing perhaps eighty-five percent, or sixty percent reacting ethically to a slightly altered situation with slightly different options. The figure of seventy-four percent thus depends substantially on the particulars of phrasing in the query, and should not be taken as suggesting that three-quarters of lawyers are ethical in a more general sense.

However, a comparison of bar and student replies to the same situation is exact, since the arbitrary structuring of circumstances applies to both. The fact that seventy-four percent of the lawyers and eighty-four percent of the entering students chose ethical resolutions cannot tell us how many of each were more generally ethical. But the difference of ten percent between the two does show quite exactly how different the two groups were from each other.

Table 1 compares law school entrants with bar members in each of the five ethical situations. The percentages of ethically compliant attorneys varied widely indeed, from twenty-five percent to seventy-four percent. Yet they were roughly matched on each matter by the proportions of entrants: The differences were ten percent, ten percent, eleven percent, sixteen percent, and five percent. On average, the gap was ten percent. This broad similarity of profile between entrants and attorneys offers little intimation that entrants as a group were adhering to distinctly different standards than those of the attorneys, or that they were substantially ignorant of these standards, or disapproving of them. In any of these contingencies, the pattern of their views would have been in greater disharmony with the stance of the bar than it was in reality.

In fact these entrants, far from revealing themselves as untutored neophytes or disapproving laymen, as a group were already in greater consensus with the profession's going standards than was the profes-

TABLE I

THE ETHICAL STANCE OF 943 LAW SCHOOL ENTRANTS
COMPARED TO 801 METROPOLITAN LAWYERS

	Percentages giving the ethical response	
	Entrants	*Lawyers*
Not condone payoff	84	74
Purchase stocks with safeguards, or decline to purchase	78	68
Not accept title company's commission	62	51
Not oppose a former client	28	46
Not accept unearned referral fee	20	25
Average percentage of ethical replies	54.4	52.8

sion itself. In each of the first three matters in Table 1, a majority of attorneys adhered to the officially approved view; a still larger majority of entrants shared it. In each of the last two a majority of attorneys adopted the officially unsanctioned stance; again yet a larger majority of the entrants agreed with them. To the extent that going ethical practices are a criterion, the beginning students already possessed the ethical standards of the bar in numerical oversupply.

The entering classes were not completely untutored, in another sense. The average level of compliance with official legal ethics among these students, 54.4%, was closely similar to the general compliance level recorded by the sample of attorneys, 52.8%. In this broad acceptance of the Canons of Ethics, our five comparisons together suggest, the entrants already matched the practising bar closely indeed.

Thus the data hint that the occupational ethics of the legal profession may not be as distinctive from those of other vocations, or of the lay world, as some lawyers believe. Or what amounts to the same thing, if the various realms of society from which a class of law recruits is drawn are diverse in ethical values, they may deposit at the law schools' doors a group whose ethical profile resembles that of a practising bar which is also diverse in its ethical viewpoints.

III. Changes in Law School: The Student Body as a Whole

While the entering students already possessed an aggregate oversupply of the profession's operating ethical principles, they were clearly not a group to whom nothing might remain to be taught. On each of the five ethical matters, a substantial number of entrants expressed unethical views. What did the law schools actually accomplish toward changing these students? Or to reflect more exactly the report that our data will make, how did the class of 1964 change from the time it entered law school to its graduation?

Two kinds of change should be described. First, the difference between the class overall at its entrance and at its graduation reflects the net change, the pattern for the group as a whole. Second, change by the individuals in the class, when added together, describes the impact of the three-year span on the separate members. As will shortly be made clear, the two kinds of change are likely to occur in different measure.

Comparisons of the students' overall entering and graduating stances are made in Table 2. At each of four schools the class of 1964 recorded five ethical views as entrants and again as graduates, for a total of twenty before-and-after comparisons. On the average, taking all of these twenty differences together, the class was just 6.4% more likely to adopt an ethical stance at graduation than it had been at entrance. This would mean that if all ethical positions had changed equally at all schools, each class at each school would have a net addition of thirteen more members out of each 200 graduates adhering to each value than had at entrance. If we were asked to summarize our data on ethical change as best we could in a single number, this one would be our choice. Whether this net addition in ethics should be considered quite a lot or only a little depends not upon the data but on the reader's point of view. To those who believe that large-scale ethical inculcation is a characteristic institutional accomplishment of our law schools, the data offer no support. To others who are pessimistic about the ability of professional schools to teach ethics at all, evidence from four of them that a small but noticeable increment in the general level of ethical conformity did occur may be reassuring.

Actually, all of the standards at all schools did not change equally. The twenty separate change figures ranged from a maximum of twenty percent, the increase in adherence at School D to ethical safeguards surrounding the syndicate-sale stock purchase, to a low of minus two percent, the slight decrease at School C in ethical handling of the proffered title-sale commission (and three others). The changes, arranged from largest to smallest, were:

20%	8%	3%	—2%
18	8	3	—2
16	7	2	—2
13	7	1	—2
10	7		
10	5		

In six instances, or less than a third of all, a net shift of ten percent or more occurred between entrance and graduation; on only these matters were there as many as ten new adherents at graduation among each

TABLE 2

NET CHANGE AMONG THE CLASS OF 1964: ETHICAL REPLIES
AT ENTRANCE AND GRADUATION, FOUR LAW SCHOOLS

	Percentages giving the ethical response		Increase in class's ethical percentage over the three-year span
	At entrance	*At graduation*	
Ethical response			
Not condone payoff			
School A	86	89	3
School B	86	88	2
School C	83	81	—2
School D	84	87	3
Purchase stock with safe-guards, or decline to purchase			
School A	78	88	10
School B	84	91	7
School C	72	80	8
School D	76	96	20
Not accept title company commission			
School A	70	75	5
School B	68	69	1
School C	57	55	—2
School D	51	69	18

100 students. In an additional six instances, a net increase of at least five percent was recorded; here, at least five or more new adherents per 100 were to be found. Among the remaining eight instances, four extremely slight shifts in an ethical direction were balanced by four equally slight shifts toward the unethical stance. In sum, in a minority of instances a fairly substantial body of students had acquired the official ethical stance, but in a sizable majority either a small or a negligibly slight ethical trend occurred. It should be said again that these results reflect quite accurately the outcomes in a much larger array of ethical and value comparisons made between entering and

	Percentages giving the ethical response		Increase in class's ethical percentage over the three-year span
	At entrance	At graduation	
Ethical response			
Not oppose former client			
School A	30	37	7
School B	29	45	16
School C	26	39	13
School D	25	35	10
Not accept unearned referral fee			
School A	22	29	7
School B	21	28	8
School C	16	14	—2
School D	22	20	—2
Average percentage of ethical replies, all respondents at all schools	54.4	60.8	6.4
Number of responding students			
School A	298	288	
School B	188	134	
School C	247	188	
School D	210	170	
Total, four schools	943	720	

graduating law students in the 1950s and 1960s: In this entire body of data, for a handful of particular precepts there were substantial changes over the law school span. Four or five times as many matters showed small or negligible change.

As here, in the more complete data the change recorded was far and away most often a movement toward the officially prescribed conduct, as set forth in the Canons of Ethics and implemented in formal opinions of the organized bar associations. Even when a majority of practitioners disregarded the approved practice, as in two of our five situations, the trend among law students was toward the officially approved standards, rather than toward going practice. These four law schools, when they had any impact at all on students' ethics, exerted influence in the direction of the profession's ideals rather than indoctrinating further the current operating stance of practitioners.

DIFFERENCE BETWEEN MATTERS. When the five matters are considered separately, a further profile emerges. Table 3 shows that these changes, though always in the direction of approved standards, varied noticeably in amount. For two, an eleven percent net increment was recorded, but for two others, the change was only two percent and three percent. As these figures reflect the continued trend at four law schools, we are tempted to speculate that law schools in general may convert students to certain types of ethical principles more successfully than to others. Some precepts, whether more frequently exemplified in law school classes, more deeply felt by law school teachers, or more unanimously supported by whole faculties—or more urgently put forward by classmates, lawyers outside of school, and others—may be brought more saliently into students' experience during their three years in attendance. And the student body may be more amenable to persuasion on some principles than it is on others. (If our figures are a criterion, however, the degree of such openness is not foreshadowed among entrants by the extent of initial agreement to a principle.) Our data, of course, can only hint at these possibilities.

It should be added that the change would appear considerably larger if it were expressed as a proposition, not of all students, but of the fraction of these students who had been opposed to the ethical stance as entrants. How many were converted, considering that some were already ethical and so already foreclosed at the outset to possible conversion? Concerning the payoff, for instance, the two percent net shift among all students represents a conversion of one-eighth or 12.5%, when considered as a segment of the sixteen percent of entrants who did not already subscribe to the ethical view on this matter. Similar measures show a net conversion of fifty percent in the stock purchase matter, thirteen percent on the title company commission, seventeen percent for the former client issue, and four percent for the referral fee. To use a rather elastic summary statistic, a net average of 19.2% of the widely varying entering proportions expressing unethical views had shifted to the ethical stance at graduation.

To those who fear that professional schools destroy idealism among their professions' recruits, these data again offer no support. On the contrary, when the focus is limited to the influence experienced by those not already in accord, the figures begin to be impressive.

TABLE 3

AVERAGE CHANGE FOR EACH ETHICAL PRINCIPLE,
AND FOR EACH SCHOOL, BETWEEN ENTRANCE AND
GRADUATION

	Average percentage	
	at entrance	*at graduation*
Ethical response, averaged for four schools		
Not condone payoff	84	86
Purchase stocks with safeguards or decline to purchase	78	89
Not accept title company's commission	62	67
Not oppose a former client	28	39
Not accept unearned referral fee	20	23
School response, averaged for five ethical situations		
School A	57.2	63.6
School B	57.6	64.2
School C	50.8	53.8
School D	51.6	61.4

DIFFERENCES BETWEEN LAW SCHOOLS. How did the schools compare? The four entering classes were not sharply different from each other. In Table 3, the average amount of "ethical response" among entrants to School A was 57.2, among those to School B 57.6%, to C 50.8% and to D 51.6%. Each of these numbers by itself means little. But when compared, they provide an indication of the degree to which one or another of the entrant classes was leading or lagging in general level of initial conformity to legal ethics. The fairly close similarity of the four numbers suggests that the four classes, while clearly not identical in profile, were not greatly disparate in this general stance.

We now add that the four schools have been presented here in order of standing. School A is one of the nation's most prestigious law schools, B is less universally regarded as outstanding but is of markedly high rank, and D, lowest of the four, is generally considered a school of perhaps below-average reputation. Assuming that their reputations reflect the technical quality of these schools, and recognizing that A and D stand some distance apart in this attribute, we can conclude from the averages that the two technically superior law schools were able to attract an ethically somewhat superior group of professional candidates. On this, there is no way to know how well the four schools reflect trends among the nation's many dozens of law schools. As the four schools in this study are all located in very large cities on the Eastern seaboard of the United States, other types of schools—perhaps those in other regions or in less urbanized environs—may of course follow quite different patterns.

The data also reveal that within the bounds of the limited change found in our studies, the four schools varied noticeably in their impact on student ethics. The average change between entrance and graduation of 9.8% at School D was largest, and of 3.0% at School C smallest. In other contexts, these figures might not be impressive: none of the four institutions exerted ethical influence broadcast. But students at one school did record more than three times as much change toward ethical standards as those at another.

At least among these four particular schools and five particular precepts, the quality of the institution was not consistently related to the extent of value inculcation. But it was at the lowest-ranking school, now, that the greatest change was recorded. Observers of the undergraduate scene in education sometimes ponder the possibility that the main advantage of a leading college over an average one may be its ability to attract a more able group of applicants. Once the initial difference is discounted, the "good" college may do no more for its students than the "weak" one does. A similar observation might be directed to the undoubted ability of a top law school to draw a technically more able group of recruits with similar outcome. In the ethical realm our four schools started from rather analogous baselines—but achieved ethical results that were unrelated to their technical repute.

IV. Individual Change

The data described thus far have dealt only with the net class change, the difference between the percentage of all interviewed entrants and (not invariably the same individuals) all interviewed third-year graduating students, in the class of 1964. This is a characteristic of the class rather than of its individual members. Considerably more changes might well be made by individuals than the net change would intimate.

To illustrate, let us consider the query about the title company commission. Table 3 showed that sixty-two percent of 943 responding entrants at the four schools gave an ethical reply, while at their graduation sixty-seven percent of the 720 respondents did so. A smaller group of 581 students gave definite replies to the query on both occasions. Among them, exactly the same percentages, sixty-two percent as entrants and sixty-seven percent as graduates, also did so. The smallest possible number of individual changers would be found if all the original sixty-two percent held fast, and five percent among the remainder shifted ground. But many more individuals could change, with the same net result. At a maximum, all thirty-eight percent of those originally responding unethically could switch to an ethical view, while all thirty-three percent of those ending with the unethical view could have started out as ethical. Thus, to produce a beginning total of sixty-two percent and an ending total of sixty-seven percent, the amount of individual change could have been as small as five percent or as large as seventy-one percent. For both, the net change in the class as a whole would remain five percent. In actual fact, twenty percent of the 581 students switched to the ethical stance, and fifteen percent to the unethical; thirty-five percent of the class members recording before-and-after views had changed them.

Clearly, this aspect of change cannot be overlooked: Granted that much of the movement will be in opposing, and in a sense mutually-cancelling, directions, a small net change can mask a considerably larger amount of individual change. If the size of the net ethical change has real implications for legal education, the amount of individual ethical change has further and separate importance.

Table 4 gives figures for the five ethical matters. It will be noted that some of the percentages for the 581 repeaters differ slightly from the percentages given in Table 3 for all respondents. (Rather interestingly, the students who were faithful respondents to the study were sometimes slightly more ethical as a group than those who could not be reached consistently.) In general, the actual frequency of individual change is about half way between the absolute minimum and the absolute maximum that would be possible.

TABLE 4

AMOUNT OF INDIVIDUAL CHANGE AMONG 581 STUDENTS
BETWEEN THEIR ENTRANCE AND GRADUATION

Ethical Responses	Percentages giving the ethical response		Amount of individual change		
	At entrance	*At graduation*	*Lowest possible*	*Highest possible*	*Actual*
Not condone payoff	86	89	3	25	17
Purchase stocks with safeguards, or decline to purchase	78	91	13	31	23
Not accept 15% commission	62	67	5	71	35
Not oppose a former client	30	41	11	71	41
Not accept unearned referral fee	19	24	5	43	29

Two possible situations, that might have produced the net overall changes found, did not occur. The data did not reveal a group of already compliant entrants that remained stable during the three years of school, with a very small group of converts added to them by graduation. These law schools do not produce the net change that occurs by holding steadfast all those who initially possessed an ethical view and inducing a small fraction of their classmates to join them. At the other extreme, no wholesale turnover in viewpoint occurred, as though all entrants had undergone attack by a faculty dedicated to moral shakeup.

It is not desirable to discuss here in detail the forces to which these changes were responsive. Two situations are possible. For one, recorded change is not necessarily true change. If large numbers of students answered the ethical queries in an uninvolved and casual manner, a sizable total individual "change" would be obtained, misleadingly. In truth, some students may indeed have answered at random. The questions dealt with hypothetical events that could not arise in the student's contemporary life.[4] But the consistency of the net trends, moving always toward a more ethical group stance, indicates that such disinterested response was not too widespread, or it would have produced random overall trends as well.

The substantial turnover of individual views is more likely the product of powerful counter-currents, each influencing separate and substantial numbers of students. For example, the school experience doubtless serves to inform most of those who enter its doors ethically uninformed; automatically a group of indoctrinated "converts" is thus created. At the same time, among the others who are ethically knowledgeable at entrance some might be induced by comparatively poor standing to develop more cynical views on ethical matters.

Again, students who were in continuing and satisfying informal contact with their professors may have been happy to accept and absorb the teachers' ethical precepts. Those who for whatever reason were

[4] Of course, such issues *have* to be largely hypothetical when posed to law students. They are not allowed a license to practise and must confine their experience with real law and real clients to such things as Legal Aid work or a summer job in a law firm, with a licensed lawyer in charge. An interesting problem arises for consideration: Are there homologous ethical decisions in the student's actual life, decisions which prefigure the ethical dilemmas of later practice? If so, these anticipatory ethical experiences may be more meaningful to the student, and a more important shaping influence, than the hypothetical dilemmas he encounters in a legal profession course—or in a sociologist's questionnaire.

isolated for personal associations with the faculty might tend to isolate themselves also from faculty ethics.

Such conflicting currents, we would hazard, are not uncommon in professional schools. Furthermore, they may inhibit the growth of certainty and deep belief in ethical precepts. When asked how sure they were about what they would do in the conflict situations, concerning three of the five matters, students were slightly less often certain as seniors than they had been as entrants. The law schools, this suggests, did not deepen students' feelings of commitment to their ethical principles in any classwide sense.

V. Graduating Students and Practicing Lawyers

When it took up formal law study, the class of 1964 was almost identical to the practicing bar in its general conformity to principles of legal ethics, at least as indicated by conforming responses to five particular ethical dilemmas. As the students became somewhat more ethical in viewpoint over their three years of schooling, the general contents of Table 5, comparing the ethical stance of the class at graduation with the bar, cannot be a surprise. But the specifics deserve note. On three of the matters, the students were now substantially more likely than the lawyers to adopt the ethical stance by margins of twelve percent, sixteen percent, and twenty-three percent. On the remaining two they still trailed the bar members, though by but three percent and seven percent. Comparing the average percentage of ethical replies, a rough indication of the *comparative level* of ethical adherence, the students who had been much like the attorneys were now more ethical by an eight percent margin.

Several conclusions are suggested by this finding. At the least, some of these students will be exposed to pressures from competitive older colleagues to cut ethical corners once they enter actual practice. And they may learn, if practitioners' own reports in the bar study are a criterion, that in some matters they will be less likely to respond ethically to a real dilemma than to a hypothetical one.

Law schools may find profit in this comparison. Some experts believe that the best way to teach law students the ethical ideals of their future profession is to put them into the courts and law offices, as apprentices and assistants to practicing attorneys. Again, if the New York bar data and our own are a fair criterion, a broadcast exposure to the practicing profession could not achieve this result. Such a "legal clinic" approach to the teaching of legal ethics, unless designed and implemented with great sophistication, may be bound to be a disappointment.

TABLE 5

THE ETHICAL STANCE OF 720 GRADUATING THIRD-YEAR
STUDENTS COMPARED TO 801 PRACTICING LAWYERS

	Percentages giving the ethical response	
	Third year	*Bar sample*
Ethical response		
Not condone payoff	86	74
Purchase stock with safeguards, or decline to purchase	89	68
Not accept 15% commission	67	51
Not oppose a former client	39	46
Not accept a referral fee	23	25
Average percentage of ethical replies	60.8	52.8

On the other hand, it may be futile to try to shield students from the ethical condition of their profession. By graduation many law students have had employment with lawyers, and have been in position to observe going ethical practice for themselves. Whatever else the faculty and administration of a law school may do to encourage ethical conduct among their students, insulation from the norms of the current-day profession is probably not possible.

Appendix: The Ethics Situations and Reply Categories

In the law school version, for each situation students were also asked how well they understood the situation and how sure they were of their response. These queries, illustrated in the text for the revenue agent situation, are omitted here. Labels have been added to show the ethical replies, (E), and the unethical, (U).

(1) Payoff to Internal Revenue agent. Quoted in text.

(2) Lawyer A, attorney for the receiver of the Doe Corporation, negotiated a sale of all of the corporation's property to a syndicate for a large sum of money. The sale was approved by the court and was at the best price obtainable. The syndicate then turned over the property to a new corporation. Prior to the receiver sale the syndicate had a general understanding with A that he should receive an interest in the new corporation. Some months later, after the receiver sale, A is given the opportunity of purchasing stock of the new corporation for which he would pay the same proportionate amount as members of the syndicate.

Would you (as A)

—purchase stock in the new corporation (U)

—purchase the stock, but only after getting the consent of the court (E)

—purchase the stock, but only after getting the consent of the receiver of the Doe Corporation (E)

—purchase the stock, but only after making a full disclosure to all parties (E)

—not purchase the stock (E)

(3) Lawyer A represents the buyer in a real estate transaction in connection with which he helps to obtain a title insurance policy for his client. After the transaction is effected the title company sends A its usual fifteen percent commission on the price charged the client for services rendered.

Would you (as A)

—accept the commission but take it into consideration in setting the client's fee (U)

—accept the commission and inform the client (or with client's prior approval) (E)

—accept the commission but deduct the amount from the fee and indicate it on the client's bill (E)

—accept the commission without informing the client (U)

—refuse the commission (E)

(4) Smith and Jones, partners in several business ventures, have been represented by Lawyer A on both business and personal matters. A controversy has arisen between Smith and Jones, and Smith retains another attorney to commence legal action to dissolve the business partnership. Jones asks A to represent him.

Would you (as A)

—decide to represent Jones (U)

—represent Jones, but only if there is no confidential information involved (U)

—represent Jones, but only with the consent of Smith (E)

—decide not to represent Jones (E)

—decide to represent Jones in an effort to bring about some reconciliation, but bow out when such efforts fail and legal action is instituted. (U)

(5) Lawyer A refers a matter to Lawyer Jones for which A accepts a one-third referral fee. A's only connection with the case has been to hear the client's story, phone Jones and inform him that he is sending over the client on the matter in question. A has no further contact with the client or with Lawyer Jones in this matter.

Would you (as A)

—accept the one-third referral fee (U)

—take more than a third (U)

—take less than a third (U)

—accept the referral fee, but only if the client's fee is not affected (U)

—not accept the fee (E)

Chapter 10. THE PROBLEM OF MORAL EDUCATION FOR THE BUSINESS MANAGER

by Edgar H. Schein

WHEN we refer to the moral[1] education of the business manager, we may have one of three different concepts in mind: 1) education for general character which would reflect itself in moral behavior in any occupation; 2) morality in the *process* of education itself, an educational process which *exemplifies* the moral values to be taught; and 3) the teaching of a particular value system as part of the general preparation of a candidate for a particular occupational role. This paper will focus on the third of these concepts—the teaching of particular values in the process of socialization for an occupational role.

I have chosen this focus deliberately in order to stimulate research on moral education in the business realm. Such research has been carried out in the fields of medicine, dentistry, and law, but is lacking in the business area. I suspect that one reason for this lack is the difficulty of clarifying what are moral questions and what are moral solutions for business managers. My attempt will be to provide some clarifying categories drawn from a sociopsychological frame of reference which, I hope, will make it possible to select research questions and testable hypotheses which are relevant to the moral realm, whether we are talking about the behavior of practising managers or the teaching of management.

I. Some Categories for Classifying Moral Values Relevant to the Business Manager Role

Moral or ethical behavior and the values from which such behavior derives are often believed to be generalizable across all kinds of situa-

[1] For purpose of this discussion I will not distinguish between concepts of "ethical" and concepts of "moral." The two words will be used interchangeably.

tions and all kinds of human relationships. Yet most research on such behavior consistently finds that people apply different standards to different situations, suggesting that moral standards are not as general as one tends to believe. For example, killing is wrong, yet we may do it in wartime or in self-defense. Stealing is wrong, yet a prisoner of war may steal from his captor. Lying is wrong, yet we may and are supposed to lie if we must do so to protect someone's self-esteem. In the recent cases of price-fixing in the electrical industry, this point came out in the defense argument that the forces in the particular situation offered the executives no choice but to collude, just as the soldier has no choice but to try to kill the enemy.

If we accept the argument that one must analyze values and moral standards in reference to *particular* situations or relationships, we can next ask, what kinds of categories would help us to classify such situations?

My major classifying principle will be to consider who is involved in the relationship, or with respect to whom is the behavior being judged as moral or immoral. Following a detailed discussion of this classification, I will discuss briefly some additional issues such as who benefits *versus* who gets hurt, the closeness of the behavior to the consequences thereof, the reversibility of the behavior, the problem of intentions *versus* effects, and sins of commission *versus* sins of omission.

A. WHO IS INVOLVED? THE MULTIPLE CLIENTS OF THE MANAGER. There are a number of ways of defining a profession. One of my favorites comes from the sociologist Everett Hughes [2] who has stated the simple proposition that a professional is someone who knows better what is good for his client than the client himself does. This definition includes the more usual definition that the professional has had extensive training in a body of knowledge and skills which he exercises on behalf of his clients.

If we examine this definition in reference to the well established professions of medicine and law, we find that the value or moral issues of the profession tend to be defined around the relationship with the client. Both doctor and lawyer receive moral training in how to exercise responsibility in their relationship with clients, how to work for

[2] E. C. Hughes, *Men and Their Work*, Free Press, Glencoe, Ill., 1958.

the client's welfare even if this means the sacrifice of self-interest or the compromising of some other value. Doctors are expected to make economic sacrifices if the patient's welfare demands it, to ignore the welfare of their own families if midnight calls require their services, to lie to their patients about their conditions, and so on. Perhaps the best example comes from the prisoner of war camp where the doctor's oath required him to treat enemy officers in clear violation of the patriotic standards of the POWs who were witness to the behavior and who viewed it as traitorous.

If we accept this definition of professionalism—knowing better what is good for the client than the client himself—we may speculate that it is the *vulnerability of the client* which has necessitated the development of moral and ethical codes surrounding the relationship. The client must be protected from exploitation in a situation in which he is unable to protect himself because he lacks the relevant knowledge to do so.

In recent years we have tended to view the business man and industrial manager as becoming increasingly professionalized. There is a broader base of technical knowledge and skills required to be a manager, a longer period of training for managerial responsibility, and a greater tendency for managers to be able to move from one type of organization to another, implying that managerial skills are quite general. If then the manager is becoming a professional, who is his client? With respect to whom is he exercising his expert knowledge and skills, and who needs the protection against the possible mis-use of these skills?

1. *The consumer as client.* Business generates products and services which are purchased by various types of consumers, raising the obvious possibility of exploitation of the consumer. Traditional economic theory minimized this problem by assuming that the marketplace was an automatic arbiter of prices and quality, hence the businessman enjoyed no special power relative to the consumer. *Caveat emptor,* let the buyer beware, was a not so gentle reminder to the consumer to exercise what power he had to prevent himself from being exploited. This assumption in turn legitimized any practice which any manager wished to engage in *vis-à-vis* the consumer, and thereby bypassed the moral issues altogether.

The point is well made by the story of the storekeeper whose son asked him what it meant to be in moral conflict. The father replied: "If a customer comes into the store and looks at some material, and asks how much it costs, and I tell him it is $1.00 per yard, and he asks for one yard, and pays me the dollar, and as he is leaving the store I discover that there are two one dollar bills stuck together—then I face the moral conflict—do I tell my partner about it or just keep the extra dollar."

Many economists argue persuasively that the traditional economic assumptions have never been validated by experience, that the market-place has not been able to curb the power of the businessman *vis-à-vis* the consumer, that the consumer has not been in a position to know what he was buying, hence was, in fact, in a relatively vulnerable position. Thus we have seen the development of formal codes, laws, and informal ethical standards pertaining to cleanliness in production processes, weights and measures in packaging, openness in stating contents of products, truthfulness in making advertising claims, rights of consumers to sue businesses for the return of their money if they have been cheated, and so on.

Clearly then, one whole area of values deals with the relationship between the manager and consumers, and one area of moral training for the individual manager concerns the development in him of a sense of responsibility to his customers. Whether or not graduate schools of management actually attempt to inculcate a sense of responsibility to the consumer is an important question for empirical research. Our own school, if it touches the area at all, does so implicitly. Courses in marketing tend to focus heavily on the technical issues, not on the moral ones. I would hypothesize that most of our faculty would assume that the requisite set of responsible feelings and values are already "built into" our students, hence do not have to be a subject of concern in graduate courses.

2. *The stockholder as client.* The consumer is a client of the manager only in a very limited sense. Most managers do not deal directly with customers, and only a small percentage of their decisions have anything to do with the final consumer relationship. Instead, one often hears the assertion that the manager's only responsibility is to the stockholder.

According to this concept the manager is a person who uses his expert knowledge and skills to bring to fruition some ideas about how to build or develop a product or service for profit, to implement these ideas, and actually to generate a reasonable rate of return on the investment of the stockholders. The client-professional relationship is here defined as primarily an economic one, and the vulnerability of the client lies in the possibility that the manager may misuse, misallocate, steal, or otherwise mishandle the economic resources entrusted to him.

Deriving from this concept is a second area of potential moral training, having to do with embezzlement, misappropriation of funds, not taking advantage of inside finanicial information, nepotism, and a variety of other behaviors which have in common that they reduce the profitability of the enterprise and thus take advantage of the stockholders. The power of the stockholder to protect himself is greater than that of the consumer, however. He has a potential organization through the annual meeting and through his representative body, the Board of Directors. He can and often does demand more direct surveillance of the financial activities of the mangers to supplement those of regulatory agencies such as The Security Exchange Commission.

3. *The community as client.* A third client of the manager is the community, viewed broadly as the individuals and other organizations who are in some way interdependent with the business enterprise. The individuals in the community who depend upon the company for jobs are vulnerable to discriminatory hiring policies, the suppliers are vulnerable to discrimination, exploitation, and bribery, and the community as a whole is highly vulnerable to economic loss if the business moves or conducts its affairs in such a way as to minimize the economic return to the community. It can bring in its own labor force, refuse to buy supplies or raw materials from local vendors, fail to support community activities, and so on.

It is interesting to note that in this value area, as in the others, the legal sanctions tend to be applied in those areas where vulnerability is at a maximum, such as in the area of discriminatory hiring practices or minimum wages for employment.[3] The more difficult moral decisions occur, however, where ambiguity is greater such as in the process of

---

[3] One might hypothesize that legal sanctions tend to develop when a) vulnerability is at a maximum; b) there is a specific identifiable target who is potentially vulnerable; c) the manager's behavior is potentially observable and unambiguous; and d) there are immediate or short-run consequences of the managerial behavior.

defining what the economic responsibilities of a company are if it is the sole employer in a community.

A special case of the community as client results when businesses have overseas subsidiaries and the managers become not only representatives of the particular organization *vis-à-vis* the local foreign community, but become representatives of the United States as a nation with a certain kind of value system. In this situation it is often not clear who is more vulnerable—the local community, the business enterprise, or the United States by having its image tarnished. Do we expect the overseas manager to uphold the values of service and community development, the values of efficiency and economic growth for the business, the values of democracy and free enterprise, or the values of nationalism, patriotism, and allegiance to the United States? These values can and often do come into conflict with each other. What is best for the local community, for the business, and for the United States are often not the same things.

We have had to face this issue in the Sloan School when we were selecting candidates for our Fellows in Africa and Fellows in South America programs. In each case our graduate was expected to become an employee of the local government and to convince it that he could be trusted. He had to have a value system which would permit him to work on behalf of his employer, even if this meant short-run disregard of United States interests, as in the case of planning a local development program which might draw most of its financial and technical resources from the Soviet Union if these were more accessible than their United States equivalent. One thing we were clear about in our selection—we could not afford to send super-patriots or individuals whose prime motivation was to export their own concept of American values to another culture. Whether or not our Fellows faced such conflicts and how they handled them if they did, is an important research question which we are currently trying to answer.

4. *The enterprise as client.* A fourth client is the enterprise itself—the organization which employs the manager.[4] With the increasing ten-

---

[4] Since the organization is an abstraction, can one view it as a client? I believe we can treat it as an "object" in the same sense in which clubs, fraternal organizations, political parties, country itself exist as objects to which we give loyalty, and attention and from which we obtain material and symbolic rewards.

dency to analyze business organizations as complex social systems comes an increasing tendency for the manager to view himself as being basically responsible to the system as a whole. He is responsible for its efficiency, maintenance, effectiveness, and growth. He is expected to make decisions on behalf of these values even if they run counter to the short-run interests of consumers, stockholders, and the community.

The important value referent becomes the organization as a whole, and the assumption is made that in the long run what is good for the organization will be good for the consumer, the stockholder, and the community. Considerations of profit, consumer benefits, community involvement, and so on are subordinated to the ethic or values of efficiency and growth, based on criteria of the "health" of the organizational system. What is required of the manager is commitment and dedication to organizational goals.

Thus, whether the manager decides to hire only certain kinds of employees at certain very low wages is based not on moral considerations in the usual sense, but on considerations of what is required to produce the product efficiently. I know of one industry that has solved this dilemma by moving to countries where labor was cheap and no legal sanctions existed concerning hiring practices.

Teaching the importance of commitment and loyalty to the enterprise as values may be particularly important because the enterprise, being an abstraction, is not in a good position to control such behavior. It is highly vulnerable to low commitment, indifference, disloyalty, apathy, sabotage, and treason. Business organizations cannot apply legal sanctions against such behaviors as easily as nations can and do through their governments. Businesses can only fire the apathetic person, but if apathy is widely spread through managerial ranks there may be a tendency not only to condone such behavior but to develop practices of concealing it from top management, the Board of Directors, and the stockholders.

Most of the technical courses in a business school probably take the values of enterprise efficiency and growth for granted. Organizational goals are accepted as given; the only problem is how best to achieve them. If ethical or moral dilemmas are involved in the choice of means, these are either ignored or settled by recourse to whether the means are in fact illegal or not. If the survival of the organization depends upon it, even illegal means are sometimes condoned with the argument that the law is not fair in the first place.

5. *The subordinate as client.* A fifth type of client of the business manager is his subordinate-employee. Many kinds of managerial behaviors labelled as immoral or unethical deal with the superior-subordinate relationship-paying starvation wages, excessive working hours, unsafe working conditions, withholding a promotion or raise to enforce subordination, arbitrary layoffs, and so on. Employees as clients have been so vulnerable to these kinds of behavior on the part of their managers that they have had to band together and, through unions and the passage of protective legislation, reinforce their own position.

Thus, much behavior formerly labeled immoral is now defined as illegal, but the issue is not settled in that a more subtle counterpart of each of the above kinds of behaviors is possible. Bosses can still threaten their employees with the withholding of rewards or subtle punishments; they can still exercise arbitrary and unfair authority; they can play favorites, fail to give credit where credit is due, persecute someone until he quits, steal their subordinates' suggestions, fail to mention their best subordinates for promotion, and so on.[5]

As one story puts the issue, a company wanted to institute a new benefit program which was more favorable to employees. All employees signed up except one older clerk who held up the entire proceedings by refusing to sign. His boss told him of the great benefits but to no avail. The boss asked the vice-president to try, but no amount of persuasion could get the old employee to sign. After several more futile attempts to get the man to understand the benefits, the president himself was told about the case. The president called the old man in, sat him down at the desk, put the paper in front of him, and said, "Listen you S.O.B. Sign that paper right now or you're fired." The old man signed. The president, somewhat puzzled, asked him why he signed so readily when others had had such difficulty getting him to sign. The old man said, "Well, sir, you were the first one who really explained the program to me."

---

[5] William Evan points out that in organizational life employees do not have the protection of due process of law and a system of appeals as they do in the larger society. See William M. Evan, "Due Process of Law in Military and Industrial Organization," *Administrative Science Quarterly,* volume VII, 1962, pp. 187–207.

The values implied by traditional management theory have always held that the boss is the boss and should only do that which is good for the enterprise. The argument has been that managers have no special obligations or responsibilities to workers and/or managerial subordinates beyond those specified by the contract or law. The human relations movement, on the other hand, has usually been viewed as an attempt to reverse this trend and to argue that managers are responsible to their subordinates, should consider their needs, should treat them as human beings not merely as interchangeable economic resources, and that they should do this because it is right in and of itself in a democratic society.

A third position which many human relationists/behavioral scientists claim for themselves is that managers should consider the needs of their subordinates not because it is basically immoral not to do so, but because it will in fact lead to greater economic and productive efficiency on the part of the enterprise to do so. Since commitment, loyalty, and energy are desirable in employees for good organizational performance, it is argued that these are most easily obtainable by treating people fairly, considering their needs, and attempting to enhance rather than weaken their sense of individuality and contribution to the organization.

We have here an area where values and science overlap to an unknown degree since the evidence is not yet clearcut whether in fact people will generally perform better if trusted and treated well, or whether this happens only under certain special conditions. If the latter is the more nearly accurate statement of where our scientific knowledge leads, the manager is in the difficult position of having to be a diagnostician in an area where it is not at all clear whether the issues are scientific or moral.

What we then teach in a school of management may well be a function of whether the teacher is an economist who leans toward traditional assumptions about economic man or a behavioral scientist who leans toward assumptions of a complex man capable of a variety of involvements in organizations.[6] In our school we teach both positions.

[6] See Edgar H. Schein, *Organizational Psychology*, Prentice-Hall, Englewood Cliffs, New Jersey, 1965, for an elaboration of this position.

6. *The peer and/or boss as client.* A sixth type of client for the manager is his peer and/or boss. I am assuming that the manager is by definition a part of an organized enterprise, and that any organized enterprise depends on coordinated behavior from all its members. The nature of organized effort thus makes the members of the organization highly interdependent, and therefore highly vulnerable to certain kinds of behaviors *vis-à-vis* each other. For example, the boss is highly vulnerable to having his subordinates lie to him about what is going on in those portions of the organization which he cannot check on directly. Peers are very vulnerable to having negative information about themselves passed on to their boss, which is one aspect of the set of activities generally referred to as "playing politics."

Where departments of a single organization are arrayed competitively with each other, the manager of each may be motivated to exaggerate the virtues of his own group and devalue the other group, and may implement the motive by falsifying figures, by failing to pass on key information, by subtle distortions, and the like. All the pathology of intergroup conflict in society and community can play itself out inside the organization, with managers being tempted into various kinds of questionable behavior *vis-à-vis* their peers and superiors.

Part of the value dilemma in this area is that we do not have clear ethical or moral standards pertaining to collaboration-competition. Not only is it not clear in our society how far one should go in defining the game as being a competitive one, but it is not clear how far one can go in bending or breaking rules in the process of trying to win. We say that free enterprise is by definition a competitive game, and that competition is good for all the various enterprises engaging in it, yet we find that competition breeds behavior which is clearly harmful and against which society must protect itself. For example, for a company to win over a competitor may mean to reduce its costs by cutting its labor force, compromise on quality of product, make untrue advertising claims, sabotage the competitor, etc., to the point where government intervention becomes necessary to redefine the rules of the game.

Most companies assume that the productivity of individuals as well as departments within their organization can be enhanced by having them compete with each other. Rarely do they observe until it is too late some of the costs of such competition in the amount of distortion of information, hiding of failures, falsification of figures, empire building, and mutual mistrust among managers presumably working for the same enterprise. Are these managers immoral, or does competition stimulate certain kinds of behavior which are well within the rules of the *competitive* game? It is only in the context of attempting to work together collaboratively that some of these behaviors look questionable.

I would state the hypothesis that most schools of management start with the values of individualism and competition, rarely examining the consequences of these values inside the enterprise. Group effort, collaboration, and cooperative coordination tend to be viewed as fuzzy inventions of the behavioral scientists, not as cencepts to be taken seriously. The only group in our faculty that believes in the effectiveness of *group* incentives (which force cooperation among workers) is the labor-relations—organizational psychology group. The economists, mathematicians, marketers, and so on are clearly in favor of individual effort and individual incentives, and, by implication, the ethic of competition.[7]

7. *The profession as client.* A final type of client can be thought of as the profession with which the person identifies and to which he belongs. To the extent that management has become a mature profession with clear standards, the individual manager can judge his own behavior against those standards, regardless of the requirements of the various other client systems. In a sense the manager then becomes his own client in that he protects his own self-esteem and his professional identity at the same time that he upholds the profession. However, the profession as client may not solve the problem of identifying moral standards in that the professional standard may merely be to try to serve the various other client systems as well as possible.

Summary and implications. The various "clients" of the manager have been represented in Figure 1. The manager as a professional has obligations and responsibilities to each of these clients. This very fact has a number of implications:

1. The managerial role, in contrast to many other professional roles, tends to be defined in terms of a system of *multiple clients.* It is not yet clear in the profession which clients, if any, are to be considered the primary ones.

2. Because the values which underlie the different manager-client

[7] Edgar H. Schein, "Attitude Change during Management Education," *Administrative Science Quarterly,* volume xi, March, 1967.

relationships differ from each other, creating potential conflict situations, and, because we have not yet defined primary client responsibilities for the managerial role, *we cannot specify a single set of values and moral behaviors for the manager.* The search for such a single value system is doomed to failure until we define to whom we ultimately want the manager to be responsible.

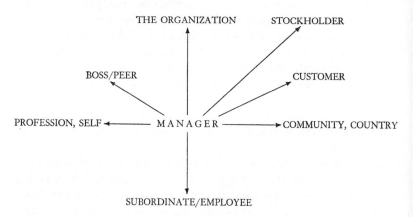

FIGURE I. VARIOUS CLIENT SYSTEMS TOWARD WHICH THE MANAGER HAS RESPONSIBILITIES. EACH ARROW DEFINES ONE AREA OF VALUES AND MORAL BEHAVIOR.

3. The responsibilities *vis-à-vis* one client system often require the compromising of responsibilities to another client system. Just as members of organizations have often been found to suffer from role conflict because of the multiple links they have to others, so they suffer from potential *value conflict* or *moral conflict* because of the conflicting responsibilities do different client systems.

4. Because of the potential value conflicts which the manager faces, we cannot glibly label his behavior as moral or immoral in any particular situation. We must know the *frame of reference* within which the behavior occurred in order to judge it. In other words we must know which of several values the individual was trying to implement before we praise or condemn him.

5. By classifying types of behavior in terms of the client relationship

which is involved, we can study empirically the kinds of values managers hold, and how these vary as a function of other variables such as rank, type of job in the organization, age, prior experience, and so on. It would be extremely valuable to know, for example, whether managers are more likely to view as immoral, behavior which hurts a consumer than behavior which hurts a subordinate, and so on. At present we have no value theory which would be able to make any predictions about this sort of question.

6. The nearest thing to a superordinate value is the assertion that the manager is ultimately responsible to the enterprise. Much of our teaching seems to be based on this premise, and most often when managers are under attack they seem to retreat to this as the ultimate defense—what is good for the company is ultimately good.

7. If indeed we are moving toward an organizational ethic of the type implied above, it becomes essential to study carefully the implications of this "ultimate" value position. If managers are taught primarily to respond to the needs of the organization, will this undermine or subvert other important values or are the needs of the organization indeed compatible with the needs of the consumer, the employee, and the community?

B. WHO GETS HURT AND WHO BENEFITS? A second way of classifying moral value questions is according to the criterion of whether the immoral behavior involved is defined as immoral because it unfairly benefits the person doing it, or unfairly hurts one or more others who are affected by it. To exemplify the distinction, discriminatory hiring practices or personal prejudice leading to unfair treatment of an employee are immoral because they are unduly harmful to the recipient of the behavior. Embezzlement on a small scale, theft of company office supplies, financial gain due to inside information, accepting bribes or kickbacks from suppliers, etc., are immoral because they are unduly beneficial to the person committing the deed. The latter type of behavior may in fact be doing no one any visible harm in the short run. But it implies that there are certain categories of rewards to which people are not entitled or certain means of obtaining benefits which are not sanctioned regardless of whether anyone else is harmed or not.

A closely related issue concerns whether the potential harm from an immoral action is directed at a particular individual or small group, or whether it is widely distributed among an anonymous mass. I would conjecture that we tend to label behavior as immoral much more readily if the harm is directed at *particular others*.[8] Thus, to cheat a customer in a face-to-face relationship is considered to be more immoral than to cheat an anonymous mass of customers as in mislabeling a package. To fire twenty particular men from a hundred man work force is considered to be more immoral than to order an arbitrary twenty percent reduction in the labor force and draw names out of a hat. Stealing office supplies, tools, and materials from the "company" is not as immoral as stealing a single tool from a fellow worker which may make his job more difficult to perform.

The double standard we use in this regard is illustrated by the story of the man whose son came home from school complaining that a friend had taken his pencil. The father told his boy that it was probably accidental, not to worry about it, and gave him another pencil. The next day the boy reported that the friend had again taken his pencil. Once more the father played the issue down and gave his son another pencil. When the behavior was repeated a third and fourth day, the father finally got mad, called the friend's father and said, "Look, Fred, my boy tells me that your boy has been taking his pencils. I want you to see that this stops. It is the principle of the thing which is bothering me, not the pencils. I can get plenty of those at the office."

It is not clear whether the tendency to condone cheating or stealing with respect to a large anonymous mass like a company comes about because of the belief that the anonymous mass can somehow afford it, and that it is not really hurt, or whether it is simply easier to commit hurtful deeds when the hurt party is not there to reproach or induce guilt. The latter position would lead to the proposition that the greater the physical or psychological distance between the manager and the client, the easier it would be for him to commit irresponsible hurtful acts toward the client.

[8] Both "helping" and "hurting" are *interpersonal* concepts with limited meaning when applied merely as a trait like "helpful" or "mean." They become meaningful as we specify *who* is hurt or *who* is helped.

Some recent experiments by Stanley Milgram [9] support the idea that morality is easier to give up as psychological distance builds up between the person hurting and the person hurt. In Milgram's experiments, subjects are asked to give extremely painful electric shocks to a partner whenever he makes an incorrect response on a learning problem. In fact there is no partner, but the subject believes that there is one. Not only did Milgram find that a surprisingly high number of people will give extreme shocks to partners in this situation if ordered to do so by the experimenter, but that they are more likely to do so, if they cannot see, hear, or feel the reactions of the partner. In other words, fewer subjects will obey the experimenter if they can hear moans whenever they give a shock, and still fewer will obey if the "partner" holds hands with the subject and clenches the hand strongly every time the presumed shock is delivered. Apparently we *do* find it easier to be cruel if we *don't* have to witness the effect of our cruelty.

If this phenomenon is general, one might suppose that the manager is most likely to be moral with his immediate subordinates, peers, and superiors, and least likely to be moral with customers (unless he is in sales), the community (unless he is in public relations), and stockholders (unless he is a large one himself or the treasurer who must report to them). It suggests also that one of the most effective means of curbing immoral behavior or training for morality is to maintain close contact between the manager and those clients toward whom one wants him to be particularly responsible. In conflict situations, one might predict that the person will choose behavior which will be least hurtful to those "clients" (including the person himself) who are psychologically closest to him. [10]

---

[9] Some conditions of obedience and disobedience to authority in Stanley Milgram, *Current Studies in Social Psychology,* edited by I. D. Steiner and M. Fishbein, Holt, Rinehart & Winston, Inc., New York, 1965, pp. 243–262.

[10] Robert Kahn has suggested the further implication of organizing our enterprise as small units, possibly federated into larger ones, to insure a maximum of close contacts among managers and their various clients.

One might speculate that the *motivation* to help or not hurt comes from the *feelings* of compassion, fear, or guilt, not from a *rational* assessment of need or vulnerability. We are more likely to give something to a beggar who confronts us than a starving country which may need our help more, but which arouses no direct feeling in us. In any case this is an hypothesis worth testing.

A further hypothesis would be that we tend to view either self-enhancement or hurting as more immoral if the person is viewed to be acting on his own behalf rather than as an agent or representative of some group. One of the commonest defenses against charges of immoral behavior is that the person was only carrying out orders (as in the Milgram experiment and the Nuremberg trials) or was only representing the best interests of some other client system with which he is identified.[11]

If this last hypothsis is supportable, it has implications for how we train members of any profession. To the extent that we teach them to identify with groups, to allow themselves to become representatives, and to develop loyalties, to that extent we are encouraging them to abdicate more personal concepts of responsibility. Perhaps one of the functions of professional associations is to "drain off" the belongingness needs of the individual professional lest he join a group which will bias his moral judgments.

C. SOME ADDITIONAL CONSIDERATIONS—REVERSIBILITY, SINS OF OMISSION, AND INTENTIONS VERSUS CONSEQUENCES. When we consider society's judgments with respect to certain categories of immoral behavior, it appears clear that not only is the amount of harm and the fairness of the deed considered, but that irreversible harms are more severely judged than reversible ones. Thus killing is most severely punished because it is most harmful and totally irreversible. Rape, maiming, and other physical insults fall under this same umbrella. Do they have a counterpart in the realm of managerial behavior?

Blacklisting a fired employee and thus depriving him of a livelihood, driving someone out of business by unfair means, ruining a colleague's career by a whispering campaign which destroys his reputation, and stealing a patent, all have a certain quality of irreversibility, but the judgment is not too easy to make in many cases. It is easier to identify the clearly reversible cases such as those which involve cheating a customer (where the customer can recover his money), fraud (where the injured party can sue for damages), or accepting a bribe (which the person can be forced to return).

---

[11] I am indebted to John Thomas for this point.

The most difficult judgments arise in situations where it is not easily determinable what harm was done. Suppose a supervisor deliberately gives low ratings to an employee whom he dislikes even though the employee's performance is excellent. If the low ratings cause the employee to be passed over for promotion, he has clearly been harmed, but neither he nor the boss may know whether or not this has actually occurred. As was noted previously, employees in organizations do not have the protection of anything comparable to due process of law. The manager especially is highly vulnerable with respect to higher levels of management, and has few channels of appeal in most organizations. Hence even if immoral behavior were reversible in principle, it often would not be in practice.

In discussion with Robert Kahn another dimension was identified which poses difficult judgment problems. The dimension concerns essentially the distinction between sins of commission *versus* sins of omission. Most of my discussion so far has taken its examples from sins of commission—some clear behavior which was irresponsible with respect to some client. Yet many kinds of situations become unduly hurtful or beneficial only if the manager does *not* do certain things.

For example, the manager may not transmit his positive evaluation of a subordinate and thus undermine the subordinate's chance for promotion. He may fail to report to the production manager information received from customers pertaining to defects in a product, and thus make the production department more vulnerable to criticism. He may leave slipshod practices in the organization alone rather than correcting them, thus weakening the competitive position of the company. He may fail to report a potential problem in a product to the customer, thus endangering the customer. Failing to inform car buyers of possible safety hazards in certain models, or failing to notify the National Aeronautics and Space Administration of weak spots in a missile system or booster would be extreme examples of this sort.[12]

How do we tend to judge this category of "sins of omission?" Two criteria which appear to be involved are 1) the amount of potential harm that can result from the omission, and 2) whether or not the manager knew that he was withholding behavior and knew of the

---

[12] The obvious more general case is the passive behavior of the witness to a crime such as in recent cases in New York City, failing to help where help is needed.

potential consequences. In the case of commission we generally hold the person responsible for the consequences whether he knew what he was doing or not. "Ignorance of the law is no excuse." But in the case of sins of ommission, ignorance or good intentions appear to be more sound defenses. If this hypothesis is supportable, it suggests that specific training in thinking through the consequences both of acting and not acting becomes an important part of professional training, particularly for the manager.

It is my impression that such training is indeed heavily emphasized in graduate school. Without stating specific value criteria for the student, we emphasize being able to think through various courses of action and accurately assessing consequences in order that the person should learn how to implement those values that he holds.

I. Concluding Remarks

I have tried to clarify the issue of moral education for the manager by pointing out the inherent difficulty of classifying what is moral and what is not for this emerging profession. Not only is it not clear to what client the manager is ultimately responsible, but it is difficult to judge the amount of benefit or harm, the effect of psychological distance from the client, the obligations of the manager to do more than avoid illegal or clearly immoral actions, and intentions within a given frame of reference. All of these difficulties should make us cautious in glibly labeling particular managerial acts as moral or immoral.

On the other hand, the issue cannot be dismissed merely because it is difficult. We should vigorously pursue empirical research to clarify the conditions under which different kinds of behavior will in fact occur and how various groups in our society judge these behaviors. We should determine what kinds of value positions are held in our professional schools of management and how these jibe with values in business and in the larger community. And we should stimulate inquiry among students themselves to begin investigation of the educative process on the part of its recipients.

Until we have more data, we should attempt to discern what the trends are in our present educative process. I would like to conclude this paper by pulling together some of these trends, as I see them from the perspective of our own Sloan School.

1. Most faculty members tend to avoid the value issues, concentrating instead on what they call "analytical approaches" to problemsolving. This means that goals are taken as given and the focus is on how best to achieve the goals. The emphasis is on means and how to choose among competing means in terms of criteria of efficiency. A corollary emphasis is to "know the consequences of your own behavior" and choose means appropriately in terms of rationally assessed consequences.

2. If the faculty member is pushed on the value issue or asked what the ultimate goals are toward which the means are to be used, he would most often choose the enterprise as the relevant client. The goals are to maximize the economic performance of the enterprise or to insure the survival and growth of the enterprise as a social system. The values are efficiency and effectiveness. I am not aware that any course seriously questions whether any given enterprise should in fact exist or not. Such questions are treated as being outside the realm of most of our courses.

3. If asked about other clients such as consumers, employees, and community, the faculty member would tend to respond that "other courses" worry about these unless it happens to fall squarely within his own area. Thus, obligations to employees are the concern of psychology or labor relations courses, not economics or mathematics. Within the area, the pragmatic means emphasis tends to be maintained, however. Speaking for my own area of organizational psychology, I would tend to justify moral behavior toward employees, colleagues, and superiors on the pragmatic basis that such behavior insures better organizational performance, thus seemingly removing the question from the moral realm.

4. A recent survey of the beliefs and values of our faculty revealed that in a number of areas there were considerable differences as a function of teaching area. If these findings are reliable, it suggests that even though we may as individual teachers try to de-emphasize the value questions, we do in fact feel differently about certain basic issues and students probably are well aware of this. I also have evidence that

students are in fact influenced by faculty beliefs and values. But, since we differ as a function of teaching area, we influence the student differentially as a function of which courses he takes.[13]

5. If we have within the school a kind of pluralism with respect to values, the ultimate responsibility for value choice seems to fall to the student himself. Either we force him through a pattern of required courses to expose himself to a variety of positions which he must then integrate, or we let him choose his own courses and thus force him to make value choices during the process of education itself, or some of both. In the Sloan School I believe we do both, but we do not provide a clear forum during the student's second year of education for integrating the diverse points of view or forcing an examination of value issues. The fact that such integrative courses have been difficult to design and to teach may well reflect the difficult value questions with which they would have to deal.

13 Edgar H. Schein, *op. cit.*, 1967.

IV. SUGGESTIONS ON CHARACTER EDUCATION FOR THEOLOGIANS AND CLERGYMEN

Chapter 11. NEW STRATEGIES IN CATHOLIC SEMINARY TRAINING

by Robert O. Johann, S.J.

CATHOLIC SEMINARIES are at present undergoing a profound reformation. This reformation concerns not only the academic structure of the seminary but also the whole style and concept of priestly formation.[1]

On the academic side the effort in this country is to bring the seminaries more closely in line with the standards and practices of American colleges and universities. Indeed, in order to overcome the isolation that has characterized the Catholic seminary in the past, there is a move afoot to do more than merely parallel in the seminary the academic procedures of secular institutions of learning and to seek actual integration with them. The idea would be to move the Catholic seminaries to the secular campuses where they would become schools of Catholic theology with their students enrolled in and receiving their degrees from the secular institution.[2]

Needless to say, such a course would involve the complete revamping of still current notions of the training of priests. Although this revamping is already under way, it is still in its early stages and has a long way to go. In the following paragraphs I wish to address my remarks to the strategies, implications, and problems of this larger development.

[1] The various trends reported in the present paper are amply documented in recent studies of seminary life. See, for example, Stafford Poole, *Seminary in Crisis,* Herder & Herder, New York, 1965; *Seminary Education in a Time of Change,* James Michael Lee and Louis J. Putz, C.S.C., editors, *Fides,* Notre Dame, 1965; Walter D. Wagoner, *The Seminary: Protestant and Catholic,* Sheed & Ward, New York, 1966.

[2] Variations on this theme are developed in James Michael Lee's "Overview of Educational Problems in Seminaries" in *Seminary Education in a Time of Change, op. cit.,* pp. 82–169.

I.

The present ferment in the Catholic seminary is part and parcel with the general ferment in the Catholic Church. The Catholic Church is in process of moving toward a larger understanding, and practical recognition, of the rights and prerogatives of individual freedom and initiative. It is moving from a morality of conformity to one of creative responsibility.[3]

The individual person has, to be sure, always had a central place in Catholic thought. It is the individual person who is created and loved by God and called to eternal life. But although the importance of the individual in the eyes of God has always been recognized, his vocation as an individual in this life and in relation to temporal structures has not been equally appreciated. His role was thought to be that of conforming to the will of God as manifested in the given structures of nature and society. Individual initiative and responsibility were played down in favor of obedience and submission.[4]

The Second Vatican Council, however, has taken a new tack. Without elaborating a wholly new philosophy, indeed without being explicitly aware of all the implications of its new stance, it has accepted from contemporary culture the idea of human intelligence as fundamentally creative. The norm for human behavior is not the world as it is, but as intelligent love can make it; not conformity but social reconstruction, both inside and outside the Church, is the order of the day. Man's responsibility extends to the very shape of society; he is called to be a reformer. And since the passage from one state of affairs to another requires the intervention of critical intelligence and individual initiative, the individual person has newly come into his own.

This what lies behind the new personalism and worldliness manifested in the decrees of Vatican II. This is also why so much stress has been placed upon the need for dialogue between the various elements within the Church and between the Church herself and the world.

---

[3] The signs of this trend are, to be sure, frequently offset by official actions, which is precisely the source of the great confusion among Catholics today.

[4] I have developed this point in my *The Pragmatic Meaning of God*, Marquette University Press, Milwaukee, 1966, pp. 9–12.

Man is viewed as involved in a process of creative interaction with the world, a process which in the measure it is illuminated by human intelligence can give rise to genuinely new and ever more satisfactory meanings. Henceforth, doing the will of God is inseparable from the intelligent re-making of prevailing institutions.

II.

The profound shift in Catholic thought which found expression in Vatican II is inevitably having its repercussions on the whole idea of seminary formation. Indeed, the very presuppositions of past practice in this regard are being called into question.

The largely defensive stance of the Church toward modern culture, which characterized her outlook and practice in the past century, gave rise to a prophylactic type of priestly training. The candidate for the priesthood had first of all to be isolated from all contact with the world. Hence, houses of formation were built in the country, where there would be little coming and going, and where what coming and going there was could be strictly supervised. In this atmosphere a twofold formation was pursued, academic and spiritual. The academic curriculum was devoted by and large to philosophy and theology and its point was to give the seminarian a firm grasp of Catholic teaching in these areas. He was expected to master a strictly codified and therefore much too limited (although it was not recognized to be so) version of the long tradition of Catholic thought. In line with the general stance of the Church, the emphasis was defensive and apologetic. Each thesis was accompanied by a refutation of any current in contemporary culture that might be opposed to it. The Catholic priest was supposed to know the Catholic position on all matters philosophical and theological and in the light of it be able to dispose of all contrary views. Needless to say, such a formation became heavily dialectical and more verbal than real.[5]

But the protective and other-worldly attitude of the Church was even more manifest in the spiritual formation she gave her priests. The

[5] See the chapters, "Theology in the Seminary Curriculum" by John L. McKenzie, S.J. and "Philosophy in the Seminary Curriculum" by Robert O. Johann, S.J., in *Seminary Education in a Time of Change, op. cit.*, pp. 405–428, 451–478.

spiritual life was conceived less as a way of relating to the world than as a matter of withdrawing from it. It, too, was something strictly codified and regulated, a style of life spelled out in a myriad of rules and prescriptions to which the seminarian was expected to conform. The spiritual was a separate and distinct domain which one entered through observance of prescribed forms. The suitability of a candidate for the priesthood was measured in terms of his conformity to the fixed pattern. A failure to conform meant expulsion. Thus spiritual formation and the effacement of individuality in the overall conduct of one's life were practically identified. To be admitted to the priesthood, the candidate had first of all to prove himself a good seminarian, and a good seminarian was one who submissively accepted the established order.

III.

The effect of the new spirit in the Church on all this would be hard to overestimate. It has practically turned the seminaries upside down. For it must be remembered that what is going on in the Catholic Church today is not simply the imposition of a new orientation from on high; this new spirit is not simply the result of a new set of rules. It results, rather, from a new experiential grasp by all levels of the Church, but especially by the younger elements within it,[6] of the inadequacy of the former stance in the contemporary world. What Vatican II did was to recognize in principle this inadequacy and to sanction the search for new forms. Perhaps nowhere else in the Church than in the seminaries themselves is the search being carried out with more eagerness and enthusiasm.

It is one thing, however, simply to reject old patterns and styles; it is quite another to find a viable way of getting along without them. It is easy enough to say that isolation is "out" and involvement, intellectual and practical, is "in"; that religious formation, and much less religious life, can no longer be conceived simply in terms of conformity but must allow full scope for individual initiative and responsibility. But it is not so easy to see what all this will mean in practice. The difficulty

[6] As Walter D. Wagoner remarks: "The present generation of seminarians, given half a chance, will overtake and outrun all of us" (*op. cit.*, p. 190). I have tried to spell out this new experiential grasp in my *The Pragmatic Meaning of God*, pp. 2–20.

here is the one of devising a new and positive concept of religious life and service.

The goal by itself of providing more adequate intellectual formation for priests is not hard to meet. We have already indicated the growing determination on the part of Church authorities to immerse seminarians in the university life of the country where they may be exposed to the most rigorous standards of intellectual competence and achievement. Nor is it a difficult matter simply to relax the rigid formalities of seminary life, to eliminate the multiplicity of rules and regulations, to put the seminarians more on their own and give them a voice in the determination of seminary policy.

As a matter of fact, all this is being done. The seminarian is being more and more assimilated to the college and university student who is preparing himself intellectually in a certain specialized field of endeavor. However, for lack of any positive notions of how to go about it, the idea of a specifically spiritual or religious formation for priests is being called into question.[7] This is the tendency which lies at the root of the present crisis in American Catholic seminaries. For it runs counter to the whole idea of seminary life and, carried to its logical conclusion, could mean the elimination of seminaries altogether. The only thing that would distinguish a candidate for the priesthood would be his area of specialization pursued at some already existing center of learning.

IV.

Although such an eventuality cannot be excluded from the realm of possibility, it is not the one that in my opinion will prevail. Nor do I think it should. For the priest is not simply a technician in religious matters, nor can religion be simply reduced to an intellectual discipline. The priest is at least supposed to be a leader in the religious life of the community. Even if that religious life is no longer to be conceived in terms of objectivist conformity to set and determinate structures, it will hardly be promoted by a kind of subjectivist individualism either.[8]

---

[7] Not only do the seminarians themselves tend to resent the idea that they need to be "spiritually formed," but the notion of "formation" itself seems to many to be at odds with the contemporary stress on individuality and personal fulfilment.

[8] This is the point of my short essay "Subjectivism," *America,* June 25, 1966, p. 876.

This, indeed, is the dilemma confronting the Catholic Church today, both at large and especially in her seminaries. The widespread rejection of universal and fixed patterns as essential to religious life, with little experience to go on of something else that religion might mean, is resulting for many in the adoption of an individualistic humanism as the only alternative. The extreme of objectivism is being replaced by an extreme subjectivism. What is needed is some way of moving beyond both these extremes, a way of achieving genuine communal solidarity without subordinating individual persons to structures, and a way of achieving a genuine personalism (with its respect for the creative initiative of individuals) without the dissolution of community.

Perhaps the most interesting strategies for coping with this dilemma are those which are aimed at devising new styles of community living. Community in the Church is being conceived in more dynamic terms than heretofore, less as a state and more as a process. Vatican II has dropped the notion of the Church as a perfect society and reemphasized its scriptural description as the pilgrim people of God. The unity of this people does not consist in their dedication or adherence to a common structure, but in their faithful service to a Lord Who is beyond all structures. They come together to celebrate His name Who is the unifying focus of the whole order of persons, in Whose love they are united to one another as persons, and Whose service consists in the intelligent re-making of the world in His image (which is that of personal community).

What is new here is that the notion of creative intelligence is being introduced explicitly into the context of community life and is itself being interpreted in communal and processive terms. The intelligent thing to do in a given situation (*i.e.,* what God expects of us as intelligent creatures) is no longer that simply which authority prescribes, nor that merely which some individual takes it into his head to do. It is rather that which is intelligently arrived at through a process of dialogue and discussion by the community as a whole. Liturgy and dialogue thus become the two key notions in the new orientation: the celebration together of the common focus of our personal energies, and the continual interaction of those energies for the purpose of improvising an ever more adequate response to the various situations in which the community finds itself.

Dedication to religious life, therefore, no longer means the adoption of a codified system of regulations. It is rather to participate in a common commitment (whose structures and instrumentalities are to be devised—and revised—along the way) to the continual promotion of human community. In this connection, the notion of authority in the Church is being re-interpreted along more scriptural lines. It is being viewed less as a matter of controlling power and more in terms of a service of unity, a kind of catalyst of concord and consensus, that in and through which the members of the community can think their relationship to one another and articulate a common course.[9]

V.

If these ideas make sense, then it would seem that there is still place for the seminary in the training of priests and one may still speak of spiritual formation as something over and above intellectual formation. In the light of what has been said, the seminary would be an on-going experiment aimed at achieving genuine personal community in the light of the Gospel. Over and above his personal commitment to Christ and his dedication to study, the candidate for the priesthood would be asked to commit himself to the process of community life itself. Because of its dialogic character, this process would free the student from the isolation of his own subjectivity without oppressing him with any fixed or rigid forms. His spiritual formation would consist in his participation in the on-going life of the group itself. The continual improvisation of a life-together-with-others, liturgically celebrated and practically implemented, would provide a concrete education in the realities of Christian living for which no purely intellectual efforts could substitute. It would also provide a more realistic basis for the screening of candidates, one that is more in accord with the actual life they will be called on to lead and the sort of work they will be called on to do.

So far as I know there are no Catholic seminaries where the ideas I have suggested are being fully carried out. There are, however, a good number moving in that direction. Moreover, they are supported by the

[9] *Cf.* John C. Murray, S.J., "Freedom, Authority, Community," *America*, December 3, 1966, pp. 734–741.

implicit philosophy underlying the decrees of Vatican II. Although this philosophy still has to be worked out in detail, its lead ideas are already abroad and having an effect. They have already generated a great deal of excitement and hope.

Chapter 12. *A TURNINGPOINT IN PROTESTANT THEOLOGICAL EDUCATION*

by Robert W. Lynn

IN W. H. Auden's poem, "The Age of Anxiety," "Emble" speaks of his situation:

> To be young means
> To be all on edge, to be held waiting in
> A packed lounge for a Personal Call
> From Long Distance, for the low voice that
> Defines one's future. The fears we know
> Are of not knowing. Will nightfall bring us
> Some awful order—Keep a hardware store
> In a small town. . . . Teach science for life to
> Progressive girls—? It is getting late.
> Shall we ever be asked for? Are we simply
> Not wanted at all? [1]

I have often been reminded of these lines when working with Protestant theological students. For a Protestant seminary these days is something of a "packed lounge." Like others in his generation, the theological student wants to be (as the saying goes) "where the action is." Our young Emble often invokes the vocabulary of change; he speaks of "crisis," "breakthrough," "revolution," and the other words that express the characteristic cant of our time. Yet it is difficult for him to see how the church in its ministry can be "where the action is." And thus he awaits with growing perplexity that "call" that will define his future.

So do his theological teachers, whenever they contemplate the future of the seminary. They sense, however inchoately, that a new kind of

---

[1] W. H. Auden, *The Age of Anxiety,* Random House, New York, 1946, p. 42.

theological education is in the making. My purpose in these brief remarks is to define that new situation and its novel challenge.

I.

First let us consider the most obvious signs of change in the profession of the ministry. Here I speak of profession in two senses of the word.

1. In the older sense of the word, a profession denoted the activity of one who had a message to profess. Typically the Protestant minister has been a "professor." Hence the aim of his seminary education was often induction into a theological stance, a distinctive way of perceiving God's word and man's ways. This tradition, for instance, enjoyed a recent revival when "neo-orthodox" theology was in the ascendancy. During the 1940s and 1950s many a seminary professor felt a sense of direction about his educational task. He was confident of the cultural and religious powers of the message into which he was initiating the next generation.

Now comes the "Death of God" theology. I do not regard this new fashion as a serious theological option. Its significance lies elsewhere. More than anything else the sudden rise of the "Death of God" thought reflects a larger diminution of the cultural and religious confidence of mainstream American Protestants. "Do we have anything distinctive and important to say?" That question now lurks beneath the surface of seminary life across the country.

This apparent change in the atmosphere of seminary life may represent an eventual gain rather than a setback. It has brought relief from some of the less attractive aspects of the preceding era: the mood of quick certitude, the boundless will to believe. For our purposes here, however, I would only note that this alteration of the climate of opinion has tended to shake the Protestants' confidence in the theological enterprise—and thus their sense of direction in theological education. The ensuing results are evident to many observers within and without the seminaries. These schools are now experiencing a period of drifting, of uncertain experimentation, and, in fact, a time of waiting for some greater clarity about the purposes of theological education.

2. The second and more common use of the word—profession—is to

describe a particular occupation, learned over a span of intensive, specialized training. Here, too, one can discern certain changes in attitudes toward the profession of the ministry. In the 1950s, for instance, the usual diagnosis of the problem of the Protestant pastor proceeded along the following lines: amidst the religious boom of the postwar period the minister is becoming a "macerated" person, a man besieged by contradictory expectations. He has—so the argument ran—far too *much* work to do.

One decade later the characteristic analysis of the professions's difficulties has shifted somewhat. Now one hears a litany of criticisms, all of which imply that the Protestant minister does not have *enough significant* work to do, *i.e.,* his parish duties in the tradition of a congregation-centered ministry remove him from any effective participation in the major movements and decisions of the day. (There are various explanations for the spirited participation of the clergy in the recent civil rights demonstrations in the South; one reason, though surely not the only one, was expressed in the commonly heard exclamation, "Now at last we are doing something!") The word most frequently heard when the Protestant clergy gather to discuss the situation is that frayed commonplace—irrelevance. Some of this talk, of course, springs out of self-pity. But that is not the whole of the story. Many a clergyman rightly senses that the Protestant churches are now going through a major institutional crisis. The present forms of church life subvert rather than express an authentic ministry of God's people.

There is no space in this paper to describe the spectrum of interpretation of this crisis. One example will have to suffice. Gibson Winter, a social ethicist at the Divinity School of The University of Chicago and one of the more severe critics of contemporary church life, sets forth his analysis in the following summary:

To cope with the principalities and powers, identifying their true character and manifesting their subordination to Christ, is the work of apostolate and ministry. This is the work of God's people as sign of His presence in the world. This work then falls primarily to those who are engaged in the public and productive struggle of this world. They alone have access to these powers and shape the decisions through which they dominate or are dominated by man. The understanding of the Christian message of freedom of the Christian man is inseparable from the encounter with these powers. The pastorate of the Church is the preservation of life amidst the struggle of these powers, and this work can only be the ministry of the laymen engaged in the public spheres where these powers operate. If the ordained clergyman in a residential sphere conceived his ministry as *the* pastorate, then he subverts the ministry of God's people in the world and misinterprets the saving Word by which God's people may bear their ministry.

In this sense, the private definition of Christianity within the residential milieu leads the ordained clergyman to misinterpret the pastorate as what he does in altering dispositions; ultimately this misunderstanding dooms him to increasing frustration with the seeming hardness of heart in his congregation. He finds himself cut off from contact with the enemy against whom his people struggle. He realizes slowly that he is cut off from the world in which they live. He then struggles to build a make-believe world of organizational activities in which some semblance of community can be created. When a public issue touches this private world, it glances off and the true alienation of the churches from the contemporary struggle becomes manifest.[2]

I cite Winter's interpretation because it so clearly embodies the spirit and form of the seminary's contribution to the life of the churches. In recent years the characteristic response of the seminary to the churches has been that of critic. At its best the seminary has concentrated upon its critical function within the economy of the church's life. Now, however, the aim of the seminary must be more comprehensive. The theological school of tomorrow should be able to exercise a formative power as well as the critical function.[3] By "formative power" I mean the capacity to create and exemplify new and valid forms of ministry. When the seminaries generate that kind of power, then Protestant education will have arrived at a major turningpoint in its history.

But that day is—obviously enough—still afar off.

II.

Our distance from that turningpoint is best indicated by examining two versions of the "first step" to be taken in that direction.

[2] Gibson Winter, "The Institutional Crisis of the Church," unpublished mimeographed paper for Seatlantic Consultation on Theological Education, 1963, p. 8.

[3] I am indebted to Professor Tom F. Driver of Union Theological Seminary for this distinction.

1. A few of my colleagues at Union Theological Seminary and else-where believe that the Protestant seminary should attend—first of all—to the task of religious formation. A Protestant layman, after an extended study of theological education (Protestant and Roman Catholic alike) was impressed by the way in which the usual Catholic seminary focuses upon the religious formation of the priest. In contrast, according to his findings, the majority of Protestant seminaries pay little or no attention to the spiritual development of the fledgling minister—apart, of course, from routine worship services and the advice of a consulting psychologist. A few denominational schools still maintain a pietistic community life, unrelated to the struggles of the church, while many of the more prestigious interdenominational schools have apparently decided to neglect the whole problem, often under the guise of freedom.

George W. Webber, whose views are reflected in the above paragraph, makes an unabashed appeal for the recovery of corporate discipline within the seminary:

The community of scholars, practitioners, and students is in need of a style of life that reflects in its situation the appropriate marks of obedience to Christ. . . . A key problem for Christians in our time is to discover a style of life. This is not only an academic enterprise, but involves the whole life of the person involved. In facing the task of discovering a style of life as a seminary community, all those so engaged are being prepared directly for dealing with the problem of every Christian in the world today. And such preparation is not primarily going to take place in the classroom, but in the whole context of seminary life: chapel, the discovery of personal discipline, small groups that are studying the Bible, the debate over the house rules, and all the rest.[4]

Much of what Webber says here is indisputable. In this matter Protestant educators have much to learn from their Catholic counterparts—and especially so, as the Catholic seminaries seek to reform and renew their understanding of religious formation. Even so, I remain skeptical about any singleminded emphasis on a corporate "style of life" as the *first* need of a Protestant seminary. Such a discipline is most valid when it is the byproduct of a communal effort to minister and serve in

---

[4] George W. Webber, "Where Is the Problem of Relevance Located," unpublished paper for Seatlantic Consultation on Theological Education, 1963, p. 5.

the world. Otherwise, it tends to become precious and excessively rigid.

2. The Protestant layman and his "practical-minded" pastor is more apt to suggest another approach to seminary reform. Their argument, in brief: the seminary will gain formative power whenever its faculty overcomes its scholarly isolation and begins to spend more time "on the field." This view has a simplicity which makes it seem utterly plausible. It appeals covertly to the incipient anti-intellectualistic strain in American Protestants. I believe, however, that it involves a fundamental misunderstanding of the problem. In this connection it is helpful to recall the judgment of the authors of the Carnegie-funded survey of theological education in the mid1950s. At that time H. Richard Niebuhr and his colleagues wrote:

Though it is often said that the seminaries are remote from the church, and that professors ought to take time off "to get out into the field," our study shows that this is usually a mistaken comment. Granted that remoteness from the practical life of the churches is a state of mind which may be found in some professors, generally speaking theological professors are in a very close working relationship to the churches, so much so that one is more inclined to question whether they are always in a position to take a sufficiently long and critical view of the church's condition.[5]

Doubtless the situation varies considerably from one institution to another. In some seminaries there is an acknowledged difference if not a hidden argument between the "involved" and the "uninvolved." But this tension does little to illumine the faculty's responsibility toward church and world. The fundamental issue is not involvement or uninvolvement (as these positions are often understood by theological teachers), but rather what Kenneth W. Underwood has described as "objective involvement." Underwood, in speaking of the university's relation to public affairs, has said:

It is crucial that the university recover its understanding of objective involvement in public life as distinct from "objectivity" as a state of mind. A person is objectively involved with something when his commitment to it demands and inspires the fullest use of his critical powers upon it. Thus "objective" signifies the "critical distance," the breathing space necessary

[5] H. Richard Niebuhr, Daniel D. Williams, and James D. Gustafson, *The Advancement of Theological Education*, Harper & Brothers, New York, 1957, p. 65.

for inquiry and reflection. Yet one's critical powers are exercised within the "object" of commitment. He is part of what he judges.[6]

In a similar vein I would say that it is crucial for seminary faculties to recover this orientation of objective involvement in the life of the church and world. It would be presumptuous even to imply that such an orientation is not represented on some faculties. Indeed Underwood's description makes sense to me, precisely because I have seen this kind of objective involvement in the work of some of my past teachers and present colleagues at Union Seminary. It is, in fact, the one common attribute of a handful of men who are in other respects— temperament, theological perspectives, academic disciplines, teaching methods, etc.—quite different from one another. And so I would argue that it is a determinative characteristic of the good theological teacher who educates effective ministers.

But how does this attribute of a few teachers become the common characteristic of our faculties? Is there any evident way by which it might be recovered? At this juncture the abstract character of my description becomes painfully manifest. For it is often irrelevant to advise a colleague (or oneself) that the cure for the air of unreality of work in the classroom is to "get into the field," it is equally irrelevant (and just as cruel) to prescribe that he achieve a new orientation of objective involvement. Objective involvement is, obviously enough, no simple achievement; it has multiple sources.

It is first of all a personal action, one that issues out of the depths of an individual's life in relation to God. It is expressive of his attempts to study and serve the work of God in history.

Objective involvement can also be a communal characteristic. It is prompted and sustained by the common efforts of a company of men to respond to historical events in church and world. One such occasion was the economic and spiritual depression of the 1930s, the rise of fascism and the threat of collapse into chaos in the 1940s. During those years the response of some teachers and a few faculties was a faithful embodiment of objective involvement in church and world. Their response was due, in part, to the leadership of a handful of teachers who

[6] Kenneth W. Underwood, "The University and Public Leadership," in Scott Fletcher, editor, *Education: The Challenge Ahead*, W. W. Norton, New York, 1962, p. 90.

were a lustrous example of this characteristic. Yet that response was also the work of others who discerned in this confluence of events an occasion that required the fullest use of their critical powers. The events of those years became, in effect, a matrix for their continuing education as theological teachers.

Today a later generation is faced by a similar historical occasion—not perhaps as publicly visible or immediately threatening (the crises of a "post-mature" society are seldom clearly focused), but just as decisive for our time. That occasion has been described by Winter and also by other theological scholars, *i.e.,* Harvey Cox in *The Secular City*. I refer to the emergence of the metropolis and also to the crisis of the churches that seek to minister in that metropolis.

By and large Protestant scholars seem to resist recognition of that fact. Part of the resistance is valid, for the interpretations of this new context of work have been occasionally marred by incoherencies and lapses into sensationalism. But another aspect of our resistance—and here I am speaking specifically of seminary faculty members—is trace-able to an archaic view of the church (and the metropolis). For too many of us the church, like ancient Gaul, is divided into three parts: the innercity church, the suburban church, and the small city or town and country church. Hence the analysis of Winter and others has been misinterpreted as simply a call for more able-bodied recruits to quell the disturbances and restore order in the first two provinces named above.

III.

Thus far I have sketched a rather bleak portrait of Protestant theo-logical education. But now, the reader could rightly ask, do you have anything positive to say about the shape of the seminary in the future? In these closing paragraphs I will describe two promising possibilities.

1. The Protestant seminary of tomorrow could become a center of theological education for laymen and experienced pastors, as well as for future ministers. It is a fact—seldom recognized and even less celebrated—that the present seminary often serves as a point of depar-ture for the layman into his particular occupation. In the past months, for instance, I have had reason to ferret out information about the

present work of eight Union graduates, all of whom were good friends when they graduated in the early 1960s. Now some years later they have scattered in quite different directions. To wit: one is in a graduate school of business after serving in a pastorate. Another has just completed his doctorate in politics and will be teaching in a liberal arts college next fall. The third is presently an assistant minister in a New York church where he spends most of his time composing for "off-off Broadway" shows. Another is presently engaged in African studies after spending two years on that continent. The fifth student is involved in *Operation Head Start*. The sixth student, after two years in the ministry to students at the University of California at Berkeley, is beginning his Ph.D. work in English. The seventh is a writer for *"Look."* The eighth has now turned to elementary education. I hasten to add that this group does not constitute a representative cross-section of their class. Yet it might become more typical of Union alumni in the coming years.

Some churchmen view this prospect with alarm and anxiety. They regard it as a deviation, a regrettable departure from the seminary's essential task, *i.e.,* training parish ministers. My own guess is that it could be a healthy development. The minister should not be trained in isolation from the laity (as is so often the case nowadays). Furthermore, there is an increasing need for a core of theologically trained laymen. This cadre will require much the same immersion in biblical, theological, and historical studies that now engage the attention of the seminary student.

I foresee the development of a *basic* course in theological studies that will be open to future clergy and laymen alike. After completing the initial stage, then the theological student who elects the pastorate will be given further intensive training—much of it "in the field" under the tutelage of a trained sponsor.

In this connection it is important to note the burgeoning growth of programs of continuing education for Protestant pastors. By way of illustration I would point to the policies of the United Presbyterian Church, U.S.A. In many sectors of that denomination the pastor is now given a two-week study leave each year. There is every indication that the study period will be lengthened so that a decade hence each Presbyterian minister could elect to spend one month each year in sustained and systematic study. This development will clearly alter the work of the seminary. It means, in the first place, that the theological school does not have to engage any longer in the pretence of including all that a future minister will need to know in a limited three-year program. Secondly, the seminary will be one of the agencies responsible for the continuing education of the pastor. That development will pose a major challenge to the theological schools. It will require not only an expansion of the faculty but also a thorough reconsideration of the curriculum and of the kind of teachers needed in a seminary.

If that evaluation is not forthcoming, then the theological schools will be in very serious trouble. These new responsibilities—the preparation of a trained core of laymen and the continuing education of pastors—cannot be met by simply expanding the seminary's current educational program. Such a policy would involve the dubious assumption that the present course of studies, re-tailored and reduced for "popular consumption," is appropriate fare for pastors and laymen. That procedure exaggerates the importance of the *content* of the seminary's course work and so overlooks the difference made by the pastor's present *context* of thought and action. This kind of development, if left unchecked, would lead to the sort of popularization that easily descends into vulgarization and—even more important—the dissipation of faculty energy.

2. The responsible seminary of the future will be integrally related to the university. The era of the independent theological seminary, deliberately removed from the presumed blandishments of the university, is clearly at an end. Within the past ten years any number of Protestant seminaries have been attempting to establish closer working relationships with the nearby universities. And no wonder.

Look, for a moment, at the problem of the faculty member whose assignment is "social ethics." In days past (and even, unfortunately, in some seminaries right now) his responsibility included coverage of the whole range of the social sciences and the relation of the findings in those disciplines to the theology and work of the churches. Thus he often found himself teaching in any one semester such diverse courses as "Christianity and politics," "Christianity and economics," etc. The same procedure was often evident in other parts of the curriculum, *i.e.,* literature, education, drama, etc. The result was the inadvertent creation of a bogus "Christian university" whose offerings were not up to university standards.

In the future the seminary must find ways of drawing upon the resources of the specialists in the university community. Very few theological schools—not even the university divinity schools which take great pride in their proximity to the university—have been able to make much progress on this front. The integrity of the seminary will depend, in part, upon its success in knowing when and how to rely upon the university.

These are, in brief, some of the problems and possibilities now facing Protestant theological educators. It is not easy to be optimistic about the immediate future. But that may turn out to be an unexpected advantage. The premature confidence of the past twenty years is no longer viable. The religious boom of the 1950s is over, and the troubles of the churches are becoming more starkly evident day by day. A searching and candid appraisal of this new situation may be the beginning of a turningpoint in Protestant theological education.

Chapter 13. NEW STRATEGIES IN JEWISH THEOLOGICAL TRAINING

by Seymour Siegel

Education is the leading of human souls to what is best, and making what is best out of them; and these two objects are always attainable together, and by the same means; the training which makes men happiest in themselves also makes them serviceable to others.—ANONYMOUS

They were offered the choice between becoming kings or couriers of kings. The way children would, they all wanted to be couriers. Therefore, there are only couriers who hurry about the world, shouting to each other—since there are no kings—messages that have become meaningless. They would like to put an end to this miserable life of theirs, but they dare not because of their oaths of service.—FRANZ KAFKA, *Parables*

RELIGIOUS institutions have had the reputation of conservatism and resistance to change. Yet, in the past decade no other institution in society has instituted changes as radical as those in religion. Constant and merciless self-examination is the hallmark of a living and vital institution. High religion has within itself a self-criticizing element. Judging itself by the perfection of God and measuring its achievements against His demands, religious institutions and religious people are constantly made aware of the gulf between duty and performance. This stance should be the dynamic of constant change. Religion is commitment to the Word of God which is Eternal. However, the application of the divine demands amidst the relativities of life requires the ability and the will to modify, abandon, and change customary ways of doing and thinking.

These inherent processes have been accelerated in our own fast-moving times. In a more leisurely age (though a revolutionary one, too), Edmund Burke said: "It has been the misfortune (not as these gentlemen think it, the glory) of this age that everything is to be discussed." Nowadays, everything is, and should be discussed. Jewish life in the past few decades has seen dramatic changes whose fateful consequences have not been fully assessed. The destruction of the Jewish communities of Europe which were the source of Jewish learning and piety; the establishment and consolidation of the State of Israel; the growth of the Jewish communities in the United States and the other free countries; and the rapid development of scientific and technological achievement—all of these have profoundly affected Jews and Judaism.

All of this has had its effects on the training of rabbis and Jewish scholars. They and the schools in which they are trained are part of the community. In them is reflected the uncertainties and problems of the epoch in which they live. Theological education was never in Judaism looked upon as a place of refuge from the world with its hard decisions. The rabbi forms his community and is formed by it. He shares its burdens, its anxieties, and its failures. Rabbi Morris Adler, who was tragically killed in his own Detroit synagogue, wrote in a posthumously published essay:

His (the rabbi's) is essentially a life of pathos. He suffers a score of alienations and must daily battle for his faith and hope. The rabbi, scion of a tradition and heir of a culture, must now function in the midst of a technological setting in which cultural differentiations are obliterated and traditional modes discounted . . . He sees himself shipwrecked on an uninhabited island far from the centers of life and movement. He sadly concludes that he is a member of world's loneliest profession.[1]

The rabbi's perplexities are compounded by the radical change in the function and place of the spiritual leader in the Jewish community. Leadership, historically, was invested in the hands of the scholar, the *talmid chacham* (the disciple of the wise). Public service was not properly a profession in ancient times. In the Palestinian and Babylonian communities, the officials received hardly any pay for their skilled services. The verse, "Behold I have taught you statutes and ordinances even as the Lord my God commanded me," teaches us, the Sages declared that "As I taught you without remuneration so shall you teach without remuneration." The rabbi in classical times was not

[1] *Jewish Heritage Magazine*, Spring, 1966.

a channel of grace; a recipient of charisma. The rabbi was the judge and teacher of the community. Religious rituals such as weddings, funerals, or preaching, were possible without a clergyman. The liturgy did not require—nor seldom included—a rabbi. In the classical times, the rabbi was closer to a modern day "layman" than to a religious official.

Even in later times, the function of the rabbi remained basically that of teacher and judge. The question of compensation of the rabbi became an issue when more and more of the rabbi's time was taken up in communal matters. Even when the rabbi is paid, he is seen as receiving compensation not for what he does but for the damage he sustains in neglecting his own business.[2]

Ordination was, and still is, a kind of academic degree certifying that the recipient had satisfactorily passed an examination exhibiting his competence in the law. It was only in relatively recent times, especially in Western Europe and America, that the rabbinate became fully professionalized and took on the character of the Protestant minister or Catholic parish priest. The predecessors of the modern theological seminaries usually called *yeshivot*—were totally unprofessional. They had no "practical" courses—neither homiletics nor counselling. Their curriculum consisted in the study of Bible, Talmud, and Codes. Only in a few were philosophy or history taught—and then informally. The aim was study for its own sake. Of course, if a community needed a rabbi it wanted a learned man. And where else to seek one but in a *yeshiva?* The concept of a "theological" school to train professional rabbis is relatively new in Jewish history. It dates from the nineteenth century when Jews entered the cultural life of the West. Only then was the concept of a rabbi, trained to be the leader of a congregation, formed. Secular learning and instruction in professional skills became necessary and were made mandatory. In the United States the rabbi tended to undertake all of the functions (and additional ones as well) of the Protestant and Catholic clergymen.

This development was not an unmixed blessing. The rabbi now finds it difficult to carry on his traditional function as scholar and

---

[2] See Freehof, *A Treasury of Responsa,* Jewish Publication Society, Philadelphia, 1963, pp. 80–82 and Salo W. Baron, *The Jewish Community: Its History and Structure to the American Revolution,* Volume II, Morris Loeb Fund Publication, Philadelphia, 1942, pp. 66–79.

teacher. The activities which had in previous epochs been peripheral became central and the degree of learning was not as crucial as it had been heretofore. Robert Gordis, one of the most distinguished members of the American rabbinate, writes:

Once a *brith milah* (circumcision) was performed by a *mohel* (a ritual circumcisor) with no other "clergyman" needed: a *pidyon haben* (redemption of the first born) required only a first-born male child, the father and a *kohen* (a descendant of a priestly family) in the presence of a quorum; a *bar mitzvah* was called to the Torah immediately after his thirteenth birthday even on a Monday or Thursday morning with no attendant pomp or circumstance; a wedding could be solemnized by any Jew who knew the ritual; a funeral was conducted by the family and friends of the departed who conducted the order of the service themselves. Today all these *rites de passage* have become rabbinical functions.

Therefore, the fast-moving changes in the picture of the Jewish community, together with the changing character of the rabbinate, has placed the situation of Judaism in perpetual crisis.

However, for the purpose of our analysis it is necessary to put the problem in a different way. The crisis of Judaism today in the free countries of the West has two aspects. First and foremost is the task of retaining the allegiance, and insuring the survival of the Jewish community. This resolute battle for survival is the common concern of all conscious Jews. The leaders of the community constantly are looking for ways to overcome intermarriage, indifference, and ignorance. It is not heresy that is so greatly feared, it is the assimilation and disappearance of the Jewish community. The constant worry about survival is not the outgrowth of chauvinistic affirmation (though it sometimes unwittingly gives birth to an unreasonable chauvinism). It is partly motivated by the experience of the attempts at a "final solution" to the Jewish problem which is embedded deep in the consciousness of every living Jew. It is also motivated by the strong and unshakable affirmation that the Jewish community has a task to survive as a witness to its calling to be a "kingdom of priests and a holy people."

The second preoccupation of Jewish leaders is filling this Jewish commitment, once it is achieved, with meaning and relevance for the life of the twentieth century Jew. It is felt that it is not enough to foster the allegiance and the spiritual identity of the Jew. These bottles must be filled with both old and new wine. The problem, therefore, of the Jewish community is to retain its adherents and to make their Jewishness relevant to their lives.

Accordingly it seems that the crisis in the theological schools and in the community is somewhat different than the one which we find (or at least read about) in Catholic and Protestant seminaries. In Catholicism the very foundations of the hierarchical and dogmatic structure which underlie the remarkable edifice of the Catholic Church is being called into question. In Protestantism (at least in leading centers of Protestant thinking) it seems that the theological underpinning of the church is being called into question. If one peruses the literature which rabbis write about the rabbinate [3] one comes to the conclusion that there is, among rabbis, a feeling of the worthwhileness of Judaism. The tradition (as interpreted by the particular rabbinic group) is potentially a good and vital body of teaching and practice which would render those who adhere to it happy and effective. What is missing in Jewish life is the right methodology and pedagogy to transmit this precious heritage to the individual Jew. This failure is attributed either to the seminaries which did not adequately prepare the rabbis; to the congregations which are not spiritually and culturally willing to listen to the rabbis; or to their own lack of wisdom or learning which would make it possible for them to transmit the heritage. There are few calls for a thoroughgoing reformation of Judaism. There are to be sure proposals for changes. But these changes are not radical. They are in the nature of repair, not renovation. There is a call for changing some of the features of the organization and curriculum of the theological schools; for a restructuring of some of the aspects of the synagogue; for a re-evaluation of the way the rabbi is expected to operate. However, it is not so much the theological foundations of Judaism which are perceived to be in crisis—as the structures which have been erected on these foundations.

If the previous analysis is correct, the theological schools are not called upon to overhaul Judaism completely as it now exists. They see as their primary task to translate Jewish affirmations into understand-

---

[3] The literature is by and large not available to the public. The best sources are the volumes of proceedings of the various Rabbinical groups such as the Central Conference of American Rabbis (Reform) and the Rabbinical Assembly (Conservative), and in the unpublished papers prepared for the Conferences on the Problems of the Rabbinate sponsored by the The Herbert H. Lehman Institute for Talmudic Ethics.

able terms, to retrain (or train better) Jewish leaders; and to influence Jewish laity to restructure their institutions so that the religious leader can function more effectively.

This, of course, means curricular revision. The theological seminaries are faced with the problem of enlarging the course of studies so that they not only include the ancient subjects of Bible, Talmud, Codes, etc., but also psychology, history, administration, and sociology. These needs have led to problems which have, as yet, not been satisfactorily solved. At the beginning of this century, Solomon Schechter, speaking of The Jewish Theological Seminary of America said:

We cannot, naturally, hope to carry the student through all these vast fields of learning (referring to traditional Jewish literature). . . . But this fact must not prevent us from making the attempt to bring the students on terms of acquaintance at least with all those manifestations of Jewish life and thought.[4]

The necessity of structuring the curriculum to include both the whole area of traditional lore and modern professional skills has necessitated elongating the training period of the rabbi. The average student studies for five years after the B.A. Even after such a long period, there are great areas of lack felt both by student and teacher.

The professionalization of the rabbinic training brings another problem to the fore. Judaism puts great stress on adherence to Jewish law and practices. This is especially the case with orthodox and conservative interpretations of Judaism. In the past, it could be taken for granted that applicants and students of the theological seminaries were committed to the standards of practice taught by the traditional guides. Though there was care taken to provide the student with moral and religious guidance, the older institutions could take a pattern of observance for granted. The modern synagogue and the modern rabbi have a multitude of functions. Judaism is a multiphased way of life. Students appeared who were not grounded emotionally and religiously in the ancient traditions. Seminaries then became faced with deciding what standards have to be established for the admission of candidates. What could one do with a young man who wants "to help people" through the ministry, but who does not feel himself able to

---

[4] Solomon Schechter, *Seminary Addresses and Other Papers,* The Burning Bush Press, New York, 1959, p. 20.

accept the obligations which traditional Judaism places upon its adherents? The ancient Book of Saints (*Sefer Hasidim*) said, "The rabbis should be God-fearing men." Modern theological seminaries must decide, what only God can really know, how "God-fearing" the candidate must be before he can qualify.

The professionalization of the rabbinate also led to problems of recruitment of new students. As a professional school, the seminary has to compete with medicine, law, business, and other professional institutions. In addition to asking the candidate to undertake a long and arduous course of studies, it demands a dedication and a commitment to a calling which is difficult and which involves a whole way of life and of looking at the world.

Thus problems of curriculum, theological orientation, and recruitment face seminary adminstrators and teachers. What new strategies can be called upon to help meet these (and other serious) problems?

1. *Intensification of recruitment.* Judaism has traditionally eschewed the notion that the rabbinate was a calling for those who had felt themselves "seized" or "called" to serve. There is embarrassment among the rabbis (even among those who have probably experienced such a "call") to account in any mysterious terms for their decision to enter the rabbinate. It is viewed as a rational decision prompted by desire to serve and commit one's self to Judaism and the world. It is also realized now that vocational decisionmaking comes much earlier in life than had heretofore been realized. In addition to these factors, it must also be recognized that the degree of technical knowledge in Hebrew language and literature which is required even to begin theological training, is substantial. Thus, there has been emphasis of late on beginning recruiting efforts earlier than the college years. In Judaism this effort has been channelled through the large network of Jewish religious schools (almost every synagogue has its own religious school); through youth movements—especially movements which try to include those who show potential leadership; and summer camps. At The Jewish Theological Seminary of America about seventy-five percent of the students have been exposed either to the youth movements or the summer camps. New and imaginative methods of attracting promising young people are obviously needed. But a good deal of thinking is being expended in this area.

2. *Specialization of training.* Until recently, theological training was

more or less uniform, and all students followed substantially the same curriculum. The diversity of functions which rabbis and theologians have to fill has led to the establishment of avenues of more specialized training for those who wish to follow differing roles. With the great emphasis on scholarships and learning and with the destruction of European Jewry, the traditional source of scholarly talent, it has become necessary for the theological schools to train their own faculty. This had led to the necessity of special training courses for those who have the talent and the desire to follow scholarly careers. There is still not enough diverse training for specializations in the ministry, such as the military chaplaincy, hospital work, or youth work. But indications are that this is in the offing.

3. *The restructuring of the Synagogue.* The relationship between the theological schools and the synagogues is close and intimate. The three great Jewish training schools in the United States each have large numbers of congregations which look upon them as religious and intellectual guides. Therefore, the leadership of the seminaries has persistently called upon the synagogues to restructure themselves so that the rabbi can better follow his traditional role as scholar and teacher. The literature which rabbis write about themselves (and the literature which others write about the rabbi) calls attention to the impossibility of any man adequately performing all of the duties which the modern clergyman is called upon to undertake. Eli Ginzberg, in an address to the Rabbinical Assembly, said: "How many ideas can a rabbi have? Frank Knight, the distinguished Chicago economist, has pointed out that the ablest academics are lucky if they have three good ideas in a lifetime. But a rabbi has to talk to the same congregants every week throughout the year for four decades!" These are problems not only for rabbis but for clergymen of all religions. The seminaries and the affiliated organizations have frequently called upon their constituents to relieve the rabbi of administrative and organizational detail. These calls have only infrequently been heeded, but they continue nevertheless.

4. *The involvement in "secular" affairs.* Jews are not first-time visitors to the "secular city." They have been there many times before. Yet, one of the most impressively new phenomena is the increasing (though far from adequate) involvement of rabbis and their teachers

in the great movements of our time. Jewish leaders have always been caught up in the "secular" aspects of Jewish life, such as fund-raising, Zionist activities, defense of Jewish rights, etc. But involvement in the challenging and revolutionary developments of our time is gaining more and more momentum. The mood of many rabbis is close to that of Archy—Don Marquis's famous bug—as he saw the moth fly into the flame and become a "small unsightly cinder": "I wish there was something I wanted as badly as he wanted to fry himself." The devotion of the fighters for civil rights or warriors against poverty has found its echo in the feeling of students and faculty alike that it is not possible any more to live in the academic community oblivious of what is going on around us. In a recent number of the "*Center Diary*" (#13) published by the Center for the Study of Democratic Institutions, I began reading an excerpt from a book by Joseph P. Lyford, *The Airtight Cage*. Mr. Lyford was describing life in the ghettoes of our great cities. He tells of the horror of a Negro neighborhood "where the adult is the dead child. . . . We are practically speaking unconscious of what is going on. I mean the piling up of children in the dark parts of our cities and leaving them to rot, the way we used to pile up boxes of 20 mm. guns and compasses and sextants in the jungle and leave them until sun and rain rotted the boxes and they broke apart." When he identified the street he was describing, I realized with shock that he was speaking of a street I could almost see from the window of my study in the Seminary. More and more it is becoming clear that we cannot shut our eyes to what is going on, and that theological education must bring the student (and his teacher as well) to immerse himself in the life of the community in which he lives.

5. *The need for continuing education.* With the world changing so fast and with the frontiers of scholarship becoming ever more wide, it is necessary to make the ordination of the rabbi only a pause in his education. The constant emphasis in the traditional literature upon the importance and religious obligation to study has made it easier for Jewish theological institutions to undertake programs of continuing education for rabbis. But there remains much to be done.

6. *Constant and merciless self-criticism.* The rabbinate seems to be one of the most self-critical callings. Meetings of rabbis and discussions with the leaders of the seminaries rarely involve any self-congratulation.

There is constant self-examination. The Jewish Theological Seminary of America has arranged conferences of rabbis (closed to the public) where the role and the achievements of rabbis and seminaries have been analyzed, dissected, and criticized. One of the most obviously effective strategies for change is to carry forward the prophetic function of never being satisfied with what has been achieved and constantly measuring what has been done by what must be done.

These are some of the changing aspects of theological training among Jews in America today. It would be fair to say that with all of these developments we cannot point to dramatic and radical revisions. Whatever is being done is being done within the contours of the traditional modes of theological education. This will disappoint many who will be satisfied only when the very foundations are shaken. There is, of course, great cogency to the argument that revolutionary times demand revolutionary solutions. But, on the other hand, one of the great functions of religion has been to emphasize the importance of tradition; to stand fast against the fads and fashions of each age. Every new wind does not necessarily have to blow the house down. Indeed only structures with weak foundations are so affected. While religion wishes to be at the forefront of social change, it cannot forget also that it is the guardian of the values and teachings which hold civilization together. "The art of free society," writes Whitehead, "consists first in the maintenance of the symbolic code and secondly in the fearlessness of revision . . . Those societies which cannot combine reverence to their symbols with freedom of revision must ultimately decay." We cannot agree that everything prior to our time was one long amateur hour. The seminaries are the intellectual centers of the religious communities. As such they must lead. But they can lead only if they are firmly based and anchored. Thus the strategies for change are varied. Some are effective. Others need to be abandoned. But the change is taking place —at least in Jewish institutions—with a profound awareness of the responsibility to carry on the tradition in a new and changing time.

In one of the shortest commencement speeches on record, a talmudic sage admonished his newly-ordained pupils: "Believe not that I make you masters. Behold you are appointed servants." It is one of the abiding insights which religion has contributed to our lives, that it is only by serving that one finds blessing.

V. SOME OTHER APPROACHES TO EDUCATION FOR CHARACTER

Chapter 14. LANGUAGE CONSCIOUSNESS AND CHARACTER EDUCATION: A SKETCH OF A SOCIAL SCIENCE CONFLICT AND SOME RESOLUTIONS

by Arthur J. Brodbeck

*Language is concerned with the prominent facts . . . These prominent facts are the variable facts . . . They vary because they are superficial; they enter into conscious discrimination because they vary. There are other elements in our experience, on the fringe of consciousness, and yet massively qualifying our experience. In regard to these other facts, it is our consciousness that flickers, not the facts themselves. They are always there, barely discriminable, and yet inescapable.—*A. N. WHITEHEAD, *Adventures of Ideas,* section on language

OF ALL the myriad ways we can differentiate people from one another, surely an overriding one is in terms of their breadth of vision and feeling. Some strive and stretch themselves to perceive and grasp meanings of patterns as wide as the universe; others see and take delight in mundane matters as close at hand as possible, within some small space they happen to occupy or which they find comfortably conceptually "manageable." Some take for consideration movements of ideas that begin far back in history and promise to extend far into the future, no matter how "fashionable" they may be at any moment in time; others take a moment-to-moment shift in ideas as fascinating, ignoring all the rest with regard to movement and duration. When we speak of "narrow-mindedness" and "small-mindedness," contrasting it with "large-mindedness" and "broad-mindedness," something at the very core of personality is under observation, something central for all functioning of the personality as a whole, whether only for itself or for all those in social networks of relationship to it. We can call this dimension of personality "the level of consciousness" and place it on a dimension running from broad to narrow, large to small—or, perhaps more formally, from inclusivity to exclusivity of the attention processes.

For the moment, we can leave to one side the many technical complications in measuring and assessing this personality dimension, such as the "small-minded" who turn out, when more sensitively observed, to have wittingly or unwittingly involved the whole universe in their attention span supposedly focused on small "atomic" details.[1] Let us turn, instead, from personality to culture with the same ideas in mind. The level of consciousness in groups, throughout the cultural evolution of mankind, drops and rises and varies, too, so that we can say that there are periods of history (and certain cultures within history) when groups have manifested "broad-mindedness" or "narrow-mindedness," sometimes despite, and other times especially because of particular personalities rising to eminence within such groups.

One promising index, on a cultural scale, of the striving to stretch

[1] One version of this process has been dubbed "the self-reference effect" by Harold D. Lasswell. Exposure to the wider stressing and stressful forces at work in the world is "escaped" from by withdrawal of attention and increase of indifference regarding them while intensifying attention and interest in one's own self and a small band of close companions. This is part of what is meant by "togetherness," in which people huddle together and tell themselves how well they are doing while ignoring the cries of the wider world for help and service. Psychoanalysis is often seen as abetting this process. However, one often observes that the larger environment continues to play upon the area to which attention and interest has shrunk, forcing out the same issues that occur in the wider world within the more intimate circle. Hence, the appearance of a "self-reference effect." This process is outlined in my essay that reviews the work of David Riesman ("Values in *The Lonely Crowd: Ascent or Descent of Man?*" in S. M. Lipset and Leo Lowenthal, editors, *Culture and Social Character,* Free Press of Glencoe, New York, 1961). Looking back at my essay, however, it often seems to me it misses something implied in Riesman's writing over and above that to which I point there. We are quite possibly moving in America away from hero figures produced by a sharp separation of evilness and goodness in life, to which "heroes" brought relief by fighting clear-cut battles against villainy. Instead, as in the "new Wave" films, we have a cult of the "anti-hero"—or so it seems—in which everyone is seen as gray, neither essentially moving toward the Common Good or away from it, but whatever eminence is achieved is always depicted as "a gray eminence," a half-hearted compromise with ideals or villainy. President Kennedy, in this sense, is not "representative" of modern times, and affords a contrast to it. In the terms used here, such a change of group atmosphere reflects a lessening of attention to the rectitude value in social process (or a new way of experiencing it) as I point out in a more general way in the essay on Riesman's work.

awareness from a prior narrow and confined condition are all the signs that indicate a marked upgrade in language consciousness. Language is the vehicle by which man expresses to himself and his fellow man what his rich array of private moods and images are like. When a great deal of experimentation and discovery goes on in cultures regarding language usage, it is likely that the life of mood and imagery is undergoing a lively and rich expansion in range and variety, accompanied by an intense inner demand that this expansion be allowed to work itself out quite fully. The ego observes more about the ego than it had before (since an ego can take itself as an object) and in the process finds potentials and patterns in itself it did not previously articulately discover, particularly potentials for communal identity that exceeds boundaries conventionally established. The "flowering" of concern with language both reflects and abets and aids this creative process, gaining momentum as the "contagion" reaches out to consolidate more and more personalities and to form a stable cultural pattern for a prolonged stretch of time.

1. A "New Age" of Language Consciousness

At the present period of our cultural growth, if we *do* use this language index of a shift in the collective level of consciousness, we are at some remarkable high point in human history, almost "a new age" of language discovery. At this high point, we perceive language where we never had before (in animals, among plants and trees, and if Teilhard de Chardin is right, perhaps soon we shall find rudimentary linguistic processes among even some forms of rocks and stones). Along with this, we have had a host of inventions of new and presumably better languages to replace those whose precision man once thought was beyond perfecting (the supplanting of Aristotelian logics, for instance, by the many new functional logics that have been proliferating endlessly). We have begun to grasp new understanding and appreciation of ancient languages, long objects of contempt, so that what was in them that was formerly "meaningless" and "nonsensical" is now suddenly of immense modern importance, a prime example of which is Velikovsky's use of ancient myth to reconstruct the evolution of the earth in relation to other planetary bodies as "crisis-ridden." The scientific predictions that resulted from Velikovsky's controversial respect and interpretation of ancient myth has conflicted with contemporary theoretical natural science, as Edison's ideas once did with what the Universities thought "possible," but so far his ideas have received an impressive amount of validation.[2] Now that the biological basis of memory has been uncovered, there is more and more reason to take seriously the notion of "a body language" and a "somatic language" in ways that Sigmund Freud speculated about without being able directly empirically to confirm, except in the crudest kind of inferential way. We are confronted with "machine languages" that reflect a rapidity of thought that man might well envy, and possibly emulate in the future. The evidence for telepathy and akin types of communication is mounting, such as Montague Ullman's studies,[3] the existence of which, when comprehended in "demystified" fashion, will throw under consideration whether private moods and images are not *in and of themselves* a language and, hence, worthy of being included within the behaviorist's definition of "response."[4] Some of my own studies at the Annenberg School of Communication give support to the idea that even music, long widely considered a "non-representational" art, is a language designed to communicate referential diffuse feeling and mood patterns, sharing this "logical" characteristic with other art forms. In short, and without elaborating still further, it is questionable whether man has ever been so language-minded or had so many revolutions in language going on together in heightened form across the whole spectrum of culture. Indeed, the point where language stops (and non-language takes over) is up for new scrutiny and consideration—and, with it, the distinctions between subjective and

---

[2] Alfred DeGrazia, editor, *The Velikovsky Affair*, University Books, New Hyde Park, New York, 1966.

[3] See Montagu Ullman, *Sleep, Wakefulness and ESP*. Paper delivered to SIRE, New York Academy of Science, February 16, 1967.

[4] While B. F. Skinner seems to be increasingly more generous in his acknowledgment of moods and images as factors in human conduct, several writers have drawn our attention to his having done little to find much of a place for them in his "reflex" schemata. See, for instance, Joseph Church, *Language and the Discovery of Reality*, Random House, New York, 1963. There is no reason why moods and images themselves should not be subject to "reflex" laws or dealt with as partial components of a total reflex pattern, at least no reason given by Skinner. Furthermore, awareness of conditioning laws would presumably change the nature and the flow of moods and images and, hence, play a role in modifying such laws.

objective events, the differentiations of "mind" and "body," fast become more blurred and open to rigorous efforts at systematic redefinition and scientific clarification. (Is, for example, "psychic" energy to be considered a "different" form of energy than that dealt with by physicists? Is man capable of "individualizing" the physical energies available to him?) Given this pattern, we should be able to congratulate ourselves about the age in which we live, since our hearts and minds never have been more open in all of history toward comprehensiveness.

II. A "Social Science" Conflict?

When we push such a survey far and deep, however, we push up against a complication in the form of a paradox that quickly removes all sound reason for easy self-congratulations about how well we are doing. There seems to be some sort of unspoken idea hovering at the back of most of our minds that *improved understanding of communication will produce a better world.* The complication and the paradox arise from the fact that the period of high language consciousness in which we live is characterized by one of the most widespread and intensified expectational systems of potential and actual worldwide violence in history, accompanied as it is by some of the most devastating instrumentalities ever invented by man to destroy not only his own species but every other form of "lower" consciousness with his own. In short, there is no indication that character processes are getting better in a time that makes it most imperative to improve upon man's past record of ethical behavior—and, in a time, when increased understanding of communication has leaped suddenly and swiftly forward to allow for a great heightening of the level of consciousness. In short, our unspoken faith in language, and the communication it makes possible, appears misplaced—for the moment, if not in the long run.

Perhaps our emerging social science may provide us with some insights as to where we could have gone wrong. When we glance back at the history of social science in the twentieth century, we discover within it a "growing imbalance" over time that may explain or locate the difficulty. The modern interest in language has been accompanied by *no new discoveries and enrichments of an equivalent revolutionary nature concerning character and character processes in personality and cultural functioning.* At the turn of the century—indeed, even in the 1920s—interest in and development of the two fields—character study and language study—were somewhat more equalized and even in elaboration and concern. Since then, language study has pressed forward vigorously while the study of character development and functioning has, despite a breakthrough here and there that lights up interest for a moment and then recedes into darkness, simply not kept pace. Actually, little research about language has come forward with any relevance to character explicitly in mind and little research about character has been evolved with linguistic dimensions in mind. Given this historical pattern that appears to have recently hardened, the hypothesis could be entertained that our attention to character processes has become more blurred and confused than it has ever been by this rapid linguistic burgeoning of consciousness, seldom enhanced by the way communication processes have been studied in social science by technicalized, piecemeal fragmentation, so that, as a whole, *we are becoming characterologically more ignorant while feeling more "clever" about communication.*[5] Under such a regime, it may be increasingly more

[5] The few advances we have had in character study, such as *The Authoritarian Personality,* contain but a minimum reference to language mechanism, although "intolerance of ambiguity," for example, ought to have ignited a host of new developments in communication and linguistic research, for the ambiguity of language is so central to communication analysis when we deal with it not merely as technologists but with regard to value meanings being transmitted with varying degrees of conscious and unconscious success. Some of the reasons why interest in this body of research has shrunk over time is brought forward by a value and trend analysis of the work coming forward around that syndrome in an interesting study by Thomas Landau (*A Systematic Trend and Value Analysis of the Literature on 'the Authoritarian Personality,'* Senior Honors Thesis, Wesleyan University, 1963.) Curiously, the scientific interest in the topic drooped and withered as civil rights interest concerning the American Negro became nationally salient, and there has been a noticeable absence of use of the literature in relationship to the study of Negro-white integration issues. In order to build upon the original body of work, incidentally, we need, too, to extend the "intolerance of ambiguity" notion to the field of moods and feelings, so as to highlight the language that illustrates "an intolerance of *ambivalence,*" rather than study only image phenomena as the original researches tended to do. The emphasis upon authoritarianism of rebels associated with Edward Shils ("Authoritarianism on the Left," in R. B. Christie and M. Jahoda, *A Continuity Volume on 'the Authoritarian Personality,'* Glencoe, Illinois, 1954) could be utilized in studying much of the key symbolism arising out of "the black power" movement recently at work in America. Generally, one has the impression that the research wave around "authoritarianism"

difficult to discover or believe in "a good deed in a naughty world," while developing all sorts of urbane sophistication about self-protective autistic uses of language interpretation. In any event, such an imbalance suggests a conflict, and a conflict operating among social scientists in particular, however much it may reflect a wider conflict to which it may add as well as partake.

Social science does not merely *study* personality and culture; it also *creates* a new culture by the way it perceives, conceptualizes, and reacts to human behavior. In this sense, it can be viewed as setting one possible model for a coming world culture. The scientific outlook has grown up slowly in the world and is now slowly extending itself to deal with man in the same spirit in which it dealt with the physical world. It seeks the objectivity—which is really a shared intersubjectivity—that is geared to settle differences by infinite inquiry rather than by impulsive violence and coercion and dogma. Hence, it is not only important to consider social science in terms of the *content* or "laws" it produces. One must also consider the worth of the *procedures* used to obtain such content, procedures which themselves can be taken as content or "laws" within a growing field of the science of science.[6] These collective procedures being established will act in the future as competitors for cultural acceptance and diffusion with alternative older and possibly newly emerging procedures, all vying for authoritative position to govern human interactions. If we take social science in this

---

never sufficiently allowed for inconsistency in every personality, so that excellent tolerance with regard to one group in social life might be used to draw attention away from a rigid intolerance toward other social groups. Major differences among people could then be described not wholly in terms of intensity of intolerance toward any one minority group but, rather, in terms of which of the whole spectrum of minority groups was most likely and least likely to bring out intolerant predispositions. As the theory did not account for the full spectrum of groupings toward which prejudice might be felt and shown, it could not bring to light clearly an equivalent pattern operating with different targets of instigation and focus than those used by "racists." (One who can have, for example, an authoritarian syndrome with regard to all "theoreticians" as a class.)

[6] Bernard Barber and Walter Wirsch have edited a volume, *The Sociology of Science,* Free Press of Glencoe, New York, 1962, which touches upon many of the detailed problems of science as an emerging culture. We have been deprived of further issues of *The Natural Philosopher* (Blaisdell, New York, 1963 on), edited by Daniel E. Gershenson and Daniel A. Greenberg, which took such wider value issues pertaining to the natural sciences as in need of clarification, and sought to widen the perspective we have had about the emergence and current development of science in our lives.

serious way as a coming possible "world culture," the flaw of imbalance between character and language study that has been sketched becomes of very deep concern to us all, whether we be social scientists or not. The study of what in our collective procedures has produced imbalance should be given high and immediate priority so as to clarify, and if necessary, correct a quite possibly dangerous pattern subterraneously at work within our emerging "scientific culture." By now we know one hard anthropological truth. The early traits of any emerging culture tend to persist with tenacity and usually die hard. The postponement of our attention to a flaw may make needed self-corrections later much more expensive for us all—and increasingly unlikely.[7]

III. A Key Hypothesis

Because the matter is serious, we might entertain a rather fundamental kind of hypothesis with regard to it. It is this: *Language study has been defensively designed by modern social science procedures* (procedures which include our categories of social science that analyzes everyday language by those linguistic concepts) *in order to keep our attention off character and character processes.* The technique by which this goal has been accomplished, furthermore, is one of riveting our attention over-exclusively on language as *a mere mechanism* rather than as a process which can *promote or damage* character growth and development in ever more favorable ways. What I am clearly suggesting is that this defensive collective strategy, at work at the fringes of consciousness, has now become so widely diffused throughout social science as to take on the status of *a group characterological trait.* Furthermore, not only is attention removed from the relation between character and language as such relation comes to the fore among the people studied by social scientists—it also keeps attention off our *own* social science language *as it affects and reflects our own characterological growth,* for better or worse, among those composing our brotherhood of interests and/or about to be initiated into membership. Notice

[7] In a paper called *Socialization as a Value Science and Community Law,* (presented to the Institute of Child Development, University of Minnesota, March, 1964), some of the detailed ways in which child-rearing norms developing out of current socialization research could subtly subvert community norms, was stressed.

the hypothesis is being entertained about a pattern of practices that will, in the future, claim to have worldwide application, a culture that attempts to build upon the scientific outlook to extend it to man himself as an object among objects. The flaw being highlighted, it should be noted, too, is one that moves character processes toward narrowness and not broadness of outlook, toward exclusivity rather than inclusivity, for a defensive process of selective attention and inattention is involved. The paradox resulting is plain: all this heightened discovery of language is going on in a way that vitiates the movement toward high levels of consciousness it originally promised and furthers movement toward characterological ignorance and darkness.

We owe to psychoanalysis the self-reflexiveness being introduced into this discussion. It is the thinking Freud made us familiar with when he saw both investigator and object of study as subject to the same set of laws (such, for instance, as those of "transference"). We owe to him, too, the policy position that the investigators first had to "purify" themselves of imbalance and conflict before they could lead others, and that they could do so only through more education, new forms of education, continuous, unremitting and vigilant education.[8] The leaders ("experts") in such a movement *first had to educate themselves* before they could illuminate followers ("patients" or "clients"). Since social science purports to be heading now toward the kind of "universality" associated with physical science, the responsibility for "self-education" of a social science leadership is many times more keenly to be emphasized in order to reduce conflict and imbal-

---

[8] The idea of a democracy is to reduce all coercion in social process. The problem is how to do it without resorting to coercive means—or, to put it another way, to use noncoercive means with coercive people so as to bring them around to adopting noncoercive perspectives and practices. Much hope lies in education, but education itself can be coercive, and often in more subtle ways than we are accustomed to recognize, given what we now know about "coercive persuasion." The least coercive means of education is simply to *be* what one wants others to be. In the long run, the use of coercive educational strategies to introduce democracy into the lives of the young, while extolling the virtues of democracy and noncoercion, are likely to perpetuate the inconsistency rather than the ideals given lipservice and "intellectual" elaboration. Perfecting the self of teachers, therefore, has a much higher significance for the perpetuation of democracy than it does for totalitarian cultures. One teaches best by being a model of the thought. And social change is more likely to result from a good ideal being embodied with excellence in one personality than larger groups of people campaigning for what none of them are ready themselves to embody.

ance. The Niagara of information in one area (language study) has to be related to and modified with regard to the increasingly thin drops of information in another area (character study). Are we indeed using language consciousness as a way of avoiding our own characterological flaws as members of the social science profession? How? Why?

In another context,[9] the point has been made that law in a scientific sense and law in a legal sense may be growing further apart over time. This happens whenever the social scientist does not consider to what degree his own character residually departs from the constitutional ideal of his own culture and, hence, quite unwittingly selectively arranges conditions and procedures to get scientific "laws" that support his rebelliousness (even destructiveness) with regard to constitutional ideals. These "laws" are then circulated as if they were "guides" to social practice in a prescriptive sense, as policy advice, while in reality they may be merely be disguised forms of "naked power" meant to modify social relations away from authorized norms of the democratic community toward specialized norms of leaders within the social science brotherhood. Can it be that this characterological process is what we are defensively keeping ourselves from examining by the imbalance at work within our current procedures? I believe in large part it is.

What do we mean by "character?" It is used here, and in tradition, to refer to the value preferences of a person or a group—a value profile, if you like.[10] Such a value profile is "carried" as a mechanism by the flow of moods and images within the stream of our experience. Hence, we are constantly *selecting* (preferring) what moods and images we permit to develop in consciousness and what moods and images we

[9] See my essay and comments in Harrop Freeman, *Legal Interviewing and Counseling*, West Co., St. Paul, Minnesota, 1965, especially "Values, the Interview and Law." It is in the legal interview that many of the lack of coherences between the legal and social science sense of law come most painfully to the fore.

[10] Surveys have been made of various student bodies—Yale, Wesleyan, University of Pennsylvania, etc.—to determine which of a systematic set of values students would *least* be willing to sacrifice for any of the others and which they would be *most* willing to sacrifice for any of the others, using this method of cost-gain analysis to shape a value profile. Generally, the *wealth* value among all student groups is placed *last* in such a value analysis, although the top value varies widely from one student body to another. *Power*, incidentally, tends to rank *low* and *enlightenment high* as value preferences. Exceptions to these trends in terms of particular individuals in a student body appear and are often of high clinical as well as sociological interest.

will pay attention to through naming them. Moods and images *are* how values appear to personality, both the value of the self for the self, as well as the value of it for others and they for it. The way moods and images are *ordered* (given some "internal government") and arranged in streams of consciousness (within particular environments) gives us the value profile or character of the person. We have only to follow the flow of language—words and word-equivalents such as gestures—in people or in groups, to discover what this internal government is like, always subject, of course, to our own deficiencies in interpretation and increasing skill with practice. It is the education that goes into establishing a particular pattern or ordered arrangement of moods and images which is, thus, to be considered character education. Language enters to shape the order and not only to express it. In short, as A. N. Whitehead emphasized so masterfully, apart from the images and feelings ("experience") that give words and gestures value, language is "nothing, nothing, bare nothing." If the character flaw in our education has been correctly diagnosed, a sweeping reform is now necessary to introduce into all of the language entering into education at all levels of maturity (and preferably at the most advanced levels first) that will remove the flaw, wherever it can be found to exist, that allows social science law to deviate from constitutional ideals. We can best do so by becoming increasingly aware of how our moods and images get ordered by, and once ordered, get expressed by languages of any and all sorts, from the most abstract mathematical signs to the most nonverbal artistic devices. We need, in short, to put social science back in social process again, rather than let it "sneak around the corner" of objective examination of its character processes, by touting all the technological elaborations it often uses as disguised ways of smuggling values, not always unwittingly, into the social process in terms of objective, descriptive poses of announcing "law."

IV. Feeling: The Missing Link

This call for more responsibility has itself operated upon my own development as a social scientist. Given the definition of character education before us, I have searched the social science literature to discover where the seed of imbalance may lie, and in the process made some modest contribution to the comprehensive vision of social process Harold D. Lasswell and I have shared.[11] In almost every "fashionable" theorist—Skinner, Piaget, Freud, Parsons, etc.—there is a curious neglect of the study of feelings ("moods") as they are shaped by and shape socialization of the personality and enter into culture at all educational levels. Of imagery, there is now an endless amount of empirical and conceptual elaboration in most existing theories at all part of the "new age" we depicted. When it comes to feeling processes, however, one finds in almost all only an occasional article or an interesting isolated passage in which feeling suddenly "catches" attention, only to fade away without successful integration into the whole structure of thought, nor do the remarks seem to play much strategic direction in guiding empirical research investigations. Instead, the resort is to concepts like "drive" or "need" or "want" which take over where "feeling" is more obviously appropriate. These "other" notions leave ambiguous whether one is referring to a physiological event or to an experience, whereas the word "feeling" makes us pay attention to experience itself.

As I have pointed out in other places,[12] much of the difficulty appears to lie in a dogma which pits feeling ("affect," "emotion") against thought ("cognition," "reason") rather than considers feeling as an intrinsic part of a thought process or considers the thought process as guided by feeling. However, in our distinctively American philosophical pattern Peirce, James, Dewey, even Whitehead, all made feeling a key factor in the origin and correction of thought patterns. Somehow, our social science has "resisted" them. There are signs, however, that we are at last ambivalently breaking out of a

[11] A central volume, *Constitution and Character,* is meant to examine all of socialization study in terms of bringing law in the legal sense and social science law closer together. An additional volume, *The Role of Mood in Self and Society,* will be undertaken by me to elaborate upon the first volume in ways that allow the social psychology of feelings to be given systematic treatment. A chapter in "Policy Science in the Classroom," written together with V. Clyde Arnspiger and Ray Bucker, and now at press [1967], gives a first systematic classification of the spectrum of moods and feelings.

[12] See Arthur J. Brodbeck, *Notes on Mood as a Factor in Teaching and Learning,* *"Urban Review,"* June, 1966, a more condensed version of "The Position of Mood in Modern Education," a paper prepared for the Conference on Science, Philosophy and Religion, May, 1966, and to appear in *"Urban Education,"* University of Buffalo, in their June, 1967, issue.

"drive" (mechanism) frame of reference toward a "feeling" value frame of reference when one examines the newly emerging work of Joseph Church,[13] for example. It is usually a half-step taken, but one which moves us further along to where the program of self-education we ultimately need becomes more and more possible.

Why should the study of feeling be the missing link between character and language study? The very tendency to *bifurcate thought from feeling* when acts of intelligence are under study helps keep language and character processes in isolation from one another. Language is taken to be centered around imagery ("cognition"), reaching high levels of skill when language approaches mathematical and logical form, levels that imply exceedingly abstract imagery or models. Character, on the other hand, is more likely to be associated with the ways in which flows of feeling—and especially the "crisis" in such flows that break out dramatically as "emotions"—are controlled and otherwise managed. Surprises are before us, however. One preliminary study of mine suggests that very abstract thinkers, when their work is going well, are guided almost solely by very refined states of feeling with little or no abstract imagery present. (They do tend to have intense dramatic dreams, however, during creative periods.) Furthermore, study of various persons of impeccable character suggests that their "control" of feeling is that of integrating it quickly and easily in rhythmic fashion into coalitions with images that remain stable, but quite voluntarily, rather than coercively, maintained. In short, such persons excell at forming "sentiments"—*i.e.,* stable coalitions of mood and image. The lack of coerciveness, the freedom from involuntary, compulsive merging of image and feeling, makes their flow of experience less likely to be crisis-ridden by "emotion." Hence, although there may be "pathological" cases where extreme separations occur in the flow of feelings from the flow of images, such as in "affectless" depersonalized

[13] Church, *op. cit.* "Drive" can refer either to a physiological event and to such an event known non-introspectively or it can refer to a subjective event such as "mood" or some introspective subjective awareness of a physiological event. Hence, as a term, it obscures the difference between a physiological mechanism and a value subjectivity. Mechanism analysis is used throughout social science at present as a way to keep attention off the values at work in conditioning and experiencing mechanism, as well as off value consequences. Mechanisms tend to cut across all values and, hence, like technology, lend themselves to cherished or abhorred value factors, so that one has given only part of the data when one invokes concepts of mechanism to explain facts.

states, good character is nowhere like the dogma. It is for these reasons, then, that the neglect of social science to investigate moods as part of acts of intelligence has, both within the lives of social scientists themselves and within their own body of "laws," defensively assisted them in keeping character and language study miles apart from where in reality both belong in close association.[14]

Perhaps we can put it in still another way. We have stopped feeling about and with the subjects of our studies in social science, and we have been able to block out attention to such feeling by developing a social science language that highlights little about the importance of feeling processes in personality and social process as a whole. This blockage has, furthermore, made it possible for social scientists to become more irresponsible toward what they study and to move further and further away from policy (value) science, while continuing to have a very serious policy (value) impact upon culture and personality, especially through the control of educational institutions.[15]

We tend to confuse, for instance, the creative process of discovery with the logical construction of it once a discovery has been achieved.[16] What makes so much of "education" so dull and boring to teacher and student alike, when it could be exhilarating, is that "discoveries" are taught not in terms of the dramatic experience through which the scientist has passed when in the throes of intensive creative endeavor—an "experience" that is usually thick with feeling when we study actual cases, in which dreams often play a paramount role—but, rather, taught in terms of how such dramas are reformulated carefully afterwards by those sticklers for "correct" logical expression that often write many of our textbooks and "code" our knowledge. In some research I

---

[14] At present, there is much concern about the interrelationship between the traits of intelligence and creativity, because there are often poor correlations among the two. It well may be that a concept of intelligence which included mood and feeling, and interactions of moods with images, might help to reduce the seeming independence of creativity and intelligence.

[15] Albert Hofstadter's paper on "The Structure and Ground of Responsibility," Chapter I in this volume, often appears to be utilizing a sensitive pinpointing of feeling states that differentiate the meaning of responsibility from irresponsibility, such as feelings of caring, gratefulness, etc.

[16] See in this regard the excellent discussion by Abraham Kaplan, *The Conduct of Inquiry: Methodology for the Behavioral Sciences,* Chandler Publishing Company, San Francisco, 1964.

have done at the Center for Urban Education,[17] for instance, it appears children who often do very well at public schools so as to acquire "successful" reputations, nonetheless dislike "science" much more than the "failures" do. When the culture of the schools in an age of science can confer success and failure upon students within them with regard to such reversals of scientific interest as contrasted with the larger nonschool culture, not only do we begin to suspect a failure of teaching method of the sort suggested here, but also we have cause for concern about another growing disparity between law in the two senses within school culture and outside of it. Actually, the real worth of logical reconstruction (often in terms of "beautifying" science) can only be fully appreciated when it is introduced in some close association with the "feeling" of what the creative person lived through in the process of arriving at a creative, worthwhile outcome (the "enlightenment" process), so that the student can contrast the two processes, making each more meaningful by becoming aware of the interrelated contribution of each. Furthermore, when this contrast and comparison is avoided in education as culture is passed along to the young, there is likely to be a downgrading of the kind of language that has gone into the process of discovery, much of which is more like that of "artistic" language than that conventionally assumed to characterize "science." Often words may play a minimal role, and very unusual word-equivalents take over the linguistic function, as most of the case histories of scientific creativity sharply suggest.[18] We then end up, too, with some further false bifurcations of "art" and "science" into "two cultures," each with a distinctively "different" language that does not ever invade the field of the other.[19] We witness here how dogmas—

[17] Such materials came from a preliminary analysis of data obtained from a survey of the Buffalo public school system for the New York State Educational Department. Current Center for Urban Education policy does not make available further access to data, nor to theoretical statements, arising from the field study, around which disagreements of theory and policy developed.

[18] See the lives of scientists depicted in *The Science of Life* by Gordon R. Taylor, McGraw-Hill, New York, 1963; see also Myron A. Coler's *Essays on Creativity in the Sciences,* New York University Press, New York, 1963; on the creative process across specializations see *The Creative Process,* edited by Brewster Ghiselin, New American Library, New York, 1955.

[19] The point of much of the family of works of Ernst Cassirer was to emphasize that "artistic" language is the index of a process of learning (and, hence, an "in-

innocently introduced as mere "postulates" to begin with, to be sure—can act quite unnecessarily to govern the limits of our thought and gradually falsify reality for us until our social science consciousness has become sizably damaged. Indeed, what we need to do is reduce all such "postulates" to the barest minimum and search for ways of making more and more of them matters of empiricism rather than dogma. In any event, the price we pay for allowing feeling and mood to be ignored, given short shrift, and ultimately demeaned, is much more exhorbitant than we need to pay for the grubby and suspect returns engendered by the selective inattention and defensiveness toward the affective life.

In the following discussion, we select three symptoms of the social science conflict to which we point. These are: "conceptual journalism," the containment of social psychology, and the exemption of the self from social science laws. Having given in this way more elaboration of the ideas already presented, we will then move in the remainder of the discussion toward some positive suggestions for resolution of the conflict and reduction of the symptomatology.

V. First Symptom: The Growth of "Conceptual Journalism"

Since the World War II, and beginning around the popularity mobilized toward David Riesman's *The Lonely Crowd,* there has been a steady stream of books which, while appearing to utilize the language of social science, actually employs language in a somewhat literary fashion and with journalistic styles of timeliness. The books of Vance Packard belong here, as does "The Organizational Man," and the latest examples flow from the pen of Marshall McLuhan [20] and Michael

---

tellectual" process if by that term "thought" is under reference). The learning involves feelings which become more and more refined out of initial cruder states, so that the quality of consciousness is both upgraded and expanded by art.

[20] The central work is most usually taken to be *Understanding Media,* McGraw-Hill Co., New York, 1964. Often, like other works in the *genre,* people use it as a kind of "projective technique," with society and history as the focus of fantasy. One presupposition in treating the larger social landscape this way is that every personality can be taken to be organizing within itself a whole society with a past—and, conversely, every larger community can be studied as if it were a single personality. Such presuppositions are not too far away from the visions that earlier flowed from the pen of G. H. Mead.

Harrington.[21] No doubt there are examples before World War II that fit into the *genre*. It is the frequency and popularity of such books, all more or less devoted to taking the Nation's "pulse," that makes the phenomena interesting and to be taken seriously. The function such books serve, on a collective level, is to right the relative neglect of the study of moods and feelings in social science, but often in a way in which symptoms of conflict are manifested in the process.

It is possible to label the phenomena represented by this stream of books as "conceptual journalism." All of them tend to use social science concepts, but not with definitions that stay put or even are representative of their conventional social science meanings. Instead, the concepts are stretched to carry connotations that warp their conventional meanings and keep shifting meaning as the work progresses. They are, thus, not very systematic. Furthermore, the books tend to be "journalistic," because they often prematurely reach sweeping conclusions without all the scholarly work that is first needed to ground description and interpretation, almost as if they were meeting a deadline of a newspaper that had to go to press before the phenomena being described disappeared from the scene. Among themselves, the works may differ quite widely in detail, but they tend all to be geared toward public attention and publicity and about newly appearing problems in society, which are portrayed by unorthodox uses of "professionalized" language.

All of these books, so I believe, can be best understood as ways to *clarify collective mood patterns and swings*. What *The Lonely Crowd* did more than anything else was to give a kind of conceptual sense to a puzzling mood change that developed nationally during the

---

[21] The work of Michael Harrington that drew so much attention to him was *The Other America*, The Macmillan Co., New York, 1963. One wonders why volumes that fit into the category do not take more public hold, such as Lewis A. Dexter's *The Tyranny of Schooling*, Basic Books, New York, 1964. Many report being "confused" after reading the latter volume, while they feel "illuminated" after reading the former, whereas a systematic analysis of the two would no doubt show Dexter to have done a more serious job of dealing with mood factors in social process, however much he utilizes conceptual journalistic styles. Perhaps everyone feels much more of an expert about educational matters than about the social concerns that the volumes which achieve wide appeal pinpoint and, hence, this sense of expertise keeps their attention off "unexplained" feelings and mood changes of a shared, collective nature in just such areas where one's own "intellectual" skill is trusted.

days of the McCarthy hysteria. Those who use words like "identity" and "anxiety" with any traditional professional connotations have had difficulty in understanding what Reisman was writing about at all, because his own use is often Pickwickian about such and similar terms. What his book did was to give a diffuse picture of American life that, strictly speaking, was conceptually crude and confused, but which seemed to make "sense" out of the kind of collective moods of a "lonely togetherness" that the McCarthy movement evoked in our cultural life. It also, no doubt, served to highlight many facts and problems to which our attention had been previously underexercised, although it processed these in a way that allowed little continuity with traditional social science developments.

McLuhan is now doing much the same thing with regard to the rise of the media in our lives, especially TV. The work does not hold up conceptually—indeed, McLuhan does not even ask of himself that it do so—but it attempts to say something significant about a shift of collective feeling engendered by a media change in society often in a kind of "Zen-like" language that is meant to baffle while suggesting ultimate clarity. In a way, McLuhan is introducing the important point that skill changes may produce value changes more than content changes themselves do. He has also drawn our attention to the way the sense channels are synthesized in personality and cultural patterns, when our sources of communication undergo shifts in the information channels utilized. In a sense, McLuhan is the most "representative" of the phenomena which I am delineating, precisely because the need to employ social science language in any traditional sense is totally abandoned and it is now used along with any other language merely to help him depict a collective mood pattern by a diffuse imagery. It is mood writing in which the imagery is purposely kept from becoming highly systematized.

Harrington falls, perhaps, closer to traditional social science than does McLuhan. Yet, he uses the word "culture" in a way that makes little sense to those professionals who employ it with austerity. The Negro in America is unlikely to compose "another culture"—as Harrington explicitly says—as anyone who has compared an American Negro with an African Negro is well aware, as are indeed both groups of Negroes about one another, although the American Negro may in some "pockets" of America compose "a subculture" in his emphasis upon mood and feeling, when such patterns are not readily explainable as "social class" or "interest group" differences *within* culture.

It is quite possible that one of the best ways a social science about collective moods and feelings could begin is by *analyzing the language shifts* in such "popular" works of social science as contrasted with more "scholarly" works. By no means, incidentally, do we need to anticipate that the "conceptual journalist" will turn out to be compared unfavorably in each and all dimensions, for symptoms often contain the seeds of creativity. It seems to me, for instance, that Harrington moved in *The Other America* toward the brilliant suggestion that there may be classes for every value in society—and, hence, we could use the word "poverty" to speak of "intellectual poverty," "poverty of affection," "moral poverty," "poverty of mental health," and so on, even when those being designated have "nice clothes" and TV sets. The sociologists seldom have put forward so creative an idea, although the same notion is now appearing within social science in such works as those of Nelson Polsby.[22]

Until social scientists, in any event, give more systematic attention to both stable and changing collective mood patterns—or what Lasswell prefers to call social "climates"—the phenomena of "conceptual journalism" is likely to grow and prosper, despite the symptomatology contained within it. It will continue to stretch what abstract terms there are in social science in ways they were not designed to be used, so as to perform such mood clarifying exercises, and in whatever linguistic style the collective moods themselves demand, making social science language akin to literary language and mixing the two freely together, until social science itself develops in counterreaction a more newly adequate systematic vocabulary to describe carefully collective mood patterns. A very positive way to view "conceptual journalism" is to perceive in it a growing public demand, within and without social science, to extend social science beyond the existing stage of achievements so that it can deal more adequately with the diffuse cultural flow of feelings from one group to another. Conceptual journalism attempts to do a better job of this than other cultural (and especially

[22] See *Community Power and Political Theory*, Yale University Press, New Haven, 1963.

anti-social-science) agents. It is a compromise formation that seeks to bring the kind of thinking social science represents to areas of life now left on the fringe of consciousness, often because collective moods vary imperceptibly and slowly. It is not surprising, incidentally, that so many of the conceptual journalists have very unconventional career relations to social science, because new developments are likely to be promoted by those whose career lines depart sizably from the usual routes by which thought is disciplined and trained. Indeed, the unusual uses of language among the writers of this type of literature can, no doubt, be traced to exposures to social roles that most social scientists manage to avoid.[23]

In a sense, the public wish to have its collective mood and feeling changes and shifts recorded and clarified by conceptual journalists in what seems like "good" social science language, may be taken as one of the signs that presage the diffusion of our social science culture beyond narrow professional groupings into the totality of human thought. The conceptual journalists may be read and studied most sympathetically when this process of diffusion is kept in mind. The point is that, if we had a better social psychology of the flow of moods and feelings around refined categories that discriminate one pattern clearly from another, the resulting imagery could be a great deal less diffuse and more self-consistent than it now is. A great deal of nonsense is currently circulated about "feelings of alienation" at a time when everyone is made to feel more needed than ever before, at ever younger ages, and leisure time becomes less and less possible given such demands upon one. A sizable increment in understanding so-called "alienation" rests in developing a better psychology of moods and feelings. What we do appear to be going through is a time when feelings of identity are changing to include the self in something larger than the narrow community which previously it was customary to consider, given the "expansion of consciousness" to which we previously referred. Our language for feelings (and the way feelings bear upon character) leave too much on the fringe of consciousness, so that our conscious-

---

[23] On the importance of role factors as background conditions for creativity, see my "Placing Aesthetic Developments in Social Context: A Program of Value Analysis" in *"Journal of Social Issues,"* volume XX, number 1, 1966. A theory of art as a clarifier of mood and feeling is presented there.

ness flickers with regard to these parts of our experience which shape a "rejection," nonetheless, of conventional images of identity.

VI. Second Symptom: The Struggle against Social Psychology

A clear public image of what a social scientist represents is now not particularly well consolidated, if we contrast the clear image the psychiatrist has achieved, for example. After hearing and watching different specialists in our profession quarrel with one another around narrow expertise associated with being in one or another branch of what should be a *brotherhood* of interests, and often about trivial language preferences, neither is there much ground for believing we have much *internal* sense of our *common interests* as social scientists, encompassed in any comprehensive way to form a clear image across the spectrum of research and theory from sociopsychosomatics to international relations. We may choose individuals for case study, if we wish—but unless these individuals are placed in relation to the whole,[24] such as being "exceptional" or "representative" with regard to general trends and patterns, such individual analysis is certainly bound to be inconclusive as a device for clarifying an internal and public image of the profession.

One great unifying force in social science is the slow but recently explosive development of social psychology. Indeed, it is becoming apparent that social psychology provides the fundamental data of all social science insofar as anything *empirical* is under observation. When we observe the empirical, we observe person interacting with person either in one-to-one, one-to-few, or one-to-many (and *vice versa*) relations. When many are involved, we have to "sample." Yet, it is always a person-to-person interaction we must deal with as empiricists. Of course, the data we utilize or select to observe in such interpersonal relations may be different—or processed differently—according to which branch of social sciences we happen to belong to and, hence, which policy problems we have in mind. What is distinctively "Ameri-

[24] This concern with "representativeness" was part of the top awardwinning plan published in *Television and Human Behavior,* edited by Leon Arons and Mark A. May, Appleton-Century Crofts, New York, 1963. See Plan 7, A. J. Brodbeck, and D. B. Jones, *Television Viewing and the Norm-Violating Perspectives and Practices of Adolescents: A Synchronized Depth and Scope Program of Policy Research.*

can" about our social science *is* this emphasis upon social psychology which we are gradually diffusing throughout the world, often with "outside" help, such as that which Karl Mannheim and his students proffered.

Social psychology has emerged to keep before us the fact that subjective events enter into any interaction that can otherwise be described in mere operational, behavioristic or "ecological" terms.[25] Such subjective events consist not only in images, but in flows of moods and feelings, too, as we have previously emphasized when discussing character. Objectivity about the meaning of operations is ultimately a matter of intersubjective agreement; and all the factors that create cultural, class, interest group and personality differences, whether of a crisis or non-crisis nature, shape subjective factors in such a way as to reduce the ease with which one can obtain intersubjective agreements. Hence, the study of mood and feeling is very much a part of questioning what we now consider "objectivity" and of discovering important ways to "resolve" intersubjective disagreements when they arise.

At present, however, there are still strong resistances against fully employing social psychology in the study of both individual and group behavior, although the data of mood and image is part of any social interaction occurring in any field of social study. Every attempt to "split off" social psychology from other social inquiry is employed, so I believe, as a way of smuggling in value assumptions about human interactions which no empirical study will support. Not only those who study the individual, such as biologists and psychologists, but also those who study groups, such as economists and sociologists, are subject to this indefensible strategy. The tendency to use it suggests to me

---

[25] Two recent excellent books on social psychology serve to make this point quite thoroughly. See Tamotsu Shibutani, *Society and Personality: An Interactionist Approach to Social Psychology*, Prentice-Hall, Englewood Cliffs, New Jersey, 1961; and, also, Roger Brown, *Social Psychology*, Free Press, New York, 1965. There is need for a social psychology still, however, that will place the same approach in relation to historical materials and across wide differences in the cultures appearing in history. Too often the social psychologist entertains hypotheses that are not as clearly seen as culturally-shaped by his own conditioning as they would be if he were to apply them to cultures and periods of history when the conditioning process was altogether different from his own. Such widening often helps to separate trivial from profound hypotheses worth scientific investigation, and uncovers areas of value analysis most easily overlooked otherwise.

a still ubiquitous character flaw around restricting and constricting "identity," so that the feeling and image of a brotherhood of social scientists is kept from emerging out of the defensive, and often fearful, attitudes of losing whatever false sense of power is thought to be associated with keeping social sciences apart from one another within the family of concerns. Needless to say, the social psychology of mood and feeling may be an especially sensitive area of aversion, given such symptoms that prevent wide and favor narrow identifications among social scientists.[26] One would find, so I believe, that the linguistic concepts of such restrictors of identity would emphasize mechanisms more than values and be especially adroit in smuggling in values in the guise of words and concepts that appeared merely to be describing facts, operations, pseudoquantifications, techniques, and much else that had a surface "scientific" appearance. Like most propaganda, the symp-

[26] One of the difficulties in making points of this sort is that, when put in a general form, everyone reaches out to subscribe to them readily, as though they were platitudes which do not require thought. It is only when one gets down to concrete cases that embody the general principles, that people divide up into sides and the subscription list dwindles when it costs something to stay on it. This movement from generals to particulars invokes more mood and feeling, as we show elsewhere in the discussion when focusing on the abstract doctrines and concrete miranda of social myths. Given this difficulty, let me bring out the point being made about social psychology more saliently. Administrators are often up against clashes between scientists about what is no doubt "personal difficulties" between them. It is easy to dismiss such quarrels as being "merely personal." Usually, however, there are issues about theory and method that are also interwoven into these "personal difficulties." It is the administrator who wants to duck these theoretical and methodological differences who is most likely to dismiss the quarrels as "merely personal." At the same time, he makes quick character judgments in favor of one of the two parties entering into a dispute which supports *his own bias* with regard to the differing positions the two have taken on objective, content issues, involving theoretical and methodological divergence of views. As a result, he knocks one person out of further power and another into more power *without ever examining the issues involved,* either in terms of scientific differences or of objective character assessment. The divorce of "personal difficulties" from "scientific differences," when dealing with scientists who clash over cooperative ventures, serves to *free* the administrator to behave in the most *undemocratic* way possible, while feeling, nonetheless, as though he were "above it all," while actually deeply ego-involved. Any *intense* personal difficulty arising between people flows out of their *whole* perspective, including their scientific perspective, and to divorce one from the other is to miss the way they resonate together. The impersonal is only a way of organizing the personal —or, in this case, the interpersonal. The view that impersonality is attained by pushing aside personal factors (and social psychology) is constantly found to be associated with a power personality inwardly insecure about his own worth and unable to examine his mood and feelings.

tom is utilized to convince the user of it that he is, above all, an objective judge of all he surveys, without taking any pains to make deep self-examinations from which such self-assessments could be realistically entertained.

Often, too, the appeal is to being "practical"—where the latter often means coming up with a plan based on the survey of actual and potential operations, without considering the meanings that such operations have to those required to be governed by them. Hence, the implicit *intended* meaning of the operational plan that "solves" problems is *mistaken* for the way people actually "experience" the plan. In this way, the intended values promoted by the plan are prejudged and assumed to be realized "in" the operations of the plan. Little about this can be studied because no explicit value "rationale" for a "practical" plan is provided, only the endless details of "operational instrumentation," so that the meaning of the whole cannot be envisaged by any single person governed by the plan, often not even by top planners or administrators themselves. Centralization of power in society often calls for "pushing and pulling" of people about in the social process, to which they often rebel because they do not see what the beneficial meaning for anyone within the pushes and pulls can be said to be. The strategy of neglecting social psychology in the name of "being practical" often results in resistance and resentment among those for whom the plan is intended as a solution to pressuring problems. The neglect is often, in short, its own worse self-punishment.

Among those given to such symptomatology, there is often to be found *a confusion of enlightenment with power*. People who resist planning or question the validity of seemingly descriptive materials are assumed to be of bad faith, men without good will, bent on pitting their power against the power of "reason" or "fact." Actually, however, such a view of power is itself a mistaken one. Power is an attitude, an attitude entertained between people. It is not "in" people like an organ of the body. Furthermore, power is not a cake that one can divide among a few. The sharing of power increases one's own power, so that the "piece" keeps getting bigger the more one shares it with others. One of the prime reasons for neglecting social psychology—often by putting it off in a glorified corner by itself—is that one hopes to be better off in terms of power over all values by so keeping social scientists apart. The sense of being "better off" is often calculated in terms of seeing every other expert (that is not oneself) as being power-hungry rather than enlightenment-hungry. Many times, such a confusion is merely a projection of an internal conflict within those manifesting the symptoms, projected outward in cynical fashion toward all those wishing the profession as a whole to expand and clarify their common map of knowledge, toward all those questioning the "value-free" nature of the plans and facts those manifesting symptoms have put forward with little self-doubt or humility. A fear is often converted into a fact. The deprivation to enlightenment impulses arouses power urges where they were not in operation before and what was not true to begin with is made true through a false system of perception that accompanies the symptoms of struggling against the diffusion of social psychology. Indeed, many people who feel they want "power" in social science are often surprised, after obtaining it, to discover that it was the enlightenment it entailed that they were seeking, while the rest of the trappings became a burden rather than a joy.

A great mistake would be engendered if these remarks were taken to mean that those now officially identified as "social psychologists" can be taken as somehow "perfect" integrators of social science into a brotherhood of common interests. The imperfections are all too obvious, but the direction is, nonetheless, the wave of the future. Furthermore, *all* social scientists are social psychologists, not a small band of self-appointed experts, even when their social psychological hypotheses are buried and smuggled into their work rather than made explicit. Still further, many of these buried assumptions which often "clash" with those more generally entertained by "official" social psychologists may be more relevant and useful, especially if they remain buried out of lack of skill in thinking about moods and images rather than out of a deliberate effort to bypass making them explicit. The social psychology of a good academic lawyer, so my experiences among my former colleagues at the Yale Law School suggest to me, is often much more penetrating (and quite quickly made explicit with a little assistance from a social psychologist) than the "truisms" of the "classical" social psychological studies that often grew up out of random study of, for example, the latest housing project. Indeed, often a conceptual journalist can do a much better job on the social psychology of even a housing project, because he is not as hemmed in by a great many irrelevant abstract words about mechanisms that allow the social psychology of moods and feelings to go unnoticed.

Part of the symptomatology that allows mood and feeling to get exiguous scientific study is, in any event, to be found in all those tendencies that struggle against social psychology as being a *common* interest of all social science. Social psychology may be glorified, of course, while set apart and kept from entering into "important" concerns, especially policy and practical matters, where moods and feelings are often taken as emerging only to produce lack of objectivity, rather than widening intersubjective agreement when understood and exchanged. Indeed, the attempt to conceive of human behavior in terms of mere movement and "operations" and "instrumentalities" has tended to go along with looking upon citizens as part of "a mass" or "a crowd," to adopting the language of totalitarians, where all can be stimulated to give the same response by a commanding engineer. Social psychology, which emphasizes the *diversity* of perspectives carried by mood and image, highlights facts that demand we conceive of "a public" with a spectrum of opinions which, when exchanged with respect for each other's moods and images, can produce an informed and harmonious consensus. The character flaw in this second symptom has, thus, sweeping implications for social science as an emerging world culture. As an example, the recent concern with school integration is often dealt with in terms of how bodies of different "colors" are placed in propinquity in differing types of architectural units. Left out of the picture are the social transactions between "the bodies" that alone make for genuine integration by way of modifying totalitarian attitudes toward one another.

VII. Symptom Three: The Exemption of the Self

Content consists of the laws the social scientist discovers that govern the way his subjects of study act. In discovering such laws, the scientist himself behaves according to laws of *procedure*. Since the scientist is in the social process like everyone else, he is as subject to the same laws of content (within his procedures) as those he discovers to govern the subjects he studies, unless he has taken special precaution to modify himself effectively, and then his subjects are capable of the same modification as he. We have made this point previously when stressing the defensive nature of concern with language as mere mechanism.

A whole host of character flaws in social science can be found to emerge from an unwillingness to consider the self as scientist being subject to the same laws as those governing subjects one studies—or an unwillingness to consider subjects as capable of the same modifications which one oneself has purportedly undergone. We find, for instance, Jean Piaget emphasizing extreme contrasts between children and adults in terms of socialized thought (the gradual movement toward reason and logic). Yet, his own writings are often taken to be masterpieces of unintelligible autisms, judging by the comments of some of his most admiring expositors, so that the adult outcomes are falsely pictured. Every reader of Piaget has his own collection of sentences that refuse to make sense. The Hullian psychologists insisted that all learning was a matter of trial-and-error; yet they learn about learning by the use of hypothetical-deductive systems rather than the randomized responses which govern the learning of others. The gestaltists insisted that all perceptions are holistic; yet, their own perceptions of perception was ultimately found to have left out from the whole the factor of motivation as a prime contextual determinant of perceptual content. Indeed, even the "popular" social science of C. P. Snow, itself an example of conceptual journalism, suffers from the matching; his strong case for the "rift" between the "two cultures" is undermined by the fact that he, as a trained scientist, wrote *novels* about science which were often esthetically quite compelling. In all these instances, and without elaborating further, the scientist is himself engaged in a false act of enhanced self-esteem, discounting himself from the very phenomena that he is depicting as content. His own character is left out of the picture of content being presented. Such false self-esteem is often in the service of undue pessimism, contempt for animals and children, unrealistic feelings of alienation from society, exaggerated stress on some single mechanism at work in social process and so on. Most of all, however, these descrepancies and the character flaws they serve to support are indices, so my own survey of social science theories lead me to believe, of defenses against *developing systems of ideas beyond the state of relative incompletion to which they have been brought.* They serve to "harden" theories against the further growth they call out in those using them. Since it is mood and feeling that remain most understudied across all social science theories, the symptoms serve especially, so I have found, to keep the scientist's attention off how his own mood and feeling get into his scientific studies and, hence, how they may play a decisive role among the subjects he observes and call for changes of theory.

It seems likely that *all* social science theories, when they are extended to deal with the *same* set of problems and the *same* empirical details, will be found to be *equivalent,* so that co-measurement of language of one with the other is likely to be the ultimate outcome of comprehensiveness of theoretical development of each and every promising system of ideas now before us for adoption. It may, indeed, turn out that one system of ideas is more economical than another, when both are so extended to deal with the whole social process rather than confined to different parts of it. Furthermore, theories themselves undergo useful modifications, modifications which often can be found to correct character flaws in those using them, when they are so extended rather than restricted and confined, because any detail is likely to look differently when seen in broader perspective.

In this regard, a curious notion that itself is never made a matter of empirical inquiry circulates quite widely among social scientists. It is the idea that "true individuality" and "creativity" of the social scientist is best promoted by divorcing one's language as much as possible from that already in community circulation in the profession. Many attempt to escape ever using language that could be associated with another prominent figure in the field. Such a strategy is not only misguided; it also assists the scientist to maintain the kind of discrepancies between procedure and content to which we have just referred. First of all, individuality is most likely to be promoted by exposing oneself to the whole spectrum of ideas circulating in both society and social science. Mandell Sherman [27] long ago demonstrated that those in "hill-billy"

[27] See his studies of the children of isolated "hill-billies" contained in his *The Development of Attitudes: A Study of the Attitudes of Mountain Children,* The Payne Fund, New York, 1933. One can then contrast this with how individuality is promoted by the public media in "The New Media and Our Total Society," written by Nelson N. Foote and included in *The New Media and Education,* Aldine Publishing Co., Chicago, 1966, edited by Peter H. Rossi and Bruce J. Biddle.

societies developed no "individuality," precisely because they kept in relative "isolation" from any exposure to a rich set of differences at work throughout the entire social process. The image of the creative and individualized person as a kind of "Robinson Crusoe" in the social process is supported by no empirical study, however much it appeals to wishful thinking. The emergence of Freud's ideas, for instance, can be shown to have been a gradual and mounting collective process to which many gross and subtle factors, in both the historical collective process that preceded him and the social events through which he passed, contributed in making manifest his own genius and giving it cultural recognition.[28] The urge to differentiate oneself from others is often in the service of petty ego concerns and selfishness, much more than the ennobling visions those who bypass responsible considerations of others prefer to circulate about their wish for "enlightenment" or "novelty" or other fine-sounding phrases. The urge, indeed, weakens the consolidation of a *common map of knowledge* in which gaps and errors can become plain, for the adoption of a "private" language (around which one seeks ego-aggrandizement) often masks the fact that what is being pinpointed has often already been discovered under quite other labels. Such positioning in social science is often in the service of obtaining "naked power" rather than "legitimated power," as the latter forces one to consider the brotherhood of thought in which one can find one's own true individualized and creative identity by building upon something already shared. Usually, this egocentric tendency fastens on some new "mechanism" of personality or of group functioning, promoted by some single quasi-literary and vague (but dramatic) term that is not related to *a system* of terms—mechanisms

[28] See Lancelot Law White, *The Unconscious Before Freud,* Basic Books, New York, 1960. The deprivations the creative person suffers often blind him to the indulgences operating to allow him as an ego to express a larger cultural process at work through him as a self (or "we") phenomenon. It is always dangerous to underestimate the potential actual support every individual act of creativity has at work for it in the larger social environment, while focusing on all the resistance to the act being faced at any moment. Indeed, it is often the deprivations themselves which allow for a richer unfolding of the creative perspective, and hence, often have long-term effects of shaping larger indulgences than would otherwise occur, simply because the deprivations have conditioned a less superficial unfolding of the creative vision. Indeed, social psychology makes the practice of dubbing anything a deprivation or indulgence less matter-of-fact and more a matter of seeing a particular detail as part of a larger time-space context.

which, furthermore, are often quite trivial in terms of the contribution made to the map of knowledge as a whole, sometimes even enticing attention away from many more solid and systematic prior discoveries of much the same thing. As a result, social science often acquires a bad name, because the ideas of today evaporate tomorrow, precisely because they were not part of a comprehensive system of ideas but of momentary bits of moods and feelings and of sheer empirical "fashions." To bring the examination of moods and feelings to the fore, we would soon uncover how much of our flashiest aspects of social science are the product of an individualized expression of a collective feeling or mood pattern often persistently working out of collective awareness.

Even within the same theory, one can often find this phenomenon at work. In the writings of Harry Stack Sullivan, for instance, one finds the same process being renamed as he goes along, as if each new instance were a quite different occurrence. Frequently all the renaming reflects is a difference of the mood complex in terms of which he observes the phenomena. The process is not necessarily harmful, if used self-consciously. One can "moodize" all mechanisms to bring out the different values which each mechanism can be used to promote. Sullivan clearly appears to be acting as though something utterly different by way of mechanism were discovered each time. His handling of "empathetic" mechanisms, for instance, is a good example of this kind of style of thought he adopts. Sullivan is chosen as a case here, incidentally, precisely because he is *least* prone to be lacking in self-reflexiveness and does not avoid the value concerns that are brought forward by utilizing social psychology—or what he prefers to call "interpersonal relations."

The most individualized persons in science or elsewhere will be found, so I believe, to have high language consciousness of the whole array of concepts at work in their culture and science, as well as all the variations in their style of usage. They are especially adapted to co-measurement, so that thought (a mood-image coalition and flow) can readily be communicated from one language system to another. They more easily "get into" the minds of others, rather than being baffled or paralyzed by superficial differences of naming patterns or by levels of consciousness variant from their own. They are able to assist themselves and others, therefore, to raise their conscious processes toward more inclusivity. More about the flow of one's own moods and images is brought to one's attention when such co-measurement is strengthened as a personality trait, and especially co-measurement in aligning matters of procedure with matters of content, so that a recognition of an equivalent state can be found in another or in oneself.

The symptomatology that creates lack of coherence in what one says about content and procedure can be found, in any event, to be associated with the neglect of the study of mood and feeling. Such study of feeling would "unmask" how momentary individual and collective moods erupt in a false individuality and weaken the vividness of a common map of knowledge. Such study would, furthermore, promote a sense of ultimate equivalence between all existing promising theories in social science. Such study would, still further, unmask the false self-esteem which permits the scientist to ignore his own feelings toward the subjects he studies in the interest of aggrandizing his own role. In short, the study of mood and feeling would make the scientist acquire a new sense of responsibility toward the social process in which he operates, a sense of responsibility he too often now shirks while exerting ever increasing power.

VIII. Damaged Character: The Correction of Low Self-esteem

While our discussion of symptomatology has not been exhaustive, the three key phenomena we have sketched point to character flaws that require professional attention and correction. Some of my work at the Center for Urban Education suggests to me that character flaws emerge out of low self-esteem. Low self-esteem arises whenever the young are kept in enforced isolation (such as Negro "ghettos") from one another while officially members of the same community or, on the other hand, are forced into interactions with each other (coercive "integration") in ways that give undue advantage or exhorbitant stress to some more than others because of their backgrounds. Children must both be *prepared* to give up isolation and learn to use integration opportunities as a chance for self-growth and change, and their educational systems must have some effective way of conducting such preparation in sensible steps toward a goal. "Instant" integration, by pushing and pulling around bodies of different colors, is likely only to be a perpetuation in a new form of an old disease, both of which attack self-esteem. It is just as likely that the character flaws of social scientists we have been detailing arise in the socialization and professionalization process in much the same way and require much the same antidote, even though the "groupings" are not around the color of one's skin. How does this process, which goes wrong at both ends of a continuum, really work?

The work of V. Clyde Arnspiger with college students aids us here in moving toward some refined and contextual ideas. In collaboration with me, Arnspiger has developed a theory of self-esteem and a procedure of testing for and correcting disorders of self-esteem. Every individual makes a series of value demands upon himself in terms of which he measures his worth. When the self fails to meet the demands, self-esteem tends to fall. Associated with the drop, one discovers the eruption of everything from psychosomatic disorders to disordered interpersonal relations, the variety of "problems" all serving to make achievement difficult and "excuse" failure. Supporting this drop of self-esteem is the memory stystem. One *selects* from one's own past life those memories *one expects to be better off remembering*. In those with low self-esteem and with the accompanying symptomatology, one discovers the memories are overwhelmingly deprivational as coded by either subject or another person. To remember selectively only past deprivation is automatically to lower the self-esteem, composed as it is of meeting value demands, and gives rise to self-protective devices that we call "symptoms." The symptoms provide grounds for *maintaining* lowered self-esteem, because they mitigate against the successful attainment of the demands one would prefer to actualize. They "excuse" one. Yet the worth of the self is still contained in what one has been "excused" from attaining by the symptoms. In this way, character flaws emerge.

The procedure Arnspiger devised as a corrective to such states (and all students to some extent have set "excuses" for themselves) is to get each student to list fifty memories and then code them for deprivation and indulgence in terms of a systematic list of values (which we will turn to somewhat later on in this discussion.) After doing this, they then recode the same events for any deprivations or indulgences other people entering into the events have suffered by being associated with them, including those figures thought to be depriving of the self. Having "taken the role of the other," the student then recodes the same events for value deprivations and indulgences undergone by the ego. In every case, the "failure" of the self as seen through the selective memory process is erased and replaced by an increased sense of "success." In short, the memories are perceived as more indulgent than previously. Furthermore, if a new list of fifty memories are given, they are coded by either subject or another person as more highly indulgent to the person recalling them. With these steps and with this shift, the symptoms that have long acted as "excuses" are gradually or even suddenly removed. Migraines of long-standing are no longer present; parental hated gives rise to compassion for the parent; personality traits of irritability evaporate and patience replaces them; and so on. Furthermore, all this goes on within the period of one academic semester and the results are obtained much before the end of such a period of time.

Not everything that goes on during the use of this procedure is yet thoroughly understood—although it seems in terms of results to be the embodiment of the kind of "short-term" (economical) therapy Franz Alexander searched for most of his life. Some of the main features of what happens are, however, relatively clear. The perspective one has of the environment at any point of one's life shapes and conditions the decisions one makes with regard to action toward it. The more negative that perspective, the more self-defensive and restricted are the choices of action and the less imaginative the decision process. Indeed, symptomatology arises from the discrepancy between 1) the self-demands and 2) the restrictions in the decision process one imposes upon oneself by one's perception of the environment. Symptomatic coding of these past events in terms of all values, and so including the perspectives of others more fully, allows the person to discover a whole spectrum of perspectives he might have with equal reason developed toward the memory events *other* than the more primitive ill-considered ones he brought to them and which unduly narrowed his decisionmaking abilities in the course of his life history. Given this wider range of alternative "interpretations," many ways of handling such events other than those he used open up so that there is less feeling of "constraint" upon the decision process. The possibilities of "success" are greatly enhanced. A "repetition compulsion" has, therefore, been surrendered to "imagination."

Often, of course, the memory of the event is incomplete. By having to code for others in it, the student remembers more of it. What was a deprivational event for him may have been even more so for the other persons, even when they acted destructively toward him. As the full context emerges, the power the person whose memories are being self-surveyed has to deprive and indulge others emerges—not merely their powers to indulge and deprive him. He begins to sense he is a value-producer and not merely on the target side of value indulgence and deprivation. The sense of being rich in values is enhanced; the sense of others being in need of values is heightened. Along with this shift, the ideals for the self are likely to reemerge from where they were buried under a damaged self-image and the student wants to commit his life to something, more than he wants to protect himself from being damaged further. A positive image of the self and positive feeling for the self come forward, as ideals or self-demands once again make their appearance and press for elaboration. These ideals for the self probably have always remained on the fringe of consciousness in the form of insistent moods and feelings that no amount of attention to "symptomatology" can ultimately placate.

Some patterns of deprivation do not seem to respond as readily and fully to the procedure as others do, so that, for example, students with severe deprivational memories in the area of rectitude (being made to feel guilty), while showing improvement, do not as easily rid themselves of symptoms or stabilize gains. In some cases, however, there are dramatic shifts of symptoms that had previously been impervious to change by more traditional methods—such as students having long-standing ulcers or tics—which disappear for the remainder of the undergraduate career. (Longer followup studies are now being contemplated.)

Character can be looked upon in part as "the dream" one has for making one's own life meaningful. This is a future ideal toward which one's decisions from day to day are directed. A life is characterless that is aimless and that has no "dream" or ideal to which it is committed, other than moving from moment to moment in time around fragmentary details that press upon one with a sense of immediacy. In survey-ing dream theory in one context,[29] I have pointed out how much responsibility begins in dreams, often indeed the most pressing respon-sibilities that shape our character. What stands in the way of actualiz-ing an ideal creates character conflict, if there has been no preparation for lack of indulgence or for meeting deprivation without "giving up." The resolution is often to lower self-esteem, support the lowering by an exaggerated deprivational memory system, and "excuse" oneself by symptoms. In this way, the best of our dreams are "compromised" or otherwise altered to protect the self against all potential future failure. There are, of course, environments which act irrationally so that they create self-doubt about any reasonable chance of success. Yet the per-spectives taken upon even an inimical environment can be such as to see the depriving agents as even more damaged than the ego they wish to damage by becoming aware of how that ego is part of a larger ideal self, a future "we."

To be precise, we ought to differentiate between security and self-esteem. Self-esteem refers to the sense of being *worthy* of indulgence and deprivation or absence of indulgence and absence of deprivation. Security refers more simply to the expectation that one *will* be deprived or indulged. One may have high security but low self-esteem. A regime of socialization that arises from "pampering" a child may produce such a pattern, for indulgence is seldom made contingent upon achievement of any self-defined goal. So, too, one might have high self-esteem but low security. A socialization regime in which the socializer always appears to be on the side of one's self-defined goals but constantly blocks their achievement, is a subtle and insidious form of "rejection" that gives rise to this second pattern. Unfortunately, the self-esteem memory procedure is not yet refined enough to differentiate out these two distinctive variables clearly, although as "exceptional" cases arise, they will no doubt help uncover imperfect relations between self-

[29] See my *"Commentary"* article, "In Dreams Begin Responsibilities," in the July, 1956, issue. Alfred Adler put an emphasis upon understanding the dream in terms of the feelings it symbolized, although he had no systematic categories for mood and feelings, and tended to constrict his attention to features of the dream that accentuated his polemical differences with Freud. It is interesting, however, that he used feelings as a way to reduce emphasis upon repression, the mechanism so central to psychoanalysis.

esteem and security. Ultimately the thought behind the procedure and the procedure itself will be refined by dealing with those who respond to the device with some novelty and lack of improvement.

The research serves to make clear, in any event, why enforced isolation and coerced "instant" integration both make for damaged character. In the first case, there is no available memory material of the appropriate others to allow for correction of the faulty self-image arising out of isolation, except imaginary or "screen" memories. (Indeed, false positive images of the self can develop this way.) In the latter case, the memory material is thick with negative and deprivational exchange. Character damage can be lessened most, however, when the variety of persons contacted are wide rather than narrow, and when the initial contacts are more indulgent than deprivational and, hence, deprivational perspectives are less easily and readily maintained toward those defined as different from the self.[30]

In this regard, there is some reason to believe that prejudice acts to soften the impact of failure. As the American Negro, like the stream of other ambivalently accepted persons before him, is provided with reasonable opportunity to demonstrate merit, the symptoms of character disorders, including somatic ones, may sizably increase, for a deprivationally geared and prejudiced society can no longer be used as an excuse to lower security and self-esteem. The responsibility for dreaming and for making good on dreams will intensify—and, with it, less "realism" of any and all excuses either for not striving toward such

[30] The Arnspiger technique allows one to "place" memories that support self-esteem in various age periods of the life history, as well as to categorize the type of figures entering into the memories at each age period in terms of their conventional value role in society. There is some evidence to believe that extremely neurotic subjects have few memories before early adolescence, while psychotics tend to be overwhelmed by the appearance of very painful memories from very early childhood which have little or no bearing upon the current situation in which they find themselves. The memory features of the normal person is selective—*i.e.,* he tends to choose from among all the age periods those memories which best bear upon the current situation in which he finds himself. With a selective group of students, I have extended the technique developed for life history memories to cultural memories. Fifty remembered events in American history were chosen by each American student and, then, subjected to much the same corrective procedure, with the added change of the student first having to choose whom he identified with in each remembered event. There was a marked change in cultural self-image induced by the procedure and, generally, more sanguine future expectations for America.

high character intentions or for endless procrastinating under the fear of possible failure. Some crosscultural data that I have seen tends to support the idea that, as opportunity *improves* for any group from a prior low state, rises of character disorders, such as suicide, appear. The intervening factor seems to be a faulty self-esteem proportional to the heightened dream, where "excuses" for refusing fully to entertain the dream or make good on it become less and less realistic. Women, for instance, show more symptoms—such as increasing suicide rates—in cultures where they are achieving more equality. A potential factor operating in such cases may be the attempt to "ape" or "imitate" the way men play roles long closed to women, when the roles are opened to them, instead of developing a unique feminine style of conduct. There is much speculation at present that women may fast be returning to the prominent positions in all institutions in society which they are often alleged to have occupied in early history, and when doing so, will transform institutional life toward harmony and affinity and away from competition and egocentricity by adopting a pattern of complete selflessness. The symptoms reported may be merely the temporary "costs" of moving from one state to another, where transitional periods are characterized by "aping" stereotyped male patterns (or using femine "guile") due to self-esteem disorders. In short, the possibilities that promote more freedom to move upward in one's level of consciousness anywhere in the social structure for groups or for persons, are likely also to increase frustration initially for them. Character is indexed by whether they make use of the increased possibility and how they handle obstacles to the dreams such possibility promotes. Self-esteem must be maintained at high levels to do both well—to dream and to actualize the dream at ever higher levels of conciousness. Those higher in the process, due to opportunity and the ability to overcome barriers, can reach back to take along others with them. In so doing, they create an environment in which they themselves can rise still higher, because the damaged self-esteem around one ultimately puts limits on the degree to which one's own may grow. Only a false sense of high self-esteem can continue to rise, if it is purchased by damaging the self-esteem of those also striving to grow with and by one, when using indifference or actual negative attitudes toward them.

Children and students ultimately become social scientists. The processes we have been surveying pertain, therefore, to them, both in terms of discovering disorders of self-esteem and correcting them. Every character flaw at work among social scientists is traceable in principle to a deprivational memory system they harbor. Indeed, there is reason to believe that it is mood and feeling that shape what memories we selectively choose to recall among the millions we store and, hence, mood and feeling which give support to high or low self-esteem. We tend to remember past events that "fit" into current mood complexes and ignore all the rest. Without understanding what positive and negative mood patterns are representative or exceptional among those circulating in social science circles, we are without an essential key to unlock the door to the way past socialization is being carried forward and permitted to distort and disorder the current flow of social science laws by the way experience is selectively retained to shape inquiry. It is to such matters we need now turn.

IX. *The Multivalued Personality: A Social Science Ideal*

There are two related processes by which character develops and in which language plays a role. One is more or less "unintended." Thus a child may develop the same evaluation of foods as a parent, without the parent wishing to have that evaluation pattern appear in the child. We call such processes that go on, more or less unconsciously, "socialization." However, we also include within that major rubric more intentional processes called "education"—*i.e.,* where during wartime, for instance, we wish to inculcate with conscious intention a positive evaluation of certain types of food that are plentiful in place of those that are scarce and which were previously preferred. As character refers to value preferences, it is clear that it is formed by unconscious processes subsumed under "socialization," as well as by those complementary processes we call "education." Ideally, character education seeks to bring more and more of the unconscious process of character formation and expression into the light by making it intended and understood rather than allowing it to go on "outside of consciousness." Adelaide Johnson [31] has put forward the key hypothesis, however, that

---

[31] See her article on "Juvenile Delinquency" in *The American Handbook of Psychiatry,* edited by Silvano Arieti, Basic Books, New York, 1959.

unconscious processes of socialization of character are really *unconsciously intended* by the socializer, despite the latter's disapproval of the character that emerges from the socialization regime. She has buttressed the hypothesis with very impressive evidence. Parents and adults have acted toward the young in a way which makes delinquency what the elders appear to be calling for. Indeed, one could extend her hypothesis to whole societies, as I have in a paper on the juvenile delinquent as a decisionmaker,[32] *so that delinquent patterns arising in a society can be viewed as what groups in conflict (such as conflicting class groupings) unconsciously intend as the character outcome of their conflict,* acting as groups do upon and through socializers. We have all subtly participated in the decision process unwittingly or wittingly to create the delinquency among the young we sometimes abhor when it is witnessed. Every adult is a socializer until proven "innocent." Perhaps the turmoil among students at our higher institutions of learning is exactly the kind of character expression we, as educators, in our conflict with other groups in culture, unconsciously wish to bring out in them, as the parents in the Johnson study are shown to do. Be that as it may, the point emphasized here is that character education strives to make much, much more of character development and outcome a matter of insight, both on the part of individuals and groups, rather than resting content with letting it go on in ignorance and at the remote periphery of attention.

It is precisely here that language plays so key a role. We are more likely to notice what we have "a name" for and the kind of "names" we have shapes what we do notice. The import of this idea is that, *unless we have names for all the value experiences in a society, we shall run the risk of having some part of character development operate outside of consciousness.* It is for this reason that those of us interested in character education have been working with an economical but comprehensive list of value categories. The striving to be nonselective disciplines us to leave no important value in society outside of any partial scrutiny of character. We start not with instincts and physiolog-

---

[32] See my paper delivered to the Fifth International Congress of Criminology, Montreal, September, 1965, called "The Delinquent as a Decision-Maker: A Depth and Scope Analysis." The paper grew out of the monitoring of dreams of youth (in trouble with authority) within a sleep laboratory. The dreams were then studied for their decisionmaking characteristics, and related to sociological data about the subjects.

ical units of desire but with the most advanced institutional outcomes of civilized man. When these institutions are surveyed, we find we can list their goals in terms of eight values: *power, enlightenment, wealth, skill, well-being, affection, rectitude, and respect.* The appendix provides systematic definitions of these terms. Character can be considered to be "governed" in individuals by any one (or more) of the values.[33] Language learning shapes such different "internal governments," and language expresses such character governments once they have been stabilized. It can, too, shape and reflect farseated changes in character that are dramatic and "emotional" or crisis-ridden in nature. Indeed, one of the surprises of a study[34] I have done on children's reactions to the assassination of President Kennedy was how stable coalitions of mood and imagery in relationship to the Presidential figure were so disrupted by the event that "emotion" was not the worst index of a character shake-up. Instead, the very soma was thrown into shock in many cases, often without much immediately refined feeling and with only confused imagery flowing through the mind. There appeared to be much more stable sentiments built up toward President Kennedy among the very young than there had been, for instance, around President Roosevelt, if we can take the difference in how "noticeable" young children's reactions were to both deaths, equally strongly felt by the adult populace. In this sense, every adult "public" figure that enters into the life of a child, no matter how less intimately than a parent figure, may nonetheless play the role of socializer and, hence, shape character. It would repay our attention to consider to what degree the mass media, and more intimate socializers, provided language in connection with the recent Presidential assassination that could have given it any beneficial as compared to damaging effect upon the character of young persons, providing for character education rather than uncon-

[33] Thus we may have the economic man in whom wealth considerations are paramount, the religiousizing personality in whom rectitude considerations are paramount, and so on, through all of the values, as each governs the rest in hierarchical order.

[34] See my paper delivered to the Conference on "Children's Reactions to the Death of the President," sponsored by the Albert Einstein College of Medicine in April, 1964, and called "A Public Event as a Socializing Agent: Case Study of Pre-Adult Reactions to the Presidential Assassination." The psychological reactions of children and adolescents to a crisis in national authority were taken as providing some insights into "internal governments" of personalities at various points of approaching mature years.

scious character outcomes.[35] Certainly, the use of poetry in connection with the Presidential death seemed to be unusually great among both socializers and the young (despite our American culture reputedly being "nonpoetic"), which suggests a language process at work much closer to "feeling recognition" than customary.

If we are to broaden consiousness, in any event, we must audit how much of all our language in socializing young persons overconcentrates upon some values and underconcentrates on the others, as well as audit all the language young persons begin to use in terms of how much it overexpresses some values and underexpresses others. In a democratic society, character education must fit a democratic constitution. A democratic character is *multivalued* rather than *monovalued*. This does not mean that some one value (or a few of them) does not govern all the rest in each individual so as to produce distinctive and individualized personalities. We want to encourage in a democracy rigorous pursuit of *specializations,* all types of "internal" governments that vary one from the other in the key value of the whole. However, we do not want to produce character types that have little or nothing *in common* with all the others and, hence, can only "impose upon" rather than "take account of" the other "specialized" character types. Multivaluedness results when we interact with all the diverse types, and expect to continue to do so in the future, and in both instances with some realistic minimally coercive success. Such diversified interaction across character specializations helps produce more insightful individuality, not more unthinking conformity, for it calls attention in the self to what is present in the "others," present more weakly or more strongly, as well as directs attention to the opposite arrangement. What

[35] There is some reason to believe that a life and death crisis surrounding the Presidential figure appears every twenty years in American life with rhythmic regularity. Insofar as violence toward the Presidential figure is a result of socialization, there may be some intergenerational unconscious process with regard to building *climates of character* that "erupt" in violations of public order in American life, especially when one considers that childrearing norms are constantly changing and "new" norms may be imperfectly incorporated among those experiencing the full norm shift in their socialization interactions. Such a view would require us to broaden our vision so as to see violent fantasies widely circulating toward public authority figures, out of which overt expressions of violence emerge, and to assess rises and falls of such dimensions of feeling and fantasy in relationship to socialization experiences of norm changes within each generation of citizens.

America has prided itself on has been a public school system that purports to do something just of this nature. Young persons of different classes, different interest groupings (such as religious and racial ones), different subcultures (such as immigrant groups), and different personalities (introverted and extroverted) with different degrees of crisis (parental divorce or death) in their lives—all were supposed to meet together to "pool their minds" in the public school classroom that passed on to them a common heritage. Distinctive character patterns went along with these predisposing differences and the interactions were often viewed as beneficial to the sharpening and sharing of values preferred by each. Any realistic look at urban education in America, and not *only* in the past, demonstrates quickly with what wretched imperfection such a vision has been actualized. Indeed, part of the function of "Educational Parks" which are now on the horizon of urban education may be that of finding congenial, effective ways in which the original image of democratic schooling can be more fully actualized, although so far the curriculum and pairing of youngsters within such structures gets much less attention than the physical aspects of the structures themselves. They promise to revolutionize character education, if planned with democratic character in mind as a deliberate outcome.

In any event, the task of education is to bring insight and understanding to a larger proportion of socialization processes, so many of which ordinarily go on outside of consciousness. What we call "the unconscious" is probably only what has passed through consciousness too rapidly and quickly without concern for meaning. Building a language awareness of all values that go into the social processes that mold and express character can reduce the worst of such thoughtless influence. At present, psychoanalysis has no systematic way of handling values. Hence, it produces only *random* results upon the character of a people, emphasizing *mechanisms,* that can cut across all values (we can "project," for instance, benevolence as well as malice), quite apart from *intentions* or *outcomes.* As part of such a perspective, we need to analyze even nonverbal languages for the way value meanings are represented in them.[36]

---

[36] The heightened awareness of animal languages as contained, for instance, in Adolph Portman, *Animals as Social Beings,* The Viking Press, New York, 1961, tends

Personality can be differentiated from character as including *how character is expressed*. It is not enough to have "good" character and a multivalued perspective. Without an effective way to actualize it in all interpersonal relations involving any other character types, both for favorable outcomes to the self and others included in the perspective, character signifies nothing of any known operational importance. The man of integrity who runs away from any discomforting confrontation with those he abhors may be a fine person within limits—but to limit oneself in this way is gradually to weaken integrity. One's good reputation is being acquired at the expense of others "excluded" from its test and assessment.

Character is also the way by which *personality is evaluated*. All of the operations of the individual are continually being assessed in terms of the outcomes they produce upon others (or the self) and these outcomes are then compared with the dominant patterning of conscious intentions. By millions of such social transactions, a style is built up which becomes characteristic of the personality. Often we can most quickly notice the dominant value that governs character by watching a person's gestures, use of the face, body posture and walk, and, of course, voice characteristics.[37] The affection personality may have a warm, clinging, seductive voice even when speaking of murder and money. Style is often taken as "the mark" of a man. But the content of his language is also his "mark." Indeed, it is often *the discrepancy* between style-value characteristics and the preponderant value-content of what is being linguistically expressed that gives us strategic clues to *character disorders*. A strategic hypothesis here is that *the more mono-valued the character structure, the more discrepancy there will be be-*

---

to accentuate the way other than traditional signs can function as sign substitutes to convey values. When such materials are value analyzed, it appears all human values operate at the animal level, with the possible exception of respect. The latter value often appears to be peculiarly "human," at least to the extent that is highly elaborated upon by us and even though it may still be imperfectly integrated in existing personality and culture. However, the play of attention in animals may be a primitive form of the respect value operating at subhuman levels.

[37] Some indications will be found discussed in *Style in Language*, Massachusetts Institute of Technology and John Wiley, New York, 1960, edited by Thomas A. Seobok. A little known exploration is that of Paul V. Moses, *The Voice of Neurosis*, Grune and Stratton, New York, 1955, in which voices are "coded" for style characteristics bearing upon character and value.

tween style and content, when the personality is observed carefully and in diverse situations. Style is, of course, a "nonverbal" language and, hence, we are comparing language systems at some odds, or integrated with, each other in the same personality (or, for that matter, the same group, because we can speak of "national character" as Alex Inkeles has demonstrated so masterfully).

We have seen that character education concerns the ordering of the flow of moods and images, so that preferred intentions are allowed to govern all other intentions. The monovalued personality carries this process to the extreme of not including, even weakly, within the internal flow, values which are *not highly preferred* but which are *relevant* to the situation. The multivalued personality is more likely to allow all relevant values to flow through his subjective awareness, however much he, too, selects some one (or more) preferred intentions to govern the rest.

If the meaning of character education is so taken, we can then ask: how does education as a whole differ from character education? The answer lies, no doubt, in the possibility that *some teaching and learning practices may involve no procedure or outcome which assists the learner to order his subjective events in any different or clearer way than he had previously.* Indeed, much of the charge about a state of "imbalance" in social science, both as a procedure and as content with which we began, can be reformulated as saying that too much of our own self-education in social sciences is at present education which has little or no explicit concern with providing an internal order to our subjective events that improves upon whatever patterns or order it was we initially brought to our social science training.

Such judgments seem too harsh, in any such wholesale form. No doubt, there is in the process of becoming a social scientist *some* changing order in experience introduced. The way in which this comes about is more like the unconscious processes of socialization, however, than it is like the conscious intentions of education. Concern with mechanism, facts, operations, and the medley of abstract words that are part of social science, may be a disguised way of changing character, much like the way food preferences are transmitted from parent to child. The very escape from value concepts in social science is, thus, in the service of value transmission in an unwitting way, under the guise of operational or mechanism analysis. Moods and images are being selectively highlighted within (or dimmed from) internal inspection by the categories of language that service a supposedly "value-free" social science orientation. In such a case, if what is called social science education amounts to something more than "mere words," it *is* shaping character, because it affects the arrangement of subjectivities. But this shaping process is probably *very random,* so that each branch of the social sciences (and even each "school" within each branch) is getting a wholly *different* order of feeling and vision about the social process, with only a minimum chance to reduce the differences by intensive interactions across branches and between schools of thought. The point is that any education of any meaningfulness cannot help but shape character, whether it chooses to or not. Even more, it is nonsensical to call anything "education" that is not a *conscious intention* to modify character. Nothing "merely semantic" is involved here. Teaching is observable, along with the conscious and unconscious dimensions of it. Learning is observable, along with the meaningful or meaningless evaluation of it by students. Character traits that go into the teaching and that are part of the outcome of learning are observable. We are clearly dealing, therefore, with pragmatics, with a conditioning process that can be studied by research quite easily.

It is important here to remind ourselves that if there is any such phenomenon as "public order," it is carried by personalities in their interactions with each other. The "internal order" of the subjectivities of such interacting individuals, when they match, is all that can be meant by "public order." Common expectations about value processes are shared by these "matched" internal orders. The "public order" in legal documents may not be the effective "public order" when examined empirically by social psychology. Furthermore, the internal order produced by social science training may not do much for the character of the person being trained to make out of him any outstanding exemplification of public order. No argument is being made here for the support of the *status quo.* On the contrary, there is reason to think law is now practiced by authoritarian personalities—who use law not for purposes of extending justice in the service of democratic principles, but rather for the shabby purposes of protecting existing elites within democratic societies, regardless of how much they practise democracy.

The work of Weyrauch [38] has brought such problems squarely to the fore of attention of legal circles.[39]

In a different way, when social scientists put technical matters over and above value clarification and integration in society and in their own lives, they, too, act to support a *status quo* situation. One of the reasons social science has survived, so many cynics believe, is that it has so often been concerned with the trivial. Yet in both legal and social science circles, it is quite possible to have "naked power" effects, when routine word manipulation and technical concerns of measurement do unwittingly modify character so that it departs not only from a *status quo* but *in a direction still further from an exemplification of our constitutional perspectives*. This matter has been discussed elsewhere.[40]

These remarks clearly have a positive direction: How can *all* of education take on the character, and diffuse it to those exposed to it, that is in line with the principles of our democratic constitution? The problem is certainly vast. Here, I wish to concentrate upon Freud's insight that all serious and sound modifications of education begin with the self and the profession identified with the self, our emerging—but not quite mature—social science. We must learn to educate by *being* what we advocate.

X. Linguistic Patterning of Social Science

The flow of imbalance in our social science development is to be corrected, so we have previously been led to believe, by *self-study* of

---

[38] Professor Walter Weyrauch has used psychoanalytic method to deepen value analysis of representative members of the German legal profession in his *The Personality of Lawyers*, Yale University Press, New Haven, 1965. The personality predisposition he sees at work as a result of socialization and professionalization is an intense need to maintain the *status quo*, no matter what the culture, and all values are used to this overriding end.

[39] There appears also to be a countervailing personality type attracted to law that one could call "xenophilic" (see Arthur J. Brodbeck and Howard V. Perlmutter, "Self-Dislike as a Determinant of Marked Ingroup-Outgroup Preferences," in *"Journal of Psychology,"* volume 38, 1954) and which tends to gravitate toward criminal law and the defense of criminals. These "types" may be merely opposite sides of the same character coin.

[40] See the concluding section ("Alternatives for Public Order") in Myres S. McDougal, Harold D. Lasswell, and Ivan A. Vlasic, *Law and Public Order in Space*, Yale University Press, New Haven, 1963.

social science as a modern movement, with its array of key figures that broaden and narrow consciousness of the rank and file, often in subtle as well as rather direct ways. As part of this study, the socialization histories of outstanding figures, as Lasswell [41] has demonstrated, can be of enormous usefulness in explaining and deepening insight into adult patterns of playing professional roles. Of course, the pressure of events upon social science from "outside" institutions and public happenings that bear down, sometimes quite demandingly, limit or expand character predispositions as to visible external expression (although not to private fantasied expression perhaps). Any response pattern, such as that of character expression, is, after all, a function of both prior pre-adult training and a current environment playing upon the institution in which one acts. [42] These "outside" influences, however, do not always act evenly across the spectrum of the social sciences, due both to historical defenses built by each field in its evolution and the way these defenses act to "protect" the character predispositions of the members. Although, if we are contextual, the environment of any social science, as well as its own history, complicates matters, it is still possible to trace the expression and growth of character potentials of a membership by

[41] See his "Approaches to Human Personality: William James and Sigmund Freud," in *"Psychoanalysis and Psychoanalytic Review,"* volume 47, 1960, for one example of his many brilliant uses of biographical materials of elite figures. In order to differentiate the *enlightenment* from the *skill* personality in science, a comparison of Tesla and Edison would be particularly instructive, since both came to prominence about the same time, somewhat competitively, with Tesla more subjectively illuminated by the principles of his discoveries, whereas Edison tended to use a more trial and error set of techniques, the difference due perhaps to differing exposures to the academic world, although both maintained relative independence from that world.

[42] In a sense, one never "tests" an hypothesis. Rather, one selects certain predispositions and certain environmental conditions under which an "hypothesis" *comes true,* in the sense of eliciting a predicted response. Hence, all "testing" of hypotheses can actually be conceived *as a policy approach* in which the investigator fails or succeeds in finding the right combination of predisposition and environment by which to get a specified response pattern. Often the predisposition factor of the personality is overlooked in stating results because it is *widespread,* and only when the same hypothesis is tested in a quite diverse culture, does it rise again to the prominence it plays in reality, for the same conditions do not give the same results where culture has molded personality predispositions in quite different ways. In this sense, several alternative hypotheses linking the same environmental condition to differing response patterns could all be true, once the variation in predispositions is accounted for fully. Realization of this process as part and parcel of the social sciences, makes it unthinkable that one can discover "universal" laws, although general laws are, of course, obtainable.

discounting for the shifting environmental influences or showing how environmental pressures are handled differently depending upon character predispositions of individual members or of one social science as contrasted with another.

Key theorists who have made sizable and widely recognized contributions to each value area of social process should be especially studied for contributions to a science of social science. The initial assumption can be made, always subject to intensive empirical check later, that the content interest expresses a key value preference. We can line up theorists this way across the spectrum of the social sciences. In terms of *rectitude,* one can select the prime theorists in psychology, anthropology, sociology, political science, psychiatry, and so on, who have made their major reputations around the study of religion and responsibility in the social process. One can, then, extract from such cases as emerge shared linguistic features. Exceptions will be noted—often traceable to the influence of a common practice within a field of specialization (psychiatrists seldom at present write "mathematically," for instance). Such generalizations can be further crosschecked against another group of theorists whose dominant contribution may be in another value content area, such as social class and other *respect* institutions and patterns of practices. In this way, we can begin to build up the beginnings of self-study of how character shapes language within social science, based upon some first simple assumptions.

Refinements can then be added. Social science has a history—and we can detect changes in the way each value area is linguistically managed over time. In the area of rectitude, for instance, earlier work on the pyschology of religion appears drastically different in both the concepts involved and the style of discussion than more recent discussions, as Louis Schneider and S. Dornbusch have shown.[43] These

---

[43] See Louis Schneider and Sanford M. Dornbusch, *Popular Religion: American Inspirational Literature,* The University of Chicago Press, Chicago, 1958. At present, all religious institutions appear to be undergoing still further deep value changes. The surveys we have indicate that America is one of the most religious nations in the world, so we would expect to find reverberations of this process within social science thought diffusing from stirrings in religious institutions. When one studies the "fads" in motivational analysis in social science, one notices how each type of drive has arisen at a time when it was a major component of a public issue. Thus, the *hunger* drive was emphasized during the depression; the *aggressive* drive during the rise of fascism; the *anxiety* drive as America was drawn into World War II; the *dependency*

historical changes often reflect socialization changes in the personality specialized to rectitude—and to enlightenment about rectitude.

Shifts of such sorts may, however, also reflect recruitment changes, rather than only socialization changes. Thus it is possible that earlier work in a given area of value was more likely to emerge with some distinction by those coming from one culture or subculture, whereas later work reflects the movement of a new cultural or subcultural group into the value area. Earlier work may have been done by upper-middle-class individuals, whereas later work emerges from lower-class upwardly-mobile persons. Women may have dominated later, whereas men did earlier, in the value area. Those from more conventional religious backgrounds may have been part of the earlier theorists and researchers, whereas later the more "unusual" religious backgrounds may send members into the field. The inhibited and overcontrolled personalities may have gradually been replaced by more impulsive types later. Those with severe crises in their lives (early parental death, or adolescent victimization) may have given rise later to those with little history of crisis in their socialization. All such differences in background can be subsumed under the five general categories of *culture, class, interest group, personality,* and *crisis.* It well may be that a character structure specialized, let us say, to rectitude content in the adult years will be relatively rarer in one sociological socialization position than in another at any one time (or even over time). Hence, the shifts uncovered may point to linguistic changes that are due to an unusual route of entrance. The linguistic variables associated with the "unusual" sociological position may be carried into the value positioning within social science to "transform" thinking within that content role.

The systematic analysis we have been outlining thus far has involved three of five forms of problem-solving: *goal thinking, trend thinking* and *condition thinking.* All three help to refine self-analysis of social

---

drive with prolonged separation of families during the war; the *conformity* drive during the McCarthy period; the *achievement* drive during the space race with Russia. In short, all of this nonpolicy and detached, academic research interest is unwittingly responding to larger public events of immense policy significance. The "unconscious" of social scientists is much more policy-oriented than their theories like to honor. We are about due for some new drive's "fashionable" term—and it may be related to religious crises now stirring.

science with regard to the interactions between language and character. We have been emphasizing, however, primarily how language expresses character.[44] A similar analysis could be made in which *the direction of interest was reversed*. The language we use calls attention to moods and images designated by them, as we have mentioned before. What we do not name, we are less likely to notice, or only to "see" in such a way that it passes too rapidly into "unconsciousness" without our first assessing its significance. Such unrecognized flows in the "stream of consciousness" stand less chance of becoming regular voluntary governors of the internal order of the stream. If we *change* our language, our character is likely to be shaped by the changes.

Our concern in such a reversal will be to add to our forms of thinking that of *projective* and *alternative* thinking. If our systematic analysis of trends and conditions suggests that a given field of value concern is developing in such a way that it is slowly losing effective contact with the other value fields,[45] it may be that, without intervention, the projections ahead will predict that the situation for us will worsen and communication across that value field and others will grow increasingly problematic. Given such dangers to our own multivalued character as a newly emerging group with a distinctive scientific culture, it is possible to think of revising language systems operating in the value area now in danger of "splitting off" from the rest, and of giving more attention to language elaboration in the rest of the value areas that accentuate the value area in danger of moving apart in isolation. No doubt, any uneven configuration of development and interchange among the value areas is supported by a host of nonlinguistic factors not quick to undergo modification. Yet, particular personalities can always be found who are willing to move in countervailing power directions in the interest of the whole community of minds, facing resistance to linguistic change with benevolent compassion and vigilant

[44] For some of the ways in which intentions and language express value tendencies associated with power intentions and outcomes, see *The Language of Politics* by Lasswell, Leites, *et al.*, The Massachusetts Institute of Technology Press, Cambridge, Massachusetts, 1965.

[45] Any person can perform this assessment for himself as part of his profession. A technique for so doing is given in the essay "Self-Observation: Recording the Focus of Attention," in Harold D. Lasswell, *The Analysis of Political Behavior*, Routledge & Kegan Paul, Ltd., London, 1948.

observation of empirical details. Indeed, part of the training of social scientists ought to consist of some preparation for occupying roles that require wide identification plus opportunities for developing viewpoints that correct group flaws with a minimum of coercion but against opposition. As Dentler once put it,[46] men to be "good" must surmount institutional conditions—and in so doing, learn to reconstruct institutions, preferably by "insight."

The continuing program of self-study of social science as a whole, as well as of any discipline within it, is meant to discover and correct gross departures from multivaluedness. Perhaps one matter of style deserves special consideration, among the many other dimensions of linguistic patterning having to do with values that will come to the fore within such a program. Mood and feeling may dominate imagery or imagery may dominate mood and feeling, so that the "internal governments" of individuals or groups can be differentiated in such terms. The referential pattern of moods and feelings is likely to be very diffuse, so that all objects in the environment, including the ego itself, are made to enter into the mood being entertained, when mood and feeling dominate a style of awareness. On the other hand, the mind may seize upon a certain part of the environment for concentration through imagery, allowing no shift of mood or feeling to distract one from such selective attention and utilizing any mood shift to maximize clarity about the field selected for fixation of attention. A character described as "romantic" is likely to be the mood-dominated one and the styles may be congenial to it that are like, for instance, those of "free association." A character described as "classical" is likely to be an image-dominated one and the styles associated with "logical analysis," for example, may be congenial to it. Intermediate character types who integrate or alternate between the two other types can, no doubt, be located. These intermediate types may be responsible for corrections in the extremes to which the other types can go, perhaps by highly refining the observation of mood and feeling or by the invention of new logics. Precision

[46] See his "Can Men Learn to be Good?", a paper prepared for the Conference on Science, Philosophy and Religion, discussion at Lake Mohonk, May 22–24, 1964. The attempt to "institutionalize" the reform of *other* institutions can, however, bring out *the very characteristics in the former* one is "warring against *in the latter,* resulting in a "confused" perspective toward where one is going with reform and a resulting instability of effort arising from internal conflict.

and suggestiveness in the use of language would probably be associated with the two diverse character types centered around classical and romantic attitudes. While we are dealing here with *mechanisms* of preference for mood or imagery, and not with value choices necessarily, there may be at any time in the flow of research pertaining to any value a movement toward or away from classicism or romanticism and sudden appearances of intermediate types of thought. Generally, shifts toward romanticism might be expected to be associated with the discovery of new value connections among values and with the exhaustion of classical ways of examining any one value in the social process, whereas shifts toward classicism one would expect when many new connections had been established and they were in need of better and more nearly precise formulation and evaluation. Intermediate phases might be taken to develop with regard to any value when many intense value conflicts had been discovered relating to that value. Hence, interest in these shifting styles, while actually a matter of observing mechanisms, could nonetheless be of use in giving us some idea of stages and problems in the development of multivaluedness with regard to each value specialization.

XI. Myth and Mood in Social Science

While our discussion of the linguistic patterning of social science has been concerned with detecting and modifying flaws in group character around departures from multivaluedness, it has not particularly emphasized the study of mood and feeling, except with regard to mood mechanisms associated with stages of movement toward or away from multivaluedness. It is now possible to add this key concern. There are two major ideas by which to do so. Every theory can be looked upon as a myth, where the word "myth" is *not* used in a pejorative sense but only to describe the key terms by which the world of social process is conceived and by which basic meaning is discovered at work within that world. The second key idea is that, once theory is taken as myth, it is possible to see that mood and feeling enter into all myths in the sense of making them emotionally compelling, by graphically concretizing them through empirical application.

What do we mean by a myth? Every myth can be taken to be a

fantasy, some highly elaborated and others only sketchily presented. What we call reality is a shared fantasy or myth. Myth has three basic components: *doctrine, formula,* and *miranda.* Doctrine is composed of the most generalized visions associated with key symbols of a myth that gives a basic picture of the world to which the myth relates. Formula are the "if, then" statements—the laws or rules—that support the generalized visions. They usually allow for statements of conditions under which they do *not* hold, and hence, have contingency characteristics. Lastly, miranda consists of all those particular examples that illustrate both doctrine and formula, giving us vivid and dramatic examples of what is otherwise referred to more abstractly or vaguely.[47]

Every theory has all three components. There are always key symbols that are associated with some general vision of the world. There are the detailed "laws" generated by this vision which tend to support the outlook. And, there are, finally, the numberless cases, experiments with and surveys of particular persons, that illustrate the laws and generalized visions. As we move from doctrine to miranda, we move from the abstract to ever increasing detail and concreteness. It is around this last component of myth that mood and feeling are likely particularly to dominate.

Some of my own research on the influence television has upon the lives of people [48] has helped to clarify some of these points. It is more usual than not to set television apart from reality as composing "a myth world." Myth is usually used, when so doing, to refer to whatever the

[47] In conjunction with a survey of pre-adult and adult reactions to television in which I am participating at the Center for Urban Education, I have written several programmatic papers that many have found useful in understanding media in our contemporary lives. Two of these are "The Measurement of Myth in Media Materials" and "Notes on Research as Myth Analysis," December, 1966. The entertainment components of the media consist of all those heroes and villains who exemplify in a particular way what it feels like to live in conformity with (or in violence of) a more general set of rules and world view associated with an abstract formula and doctrine.

[48] Television acts for social myth as a whole in the same way the reports on interviews or experiments act for theory as a whole. Furthermore as the key terms of social myth and theories about human behavior can often be found to be similar, and will become increasingly similar as social science provides a new culture, it becomes difficult to maintain clearcut boundaries between entertainment and learning. Furthermore, there may be greater equivalence between the "technics" associated with providing attractive media entertainment and those associated with obtaining compelling knowledge from the interview and experiment than we now choose even to suspect.

speaker does not consider "his" reality. But such judgments tell us as much about the myth of the speaker as they do of the truth or falsity of what is being judged. It seems infinitely more useful for television research to adopt a less judgmental and a more descriptive approach to the study of television as a myth. If one does so, it becomes apparent that most (not all) of television programming consists of but one component of myth—*i.e.,* miranda. Rather than pitting that one component against the rest of "reality," it is possible to see television and reality interacting, in the sense that dramatic entertainment programs provide *illustrations* for doctrine and formula circulating widely in other portions of social process. The programs provide negative and positive illustrations of the meaning of these more abstract components of myth in terms of heroes and models that exemplify the "teaching" at a level where one can *get a feeling* for what it is like to *live one's life* in terms of a myth. Indeed, if one carefully content-analyzes most entertainment programs on television, one discovers traces of the doctrine and formula within the program to which it is linked as miranda. Given this perspective, it becomes exceedingly difficult to separate television from the real world, because together they are building up a mythic perspective, and how any one component of that environment can do so depends upon what all the rest are doing. Dealing with television by itself—and certainly as "in opposition" to reality—simply does not allow us to understand a total pattern of which the endless media details are only a part and from which totality they often derive their meaning. When this way of tuning into the public media is adopted, furthermore, it becomes possible to understand more fully why people spend so much time with so much we consider dull in television programming. They are strengthening an outlook on life at the doctrine and formula level through repeatedly feeling their way into it in terms of graphic and dramatic illustrations of the abstract features of the outlook. There may, of course, be a myth for every value, as well as a myth that deals with all values and their interrelationships. In any event, the role of miranda is to drive home support for a total myth at the feeling level, whereas doctrine and formula tend to be less obviously specialized to feeling and more to imagery. Miranda gives a pattern of feeling that supports and makes meaningful at deeper levels the imagery promoted by doctrine and formula.

Furthermore, miranda is not necessarily offered as "truth," but as an illustration of the more abstract components of a myth. It serves to clarify the general myth, to give a way of living or embodying it, not to "prove" the myth.

As Mannheim [49] long ago brought to our attention, myths vie with each other for authority. Indeed, he looked upon myths which supported a current elite, even a scientific elite, as "an ideology." Counterposed to such myths, there were those of challengers of elites, circulating a body of ideas that were spoken of as "utopias." There are those who believe that the role of the artist in myth change can be particularly strategic, often making politics in any orderly sense well nigh impossible, for the artist keeps experimenting at the miranda level with new myths in which the doctrine and formula may not yet have become elaborated and stabilized. Hence, tension is being intensified totally at the feeling level. In this process of the circulation of ideas, utopias became ideologies and ideologies took on utopian characteristics over time as differing groups fell from and rose to power.

If we now look at scientific theories with this general analysis of myth as a background, it is clear that it takes a certain amount of time for any new theory acting as myth to be elaborated as miranda. Much of the cry for "operationality" is often only a cry for allowing the listener "to feel what it means" to entertain the doctrine and formula of a new myth that has not yet been sufficiently dramatized by application to many cases. The miranda that supports the whole has not yet been thoroughly developed through endless research elaboration. One discovers, too, at scientific meetings of social science groups how much time is spent in such *feeling exchanges* around the latest research studies ("facts") that operate as miranda for such groups, much as television does for the public at large. It is an exchange of anecdotes, similar to that regarding media programs, an exchange rich in feeling —and often thin in doctrine and formula in an explicit way. It is at this factual, operational level that mood and feeling most operate in social science and, hence, where value is most likely to be smuggled in,

[49] See Karl Mannheim, *Ideology and Utopia,* Harcourt, Brace, New York, 1936, for the full elaboration of this view. The implications arising from this initial work were further detailed in later volumes, such as *Essays on The Sociology of Knowledge,* Routledge, Kegan, Paul, London, 1941.

even when not honored in the doctrine and formula of the theory.

It is simply not enough, therefore, to audit social science practices for multivaluedness in terms of linguistic patterning alone. We must also investigate what feelings are receiving elaboration at the miranda and research level of fact collection. There are many indications that respect feelings are often confused with affectionate feelings in much research organized around the linguistic concepts of "dependency," for example.[50] And the price paid for the confusion at the miranda level is that the laws circulating in the theory which might otherwise be validated are not confirmed because of no sensitive discrimination of values and feeling at the level of operations. If respect ("attention getting") had been separated out from affection ("warmth") feelings, the laws might appear clearly confirmed. The conditions of setting up a study may, furthermore, evoke some feeling patterns more than others and, hence, lead to confirmation for a law (and a vision of some part of social process) that would otherwise not be validated, had other feelings been evoked by a slight change in conditions. Unwittingly, the researcher has smuggled in values to support his views, by the way he has arranged conditions to evoke selectively one set of feelings more than any other set, where that one set gives results that the others would not give. Yet no awareness of this feeling process enters into the report of findings.

No need is served by endless elaboration of how mood and feeling operate at the level of operationality and fact. The general point about the miranda component of all theories is clear. Our program of self-study that calls for discovering and correcting flaws in multivalued group character must be extended to the miranda level and cannot stop at the level of the key symbols of doctrine or the relations between

[50] See *Patterns of Child Rearing,* Row, Peterson, Evanston, Illinois, 1957, written by Robert R. Sears, Eleanor Maccoby, and Harry Levin. Sears has given repeated attention to the difficulty of measuring "intentions" (or value meanings) although he has, as yet, not moved toward adopting any comprehensive set of categories by which the intention lying in back of any operation or response pattern could be best conceptually captured. If one were to apply all the existent "drive" concepts to any operation or response pattern (and usually they are applied one concept at a time, rather than as a systematic battery of concepts), so many of them would apply to any one response pattern that the current ambiguities in "drive" language would come squarely to the fore and give rise to more systematic value thinking.

abstract variables that enter into formulas. If mood and feeling are also to be included, we will need to extend the program of self-study to how mood and feelings of the scientist get into the miranda of his fact collection and distribution, both directly and in terms of how he evokes mood and feeling in his subjects by the condition he arranges in order to study them. Often this is the "artistic" side of social science.

XII. Anxiety and Character Integration

Escape from the trivial and superficial, whether of the grand theories or of the tidy little detailed studies in social science, is brought squarely to our attention in the quotation from Whitehead with which we began. Our suggestion has been throughout that more attention to character as part of the background of language consciousness will assist us in reducing outcomes that are merely commonplace and trite, however comforting they can be taken to be. It seems possible to add a particularly vivid illustration of this principle that may be especially important for us all to consider and in terms of which we may conclude this discussion.

Freud was led to place a heavy emphasis upon those "crises" in the flow of feelings which we label "emotions"—and, in particular, that singular affect of "anxiety." As Magda B. Arnold has remarked,[51] anxiety appears to be an emotion whose physiological pattern is totally unlike the character of all other emotions. Freud wanted to compare anxiety with fear and, hence, to make it merely a higher level of a *well-being* crisis in the flow of feeling, an emphasis further sharpened by relating it to lack of pleasure associated with sex and the impulse life.

The discovery of "anxiety" is, indeed, a major one. The theory to explain it may be much less worthwhile—and Freud's difficulties in making his explanations somehow "fit" his own experiences with the

[51] See especially the second volume of Magda B. Arnold, *Emotion and Personality*, Columbia University Press, New York, 1960. It is curious that Arnold in her comprehensive work never clearly hits upon the vision that emotion is merely "a crisis" in the life of feeling, a life that otherwise acts to guide intelligence until it is incapable of being further integrated and breaks out as an "emotion," a disturbance in the internal ordering already achieved as routine.

affect, suggest that his theoretical images regarding it never felt altogether right to him.[52] As part of an advanced seminar at the Annenberg School of Communication, students began to make systematic
observations of their moods and emotions—and, in the process, hit
upon some discoveries about "anxiety" that began to make much sense
and which have since proved prepossessing.[53] A continuum emerged
that moved from anxiety to joy. It seemed to be a continuum of
emotion associated with *enlightenment,* and which appeared to have
little or no relevance to any well-being dimension of the sort Freud
searched for in his theories about the affect. Joy, for instance, had little
relationship to indulgence in pleasure—past, present, or future. Nor did
anxiety appear to be associated with deprivations of pleasure. Indeed,
anxiety was often highest when the mechanical pleasures of well-being
abounded in the lives of the students. The relationship instead appeared to be associated with a state of consciousness itself. Joy came
when the significance of one's life seemed to be silently felt and everywhere experienced in the "rightness" of one's images, but particularly
deeds, toward others or even toward the physical environment.[54] Anxiety, on the other hand, was evoked when the meaning of one's life
seemed cloudy and confused and where no action seemed to feel right.
(Perhaps Freud's writings about anxiety are themselves examples of
a state of "joylessness.") In periods of anxiety, there was a feeling of
something "missing" that one could not make a good deal of sense out
of in terms of the nature of the situation one was in, because the
setting was often a very fortunate one. The feeling of "joy" tended to
be wordless, even imageless, because there was no set of "objects"
associated with it or even a sense of having to find such; the feeling of
"anxiety," on the other hand, tended to be a very word-conscious one
and somewhat overrich in bustling images. Joy was often associated
with a sense of being a "natural" meaningful part of the whole

[52] A discussion that particularly calls our attention to such matters is Percival
Bailey, *Sigmund The Unserene,* C. C. Thomas Co., Springfield, Illinois, 1965.

[53] Mrs. Lillian Bregman and Mrs. Carole Brown were two particularly strategic
students in consolidating group findings into useful generalizations in the graduate
seminar to which the study of moods and feelings was central. Mr. Tristan Campbell,
Jr., has put some of these ideas to work in value analyzing music.

[54] Several students reported a strange, unaccountable feeling of "joy" in emergency
situations where they felt in absolute command of themselves and able to avert danger
under harrowing conditions, such as when a car went out of control.

universe—anxiety with having little place or not having a clear position (or still worse, of having an "artificial" position) within the world.

It is premature to put forth a theory that has slowly emerged from this initial group insight. However, it has long seemed to many of us that what we call "consciousness" can be either a mood or an image, rather than some kind of additional subjective factor. If so, "joy" may be one way in which consciousness as a mood is experienced, while "anxiety" may be a major way in which consciousness as a mood is negatively experienced, just as "guilt" is a negative way in which rectitude feelings are experienced. The fact that language in a conventional sense was most often not a necessary part of a state of joy, seems inordinately important, reminding us of all we have heard about "the limits of language"—and, when we contrast the language-consciousness of states of anxiety where internal or external streams of talk were prominent, the "pregnant silence" of the mood of joy takes on a dramatic character. It suggests the kind of consciousness in which the background is never allowed to evaporate by undue emphasis upon what is made foreground—a vivid sense of contextuality at the feeling level which makes all and everything understandable.

Anxiety has long been used as an index of a lack of character integration. The ego in development has endless opportunities for forming alliances and antipathies with every person and group it encounters (my family, my friends, my town, my club, my nation, etc.). Often these multiple selves are only imperfectly integrated, for my family may stand for things my club abhors and my friends think are senseless. The ego is constantly searching for an orientation toward all these possible mergers and resistances which feels right for it. The continuum of anxiety and joy reflects, no doubt, movement away from and toward the right balance of identity in which all becomes less or more meaningful for character as a whole. When found, even momentarily, one has a distinct sense of individuality that integrates all of these demands. Yet, the joy experienced is not traceable to (but, nonetheless, might originate in) a prolonged process of "intellectual" analysis. The character integration appears to be achieved wordlessly.

On this note, I leave the topic at a place where social science may not yet have adequately pioneered. There may be more languages than are dreamt of in our social science categories and our emphasis upon "intellectuality"—and, if there are, it would appear the kind that induces "joy" has the capacity for even more inclusiveness than we have any right to expect from those word-centered ones with which we are most familiar. Perhaps our friends from the Eastern part of the world have contributions to make which can assist us here. I am reminded that many have predicted our world might be moving in the future away from the kind of activism associated with the West toward more internal contemplation, although few have emphasized the role that feelings might play in such a movement as contrasted with the emphasis upon images. The cultural consequences of full integration of the East with the West, as diverse traditions meet and merge, could be *not* a retreat from science, but *a totally new vision of science as character building.* To be a scientist may mean to control feelings of irritation, of impatience, of ego-assertion, of envy, and much else present in the subjective life, as part of character which stands in the way of "objectivity." To be a scientist may mean to develop feelings of compassion, of trust, of courage that contribute to ultimate intersubjective agreement and objectivity. Hence, we may find our concern with "scientific method" has overconcentrated on "rules" of procedure that emphasize "technics," whereas the lasting advances under the symbol of "science" may have come out of good character and a generous government toward feelings. There is much reason at present to believe the actual conduct of scientists is nowhere near what their scientific ideologies make such conduct out to be. By "intellectual" analysis, one may prove and justify anything through word play and games. Using "the language of the heart," one's intellect may be employed to perpetuate and perfect good character. In any event, there is much in the cultures of the East, however mismanaged there, that may help to strengthen the science of the West wherever it strives, not to engage in ego-aggrandizing "self-congratulations," but in expressing and resolving "the Divine Discontent" still at work in it. There is much reason to doubt that the conceptions of "objectivity," East and West, will ultimately turn out to be quite so different as they now look. Indeed, many see in American pragmatism only another form of Eastern metaphysics, which when taken over by mere "intellectuality" helps mask this equivalence and results in an absurd kind of "metaphizzling" with Eastern word play substituted for our own, vitiating in practice what is most cherished in the history of the cultures from which the concepts came.

Perhaps one of the procedures now open to mankind for perfecting the culture that social science will ultimately require for successful world diffusion is one that concentrates upon *conditioning pre-adults not to be conditioned,* a procedure to reduce internal and external coercion as drastically as possible.[55] With a few years, it seems likely that we will be able to evoke *every* value in the form of feeling during infancy by, for instance, exposing infants to musical selections specialized to each feeling form of value within a culture. Along with this, it seems possible that general simple drawn images associated with each value can be isolated. The infant can, thus, be conditioned to experience every value in the form of feeling in association with every "image picture" representing each within the whole array of values, and *vice versa.* The range of experience open to the infant by so doing will permit high multivaluedness at the very start of life—and a more voluntary development of preference or "sentiment."[56] Given this

[55] See my paper prepared for the members of the Conference on Research and Teaching in the Field of Infant Development, Merrill-Palmer Institute, February, 1967, called "Opening Up The Study of Infant Development To Value-Institution Analysis." One is constantly struck by how research on infant development makes minimal reference to adult outcomes, so that, for instance, a study on "reactions to strangers" is dealt with as "a stage" of socialization, rather than creating predispositions for various reactions to strangers at the adult level. Slightly different criteria of the stranger operate in terms of institutions being considered at the adult level, and this helps to "mask" adult outcomes of infant problemsolving.

[56] Every stable person has sentiment—*i.e., voluntary* coalitions of feelings with images of objects. Sentimentality is to be differentiated from this "normal" process by its coercive and involuntary nature—*i.e.,* the coalition of a feeling with an object (or *vice versa*) is the only possible one the subject can consider or experience. The earlier work on character introduced the notion of "sentiment" to handle the patterning and ordering of images and feelings in experience and saw it as an outcome of a learning or socialization process. See, for instance, William McDougall, *Introduction to Social Psychology,* John Luce, Boston, 1926 edition. Unfortunately, the distinction between sentiment and sentimentality is not always prominent in such writings, for so much of it was organized around concern for "instincts." Furthermore, "emotion" was not seen as a "crisis" in the organization provided by sentiments and sentimentalities, nor that a more "emotionridden" personality would be likely to emerge when substituting sentimentalities for sentiments in the socialization process. Much of the anti-Freudianism of these early character theorists, furthermore, seems unfortunate. Every value in the form of feeling can enter into sexual relations and around any object toward which a sexual impulse is mobilized. A study of urban pornographic literature made by students at the Annenberg School of Communication demonstrated, for instance, that about ninety percent or more of the feelings entering the sexuality in such hard-core pornography were those of mere power and well-being, whereas the feelings entering into the frank sexuality depicted by writers such as Edmund Wilson were of a wide and rich value range, so that every value was touched upon as it entered into sexual

early training, later attempts by conventional conditioning techniques are less likely to succeed in inculcating "sentimentalities"—because the internal "responses" (mood and image) are not open to controlled manipulation as easily.[57] What this means is that early education will put heavy emphasis upon what we now think of as "art." But it is actually *character* that is undergoing molding by these artistic exposures. As matters now stand, simple intellectual skills become the first step in an education, before the emerging character has even developed any rudimentary sense of what general directions of values are considered suitable and attractive, because no full environmental opportunity to explore value combinations has yet been given. In this way, skills are passed along from old to young without questioning their relevance to emerging character and value preference. Teachers of Negro children often have this relevance of "intellectual" skills questioned, because no background has been provided which makes such skills "automatically" taken for granted as "the" essential ones for all character orientations. In any event, the crude attempts some of my students have made to apply to their own children (at the very start of a life of symbolic functioning) value materials of this rich artistic nature, promises much for what could lie ahead in education. There is renewed interest,

---

experience. There is every reason to believe the somatic response at every phase of a sexual act varies as the feelings and images at work among the participants within it rise and intensify and become submerged and disappear; this varied, rich flow of feeling and image are a way of valuesharing and shaping or valueclashing. There exists at present no analysis of this process as it affects extreme success in sexual relations during which the soma continues to feel "pleasure" for prolonged periods after orgasm, and as it affects failure such as mechanical orgasm with varying degrees of somatic dullness or pain.

[57] There is a sizable literature demonstrating that exposure to *meaningful* materials, as measured by adult criteria, during the infancy period has quite lasting and powerful effects, even though the infant cannot be said to "know" the meaning of the symbolic exposures in anything like a complete adult sense. Feelings are, of course, *diffuse* (nonspecific) references to the environment or to the self. Hence, much language learning during infancy seems initially centered around "the speech melodies" or "music" used by the speaker rather than the content itself—or around values as communicated by feelings rather than images. Supplementary cues can, however, help clarify content or imagery. What the research indicates is that, even in the absence of supplementary cues, the image does not remain altogether hazy judging by later lasting effects ordered as sentiments. Michael Polyani, *The Tacit Dimension*, Doubleday, New York, 1966, explains such subliminal learning and leads to a theory of feelings in all learning which he fails to bring to the fore. The tacit dimension remains tacit.

at present, in the infant's development, and out of that interest many signs have already appeared that the procedures I have sketched will develop rapidly, if somewhat haphazardly. One cannot help but believe that the "language consciousness" that later appears, among those experiencing such early value exposures, will have more of the rewarding features going with "an expansion of consciousness" than the current state of "the language revolution" has yet made possible by keeping attention off character and off the life of mood and feelings, especially that form which we have called "joy."

Appendix. The Definition of Values and Other Related Terms

Power. Any concern with the giving and getting of a place in decision-making, no matter what the value issues are about which decisions are to be made. Decisionmaking is contrasted with choicemaking in terms of the severity of the deprivations and indulgences that can be imposed.

Enlightenment. Any concern with giving and getting a fuller picture of the whole environment. Hence with understanding and clarifying goals and values at work in the whole context.

Wealth. Any concern with giving and getting goods and services. Money is, of course, only symbolic of ultimate purchasing power.

Skill. Any concern with arranging the available elements into various patterns whether in terms of "beauty" or "utility" or anything else.

Well-being. Any concern with physical and psychological comfort and safety.

Affection. Any concern with giving and getting warmth and intimacy.

Respect. Any concern with giving and getting a place of distinction and of honor.

Rectitude. Any concern with responsibility toward oneself and toward others.

OTHER TERMS

Ego. Any concern with "I" and the "me."

Self. Any concern with the "we" as contrasted to the "they" and as related to the "I" or "me."

Identity. Any concern with relating the "I" and "me" to the "we" or to the "they."

Chapter 15. WHAT IS THE PLACE OF THE MASS MEDIA IN RELATION TO EDUCATION AND THE CHANGING SOCIAL SCENE?

by Louis G. Cowan

No one can dispense with an education directed expressly to the moral as well as the intellectual part of his being. Such education, so far as it is direct, is either moral or religious; and these may either be treated as distinct, or as different aspects of the same thing.

The subject we are now considering is not education as a whole, but scholastic education, as we must keep in view the inevitable limitations of what schools and universities can do. It is beyond their power to educate morally or religiously.

Moral and religious education consist in training the feelings and the daily habits; and these are, in the main, beyond the sphere and inaccessible to the control of public education.

It is the home, the family, which gives us the moral or religious education we really receive; and this is completed, and modified, sometimes for the better, often for the worse, by society, and the opinions and feelings with which we are surrounded.—John Stuart Mill, From his inaugural address at St. Andrew's.

SOME YEARS AGO, Robert Hutchins had some related and very direct observations to make about the mass media (even before television had moved into its present high gear). His position:

In our time, the impact of society, particularly as it makes itself felt through what one calls the media of mass communications. . . . is, I think, the most important factor in moral and cultural development.

I do not see how any educational system can be expected to cope with the comic book, the radio, the motion picture, the slick paper magazine, the sensational press and television. The tremendous skill and enormous resources available to these moral and cultural agencies make them more influential in molding the lives of our people than the whole educational system.

While it is rather commonplace for educators and social scientists to explore "the place of the mass media in education and the changing social scene," the question is seldom turned inward and focused on "the place of *education* in relation to the mass media in the changing social scene." The revolution in communications that is now taking place suggests that this might be a timely, worthwhile exercise.

There is considerable evidence that student involvement with television and radio alone is extensive. Available data also reveals that this is not the case with most educators. The question then arises: should educational decisionmakers get involved? The answer should be "yes."

Thus far, most of the educators seem quite willing to let the media managers operate "where the action is." But, the fact that we now have major changes in the mass media-educational relationships raises the question anew.

Some years ago, President Eisenhower warned of a different complex, the industrial-military complex, and suggested some of the problems that could be emerging. Now, there is a developing new complex (mass media and education) and those concerned with positive educational progress no longer can remain disinterested.

It has been suggested that educators not only examine the mass media but, indeed, become involved. This will require understanding and a sense of the necessary, as well as proper, involvement. Even more, "joining" will require a capacity to master the necessary disciplines. The fact that the question of the place of the mass media is raised at all suggests that there is awareness of media impact on the public and on its values and attitudes.

The statements quoted from John Stuart Mill and Robert Hutchins are but two of many that could be included that recognize the limitations that continue to confront the educational establishment. To paraphrase a well-known political campaign admonition of some years ago: educators may well have to be the "masters" and not the "subjects" of the mass media. This is not as extreme as it might seem since those in the media also are acutely aware of the freshness of thought, taste, and direction that can be important to their own future well-being. Educators may be more welcome than they think.

At any level of education, teachers are aware of the demands for the time of students while they are yet involved in formal education, as well as later. It is interesting to consider the length of time that students are in school—to reflect on the percentage of his life span that is given to formal instruction. For example, Christopher Jencks addressed himself to this point in a recent article on the future of American education. Adapting his own computations, he wrote: "The average American goes to school only twelve years out of almost seventy and" (calculating days and hours of actual school participation) "devotes only about 2 per cent of his lifetime to formal education. . . . . Academically talented or specially fortunate children (are) likely to give more of their lives to educational institutions; often as much as 4 and sometimes even 6 per cent."

Compare this with some rather formidable figures about television and radio set ownership and use in this country. As of this writing, there are approximately 72,000,000 television sets located in something more than 52,000,000 homes.

It is an accepted statistic by broadcasters and advertisers that the average home has at least one set tuned on for six hours per day. Recent radio manufacturing figures report more than 240,000,000 radio sets in this country . . . that there are some 5400 radio stations (AM and FM) offering their listening inducements every day (some statistics on radio listening follow shortly).

Considering these massive figures, it is worth noting that the academic community has retained a unique television position for itself. One personal experience may provide a tiny insight. A while back I was present at a conference attended by fifteen distinguished educators who are part of a well-known academic community. They were asked if they had television sets in their homes. Those who did not own sets were asked why.

Five of those present reported that they own television sets. In all instances they said that they watched only on special occasions (national political conventions, some sports, very little entertainment, some discussion programs, some documentaries). Two of the five owners volunteered that an important motive for purchase was to provide entertainment for baby-sitters. Those not owning sets gave a variety of reasons: "junk," "bad taste," "full of commercials," "waste of time," etc. (After some more detailed questioning, it developed that most of them had little knowledge of television programs, or that they watched television only occasionally at the home of a friend, when something of extraordinary interest was brought to their attention.)

While illustrative, perhaps, this sample of fifteen professors hardly constitutes research. In his significant study, *The People Look at Television,* Gary A. Steiner did work with a properly-selected sample probing at the same general theme. In the book, he writes this summary line: "Academicus obviously watches little, if any, television himself, and certainly does not depend on it for serious information."

Turning it the other way around in this same study, Steiner pointed out that "the average American viewer . . . has no more than a high school education, an annual income of less than $8000" (probably a bit more now since his book was published in 1963) "and he accounts for over three-quarters of all television homes and a still higher percentage of the effective audience at any given time. . . ."

In Steiner's study, which has a great many more facts than can be included here, he asked one particular question that seemed relevant: "Considering all the new inventions, new products and new developments of the past 25 years or so, which—if any—have done the most to make your life more enjoyable, pleasant or interesting?" Some sixty-one percent named television. (Base: Men-100% = 1177; Women-100% = 1246. The sample included as "viewers" the 136 non-owners who view elsewhere, and excluded only the 71 non-viewers who reported they "never watch." Total base sample of 2427 viewers.)

In quite a different, but highly revealing study, Paul Witty of Northwestern University's School of Education reported on some of his findings about children and television ("Science Education," March, 1966). Witty wrote about the Chicago area: "In 1965, almost all children had access to TV at home". Further: "In 1965, the average [viewing] was about 20 hours per week. [A weekly drop of about three hours occurred during the summer.] In the first grade, the average was about 15 hours and rose to a peak of 25 in grade 5. Throughout the investigations, 12–14 hours was the weekly average for high school pupils."

Witty, properly, did not overlook radio in his study. He reports: "Radio still attracts children despite the stronger appeal of TV. In 1965, the pupils in grade 2 stated that they spent about 4 hours each week listening to radio while in grade 5, as in grade 6, the weekly average was about 8 hours. In the high school surveys, students said that they spent about 12–14 hours each week listening to the radio." (There are other sources that doubt that the national average runs that high.)

The high school figures reported by Witty indicate a total of some 24 to 28 hours devoted to broadcasting by the students each week. (It is also possible—and not unknown—for students to turn on their radio and television sets at the same time. Nevertheless, this absorbs a fair amount of non-school time, particularly when many other duties and attractions—not including sleeping and eating—also occupy them.)

There is such a range of statistical material that these few facts must be recognized as only the tiniest fragment out of many quantitative studies. They do tend to indicate, however, that along with the annual sale of hundreds of millions of comic books, hundreds of millions of paperbacks, billions of copies of newspapers, billions of copies of magazines, huge recording purchases, movie attendance, etc. networks of communication can represent considerable modifying societal influences. This assumption was expressed by David Riesman some time ago in *The Lonely Crowd* in his suggestion that the responsibility for character formation in our society has shifted from the family to the peer groups and to what he describes as "the mass media peer group surrogates."

When John Stuart Mill discussed the opinions and feelings that surround us and referred to the capacity of society to modify "moral and religious education," (education for character) communications operated quite differently. Then there was the church, theater, books, a different sort of press and considerable letter-writing. Nothing was even close to the mass media society that we now know, yet his thesis has not been disproved despite the change that we now know or can anticipate. Perhaps one of the best expressions describing the meaning of the power of mass media comes from Professor Dallas Smythe. He sees the mass media as "the agenda setters for our society."

It is within this context that we want to know the answers to these questions, among others:

> What manner of man in what sort of social process do we want to achieve through future years?

> For what are we educating?

> What is the role of those not professionally involved?

Harold Lasswell offers a guide-line through a question that he once asked:

For the future the question is whether education and communication networks will contribute to a double liberation of man; liberation from parochial loyalty and the exploitation of violence, and liberation from the restrictions that spring from the crippling anxieties of elder generations who are uncertain of the adequacy of culture to cope with man's creativity, particularly as encountered in children and young people. A fully consummated communications revolution, if it occurs, will dissolve predispositions that block the way toward universality and diversity.

If there is agreement on these goals, the introduction of scholars into the mass communications process could have a salutary effect.

It is for this point that the journalists and the educators have a great deal in common: diversity of views, willingness to deal with a limited percent, and healthy skepticism are but three of their congenial points.

It may be that now evidence can be forthcoming that the mass media are not wedded to "safe subjects," avoiding what might be considered as transgressions and abjuring support for the established forms and customs, or long accepted and oft-repeated societal myths. This accusation persists particularly for broadcasting and films. It seems to be much less so for newspapers and magazines.

Perhaps a good illustration of response to the "popular" is one that has been given by some broadcasters. They have made clear their position that they operate in a culturally democratic society and that most programming must respond to the majority—those who give the most "tune-in" votes. Put another way, the responsibility of the broadcaster is to give the people what they want—what they choose. (This seems to be more the case with television than radio. There are now approximately 6,000 AM and FM radio stations with limited network feeds. Forced to operate to a large degree out of their own resources as independent (non-network) stations—and faced with intense competition—they offer variety in programming. The general television position, however, led to running battle between the broadcasting establishment and Newton Minow and his successor to the chairmanship of the Federal Communications Commission, E. William Henry.)

The educators' built-in acceptance of diversity and the constant experimenting and re-testing of ideas puts them at some distance from those who frame the broadcasting policies and decide—for reasons stated and unstated—to program basically for popular taste.

This inherent dissimilarity suggests that the main innovations that eventually may produce change will come from the crucible of academic testing and from the "literature"—books, journalism, magazines, broadcasting—that does not rely on "popularity" polls or sales. It is not likely that the mass media in general are going to pioneer social change —the kind suggested by Lasswell—by virtue of the massive dissemination of diverse views. [It is possible, of course, that unanticipated events (great depression, major war) might produce sudden massive changes which by creating new symbols and appeals could affect the mass media output. The question then would be: For how long?]

It is not the purpose of these observations to impose a value judgment saying that the "new" is good and that the "past" is bad, or vice versa. What is intended is re-examination of the enormous effect of the mass media in shaping or reinforcing attitudes that affect the educational process and social change. More than that, they express the view that much of the educational elite no longer can continue to ignore the mass media, particularly with the changes now at hand. If anxieties exist among thoughtful educators, it also is true that anxieties exist among the media managers or decisionmakers. They are aware of the power they possess and they have concerns for the future that their influence is shaping.

At the same time, anxieties exist among the "manipulated" and these include the consumers in the educational system—the students. This generation has been particularly subject to an unending procession of words, sounds, pictures. Coping with a bigness that seemingly cannot be resisted in a society that is simultaneously undergoing rapid physical change has produced its sets of problems.

It has been suggested that there has been developing among students a form of "loneliness"—that the college or university no longer forms the totality for life that once existed. Behavior patterns have been variously described as expressions of "alienation" or "disaffection" or "search for identity."

Student experimentation can be regarded, under whatever label, as anxiety reactions. Not content with being mere spectators and being always on the receiving end, they may test different parts of the social structure even while they are testing their own relationships to reality.

In some instances this process may be relatively easy through participation in certain established extra-curricular activities, being involved, for example, in the traditional areas of participation such as the student council, sports management, long established charitable activities.

There are certain other circumstances, however, that are fraught with problems for them. For example, we are witnessing the participation of university, as well as high school, students in the so-called New Left. Students were a primary force in stirring up the Civil Rights Movement. They are active in peace movements. Others moved into the Peace Corps, Vista, etc.

Their actions often did not comform to the traditions and stereotypes that their parents have accepted and have had reinforced by the media agents of society. There are even certain indigenous cultures that might regard them as "deviants" and not as individuals seeking— in their diverse "testing" ways—a greater understanding of society and of their places in it.

What they are doing is part of the perpetually unfinished business of society, which means that there is bound to be prolonged debate. It has a high priority among educators and communicators. When this is resolved, the students should not be the losers.

We are witnessing, then, developing stages of a new order of relationship between parts of the education and communication institutions. With these continuing problems in mind, there also are certain established circumstances that need to be examined. For example, although the Congress and the Federal Communications Commission long ago took the necessary legislative and regulatory actions to accommodate requests made by some spokesmen for education and television, there has been minimum support from the educational establishment. A great many television channels still remain vacant. No one applies.

It has been a well-kept secret that those involved have been without proper support. Hopefully, all of this will be changed as a result of the Ford satellite proposal submitted by McGeorge Bundy. By virtue of this, a new dialogue began and it is now recognized that unless sufficient funds are made available, the Second Service (Educational TV) cannot ever have much meaning. It now seems that funds will be forthcoming and this Second Service will need the talents and skills of educators. Eventually, it is believed, the impact of this Special Service will have wide and deep effects on all broadcasting, which means that a whole new opportunity for educators will be at hand.

Also, as indicated earlier, there is going to be a major realignment between the professional communications institutions and the electronics community. Here I am referring to the many technical innovations now existing or in prototype or blueprint stages.

Despite all the good-will that now exists, it is not likely that this new accommodation will be accomplished easily. Basically, there have to be widely differing points of view, which means that there will be many problems about the most effective uses of the existing and anticipated technology. Who is going to decide? For what purposes? With what knowledge or experience? These are among the other questions that need resolution if there are to be changes in policy decisions.

There is nothing new about the questions regarding the present educator absenteeism. What is new (and can be effective if this absenteeism continues) is the complex that has been established by the business community with its acquisitions and mergers.

Charles Silberman included a chart of some of the corporate actions in the August issue of *Fortune*. Among those he listed are: RCA-Random House; CBS-Creative Playthings and eleven percent of Holt, Rinehart and Winston; Cowles Communications-Educators Association and College Publishing Corporation; Time, Inc. and General Electric and General Learning Corporation ($35,000,000 investment). One important merger now pending: ITT and ABC. There are a number of others settled or pending. These combinations suggest the various elements now within the orbit of the mass media.

Chapter 16. EXPERIENCE WITH A GRADUATE SEMINAR ON PERSONAL GROWTH

by Willis W. Harman

IN THIS PAPER we address ourselves to the question of how a graduate seminar, aimed at assisting the individual student in the discovery and development of his own potentialities, might be structured and conducted. The discussion to follow stems from experience gained in conducting such a seminar at Stanford University for the past ten years. Rather than describe this particular experiment in detail, however, because each such endeavor will inevitably be the unique individual creative effort of the particular instructor, I propose to discuss the matter in somewhat more general terms.

I. Some Basic Principles

There seem to me to be several basic principles which govern such an effort. One of the most fundamental was enunciated in blunt form by Carl Rogers: *"Anything that can be taught to another is relatively inconsequential. The only learning which significantly influences behavior is self-discovered, self-appropriated learning. Such self-discovered learning, truth that has been personally appropriated and assimilated in experience, cannot be directly communicated to another."* [1] That is to say, the endeavor will be successful to the extent that the leader is a "guide, philosopher, and friend," not a teacher in the knowledge-imparting sense—to the extent that it is a seminar in the root meaning of the word, as a place where birth and growth are encouraged and facilitated.

Another principle is that in adult life the important limitations on the extent to which we realize our potentialities are self-imposed and

[1] C. R. Rogers, *On Becoming a Person*, Houghton Mifflin Co., Boston, 1961, p. 276.

lie in the deepest reaches of the personality. (Consider the crippling effect which a basic conviction of inadequacy, or impotence, or inferiority can have.) It follows, then, that the realization of the individual's highest potentialities come about through a realignment of the personality at all levels. It is a process which involves the feelings as well as the intellect. Hence feelings as well as thoughts—perhaps even more than thoughts—are pertinent agenda for the seminar discussions. This is true in two important ways. In the first place, feelings play an essential role because we have resistance, in the psychoanalytic sense, toward the unveiling of the nature of our highest potentialities. A. H. Maslow speaks of this as "the need to know and the fear of knowing." "Not only do we hang on to our psychopathology (by repression and other similar defenses), but also we tend to evade personal growth because this, too, can bring another kind of fear, of awe, of feelings of weakness and inadequacy. And so we find another kind of resistance, a denying of our best side, of our talents, of our finest impulses, of our highest potentialities, of our creativeness . . . It is precisely the god-like in ourselves that we are ambivalent about, fascinated by and fearful of, motivated to and defensive against." [2] Secondly, the experiencing of positive feelings—wonder, exhilaration, affection toward other group members, delight at a new discovery, etc.—typically accompany the self-discovery process.

A third principle is that the effectiveness of the leader of such a seminar depends less on his academic knowledge of such relevant areas as psychology and the humanities than it does upon personal characteristics such as self-awareness, genuineness, warm acceptance of others, sensitive perception, comfortableness with his own feelings and the emotionality of others, and integrity—upon the extent to which he has traversed the path upon which he would now guide others.

The implications of these principles are that the seminar for the development of human potentialities, while it may be within the academic framework and sanctioned by centuries of academic tradition, inherently has a very different setting and atmosphere from the familiar lecture hall or classroom. Thus, for example, it seems advisable sharply to limit the group size to the fifteen or so which allows for

[2] A. H. Maslow, *Toward a Psychology of Being*, D. Van Nostrand Co., Inc., Princeton, 1962, p. 58.

effective group participation. A seminar with a large table around which all can sit and see one another is a help. Two-hour uninterrupted discussions seem to have a decided advantage over twice as many one-hour periods. If it is feasible, a full-time two- or three-week retreat to a mountain lodge provides a far more advantageous setting than the best that can be arranged on the campus during the regular academic term. A carefully structured, permissive but directed, informality is perhaps a good way to describe the creative atmosphere. The seminar leader needs to be well in touch with his own feelings, and to be comfortable with the expression of strong feelings by others. Examinations, grades, and even some types of term papers seem quite inappropriate to the nature of the endeavor.

The question of appropriateness is sometimes raised—as by one of my colleagues who protested making the "classroom into a psychoanalytic couch." But this comes about because of the historical development of specialized professions which, whatever its inevitability and advantages, has resulted in an artificial fragmentation of knowledge. Thus the three functions of education, psychotherapy, and religion appear in our culture separate and relatively distinct. This may obscure the more important fact that all of them have essentially to do with the recognition and freeing of inner forces that work toward unity, health, fullness of life, and purposeful development toward ever-higher levels of conscious awareness. (And altering a value system is, in a sense, "deeper" psychotherapy than uncovering a repressed sexual drive.) Insofar as these three areas have to do with the individual's discovery of the wondrous possibilities inherent in the self and of what in life he most wants, they are better viewed together than separately.

II. The Self-image View of Personality Change

Before commenting more specifically on how a seminar on the human potentiality might be organized, let us attempt some general remarks about the processes of personality change. We assume that to make genuine progress in the directions pointed to by such declared aims as releasing creativeness, enhancing ability to communicate, increasing degree of self-actualization, improving intuitive awareness and clarity of perception, establishing consistent and authentic personal values, freeing from such inhibiting reactions as inadequacy feelings or inappropriate anxieties, and so on, we must think in terms of rather drastic re-examinations or of alterations in the personality structure.

M. Rokeach[3] provides us with a useful concept for bringing together knowledge about processes of personality change which is found in diverse disciplines and hence discussed in varied specialized jargons. He speaks of the *belief-disbelief system.* By the term belief here is meant, not what the person consciously thinks he believes, but what one would have to infer that he believes on the basis of all that he says and does. (For example, "I love all mankind" might be a claimed belief substantiated by certain obvious actions, but questionable in the light of more perceptive observation.) "Belief-disbelief systems serve two powerful and conflicting sets of motives at the same time: the need for a cognitive framework to know and to understand, and the need to ward off threatening aspects of reality . . . The more closed the belief-disbelief system, the more do we conceive it to represent, in its totality, a tightly woven network of cognitive defenses against anxiety . . . The closed system is nothing more than the total network of psycho-analytic defense mechanisms organized together to form a cognitive system and designed to shield a vulnerable mind." In Rokeach's terms, growth is movement in the direction of the open belief system—open in the sense that any portion of it is available for re-examination for consistency (which consistency includes a tolerance for paradox), and also open to and unthreatened by new data from outside which may prompt revision of beliefs. And this movement is prerequisite to, if not almost synonymous with, realization of one's highest potentialities.

In these terms, central to the personality are the primary beliefs about the nature of the self and its relation to other selves and to the universe in which it exists. This self-image is like the input signal to a feedback control system; the personality and behavior-pattern structure tend to "follow" the self-image. We become as we imagine ourselves to be. "As a man thinketh in his heart, so is he."[4] Thus we can think of personality change as depending upon change in self-image, and of the problem of realization of potentialities as fundamentally involving a change in the person's perception of himself and hence of the possibilities open to him.

[3] M. Rokeach, *The Open and Closed Mind,* Basic Books, Inc., New York, 1960.
[4] *Proverbs* 23:7.

III. Three Processes of Self-image Alteration

There appear to be at least three different processes by which these alterations in self-image and resulting changes in personality have been observed to come about. Understanding of these is valuable for assessing the possibilities and limitations inherent in the seminar situation—also for the individual in coming to appreciate the various approaches which he might give trial.

The first process is oriented toward problemsolving. Here we mean to include most of what goes on in conventional, verbal psychotherapy (individual and group) as well as the dynamics of "T-groups" or "sensitivity training" groups.[5] In essence, the individual is helped to become aware of problem areas in his life—difficulties in relationships, value conflicts, failure to feel "fully alive," and so on—and encouraged to search for the genesis of these, either in a historical sense or an existential sense. Through a meaningful, emotional relationship with another or other persons, and in a supportive environment, he comes to an increased intellectual and emotional understanding of himself. He comes to see that his problems are the direct result of unwholesome beliefs included in his self-image—the belief that he is inherently inadequate or inferior; that his feeling of self-worth depends wholly on what he can acquire by way of knowledge, possessions, position and status, esteem of others, etc.; that his existence is threatened when his beliefs or good reputation or financial affluence are threatened; that he is driven by dangerous urges of sex and hostility which must be kept under control at all times; that the criticism or ridicule of others can "hurt" him; and so on.[6] He sees also that these unwholesome beliefs are the consequences of his interpretation of life experiences which were possible of other interpretations.[7] And "seeing" this in a feeling sense,

---

[5] L. P. Bradford, J. R. Gibb, and K. D. Benne (eds.), *T-Group Theory and Laboratory Method: Innovation in Re-education,* John Wiley & Sons, Inc., New York, 1964.

[6] A somewhat similar listing of unwholesome beliefs is given in A. Ellis, *Reason and Emotion in Psychotherapy,* chapter 3, Lyle Stuart, Inc., New York, 1962.

[7] See H. Fingarette, *The Self in Transformation,* chapter 1, Basic Books, Inc., New York, 1963, for an analysis of psychoanalytically oriented therapy as a process of "meaning reorganization." Particular emphasis on the healing capabilities of re-interpretation of experience is given by V. E. Frankl, *Man's Search for Meaning,* Washington Square Press, Inc., New York, 1963.

he is able gradually to revise his self-picture and, as a result, his behavior in problem areas and in stressful situations. The process is characterized by a sort of uncovering layer by layer, as it were, the levels of the psyche, working through problem areas as they come into awareness.

A second process differs from the first in that it bypasses, temporarily, the specific problem areas and centers on changes taking place in the deeper levels of the personality. That is to say, the self-image is changed more fundamentally and directly. Changing of personality and behavior patterns follows, largely without conscious manipulation, through the much underestimated power of imagination. (The French psychologist Emil Cou wrote, "When the will and the imagination are in conflict, it is always the imagination which wins.")

One approach, used in several executive development seminars and various kinds of self-improvement groups and expounded in some detail by M. Maltz,[8] involves selection of the desired self-image by rational means, and autosuggestive techniques for feeding this image into the deeper levels of the mind. Study of "the best that has been thought and said" in humanities seminars and great books courses, contact with great works of art and with religious symbol and ritual, are all ways of allowing the experience of those who have gone before to influence the self-image.

The changing of self-image by integrative symbols which the person presents, so to speak, to himself—through dreams, fantasy, directed imagination, in the psychedelic (drug-facilitated) experience,[9] etc.—is a powerful technique which is central to the "constructive technique" of C. G. Jung and to the psychosynthesis of Assagioli.[10] It is set forth with particular clarity by one of Jung's students, P. W. Martin:[11] "The principal means by which the creative possibilities of the deep

[8] M. Maltz, *Psycho-Cybernetics*, Prentice-Hall, Inc., Englewood Cliffs, New Jersey, 1960. The same principle in a less popularized framework will be found in Roberto Assagioli, "Technique of Ideal Models," *Psychosynthesis: A Manual of Principles and Techniques*, Hobbs-Dorman, Co., Inc., New York, 1965.

[9] R. E. L. Masters and J. Houston, *Varieties of Psychedelic Experience*, Holt, Rinehart, Winston, Inc., New York, 1966.

[10] R. Gerard, *Psychosynthesis: A Psychotherapy for the Whole Man*, Psychosynthesis Research Foundation, New York, 1964. Assagioli, *op. cit.*

[11] P. W. Martin, *Experiment in Depth*, Pantheon Books, Inc., New York, 1955, p. 115.

unconscious may be reached is the transforming symbol. Anyone wholeheartedly engaging in the experiment in depth will find, as a normal fact of experience, that the unconscious repeatedly produces shapes, objects, phrases, ideas, which have this peculiar quality: if put to their right use they make possible a re-direction of energy and, by so doing, progressively transform the man who uses them." I. Progroff [12] specifically recommends avoiding attacking personal problems "head-on." Rather, he says, the best progress is made indirectly, by shifting attention "to the depth level of the psyche. There, by permitting the elemental symbol to unfold, a new quality of awareness is achieved by which the original problem is placed in a new perspective that restructures it so that it can be resolved."

If the governing image of the self—the one that is emotionally felt and imagined—is changed from one of worthlessness, or inadequacy, or precariously pent up urges, to a self-image centered on an inner Self which can be implicitly trusted, then the entire personality structure undergoes (in time) a reorganization in the direction of increased realization of inherent potentialities.

A third process of personality change is described in mystical and occult literature, but cannot be said to have formed a part of recognized psychotherapeutic procedures in recent times, until the advent of psychedelic therapy.[13] It is characterized by the fact that the person's image of himself is changed as a result of his having experiences which he perceives as transcendental and valid, as directly revealing to him higher aspects of himself of which he had previously been unaware.

One of the earliest studies of these states of altered awareness uses the term "cosmic consciousness" to refer to a broad range of experiences which awaits a satisfactory taxonomy:

The prime characteristic of cosmic consciousness is, as its name implies, a consciousness of the cosmos, that is, of the life and order of the universe . . . Along with the consciousness of the cosmos there occurs an intellectual enlightenment or illumination which alone would place the individual on

[12] I. Progroff, *The Symbolic and the Real*, Julian Press, Inc., New York, 1963, p. 167.
[13] J. N. Sherwood, M. J. Stolaroff, and W. W. Harman, "The Psychedelic Experience: A New Concept in Psychotherapy," *Journal of Neuropsychiatry*, volume 4, 1962, pp. 69–80. See also W. W. Harman, "Some Aspects of the Psychedelic Drug Controversy," *Journal of Humanistic Psychology*, volume 3, 1963, pp. 93–107.

a new plane of existence—would make him almost a member of a new species. To this is added a state of moral exaltation, an indescribable feeling of elevation, elation, and joyousness, and a quickening of the moral sense, which is fully striking and more important both to the individual and to the race than is the enhanced intellectual power. With these come what may be called a sense of immortality, a consciousness of eternal life, not conviction that he shall have this, but the consciousness that he has it already.[14]

William James wrote of this process in a classic work.[15] Further documentation may be found in philosophy and arts, in mystical literature, and in the rapidly accumulating literature on experiences with the psychedelic chemical agents.[16]

IV. Where Do We Seek?

With this much as a background, let us return to the question of how a "human potentialities" seminar might be set up. From a logical standpoint, an obvious place to start would seem to be with some sort of picture of what the highest potentiality of the individual human being appears to be. But because this must be discovered anew by each person, and because he simultaneously wants and resists such discovery, this is not such a straightforward matter as it might seem. I know of no better guideline for the search than the following: "Truth is not that which is demonstrable. Truth is that which is ineluctable." [17] Inescapable, discoverable—yet elusive because of the ambivalence toward it which is the universal condition of man.

A reasonably good beginning is provided by asking, "Where, in the vast realms of human knowledge, are we likely to find useful guidance in our search for the nature of and the means for actualization of man's potentialities?" Science, of course, and particularly the sciences which have most directly to do with man's mind and its development. But the contemporary scientific world-view, with its positivistic-physicalistic prejudice, reflects within it the resistance and denying of

[14] M. Bucke, *Cosmic Consciousness*, E. P. Dutton, Philadelphia, 1905.

[15] William James, *Varieties of Religious Experience*, Modern Library, New York, 1936.

[16] R. E. Mogar, "Current Trends in Psychedelic Research," *Journal of Humanistic Psychology*, volume 5, 1965, pp. 147–166.

[17] A. St. Exupéry, *Wind, Sand and Stars*, Harcourt Brace & Co., New York, 1940.

our highest potentialities which is part of the psychic economy of the individuals who make up the culture. Thus it is useful to examine critiques of the limited view of man which is implied in many scientific presentations.[18] Students find it a valuable mind-opening exercise to suspend premature judgment and to examine sympathetically the data of such scientifically offbeat areas as extrasensory perception,[19] faith healing,[20] teleportation and other psychokinetic effects,[21] occultism,[22] mysticism,[23] etc.

Thus scientific knowledge is, to use a phrase common in mathematical disciplines, "necessary but not sufficient" as a guide.[24] "The self-directed development of the faculties of the inner life has been almost entirely neglected in the modern study of psychology.[25] We need also to look to the humanities, and to ponder the meaning of such statements as the following: "The areas of experience with which only literature and the other arts can successfully deal are those which involve the consciousness rather than either mere behavior on the one

[18] One of the most scholarly is Michael Polanyi, *Personal Knowledge*, University of Chicago Press, Chicago, 1958, with, as a sequel, Floyd Matson, *The Broken Image*, George Braziller, Inc., New York, 1964. Others from varying points of view include the later books of the biologist E. W. Sinnott, particularly *Matter, Mind and Man*, Harper & Brothers, New York, 1957; P. A. Sorokin, *The Ways and Power of Love*, Beacon Press, Boston, 1954, in sociology; Carl Rogers and Abraham Maslow in psychology. Still more critical writing in psychology are Abraham Maslow, *The Psychology of Science*, Harper & Row, New York, 1966; Joseph Wood Krutch, *The Measure of Man*, Bobbs-Merrill Co., Inc., Indianapolis, 1954; and John Langdon-Davies, *On the Nature of Man*, Mentor Press, New York, 1961 (paperback).

[19] Especially recommended is Raynor Johnson, *The Imprisoned Splendour*, Harper & Brothers, New York, 1953. Also Rosalind Heywood, *Beyond the Reach of Sense*, E. P. Dutton & Co., New York, 1961; and J. B. Rhine, *New World of the Mind*, William Sloane Associates, New York, 1953.

[20] Ruth Cranston, *The Miracle of Lourdes*, McGraw-Hill, New York, 1955, is reliable and easy reading. The story of Edgar Cayce, *There Is a River*, by Thomas Sugrue, Henry Holt & Co., New York, 1949, is interesting in connection with a related phenomenon.

[21] Two particularly good references are René Sudre, *Parapsychology*, Grove Press (paperback), New York, 1962; and Nandor Fodor, *Mind over Space*, Citadel Press, New York, 1962.

[22] Maurice Nicoll, *Living Time*, Vincent Stuart, London, 1952.

[23] One of the best, in paperback form, is W. T. Stace, *The Teaching of the Mystics*, Mentor Press, New York, 1964.

[24] W. W. Harman, "The Humanities in an Age of Science," *Main Currents in Modern Thought*, volume 18, Foundation for Integrated Education, 1962, pp. 75–83.

[25] I. Progoff, Introductory Commentary, *The Cloud of Unknowing*, Julian Press, New York, 1957.

hand, or on the other, the impersonal forces which are supposed by science to determine that behavior. The phenomena of this area can be successfully presented only when they are organized in terms of concepts which recognize the validity of value judgments." [26] "Poetry is a form of knowledge. . . . The disciplines of poetry may be expected first to teach the evocative power of words, to introduce the student, if we may so put it, to the mighty power of symbolism, and then to show him that there are ways of feeling about things which are not provincial either in space or time." [27] "One of the principal functions of all art is . . . to bring the individual to himself to transcendence . . . to lead him to the timeless radiant dynamic that is at the heart of the world. In this sense the greatest art is learning to see in the way described by Rabbi Nachman of Bratislava: 'Just as a hand held before the eyes conceals from view the vast lights and mysteries of which the world is full, and he who can withdraw it from his eyes, as one withdraws a hand, will behold the great light of the innermost world.' " [28] All art exists to communicate states of consciousness which are higher synthetic wholes than those of ordinary experience." [29]

And then, what of religion? Not as a social institution serving to promote morality, nor as a neurotic escape from the harshness of life, nor as a highly intellectualized abstract theology, but as a living, vibrant, empirical record of man's inner experience and a guide to the most profound levels of self-discovery. What is the difference between the scientific search for truth and that in the Indian *Vedas,* the Egyptian *Book of the Dead,* the Hebrew Prophets, Plato's *Dialogues,* and St. John of the Cross?

V. Seminar Procedures

Space allows only the merest mention of topics which may with profit be read about and discussed in the progress of such a seminar—

---

[26] Krutch, *op. cit.*

[27] R. M. Weaver, *Ideas Have Consequences,* University of Chicago Press, Chicago, 1958.

[28] E. Neumann, *Art and the Creative Unconscious,* Pantheon Books, Inc., New York, 1959.

[29] J. W. N. Sullivan, *Beethoven, His Spiritual Development,* New American Library, Inc., New York, 1949.

creativity, love, freedom, acceptance, non-attachment, transcendence of opposites such as good and evil. I have found useful the technique of presenting as discussion-openers a few provocative statements such as the following:

1. ON KNOWLEDGE

Truth is within ourselves . . . and to know, rather consists in opening out a way whence the imprisoned splendour may escape, than in effecting entry for a light supposed to be without.[30]

It is only when a man has shed his egotistical self and with it his needs that he is open to a truth not specially moulded by himself nor determined by his needs. If the truth which comes to us when we are detached from ourselves is the same as is perceived by others vastly different from us in race and creed and separated from us in time, then we are as near as we can ever be to absolute truth, even considered by the most rigid standards of science.[31]

2. ON THE PARADOXICAL NATURE OF WISDOM

True words always seem paradoxical, but no other form of teaching can take its place. (Lao-tse)

The recognition of the direction of fulfillment is the death of the self, and the death of the self is the beginning of selfhood.[32]

Die and Become.
Till thou hast learned this
Thou art but a dull guest
On this dark planet.[33]

Having realized his own self as the Self, a man becomes selfless; and in virtue of selflessness he is to be conceived as unconditioned. This is the highest mystery, betokening emancipation. (*Upanishads*)

Hold well in your mind this brief word: Forsake all things and you will find all things . . . Print well in your mind that what I have said, for

[30] Robert Browning, "Paracelsus."
[31] A. Guirdham, *Christ and Freud,* Macmillan Co., New York, 1962. See also Aldous Huxley, *The Perennial Philosophy,* Chatto & Windus, London, 1946.
[32] R. P. Warren, *Brother to Dragons,* Random House, Inc., New York, 1953.
[33] J. W. von Goethe, *Spiritual Longing,* Book I of *West-Eastern Divan,* translated by John Weiss, Roberts Brothers, Boston, 1877.

when you have fulfilled it, you will know well that it is true . . . This lesson is not one day's work, or play for children—in it is contained the full perfection of all religion.[34]

3. ON OTHER LEVELS OF CONSCIOUSNESS

To me the occurrence of mystical experience at all times and places, and the similarities between the statements of so many mystics all the world over, seem to be a significant fact. *Prima facie* it suggests that there is an aspect of reality with which those persons came in contact in their mystical experiences, and which they afterward strive and largely fail to describe in the language of daily life.[35]

The important thing is to see and admit . . . that there does exist a real and recognizable fact (that is, a state of consciousness in some sense), which has been experienced over and over again, and which to those who have experienced it in ever so slight a degree has appeared worthy of lifelong pursuit and devotion . . . The question really is not to define the fact—for we cannot do that—but to get at and experience it.[36]

There are certain root experiences man never forgets . . . The first time he breaks the chrysalis of being to emerge as a conscious spiritual unit . . . is the greatest of all . . . The Overself makes no demand of man other than he open his inner eyes and perceive its existence . . . Once we push the gate of the mind slightly ajar and let the light stream in, the meaning of life becomes silently revealed to us . . . Man as a spiritual being possesses a capacity for wisdom which is infinite, a resource of happiness which is startling. He contains a divine infinitude within himself, yet he is content to go on and potter about a petty stretch of life as though he were a mere human insect.[37]

Particularly in the earlier meetings of the group, participants are asked to consider such personally relevant questions as:

What is the most significant and moving experience you have ever had? (What does your answer tell you about what you value?)

---

[34] Thomas à Kempis, *The Imitation of Christ,* Morehouse-Gorham, New York, 1950.

[35] C. D. Broad, *Religion, Philosophy and Psychical Research,* Harcourt Brace & Co., New York, 1953.

[36] Edward Carpenter, *From Adam's Peak to Elephanta,* Swain & Sonnenschein, London, 1892.

[37] P. Brunton, *The Secret Path,* E. P. Dutton & Co., New York, 1935.

What is the worst (most unpleasant, humiliating, painful, horrible, etc.) experience? What, in essence, made it so bad?

What meaning does life hold for you?

What "makes" you anxious, fearful, irritated, frustrated, angry? How?

What seems to you to be the fundamental existential (contrasted with situational problems in your life?

To whatever extent he is willing, the participant is encouraged to share the results of these ponderings. In these and various other ways he is made aware that he is being asked to set aside well-entrenched preconceptions and to approach afresh the question, "What can I be?", to see how feelings enter into thinking and communication, and to deepen the level of communication with other group members.

As the seminar progresses, individuals gain trust in the group and become more and more willing to share personally significant material. At the same time they become more aware of their own feelings and of the way in which they create them through their attitudes; but also of the value of these as signposts leading to further self-discovery. They may carry on experiments, in the group or outside, along lines of meditative introspection, active imagination, self-acceptance and affirmation, exercises in awareness,[38] and so on.

At the end, each person is asked to formulate in writing his own individual progress report or tentative conclusions, and to share orally with the rest of the group as much of this as he feels is appropriate. The following sample comments are representative:

The idea of tearing down the defenses and narrowmindedness carefully built up over most of my life has not been an easy one to accept . . . I have altered what I originally believed to be the structure of my life: a well-ordered collection of selected experiences set and evaluated against an unchangeable list of criteria, wherein man's only defense against the environmental control which held him by the scruff of the neck was organization and the avoidance of unfamiliar experience . . . At this point I feel as Wendy in Peter Pan must have felt when she screamed delightedly, "I can fly!"

---

[38] Some good suggestions will be found in F. Perls, F. Hefferline, and P. Goodman, *Gestalt Therapy*, Julian Press, New York, 1951. Also in A. P. Orage, *Psychological Exercises and Essays*, Janus, London, 1965.

The mere fact that I feel a change in myself to be necessary shows the importance with which I view this working for self-knowledge. I know the emptiness, the incompleteness I have felt for life in the past. Searching inside myself, knowing myself better, no matter how painful such knowledge may be, seems to hold an answer . . . For me it's an amazing beginning.

It is as if I have come upon a new religion, capable of originating within myself.

How can I convince anyone that after twenty years of search a few short classroom discussions and a little reading could produce any significant improvement or alteration, or gain in insight—I must record that I think I have glimpsed something that causes me to meditate in awe . . . I do not presume that what I have seen is either all, or even a significant part of reality. I do say that it is a little more than I have ever seen before, and this fills me with both comfort and wonder.

I confess to feeling a pleasurable sense of gratification when I read such reports. They indicate that, clumsy as our efforts may be, it is yet possible to provide such a situation that there may take place a bit of what might well be called the true "higher education"—in the sense that the highest to which man can attain is knowledge of himself.

Chapter 17. BASIC PROBLEMS IN EDUCATION FOR RESPONSIBILITY CAUSED BY LSD-25

by John C. Lilly

THE RISING number of young persons taking LSD-25 (lysergic acid diethylamide) brings in its wake many of the older problems faced by parents and educators in regard to the development of those factors which we epitomize in the word "responsibility." One view of responsibility is that of an inner discipline which directs the activities of the self toward attainable and idealistic goals. These goals may be directed so as to be strictly personal or they may be directed for others than one's self. The goals may be connected with only a few persons or large numbers of persons.

In the matrix of our civilization each one of us has multiple exchanges and responsibilities for many different aspects of that civilization. Each of us has a more or less fluid reference point within the structure of society. Most of us are regulated in detail by taxation, by income, by available work, by husband, by wife, by children, by parents, by governments, large and small. Each of these separate agents and agencies exacts its toll of time, effort, and money from each of us. Each of these agents and agencies has ways of enforcing its toll upon each one of us in the absence of a response and continuing responsibility from each one of us toward each one of them.

As each human being grows from the nonspeaking little animal that is born into this world to the responsible adult with his own family, he is required to expand his responsibility to the outside world again and again. Only when responsible people judge him to be unfit to accept further responsibility does the pressure to expand the areas of his responsibility decrease. There are times when one has the feeling that irrespective of the desires of the individual this inexorable process continues throughout his life.

Inside each person there is an answering to these external calls to duty. At each stage the individual tests the system to see what its limits are and how much he must respond with appropriate action, thinking, and dedication. At each young stage the various kinds and forms of evasions of responsibility are tried to the limits possible to that particular person and either rejected or further espoused depending upon the inner satisfaction generated by the evasive action.

The evasions for the young usually take the form of pursuing the most pleasurable paths and staying away from those which are found to be unpleasant or painful. However, as one grows older and more experienced, the pleasure and pain have become more than physiological experiences and have begun to attach themselves to concepts, to persons, to institutions, to real things, and to distant goals. Then one's brain has enlarged enough and become experienced enough in controlling the algebraic sign of the emotional value (plus or minus) of various systems of thinking and successes within those systems; the basic structure for responsibility has been achieved. The responsible strong self-directed individual with dedication and interest in improvement of self and in widening his areas of responsibility is the person we should keep in mind in the rest of this discussion.

Let us look at a distribution curve of responsible persons; at one end those of minimal responsibility and the other end those of maximal responsibility. This curve of the number of people with each degree of responsibility varies with quite a large number of parameters. It varies with age, with economic level, and with educational level achieved. Some of these individuals are selected by the educational system for the very factor which we are discussing; *i.e.,* the more responsible individuals with intelligence will either continue their education and complete it or will have found what they are looking for outside this system of education and have accepted responsible jobs on which they start their life's work. As John Gardner says in his book, *Excellence* (Harper & Row, New York, 1961) there is no *a priori* reason that all those with intelligence, responsibility, and dedication should pass through the college system. There are other means of reaching social and national responsible positions than through college. Gardner points out that we have people on arbitrary scales of value, placing those who have loafed their way through college higher than those who have achieved in large measure through a self-education regime. The latter makes a more valuable person than the former.

All of these considerations are relevant to the present fashion for taking LSD-25. The recent spate of bad press having to do with college students taking LSD, the withdrawal of the Sandoz Company from supplying the drug, and the new controls of the Federal Food and Drug Administration and the National Institute of Mental Health underscore this problem. One might ask: who *is* responsible with regard to LSD? *Where lies the responsibility for educating for responsibility with regard to LSD itself?*

This is a very difficult problem. In my opinion the abdication of responsibility for LSD and similar substances started in the early days (in the 1950s) when certain people began to take these substances and report their experiences in the scientific and nonscientific literature. Using the "20/20 vision of hindsight" let us reconstruct what seemed to have happened with regard to LSD over the past fifteen or so years.

First of all the effects of these substances have been known for a long time. The naturally occurring plants and fungi which are the biochemical factories for these substances have been around literally millions of years. Man has incorporated some of these into past religious rites and certain "pagan" groups have used them with telling effect in their religious rituals. In so far as we can discover, each of these groups has had to face the problem of discipline with regard to the use of these substances. A current and cogent example of the achievement of discipline in order to control the use of these substances is the Native American Church, with the peyote cult. The history of this group has been recounted many times. From the published accounts we can deduce that responsible use was achieved within the confines of a religious setting.

It may be that responsible use of these substances cannot be achieved without some sort of strictures in the direction of the religious aspects. A religious transformation of the individual may be a step on the way toward achievement of inner responsibility to himself. Let us move from the religious viewpoint to what one might call a more basic philosophical viewpoint in which one attempts to explore the basic beliefs that a given individual has and on which he really operates. In this context we will try to ignore the tendency of most persons to *say* that they believe certain things, whereas in reality they act as if they believe quite something else. In this context we are speaking of only those basic beliefs which are operationally, demonstratively existent in the behavior and in the accomplishments of the individual.

Basic beliefs are here defined as that set of basic postulates which can be demonstrated to be operative through long study and careful analysis of the behavior, writings, and vocal productions of a given individual. It is this basic structure of the individual and of his feeling-thinking machinery in which we seek the basis for responsibility and the education for responsibility.

It is this basic set of beliefs which controls the effects of LSD on the person and on what he does, thinks, and produces during the LSD state. It is these basic beliefs which can apparently be unearthed (and possibly even changed) during the LSD state. This is the desirable and at the same time the perilous aspect of LSD and of its control. The temptation to elicit, to control, and to change the beliefs of others and even of one's self at times is a seductive goal. *Apparently* LSD puts this power in the hands of those who use LSD. But this may be a delusion. LSD may release mechanisms for the construction of self-deluding beliefs.

LSD allows a person to take himself apart, as it were, and look at separate areas of belief independently of beliefs about those areas, *i.e.,* independently of his meta-beliefs. For example, if one believes, even temporarily, that one is a god in the LSD state, one becomes a god in his own imagination. One becomes one's concept of a kind of god, how powerful, how omniscient, etc., how knowledgeable a god one can be. Under the LSD state one is no longer influenced by the usual meta-belief, "I am in a class of animals known as *Homo sapiens,* not in a class above the animal class and known as gods." In the LSD state one can ignore what one knows in one area and construct a belief about another area contradicting the first and have freedom to carry out many of the logical consequences. It is of no matter how irrational or how out of step the belief is with reality or with other belief systems nearby in self. In this sense LSD can be thought of as facilitating the genesis of psychosis itself rather than causing mimicking of psychosis.

The ability to hold a very powerful nonrational belief in mind and act as if it is true within one's own mind is one aspect of psychosis. If and when the LSD state or similar states persist beyond the expected limits of six to ten hours with the known pure diethylamide substance, then may one begin to suspect that other biochemical and neurological mechanisms are activated which might possibly be similar (if not identical) to those occurring during "true psychosis."

However, since LSD-25 has been called "psychotomimetic" quite early in the analysis of its effects, we are left with this history of the "psychotomimetic drug." This judgment acts as a programming agent for all subsequent work with LSD-25. This is embedded in the literature, it is embedded in the guiding agencies for its investigation, it is embedded in the public mind and wherever one turns one is faced with this tradition of "psychotomimesis."

(A rather amusing sidelight occurred with respect to this particular view of the perils of LSD. A well-known psychiatrist was approached by a woman who was worried about what LSD might do to her mind and brain. She had been reading the literature and had read the work of this particular man. She questioned him. He answered, "I have written that LSD causes psychosis and I am sure that it does for a period of at least four to eight hours." She said, "And what do you mean by psychosis?" At that point the psychiatrist's wife interrupted and said, "let me tell you a little story which will illustrate what he means by the word 'psychosis.' One night he came home from the laboratory complaining that he was getting some sort of virus disease. I asked him to describe his symptoms in detail: as he began to describe the symptoms it suddenly occurred to him that these were the symptoms of the LSD state. He then thought back during the day and discovered that by accident he had apparently absorbed some LSD. At this point he said, 'Oh, it's just an LSD psychosis. I am going to bed and sleep it off,' which he did.")

This story illustrates what a strong-minded self-disciplined and responsible individual thinks about the effects of LSD on himself. There are weaker individuals who are precipitated into a "real," difficult-to-reverse psychosis by the drug experience; there are many such persons and we cannot be too careful with such individuals.

Another idea which has grown up around the use of LSD was started about the same time the psychotomimetic viewpoint was promulgated. This is the "religious revelation" aspect of the drug. This aspect has done as much of a disservice to our understanding of what is going on as has "psychotomimesis." We cannot take responsibility for "religious transcendental experiences" scientifically. Each of these phenomena is placed a little bit beyond the reach of proper scientific investigation.

But once again this is the state of our present knowledge. "LSD causes mimicking of psychosis, LSD can cause religious transcendental experiences."

Support has been given to both of these points of view by innumerable books writing up personal experiences under LSD-25. I call your attention to the books by Jane Dunlap, Constance Newland, M. G. Bishop, those by Aldous Huxley, and by Timothy Leary, Richard Alpert, and Ralph Metzner.

If only LSD-25 and its effects could be accounted for fully by these points of view, the scientific work would not be as difficult as it is. If we could only go along with these "wishful thinking" views of the effects, if we could go along with those who saw only these things when they took the substance, then our work would not be very difficult. We could agree that the explanations were adequate and we could drop the whole subject. But somehow these explanations are scientifically unsatisfactory. Somehow they seem to have led to "mental absolutes" which, to this author at least, seem unreasonable. What I see in the writings of these two aspects of the effects of LSD on the human mind is that I am reading *long accounts of the details of the wishful thinking* of each of the authors. I do not say that this is irresponsible reportage of inner events. I believe that these people are sincere, straightforward, and disciplined along their own lines. However, each one of them is giving us that which they wish most to be true.

One can summarize my viewpoint of this literature by saying that these elaborate constructs reflect two things from each of these persons: 1) the contents of their own memory recombined in a free associational way, and 2) the realization of their most secret and hoped-for set of goals with regard to their own basic beliefs, in so far as these could be accomplished within their own heads (Jerome S. Bruner and C. C. Goodman).

The social effects of these writings and others like them include a rather devastating and widespread seduction of young minds toward

the taking of LSD-25. The promise of "ecstasy" and "religious transcendence" to some of the youngsters is very seductive. To others the
promise of "psychotic experience" is equally seductive. Let us not forget that today adventure still beckons to the young and that this rather
old frontier of the mind is now being opened up by LSD and other
such substances for the perusal of those seeking adventure, both for
pleasure and for danger.

According to the clinical reports from various psychiatric out-patient
departments connected with universities, most of the people who are
getting into trouble with LSD and similar substances are between the
ages of approximately seventeen years and twenty-five, *i.e.,* college and
graduate students. A sufficient number of these students have read the
writings above and have established a peer mythology with regard to
these writings to the point where there is a subculture built up around
these substances. I have spoken with several of these youngsters and
was left with the impression that the motives involved are quite complex and worthy of a good deal of further study. In the light of this
kind of experience, it is high time that we instituted a thorough and
widespread scientific investigation of what is going on among these
youngsters.

Let us now turn to some other possibilities with regard to LSD-25
and the state that it produces. Let us try to arrive at objective and
scientific views of its effect upon the mind. This is indeed not easy but
I believe that it is important to try.

The objective, dispassionate, and thorough investigation of states of
mind induced by these substances is a primary requirement for science
for the next few years. We cannot eliminate the subjective report as a
source of data. We should not allow subjective reportage to become
merely an artistic and romantic medium for use only by novelists and
artists. The science of a mentality as reported by that mentality has
been neglected in academic science for many years. The encouraging
increase in cognitive psychology within certain academic institutions is
to be applauded, and, hopefully, expanded.

The subjective aspects of one's own mental functioning in adolescence is incredibly important to one's self. Many youngsters seek
guidance, seek help and seek education in this world of the subjective
and do not obtain much help from science.

The failure of science to explore this area is expressed in the present problem with LSD-25 among these same youngsters. The only maps of the territories they have are those of the artists, theologians, and psychiatrists who preceded them in the LSD-25 state. *I feel these youngsters do not need maps so much as they need a catalog of possible maps and an estimate of the probabilities of the occurrence of certain kinds of maps in this area, and maps of the dead ends and lethal traps.*

In order to construct a set of ideas which may be of help to us in educating the young in regard to the inner life with special reference to the LSD-25 state, first of all let us say that the species of *Beings* (beasts, plants, and other living intelligent and non-intelligent creatures) which one may come upon in the LSD state, have a much more flexible "zoological science" to them than does the zoology of real animals. Since the "creatures seen, felt, heard," and the "beings thought to and thought from" under LSD are literally constructs of one's own mind, the limitations in the "mental zoology and botany" are only those of one's own imagination and of the elements stored within one. From the multitude of materials in one's own memory, one can construct through imagination any conceivable apparently living breathing kind of creature. One can construct thinking machines or thinking beings or other people with any desired set of chacteristics and any desired set of powers, within the limits of one's own conceptions.

So in essence how does the LSD state differ from ordinary dreaming, ordinary daydreaming, and wishful thinking in general? It differs in the greater brilliance and the greater intensity of the projected visual images and in the greater intensity of the feelings aroused, coupled with these images, sights, and sounds. It is as if this substance puts a noisy amplifier in one's computer, an amplifier of the emotive and cognitive processes of one's mind, by means of LSD-25. This noisy amplifier gives one the subjective impression of increased powers of control over one's own thinking processes. But this is a false impression caused by the energy of the added random noise. One may not have such control but one has the impression that one does. This effect under the influence of this drug may be caused by the forced turning inward of one's self, away from a less interesting external reality and paying more attention to one's own highly active inner processes excited by the noise. A primary effect seems to be as if one's rewarding brain systems are stimulated and the punishing systems inhibited.

The important cautions, then, are that LSD-25 has a seductive history, and causes states of mind which are so seductive the subject wants to return for further experiences. Importantly the subject is wide open to influence, is very vulnerable in this state. He becomes very programmable by other persons. He is quite at the command of his own pleasurable desires and his own wishful thinking in greater measure than is comfortable to contemplate.

Long-term subtle psychological damage may result; such damage may long be hidden by the pleasure and enthusiasm engendered by the substance. It is possible that in the long term use brains are structurally damaged. Thus subjects may be weakened by this substance—attacked literally where they live. Subjects are being seduced by a chemical rewarding of mental life without working for the reward. The new stimuli for the new lotus-eaters are subtle and subtly evasive, hiding insight itself under unearned chemical rewards given gratis.

Is education for responsibility possible with the use of such chemicals? I don't know. I'm interested, and am trying to understand. Who has taken responsibility? No one, so far. A phantasy of attaining a goal, a mental imagining of achieving a goal, fully biochemically rewarded, may become a fixed belief, a way of life. I don't like the feel of it. It's wrong, somehow.

Chapter 18. THE IMPACT ON PSYCHIATRIC RESIDENT PHYSICIANS OF AN EFFORT TO SHARE POWER IN THE HOSPITAL COMMUNITY

by Robert Rubenstein and Harold D. Lasswell *

CONVENTIONAL psychiatric institutions reinforce the self-image of the hospitalized as losers, sufferers, and victims. Decisions about fundamental and pressing issues in the lives of patients are made by others without the participation of the individuals most concerned. In such an authoritarian hospital the roles of doctors, nurses, and patients are clearly defined. The "good patient" is compliant, cooperative, accepting, unquestioning, the recipient of the good, established, known things that were done to and for him by the doctors, nurses, and other staff members. He is regarded as a troublemaker, uncooperative and cantankerous, if he questions procedures, seeks information about why this is being done and that isn't, or if he presumes to take a more active position by volunteering judgments of his own about what is wrong with him or about what should be done, or about the nature of the difficulties and the treatment of other patients. One part of the hospital, the staff, does things to that other part of the hospital, the patients, "to get 'them' well." The patients comply with the expectations implicit in this hospital environment by assuming the passive role of those to whom things are done by others.

Society and the expert agents to whom it delegates such extraordinary authority over the lives of others, the doctors, justify such exemptions from democratic practice and the drastic usurping of their pa-

* THIS PAPER is based on research by the authors reported more fully in *The Sharing of Power in a Psychiatric Hospital,* Yale University Press, New Haven, 1966.

tients' rights and powers, on the assumption that those who suffer from mental illness are fragile, childlike, irresponsible, dangerous to themselves and others; not protecting them, failing to administer their affairs as dependents, would be a breach of professional obligation.

But now some psychiatric hospitals have begun to change; the "therapeutic community" has emerged. The patient is beginning to be invited to prepare himself for successful participation in the community beyond hospitalization by learning the techniques and strategies of such participation within the hospital community. Indeed, the possibility is being considered that the traditional medical model is not appropriate for the reprocessing of the defeated and the disadvantaged, and new institutions specifically elaborated in response to their needs are developing. The beginnings of this shift were prompted by convincing demonstrations of the beneficial effects of patients participating actively with staff in determining and assessing what happens in the hospital.[1] Conflicts of conscience are evoked within those exercising power, the doctors, who know but had not previously been forced to acknowledge to themselves or others the necessity of extending to all of the patient's experience the dignity, respect, responsibility, autonomy, and self-determination long acknowledged as central to psychoanalytic treatment. The fact that patients respond competently and responsibly to opportunities and expectations informed by an appreciation of their resources and strengths, and in such an atmosphere assert their dissatisfaction with being the passive recipients of the ministrations of others, renders the doctor's authoritarian position uncertain. He cannot continue to violate the canons of shared power and fulfil his obligations as a physician, for these deviations from democratic practice are no longer justifiable on therapeutic grounds.

An effort to include patients in the hospital decision-process was undertaken at the Yale Psychiatric Institute beginning in 1956. Forums developed for the sharing of information and the appraisal of the way in which all aspects of hospital affairs were conducted (patient-staff meetings, held three times weekly), and for making explicit decisions about individual patients and overall hospital policy (patient-staff advisory committee) previously made by the director and the staff without patient participation. The continuing dialogue between all mem-

[1] Maxwell Jones, *The Therapeutic Community,* Basic Books, New York, 1953.

bers of the Yale Psychiatric Institute Community, including patients, doctors, nurses, social workers, and other staff members, has since modified the functions, roles, and power positions of all participants. This report focuses upon the impact of these innovations on resident physicians. In the post-innovation period, patient-staff meetings and other innovations add to the resident's burdens by demanding that he be a participant in the life of the hospital rather than only a psychotherapist working on its periphery. His work is now subjected to greater scrutiny by patients as well as colleagues and seniors, his performance publicly appraised and, at times, criticized, his private life even more frequently intruded upon.

All the many tasks and obligations of the pre-innovation resident persist in the post-innovation calendar. However, his day may now begin with a patient-staff meeting in which issues, observations, and plans (previously confined to staff meetings) are discussed. In the patient-staff meeting he is a participant with all his patients and all other hospital patients. They observe with whom he sits and chats as the meeting begins, how he reacts to comments by patients and others, and the responses of others to his comments. He may be confronted by a patient describing, complaining about, and demanding that he account for the way he handled a patient's distress when on duty the previous evening or how he dealt with an agitated patient the previous afternoon. He may be asked to explain why he isolated or restricted a patient, or opposed a patient's request to work or attend school. His colleagues and seniors may side with the complaining patient and imply that he was unwise or unfair. A nurse, social worker, or the director may offer observations which contradict the resident's assessments and decisions. He may feel vulnerable, ridiculed, and unsupported.

Such pressures challenge the therapist to think through carefully positions he takes with his patients. In subsequent individual treatment hours, a patient may chastise him for not effectively advocating at a patient-staff meeting a request he had accepted in their discussions. Patients may be contemptuous of him because he was criticized or ridiculed by the director or his fellow residents, or they may comfort or support him in his struggles with the rest of the staff. The patient sees how others view his doctor and how he is appraised by colleagues and seniors; a more complete picture of how his doctor operates is available to him on the basis of his behavior in these forums. He may see his therapist intimidated by criticism and readily backing down, or holding to his position despite opposition from both patients and staff. The patient may determine from his own observations and participation in these forums whether his therapist takes a position or remains non-committal, is concerned about pleasing everyone, or whether he appears to have a consistent set of guiding principles in his work. If his doctor's values and expectations are very different from those of the rest of the community, they will be discernible more readily than before and may be discussed in forums in which the patient participates.

The resident's daily calendar, in addition to seminars, conferences, staff meetings, hours of supervision, and his own analytic hour, may now include attending a patient-staff advisory committee at that committee's request to explain, for example, why he supports the request of a patient to move from the closed to the open ward. In this meeting patients may, with or without the support of a nurse or the chief resident, convincingly document their impression that the patient remains too troubled for such a move, continues to need the larger staff available on the closed ward, and has remained withdrawn on visits to the open ward. The resident may again feel vulnerable, incompetent, and unprotected. He cannot lean upon his authority as physician or expert; unlike the traditional physician his judgment and power do not remain unquestioned. He must now justify his actions and decisions to the community of patients and staff.

In evenings and weekends on duty, in addition to handling hospital affairs, talking with patients who require his attention, and doing his paperwork, he is now encouraged to have supper with patients, play bridge or pingpong with them, and go through the wards chatting with them before they retire.

The impact of the innovations upon Yale Psychiatric Institute residents is suggested by the residents' responses to a list of thirty topics which might be discussed at joint patient-staff meetings and to the question whether they should be discussed. These included the "director's running of the hospital," "request by a patient for a change of therapist," "whether a given patient should be placed in special (isolation)," "a patient's request that a staff member be fired," "a nurse's or a resident's handling of a patient," "a patient's readiness for discharge or to hold a job or attend school," "promiscuous behavior by a patient," "a patient's financial problems," and fourteen other comparable topics. Seventy-five percent or more of both pre- and post-innovation residents felt that twenty-four of these thirty topics should be discussed at patient-staff meetings. Residents were less amenable to the discussion of six other topics, but a majority opposed discussion of only one question, "staff salaries." Why is the discussion of this one topic opposed by a majority? The value analysis of patient-staff meeting transcripts demonstrates that statements concerned with economic issues (wealth) arose far less frequently than other values, and much less frequently than in many other kinds of meetings in our society. Residents express their readiness to talk about "a patient's financial problems" in joint meetings of patients and staff, but oppose discussing staff salaries. Residents' salaries are very low ("grossly so," said a resident who listed it as a complaint he did not feel free to bring up with his seniors), in keeping with medicine's tradition of apprentice bondage. Their salaries do not begin to correspond with their responsibility, power, and respect in the hospital. As money is regarded as an indicator of prestige and competence in American culture, it may be expected that the discussion of salaries might undermine the respect accorded the resident, particularly where most patients and their families are of high socioeconomic position. As perennial students, in their late twenties or early thirties, with wives and children, often dependent financially on parents or wife, they are likely to be sensitive about their salaries. A related consideration is the traditional medical school policy which emphasizes the "confidentiality" of staff salaries. This restriction refers only to positions beyond residency, however. Information about resident salaries is readily available and generally known to patients.

Other topics which residents are relatively less willing to discuss in joint meetings of patients and staff (although a majority favor their discussion) are in two related groups: issues traditionally regarded as "medical," to be decided exclusively by the physician as an expert in caring for patients; and issues which concerned the private life of the resident, the disclosure of which might upset the resident and disrupt his work with patients.

The degree of mutuality in patient-staff meetings acceptable to residents is limited, but the extent to which residents are willing to participate candidly with patients in these meetings is impressive. Their reluctance reflects their seniors' judgment about what constitutes optimal conduct in these meetings, discomfort from intrusions into their personal affairs, and the threat these meetings and increased participation of patients in all phases of decisionmaking in the hospital now pose to their traditional medical role.

When patient-staff meetings were first considered, and later when decisionmaking began to shift to these meetings, residents were confused, troubled, and threatened. At each point of transition the question was raised, "How are you going to tell the patients from the doctors?" Their support of these forums and readiness to discuss freely most topics, indicates that the new hospital environment did not undermine their position as much as they feared. However, the physician, particularly the relatively inexperienced resident, is reluctant to abdicate much of his traditional authority and power until he is convinced that his fears are exaggerated and the changes serve him and his patients.

The majority (thirteen) of residents who served during the years 1954–1958 personally felt "enthusiastic," six felt "contented," and none felt either "discontented" or "very dissatisfied" with their Yale Psychiatric Institute year. This remarkable era of enthusiasm and contentment, preceded and followed by considerable discontent and dissatisfaction, was the period of the innovations. Discontent returned when experimentation and innovation began to subside and policy and procedure were again relatively stable.

The innovations modified the annual change of doctors at the beginning of the hospital year for both resident and patient. Patient-staff meetings provided an opportunity for the expression and discussion of feelings, fantasies, and rumors about the shift, as well as its implications for individual patients, and made them available to the reality-testing which staff participation facilitated. The resources of the entire hospital community were mobilized more effectively during the changeover crisis to cope with what was now recognized as a problem faced by all. Incoming residents attended patient-staff meetings in late May and June, prior to beginning work at the hospital on July 1. Their initial observing, and then gradual taking part actively, facilitated the mutual orientation of resident and the hospital community. The deprivational impact of the shift was further modified by the increased contact with the more substantial relationship each patient had with senior physicians and other members of the permanent staff. The loss of the resident with whom the patient worked in treatment was tempered by the continuation of these important relationships now possible in the hospital. Contact with physicians other than the resident therapist was not discouraged, and a broad transference extended beyond the individual therapist to include the entire hospital and its permanent staff.

Physical attacks on residents by patients were less frequent in the post-innovation period. This may reflect the increasing availability of tranquilizers and other mood-affecting medications, changes in the hospital population, and the new hospital climate which made war less necessary.

The innovations encouraged more informal interaction between residents and patients. Although this often meant increasingly meaningful contacts and gave the resident greater knowledge about the patients' hospital experience, this emphasis at times jeopardized the resident's position in psychotherapy. It was more difficult for the therapist to sustain the relative anonymity that was possible in the pre-innovation hospital. As a participant in community forums, his actions, responses, the strategies he employs, their effectiveness or failure, the positions he is committed to, the issues he cares about, and his inactivity were all available to observation by patients. His conduct might influence patients in their individual struggles with problems of assertiveness. His personal conflicts about taking a stand, now more readily evident to the patient, might interfere with the thorough exploration of the patient's own related difficulties in individual treatment. However, it may be argued that if the therapist is not able to handle problems involved in participating in a democratic society, he cannot be helpful to his patients with their similar problems, whether or not his conduct in forums is visible. In patient-staff meetings, other models are available to the patient; he may learn effective alternative strategies from other participants who are less troubled in areas where his individual therapist is limited.

The availability of others in these meetings can be used by the patient to evade what he may come to experience as a threatening closeness in his relationship with his doctor. Leverage traditionally available to the psychotherapist may thus be undermined. The patient may experience the individual therapist as the one person in the hospital who understands, appreciates his predicament, and cares, in contrast to the indifference of other patients and staff members. In the new hospital this important spur to the development of an intense relationship with the therapist was less likely to occur. A crucial question in evaluating the innovations is the importance of this element in motivation for treatment.

The issue of confidentiality is difficult to clarify in the post-innovation hospital, where sharing information with the entire community, including patients, is insisted upon. Just what information confided to the resident by patients should be shared with others? Can confidences be shared without jeopardizing the patient's relationship with the resident? The extent to which discreet, yet useful, means of sharing information were found, which were both protective of the patient and adequately responsive to the requirements of other members of the hospital community in their efforts to live and work together, was most impressive.

The therapeutic efforts of the resident are perhaps jeopardized by his more clearly secondary position in the staff. The patient may be encouraged to regard relationships with the director and other seniors, who clearly have more power and are not transient, as more important: contact with the director on rounds and in patient-staff meetings may seem more crucial than the individual psychotherapy.

The patient's image of the therapist, now derived from more informal interaction and regular participation together in patient-staff meetings, as well as contact in individual psychotherapeutic work, is less likely to be determined largely by the patient's wishes, needs, and prior experience. The transference may be diluted and its analysis interfered with by frequent, intense extrapsychotherapeutic contact. The assessment of whether or not this risk is worthwhile depends on the conception of what constitutes effective psychotherapy in the psychoses. In certain phases of such treatment, the analysis of the transference is central. However, a context must first be established in which the patient can actively bring his capacities and resources to bear and effectively participate in this phase of psychotherapeutic work. The preliminary stages of treatment are terribly difficult: engaging severely disturbed patients in meaningful contact requires patience, hard work, and thoughtful therapeutic activity for long periods. The resident may cope with extrapsychotherapeutic contact by means not inconsistent with the objectives of individual psychotherapy. He may walk with the patient, be defeated by him at pingpong, or join him over a cup of coffee, and then discuss and clarify the patient's feelings and thoughts about these events in the psychotherapeutic exchange. Work with psychotic patients demands that the therapist "be there," that he emerge as a real figure with whom the patient has continuing active contact; the silence and inactivity of the therapist appropriate at times in the treatment of the neuroses cannot be sustained by the psychotic patient.

As a result of the innovations, the functions of residents began to overlap those of nurses and social workers. The resident on the wards interacted directly with patients more often; the nurse moved closer to the resident's role as she tried to fulfil the demand that her work be more clearly psychotherapeutic. Residents were encouraged to be involved with patients' schooling and work activities and to meet with their families, previously the exclusive concern of the social worker. The social worker's increased contact with all patients was encouraged; her classically psychotherapeutic mode of interacting encroaches upon the resident's territory and is more threatening to him. Because of her professional training, longer experience, and the fact that she remains on the staff after the resident departs, the social worker is an articulate, well-armed competitor for patients' respect, and an authority in community forums. Her role now duplicated the resident's to the extent that a staff social worker, particularly successful in engaging a difficult patient in the course of working with his family, was sometimes assigned as the patient's therapist. Such stimulating confusion accompanied the reexamination of role designations and functions in the hospital; the resident, on the wards more, is often the patient's companion; the nurse tries to work with the patient psychotherapeutically; the resident talks with members of the family; the social worker may see the patient in individual psychotherapy.

An important source of the social worker's power in collaborating and competing with the resident, and in sustaining a professional image superior to nurse and patient, has been the information she obtains in interviews with patients' families, her secrets: history of the patient and his family, how they interacted in the past, and how the family responds from week to week to the patient's hospitalization and treatment. This source of power was now diluted by the resident's information-gathering in his contacts with the family. The social worker's deprivation was outweighed, however, by the opportunity to apply her training and experience with greater freedom; her work was increasingly determined by the psychotherapeutic contribution she is equipped to make, rather than the conventional characterization of what the social worker does.

The nurse is no longer the resident's confidante; her secrets, derived from observations of patients and information the resident confided to her, are now shared with the entire community. The nurse struggles to gain competence in working psychotherapeutically with patients, turns to the resident for guidance, is less awed as she becomes better informed about the once mysterious work of psychotherapy, and begins to assume a professional status closer to and in some ways competitive with that of social worker and resident.

The described blurring of roles and functions was only a beginning. The innovations opened the way for the unfettered use of nurses' and social workers' individual talents, training, and experience, and encouraged their greater participation in the fulfilment of the overall psychotherapeutic goals of the hospital. They stimulated a new sense of freedom and fostered a new, vigorous, intellectually curious pursuit of professional growth and development. Nurses and social workers began to awaken to the challenge of the new hospital and may eventually become the resident's co-workers, rather than his helpmates, in the psychotherapeutic task.

An effect of the innovations upon the residents' relations with one another was the use of patient-staff meetings as a public arena in which to compete for the respect of patients and seniors, particularly the director. Residents as a group were sometimes not active participants in the meetings. However, when a resident spoke, particularly when he was articulate and effective, other residents learned that silence served them most effectively in this competition and refrained from speaking, assuming that more profound thoughts would be attributed to them if they refrained from some of the awkward things they found themselves saying when they participated.

Patient-staff meetings made feelings between the director, other senior staff members, and individual residents, clearer to the entire community: all could know that residents A and B see things the same way and would support one another; that residents C and D were antagonists; that the director and chief resident favored resident E, respecting and supporting his positions; and that they did not respect Dr. F and contradicted or dismissed his comments in the meetings. Competition among residents now included attempts to demonstrate their greater involvement in the hospital community; they employed the stratagem of trying to engage more actively than their fellows in informal contact with the patients. Despite their competition, post-innovation residents were increasingly aware of their vunerability as a group, especially in hospital forums, and reported feeling closer to one another.

Just as the director and other members of the senior staff are now more directly engaged in the affairs of the hospital community, and more informed about each patient from day to day, their opportunities to scrutinize the resident's work and to engage with him in a continuing dialogue on his assessments, decisions, and plans have been greatly increased by the innovations. Their observation and supervision of the Yale Psychiatric Institute resident's work during the pre-innovations period was remarkably detailed; patient-staff meetings and other innovations carried this process even further. The resident's need to be well-regarded by his seniors, particularly as a competent psychotherapist, persists in the post-innovation era. However, the demands made upon him by his seniors, and the demands he makes upon himself to live up to what is expected of the proficient resident, now include the quality and extent of his community participation.

The conditions which have developed in the hospital as a result of the innovations constitute a trying work-setting for the resident. Changes in expectations include new and different criteria of competence and effectiveness. Critical areas in the resident's performance, such as his capacity to lay down the law and stick with it, to temper his judgments and modify his decisions when presented with new information, to sustain his curiosity and investment in understanding what is going on despite demands for prompt action, and thoughtfully and flexibly to coordinate his own contributions and efforts with those of patients and colleagues, are all far more available to the scrutiny of the entire community. This also applies to the inclination of an individual therapist to be either overly assertive or noncommittal and inactive. When topics which evoke a high level of anxiety are discussed in the group, the doctor's interventions are available to observation and assessment of all present. When sexual acts among patients are talked about in these forums, the doctor's views about sexual behavior and sexuality in general, as well as any manifestations of comfort or anxiety regarding his sexual role, are open to appraisal; so, too, is his total self-image in sexual and aggressive terms. Far more observable is the extent to which he is dependent upon the views held of him by colleagues and seniors or is relatively independent and self-assertive, his efforts to rely upon demagogic popularity or his emphasis upon the substance of issues under discussion, and his capacity to stick his neck out, taking whatever deprivations result from asserting himself, because he believes that his goals justify enduring these deprivations.

The heavy investment of the senior staff in patient-staff meetings is evident to residents, and it is clear that an important means of pleasing these teachers and bosses is to invest in this program. Sometimes residents make an effort to approve and respect these forums but are unable to do so in a thoroughgoing, substantial way.

The resident is deprived of the opportunities to hide and protect himself that are characteristic of conventional psychiatric hospital work. He can no longer work as if conducting a private practice on the periphery of the hospital, seeing a series of patients in his office and having his work assessed by his teachers and bosses on the basis of his own reports. His individual psychotherapeutic work remains central to his seniors' appraisal of his competence, but activities outside the office, particularly in patient-staff meetings, now compound the demands made upon him and are critical. In examining the heavy responsibilities of the pre-innovation resident it was not easy to see how anyone could adequately carry through the tasks intrinsic to his predicament. The burdens which the demand for community participation place upon the post-innovation resident, his greater vulnerability in this setting, and the different resources and strategies required of him render the new situation even more demanding and stressful. He undertakes both individual psychotherapy and active participation in the hospital community, struggles with the hardships intrinsic to each, as well as the still greater difficulties which arise from the effort to do both at the same time.

Whereas the contacts of the pre-innovation resident with the director consisted in administrative supervision, his chairing of staff meetings, infrequent appearance on the wards, and participation in departmental conferences, these contacts are now augmented by his seeing each patient regularly on rounds, a more active and direct involvement in the treatment of each patient, and participation with residents and all patients in the continuing dialogue of the patient-staff meetings. Although these changes bring the director and residents into one another's presence more often and provide many more opportunities to communicate directly, he must be shared at such times with the rest of the staff and patients, and the residents' wish for greater individual contact with him is still frustrated. The occasions on which the resident is liable to criticism by the director multiply, and the emotional stress of adverse criticism is heightened by the public context in which it occurs.

Residents' responses to the director were consistent throughout the pre- and post-innovation periods: they tended to criticize him as "authoritarian," "dogmatic," and "vague"; these complaints were made increasingly through the term of the director who served longest during the period studied, and made most heavily after the innovations. Residents emphatically recommended that the solution was to be found in increased personal contact between the director and themselves. However, it was noted that he successfully maintained communication with residents: next to fellow residents and the chief resident, they most frequently brought their complaints to him. In the residents' appraisals of overall performance, the director consistently received the highest rating of any staff member. The inauguration of patient-staff meetings, which seemed to facilitate greater communication between director and residents and to encourage a greater sharing of decision-making power by all members of the hospital community, did not change the residents' perception of the director. They still complained that he was too authoritarian, continued to press for increased personal contact with him and to regard his overall performance as superior to that of any other staff member. The director's greater participation in the affairs of the hospital did not silence the residents' demand that he be more intimately concerned with them.

The patient continues to be deprived of certain freedoms, and the hospital staff remain the expert agents sanctioned by the community to exercise extraordinary power over the patients in their care. The director continues to be authorized to deprive patients of rights and privileges ordinarily regarded as their prerogatives as citizens in a democracy, in the service of their treatment. Although he delegates some of this power to members of the staff, he is viewed as personally retaining full responsibility. As these powers are now increasingly shared with staff members other than physicians, and patients are encouraged to participate with the director and his staff in decisionmaking, a potentially hazardous departure in the delegation of power has now been undertaken by the director. While he now shares more of his authority with residents, social workers, and nurses, and takes the critical step of encouraging patients to assume more responsibility themselves, his caution in delegating power to relatively inexperienced residents extends to all members of the hospital community.

The resident's basic responsibility for determining the extent to which the rights and privileges of a given patient are limited or usurped continues. However, this responsibility is now more directly shared with patients, as well as the director and other members of the staff. Patients participate in discussing, deciding, and assuming responsibility with the resident for such questions as whether a patient should live on the locked or open ward, make phone calls, receive visitors, go out into the larger community to work or attend school. The patient continues to discuss such issues with his therapist, but action requires that he raise the issue himself in patient-staff meeting: approval and implementation require the assent of the patient-staff advisory committee. The resident's approval remains important, and his opinion is sought when the proposal is considered, but the decision results from discussion initiated by and participated in by the patient. He is free to raise questions, challenge arguments opposing his request, and demand explanations. Although, when he offers his proposal to the group, his therapist may support or oppose him, or remain silent, the patient is now less dependent upon his therapist. Prior to the innovations, the patient could not himself raise such issues for approval and implementation. He had to rely upon his doctor to raise them on his behalf at staff meetings and to report staff responses to him. If the patient's request was rejected he had no recourse other than complaining to his resident and persisting in efforts to convince him, or to press him to act again and more effectively.

These changes unburden the resident from much of the pressure exerted by patients and of feelings of guilt about confining and in other ways controlling his patients, and decrease his power. The resident is therefore also deprived of some of his former prestige. His moral conflicts about limiting the freedom of patients with whom he is emotionally involved are less intense; affection and rectitude conflicts are resolved in ways that carry the cost of decreased power and respect in the community. To the extent that the resident values the traditional image of the physician as an expert who makes the decisions and heals the patient, he suffers a deprivation of self-esteem; if this is accompanied by anxiety or symptom formation, the resident is also deprived in well-being. To the extent that he is unambivalently committed to democratic processes and has the capacity to share authority with the patient, the resident's self-esteem is increased, his preferred image of himself as physician and citizen is fulfilled, and his well-being is served.

The residents' perspectives about their power in the post-innovation hospital are expressed in their pointing to the director when asked, "Who tended to make decisions about your patients that you should have made," viewing him as the only staff member with a great deal of influence over the way things go at the hospital, and complaining that they are overruled when he disagrees about a patient's readiness for discharge. Residents imply that the hospital remains essentially authoritarian; decisions are not arrived at through democratic processes. At the same time, the residents view themselves as most influential in "determining whether or not patients get better," feel they have "as much say as they should have" in deciding most issues important in patient management, and emphatically state that they have "enough power" in making decisions about patients. Residents are still content with the degree of their power despite the innovations and complaints about the authoritarian director. They continue to say that they have enough power and influence in the face of evidence documenting the increased power of the director, social workers, and patients, and a concomitant decrease in their power within the community. They are enthusiastic about those changes in the hospital structure which have furthered the sharing of power with patients.

Residents resoundingly support patient-staff meetings; those who participated in them favor them unanimously. They emphasize opportunities provided for patients to assume more responsibility and for patients and staff to share information and compare views. The most heavily weighted reservation about the meetings concerned the possibility that they offered only the appearance and not the reality of shared power and responsibility. Although most pre-innovation residents did not think the business conventionally conducted in staff meetings could be worked out in patient-staff meetings, a majority of post-innovation residents believe that it can be done. Most residents stated that they found participating with patients in discussions of their problems and management less difficult than they had anticipated. The great majority of residents believe that decisionmaking meetings at the Yale Psychiatric Institute should consist of both staff and patient-staff meetings. Residents who participated in patient-staff meetings describe themselves as participating actively much more than they actually did. A majority favor the discussion of almost all topics in meetings with patients but oppose patients participating in the making of decisions conventionally regarded as medical. Although the residents describe themselves as bringing their complaints and criticism to staff meetings, they said that they virtually never speak up about matters of particular concern to them in patient-staff meetings.

In the predicament of the pre-innovation resident, the moral and ethical conflicts with which he struggled in exercising extraordinary power over his patients were prominent. He felt guilty about depriving his patients of their rights as citizens and about the anger which his distrustful and provocative patients evoked in him. He regarded his patients as objects toward whom it was forbidden to acknowledge or express anger and tended to direct such feelings to his seniors. He tried to cope with this guilt by evading and externalizing responsibility for the use of power. The resident's abdication of power was motivated by conflicts engendered in him concerning his preferred self-image as a psychiatrist and as a citizen in a democratic society. In the pre-innovation period he viewed his seniors as the wielders of power, and felt victimized and deprived when they overruled him or exercised power when he failed to act. But he was not dissatisfied about the limited extent of his power, although he complained about the authoritarian and dogmatic behavior of his seniors. The residents' sense of deprivation stemmed largely from feeling that their seniors did not invest enough in them. Their major complaints in this predicament concerned the behavior, particularly the authoritarianism, of their seniors, especially the director. They emphatically recommended increased personal contact between themselves and the director and other seniors as the means of improving this situation. In effect, residents were willing to accept the superior power of the director and other seniors, asking only that they be cared for and respected.

Post-innovation residents have less power. The director, through greater involvement in the day-to-day affairs of the hospital and more active, direct participation in the treatment of each patient, is more powerful. Other staff members, notably social workers, are also more powerful; their greater participation in treatment and decisionmaking is authorized and encouraged. Much of the residents' power has been relinquished to patients who now assume more responsibility. Residents welcome the sharing of power with patients: it lessens their conflicts about exercising extraordinary control over patients and unburdens them of pressures from patients who now bring complaints and demands to community forums. They complain more vigorously about the director's still greater power but continue to view the extent of their own power as adequate, and make even stronger demands for the director's affection and concern. The innovations have not modified the central importance of intensive psychotherapeutic work, nor have they affected the residents' continuing preoccupation with seniors, although the demands made upon them in order to win their seniors' approval and respect are now even greater.

Chapter 19. MORAL PROBLEMS FOR POLICE

by Michael J. Murphy

FEW GROUPS are more constantly challenged by ethical and moral questions than the police. Each decision a policeman makes in the course of his duties, and these run into dozens each working day, involves a matter of ethics, whether he realizes it or not.

Should he issue a summons to an illegally parked car bearing a politician's plate or, even more disturbingly, the P.B.A. card of a fellow patrolman? Should he break up an early morning fight between two drunks, or let them slug it out? Should he forget a violation of the law for a gratuity, consoling himself with the explanation that it was a small violation? Should he answer the call for help, or conveniently overlook it? Should he give the people of his town a full eight-hour day, or should he find a nice, warm coop?

All these are ethical questions seldom recognized by the policeman at the time or considered as involving and affecting his character. Thank God, they are almost always answered correctly and ethically. For the people of this nation are, in the main, fortunate in the caliber of men who make up their police forces.

Yet to most policemen, ethics is still just a word. This does not mean that ethics is absent from police work: merely that its practice is largely automatic and unheralded. If you were to ask a policeman whether his action in some particular incident was ethical or unethical, he would most likely reply: "Do you mean was it right or wrong?"

The police do have a self-proclaimed code of ethics, yet the true code of moral behavior of a police officer, as of any one else, comes from within and rests on a foundation of religion and conscience. The moral code for police, however, is also bolstered by the rules and regulations of his department—and by the law. The policeman may not label his act as ethical or unethical, but he is certainly aware of any breach of conduct by anyone, particularly himself.

Because he deals constantly with the law and is therefore more aware than many of his fellow citizens of the rules of society and the need for their enforcement, the policeman is—or should be—held to a higher degree of behavior, both in his official and private life. The same strict rules must also apply to all in public offices and positions of public trust. People expect more of such persons, and should not be disappointed. In short, a higher standard of behavior is expected from members of all professions, and police work is becoming a profession. The hope of the future for both public and police lies in the development of a professional police force.

To meet this growing need for a professional body within the police family, more training, higher education and constant attention to attitude and performance are the prime requisites of any police department. Fortunately the awareness of these needs is present in almost every major police department in the United States and greater emphasis is being put on training in all the arts as well as the police function. In New York City, for example, the recruit training course for every rookie is of college level. This course is of four months duration and all policemen who graduate earn ten credits toward a degree in Police Science. Every policeman must pass this course to become a full fledged member of the department. He may then continue his education at the recently established College of Police Science, the first police college of its type in the world. Here he can gear his studies to his working hours, earn a Bachelor's Degree in Police Science and continue on to his Master's. The curriculum at the College consists of more than merely courses in police science. It includes studies in economics, English, government, history, art and music, and the law. It also includes psychology, science, sociology, and speech, with continual emphasis on the art of handling people.

At the Police Academy there is great accent on public and community relations, as well as civil rights and constitutional law. Woven into these subjects are lectures on ethics and morality, with added and special courses given by the department's chaplains of the three major faiths.

These same courses are expanded at the college and the need for absolute honesty and ethical conduct is emphasized throughout the policeman's school hours. Yet while theory is fine, it must be supported by practice and the big question is: To what degree do fine thoughts disintegrate under the stress of everyday reality?

The question is not easily answered, for every man, policeman or not, considers himself as special and almost a law unto himself. Merged into the character of each human being are the hundreds of converging and ramified experiences, frustrations, hopes, and ambitions which contribute to the making of the full man. Co-mingled in the entire problem is also the fluctuating nature of each individual's reaction to a set of circumstances; solid and unyielding today, indecisive and compromising tomorrow.

The ability and desire to resist temptation, to fight against taking the "easy way" is the test of the man. Yet, sadly enough, that desire may be attacked by a host of aggravating doubts and concessions and convenient self-serving alibis which can weaken a man's ability to resist and cause him to bury his beliefs and his conscience. To the strong man this is no problem. He knows his course of action, he has studied the consequences of weakness and he refuses to surrender. His will is so strong that he is generally labelled harsh and unflexible. Just how many such strong men are there? Every person wants to be liked. It takes great moral stamina to make the right decision which generally is unpopular. Yet in this regard, police have a greater advantage then others, because most of the decisions they are called on to make are unpopular. Police work, by its very nature, is repressive and resented. Even those citizens who demand honesty in enforcement generally mean "against the other guy—not me."

The purpose of police training is to produce strong and brave men. Not men of physical courage alone, but men of great moral courage who can face unflinchingly the hoots and jeers of weaker men, who secretly respect and envy them. Every effort, every skill and talent at the Police Academy and the College, is devoted to this goal, and yet no one can guarantee the length or endurance of the lessons so intensively taught, or even the degree of absorption by each individual student.

When the police recruit enters the Academy he brings with him the end products of all the experiences and frustrations of his young life. He brings with him the prejudices he has accumulated from his friends and his family and his enemies. He brings with him all the clichés and pre-conceived notions he has absorbed at work and at school and at play. He enters either with the cynical attitude that he will listen to all "the jazz" and make his own decisions; or with a sincere desire to learn and improve.

No institution of learning has yet established an assembly line operation capable of turning out scores of similar scholastic products, and this is a fortunate thing. No one would care for a nation of robots, whether they were attorneys, doctors, businessmen, or police. The secret of education lies in the ability of the student to absorb and the skill of the teacher to meet the special demands posed by each individual student. The teacher judges his success by the responses and interest he evokes from each student and, in the long run, by the way his pupils translate his lessons in the crucible of day-to-day living.

So each teacher starts with the raw product before him and seeks to mold it to those concepts which in each discipline should produce the best. At the New York Police Academy great emphasis is placed on the absolute importance of ethics and the professional concept. Each patrolman is taught that his duty is to serve mankind; that he must be fully trained before he can practice his calling; that he must constantly practice self-discipline.

Special lectures are given on discipline and deportment as the keystone of success. It is emphasized that good discipline and deportment result in a more efficient department and bring greater confidence and respect from the public. Lectures by chaplains discuss the absolute need for integrity, courage, responsibility, and sacrifice as the ingredients of the professional policeman. Yet with all the teaching, one fact becomes startlingly apparent and is summed up succinctly in the concluding paragraph of one chaplain's discourse:

Others can advise us, and suggest, and help us, but each of us carries the sole responsibility of making the major decisions which will affect our lives, our futures, and our souls.

And so we come to the crux of the matter: the need to discover new and effective methods not only of driving home the lesson of ethical conduct, but of seeing that the messages are remembered and retained; not sacrificed to expediency and selfishness. There are no miracles available; no ready answers to be pulled out of anyone's hat. It requires constant attention, improved procedures, and always the search for more dedicated men.

The problem does not revolve around police alone. It is so farreaching that it penetrates every layer of our society and includes the entire question of the moral tone of our civilization and the state of mind of its leaders and its people. Without a climate of law and order, no society can flourish.

Without respect for the rights of others, without respect for the rules of society and humanity, the doors are open to anarchy and the law of the jungle. Tragically enough, the mere adulteration of the laws emanating from the Ten Commandments is as destructive as a planned campaign of disorder and disregard. Perhaps even more so, because disregard of the Commandments breeds contempt for humanity which swiftly erodes the foundations of good conduct and corrupts the young, who quickly learn that the easy way seems to be the best way to survive. From this evil atmosphere emerges a cynicism which justifies itself by pointing to the behavior of those in positions of authority and power who have denied their oaths and the ethical concept in favor of greed and self.

The policeman is a realist. He can live in any society and give that society the type of enforcement it seeks and, in his mind, deserves. If he finds that he can prosper best in an atmosphere of permissiveness and special privilege, he will in most cases learn to live with it. If he discovers that those in higher positions callously flout the law, he uses these examples as a salve to his conscience and goes along with the system.

One can take the most dedicated young policeman in any department, and if he learns that certain people are "sacred cows" and free from almost any sort of punishment, he will shrug his shoulders and say "what's the use?" If he issues a summons for a traffic violation and has to listen to threats from a belligerent motorist that "I'll have your job," he can smile and shrug his shoulders and do his job. But if he finds that the threat was more than just words; if he is brought on the carpet and told to be more careful, then he will, in most instances, go beyond that and not only overlook such violations but cash in on them. He appeases his conscience by saying "everybody's doing it, why not

I?" Should he enforce the law against gambling, for example, and then be admonished after breaking up a gambling combine, it does not take him long to feel that he is foolish to fight the tide—and that he should go along with it instead.

It is in these areas that only the strong-willed can survive. But there should be no such bog which sucks a man down like quicksand. He must have respect and confidence in his superiors and the value and worth of the law, if he is to walk tall in his job and private life. And, in the area of police work, the key to police achievement and attitude lies in the hands of police commanders. No superior can expect and demand moral honesty from his men, if he is morally dishonest. Such a man will encourage not only mass misbehavior, but contempt. The honest, dedicated, "tough" boss will not only be respected, but obeyed. The tone and example he sets will become the blueprint for all but the most cynical of his men. The commanding officer, in most cases, also tends to reflect the principles and precepts of his superiors who must always be of the highest and most professional types. The police service is one in which the poison of corruption spreads most rapidly, not from the roots upward, but from the top down.

The policeman's mimicking of those he should respect, but does not, is reflected in his actions and enlarges the breeding ground for similar misconduct, not only among his fellow patrolmen but among the young of the whole society. Once the new generation discovers that crime pays, or seems to pay, only the very strongest will resist temptations to become "one of the boys." Corruption spreads like a cancer, and like that dread disease, no cure has yet been found for it.

Therefore training, to me, is absolutely essential, not only for the patrolman, but for all ranks.

There can and should be more room in training for student growth. Every graduate student suffers disillusionment, loss of enthusiasm, and loss of idealism, and this is triply so in law enforcement. Such rude awakening comes speedily to the policeman who is confronted, from the time he begins to walk his post beat, with the current problems of immorality. The atmosphere has not changed much in this century; the problems have merely multiplied because of huge population growth. People have not changed, but each cultural group migrating to a city, particularly such a dynamic and changing metropolis as New

York, has brought new and varying problems with them. Chief, of course, has been the problem of race and the struggle for equality, something unheard of by the policeman several generations ago. This dramatic revolution must be understood and appreciated, particularly by police, if the fabric of our democratic society is not to be ripped asunder.

It is here that only the highest and most advanced type of teaching can bring visible improvement in the attitude of police. There must not only be rapid assimilation and understanding, there must be positive efforts by police to convince all of their sincerity and belief that their prime mission is to protect the lives and liberties of all. This area of police training is one of the most exciting and challenging of our modern age. It is being scrutinized very carefully by all segments of our society, and on the success of the police schools in conveying the message of equality and impartiality to police rests the hope of a happier society.

The answer lies in a return, and a speedy return, to the old verities; to a greater realization of the need for absolutely spotless conduct on the part of all of us. To a realization that compromise and connivance does not pay; to the understanding that the future of our nation depends on the best behavior and attitude.

This, to me, means a combination of education and example. As it applies to police, there have been great advances, but there must be even greater. Careful attention must be given to the selection of faculty for each training center for police, not only those schools of college level, but all types of institutions. The lessons to be taught must be applied in the field and constantly drilled into each policeman not only by his teachers but by his commanding officers. There must be carefully planned programs of re-training in ethics and morality in the police schools and in the police precincts, and there must be swift and stern justice to those officers who disregard instructions and orders and violate their oaths of office. There must also be a more careful evaluation and selection of police candidates and no lowering of standards, no matter what the outcry. Not only police standards but police salaries must be raised to attract and retain the best type of men in the community. Only in this way will the climate of law and order be maintained and improved and the tenets of the Policeman's Code of Ethics, which follow, become more than mere noble sentiments and window-dressing:

As a law enforcement officer, my fundamental duty is to serve mankind; to safeguard lives and property; to protect the innocent against deception, the weak against oppression or intimidation, and the peaceful against violence or disorder; and to respect the constitutional rights of all men to liberty, equality, and justice.

I will keep my private life unsullied as an example to all; maintain courageous calm in the face of danger, scorn, or ridicule; develop self-restraint; and be constantly mindful of the welfare of others. Honest in thought and deed in both my personal and official life, I will be exemplary in obeying the laws of the land and the regulations of my department. Whatever I see or hear of a confidential nature or that is confided to me in my official capacity will be kept ever secret unless revelation is necessary in the performance of my duty.

I will never act officiously or permit personal feelings, prejudices, animosities, or friendships to influence my decisions. With no compromise for crime and with relentless prosecution of criminals, I will enforce the law courteously and appropriately without fear or favor, malice or ill will, never employing unnecessary force or violence and never accepting gratuities.

I recognize the badge of my office as a symbol of public faith, and I accept it as a public trust to be held so long as I am true to the ethics of police service. I will constantly strive to achieve these objectives and ideals, dedicating myself before God to my chosen profession—law enforcement.

Chapter 20. THE CHALLENGE OF CHANGE: PARTICULARLY FOR THE ARMED FORCES

by Ben M. Zeff

THROUGH THE AGES man has had to adjust to new developments. More often than not, man himself was responsible for changes that created new challenges. When new challenges came about through the slow evolutionary process, man was able to meet them more easily than when changes came at devastating speed.

Arnold J. Toynbee, in his monumental studies, traced the rise, decline, and fall of twenty-six civilizations. One of the conclusions that can be drawn from his studies is that major civilizations that were unable to adapt to new conditions declined and fell. The same theory may apply to individuals, institutions, organizations, and associations. We can disregard the challenge of change and perhaps continue a sort of existence for another five decades, or we can respond to the challenges of the times and become a dynamic, viable force. The future rests in our hands. Let us examine some of the challenges that exist and how we might respond:

Almost overnight the weight of the Federal Government has been brought to bear on many of our serious social, political, and economic problems. Human rights, aid to education, the attack on poverty, reapportionment, Medicare, and many other important concerns will provide greater opportunities for the young and the old, for the disadvantaged as well as for the advantaged. The Federal Government recognizes the fact that it can provide some of the ideas and some of the monies to effect change. It can serve as the stimulater, initiater, and catalyst. However, individuals, institutions, agencies, and associations must recognize the challenges, must devote time, energy, and resources if these goals are to become a reality. Shall we be passive observers? Or dare we be active participants in the building of a better social order?

On the horizon loom some mighty dark clouds created by the rapidly advancing technological revolution. In reviewing the impact of automation on agriculture, it is evident that unemployment in agriculture will rise. Robert Theobold, in his book, *Free Men and Free Markets,* states that only five percent of our population will be required for our agri-industry. Unless we give serious thought to these developments, and time is precious, the fruits of our technology may come to haunt us.

The impact that technology has had on our industrial life is readily calculable. Many benefits have resulted but millions of workers have been displaced by computers and automated machines. One authority predicts that, "2% of our population will in the discernible future be able to produce all the goods and services needed to feed, clothe, and run our society with the aid of machines."

Change is upon us and will continue at an ever increasing rate; we cannot stop it, even if we wished. And if we did, the consequences would be far more detrimental than advantageous.

This year (1966) we have one million more eighteen year olds than we had in 1964. Perhaps half of these will enter colleges and universities. What are the employment prospects for the others? Huge numbers of youngsters will continue to enter our labor market for years to come. They are born; they are here!

The opportunities for continuing education are manifold. Technology will increase rather than limit our sense of freedom. It is possible that man can finally achieve his greatest potential. The future can be dark if we do nothing. However, if through continuing education we are able to exploit to the fullest man's greatest resource—the human mind—truly, the golden age of mankind may be around the corner. What role will we play? Will we be in the vanguard, or will we simply sit on our hands and do nothing?

How can we harness our strengths and our talents? Each of us can provide some answers.

Collectively, working as a team, virtually no problem should prove insurmountable. We represent many strengths and competencies which we too often take for granted or even overlook.

Charles Dickens begins *A Tale of Two Cities*—"It was the best of times, it was the worst of times, it was the age of wisdom, it was the age of foolishness, . . . it was the season of light, it was the season of darkness, it was the spring of hope, it was the winter of despair, we had everything before us, we had nothing before us . . ."

This same sense of paradox prevails today in America about automation and technological change. How incredible it would have seemed even to Dickens that a society could be concerned about the possibility of machine systems taking over production of the necessities of life! America is the richest nation in the history of mankind; and yet one-fifth of us live in poverty. We have a surplus of labor, capital, and in the production ability of both our farms and factories—and yet we have vast unmet needs in our slums and depressed areas, in medical care, educational facilities, and in urban transportation. Today we are able to control our environment as in no other age before us. Potentially we could be on the verge of a new golden age. President Lyndon B. Johnson expressed it when he said this generation of Americans in particular faces "the challenge of greatness."

Yet there are those who say that we are fast approaching a time when two percent of the labor force can produce all we need. They base their predictions on what to them seems the logical projection of the growth of machine systems that can replace man's mind as well as his muscles.

Similar predictions were made when steam engines were introduced to power the mills and carriages of the early nineteenth century. In the early 1930s the technocrats cried similar alarms. Yesterday we built roads with strong backs and shovels. Today we build them with trained minds operating enormous and costly machinery.

The can opener developed from a knife-on-a-stick into a fifteen dollar electric tool. Television came from nowhere. Aircraft grew from slow and puny ships to rockets that fly to the moon and beyond. Today even the sweeper in the factory—the man with the bucket and the broom—is likely to be using mechanical equipment. There is little work for the unskilled. Obviously tomorrow's factory hand will require even greater skills. In our tomorrows the electronic computer will be as commonplace in our society as is the telephone today.

We in America are living in extraordinary times. Perhaps there never really was a calm and peaceful period in man's history. It may be that the world has always seemed to be going through something extraordinary, and our recollection of a peaceful past is only an elemental memory of the Garden of Eden. But, even if the past were as exciting a time as ours here and now, I would still maintain that never in man's history has there been such a tremendously abundant today, nor such a promising tomorrow.

Man started with his fingers, not long ago in terms of time and space as we understand them now. Today these remarkable fingers have produced tools with enormous power. But man must keep pace with his invention. We can neither afford nor can we tolerate a tomorrow in which a skilled elite dominates a technologically illiterate mass. Nor does our heritage, or our national dreams and aspirations, permit us to tolerate compromise in striving for achievement.

Yet in the midst of these dizzying perspectives there are still with us the old problems of war, poverty, suffering, and ignorance. Our ability to master the world of matter has far outrun our wisdom in coping with social and human problems. We have over three and a half million men and women who want work but for whom a society with vast unmet needs cannot find a job.

There is no iron law that a high rate of unemployment is the price we must pay for automation. In the 1930s before true automation had been devised, we had over ten million unemployed. Today many less developed countries have unemployment rates several times higher than the United States. Conversely, Western Europe which is automating some areas of production at a faster pace than the United States has a shortage, not a surplus of manpower.

Our only defense, our only assurance that future generations will live as free men in a peaceful and abundant society, is our ability to teach and to train this and future generations in the social sciences and the technical skills that make man the master of his creation.

War is no longer a matter of muscles. Now it is largely a matter of brains, and the need for brains is not limited to a handful of high-ranking military leaders. Today all the men and women in the Department of Defense—whether they are military or civilian employees—need the education necessary to meet the startling changes in our world, occurring with such great rapidity.

From the standpoint of our national defense, the dimensions of change are enormous. In the decade between 1947 and 1957 there were more changes in warfare than in the whole of the previous century, from 1857 to 1957. In this 100 years, the technological changes were roughly the magnitude of those which had taken place during almost a thousand years previous; that is to say from about 1147, with the building of the great medieval castles.

Designing the castles, learning to use the longbow, inventing gunpowder, developing the musket and the cannons—all of these changes in warfare occurred before 1847. Fragmentation shells, steam-driven propeller-motivated ships, battleships made of iron, new ranging devices, repeating weapons, jet propulsion, the tank, radar, and finally the atomic bomb—these were some of the developments of the century 1847–1947. In the ten years from 1947 to 1957, however, a similarly astonishing change took place in warfare—miniaturization, missilery, hydrogen bombs, and automation. This dramatic geometric progression gives us a window and some perspective on the future. The United States is deeply involved in this revolution in warfare with a spectrum of instruments running from those used in conventional warfare to those used in thermonuclear attack and defense and extending to the potentials of space. We must have sophisticated military and supporting manpower to cope with the requirements posed by this broad spectrum of warfare.

Modern technology is developing so rapidly that weapons have increased in destructive power some 100,000-fold in two decades—from World War II to the present. The demands of our new technology are such that our educational resources are the very base on which we must build our modern forces. Our colleges and universities are basic resources.

Technology is only a part of the educational picture which we must bear in mind for today and the decades ahead. Technology and the training necessary for it cannot be overemphasized, but at the same time other educational demands are being made each day which are equally pressing. These demands are especially strong for education in the area of the social sciences and in languages.

No society has ever displaced so many other societies as has that of the Western World. The technological revolution of the nineteenth and twentieth centuries in the Atlantic community has changed the political face of the globe from Africa to Asia. The pressures of our time have created new countries, new ways of facing things, and new problems to be solved today in a context quite different from that of the nineteenth century.

There has been great interest in the development of capability in guerrilla warfare and counterinsurgency. But both guerrilla warfare and counterinsurgency require our officers and men to know more of languages, history, sociology, economics, and psychology than ever before.

The problems of guerrilla warfare and counterinsurgency are ones which military instruments alone cannot solve. The insidious spread of Communism requires that our military men and women participate in the rebuilding of societies in conflict, and this, in turn, means that they must know and appreciate the societies into which they are moved as instructors and planners. They must understand the structure of villages, areas, and regions. They must understand and appreciate political relationships in a way they have not had to do before. They must be able to work with other agencies of Government such as the Departments of State, Commerce, Agriculture, and the United States Information Agency, so that together our country teams overseas may bring to bear a coordinated effort to keep our friends and our allies out of Communist hands. In other words, we not only have a definite need to study technology but have at the same time the equally pressing need to understand all of the arts of communication, all of the economic interrelationships, all of the impacts of sociological change on all areas throughout the world. These are the reasons that the Department of Defense has put a new emphasis on educational programs and why they are considered essential. For the same reasons, it is vitally important to strengthen the national higher education structure.

Because of the nation's needs for better educated personnel the Armed Forces now have a difficult problem both in obtaining and in retaining the people they need. Within about two years of their graduation from the Great Lakes Naval Training Center Electronics School, almost ninety percent of the technicians return to civilian life where their skills are in great demand. Again, recently an Air Force spokesman said that while the overall retention rate for officers was forty percent, the retention rate for science and engineering officers was only about fifteen percent and for research and development officers only about seven percent. These examples illustrate that as a Nation we face critical manpower shortages which a program strengthening education would alleviate.

Today, as never before, the enlisted man must have a good educational grounding, preferably through high school, if he is to absorb training and perform effectively the demanding tasks generated by our modern Armed Forces. At the end of World War II, about one-third of all enlisted jobs were in occupations which are classified as technical and mechanical jobs in the civil economy. These fields now account for almost half of all enlisted jobs.

The equality and extent of preparation in mathematics and especially in English have a bearing on success in training and on effective performance in these and other military jobs. Moreover, of the nation's some 1,400,000 youths who yearly reach the age of eligibility for military service, about 235,000 will be unable to pass the mental tests required for entrance into the Armed Forces. Lack of educational opportunity certainly contributed to this significant social and military liability. Additionally, better educated servicemen are not only more competent but are also less likely to create disciplinary problems. Here, then, is a clearcut responsibility and challenge to American higher education: Develop new techniques for diagnostic testing, basic education, vocational and psychological counseling, and methods for motivating this segment of American citizenry which has for too long been, not forgotten, but neglected. Who is better equipped than the nation's educators to provide leadership and knowhow in preventive and remedial services for school-age youth? It is time we shelved the old wives' tale that "the poor will always be with us." We can no longer afford a society in which preliminary screening shows one out of every two selective service registrants called for preinduction examination to be unqualified.

Each year the services obtain only a small percentage of their new officers from the service academies. For the remainder, the services must, and happily do, rely primarily on civilian colleges and universities. They have been getting over 30,000 new officers a year, of which about 1,600 come from the service academies. The three academies at West Point, Annapolis, and Colorado Springs in fact are only the most visible part of a Department of Defense educational complex which ranges from recruit training to operating top-level military professional schools such as the National War College and the Industrial College of the Armed Forces. As part of the programs to meet their educational needs, the services have at any one time students in some 400 civilian collegiate institutions. The Army alone has students doing graduate work in some eighty-eight universities here and abroad. The Department of Defense must meet its requirements by conducting educational programs for training in virtually every kind of skill the twentieth century needs. Communications, electronics, languages, sociology, international relations, nuclear physics—these are only some of the areas in which the Armed Forces must possess competence.

The mission of the United States Military Academy is to instruct and train the Corps of Cadets so that each graduate will have the qualities and attributes essential to his progressive and continued development throughout a career as an officer of the Regular Army.

Inherent in this mission are the following objectives:

1. Mental. To provide a broad collegiate education in the arts and sciences leading to the Bachelor of Science Degree.

2. Moral. To develop in the cadet a high sense of duty and the attributes of character with emphasis on integrity, discipline, and motivation essential to the possession of arms.

3. Physical. To develop in the cadet those physical attributes essential to a lifetime career as an officer of the Regular Army.

4. Military. To provide a broad military education rather than individual proficiency in the technical duties of junior officers. Such proficiency is, of necessity, a gradual development, the responsibility for which devolves upon the graduates themselves and upon the commands and schools to which they are assigned after being commissioned.[1]

The mission of the United States Naval Academy is to develop midshipmen morally, mentally, and physically, and to imbue them with the highest ideals of duty, honor, and loyalty, in order to provide graduates who are dedicated to a career of Naval Service and have a potential for future development in mind and character to assume the highest responsibilities of command, citizenship, and government.

The mission of the Air Force Academy is to provide instruction, experience, and motivation to each cadet, so that he will graduate with

[1] United States Military Academy, *1965–1966 Catalogue*, p. 1.

the knowledge, character, and qualities of leadership essential to his progressive development as a career officer with the United States Air Force.

The following excerpts from the catalog of the United States Military Academy are representative of all the Service Academies and emphasize the ideals which are a way of life which each student carries with him the rest of his life.

The development of character and integrity in the members of the Corps of Cadets is a basic objective of the Academy. The Cadet Honor Code and System are officially recognized as primary means through which this objective is attained.

From the earliest days of recorded history it has been universally recognized that unquestioned integrity is an essential trait of the military leader. . . . . . . The Honor Code has never outgrown its original and simple meaning —that a cadet will not lie, cheat, or steal. The Code requires complete integrity in both word and deed of all members of the Corps and permits no deviation from those standards. Not only is the cadet expected to tell the truth on all occasions, but also to avoid quibbling or evasive statements. In the classroom a cadet does his own work. Under no circumstances will he take unfair advantage of his classmates. The maintenance of these high honor standards is the responsibility of each cadet, and each cadet is expected to report himself or any other cadet for violations of the Honor Code. . . .[2]

Because the Department of Defense has educational needs on every intellectual level, strengthening and improving the educational quality of the nation's manpower are directly related to the nation's ability to defend itself. It is therefore of special interest to the Department of Defense as a major user of the nation's manpower to encourage and support efforts to upgrade education at all levels and especially in the college and university.

Getting back to the military, there are at present some 300,000 officers and enlisted men on full-time duty in specialized training or in education programs. These men are educating themselves or being trained in all the subjects normally expected, such as electronics, radar repair, and maintenance, and infantry tactics. But the same men are doing a number of things which might not normally be expected. They are taking

[2] *Ibid.,* p. 2.

some 4,000 courses which are offered in the Department of Defense and in the several hundred universities which they attend. Some are studying international relations; others, petroleum management. Some 8,000 on full-time duty are studying one of the fifty languages offered by the Department. Still others are taking courses in business administration, nuclear physics, taxonomy, naval architecture, automatic data processing, and a number of other subjects not traditionally associated with military requirements. As a matter of fact, the services have hundreds of officers doing postgraduate work in more than a hundred universities from Maine to California and from Wisconsin to Texas. This point is stressed because the interest of the Department of Defense in education is not as widely known or understood as it should be. There is still a lack of awareness of military efforts and contributions to higher education.

Quite apart from military manpower, the Department of Defense is one of the nation's largest employers of civilian manpower. About one million civilians are employed directly by the Department in shipyards, depots, laboratories, test centers, posts, camps, stations, and shore establishments of all kinds, all over the world. The spectrum of skills needed is about as broad as would be expected in an enterprise so vast. Significant percentages of scientists, engineers, managers, and other highly skilled persons are needed—and again these are the products of civilian colleges and universities.

The Armed Forces have done considerable research into the production of educated people. They consider it as important as the production of weapons. The military does not shy away from the idea of education as a technology. It believes firmly that the scientific revolution has a great deal to offer in improvement of techniques of education. In fact, the military has developed some new methods and techniques specifically adapted to needs of adult learners. The Air Force has been experimenting with and using programmed instruction for more than thirteen years. All of the services have been using correspondence and self-study programming for many years. They have been accumulating theory, knowledge, and practice, and are convinced that a man can learn with these techniques.

The interest of the military establishment in education is, of course, nothing new; from the very beginning in our country the military has understood that a love of learning is a military necessity. It has understood very clearly that the military must be on the very frontiers in matters of training and education, just as it must be on the frontiers of technology on the one hand and, particularly today, of economics, politics, sociology, and psychology on the other. The basic mission of the Armed Forces in peacetime is training and education. Because they have had to be educational innovators, they have made a number of contributions to civilian education.

It was through the United States Military Academy at West Point that civil engineering was introduced into other colleges and universities in this country. Mechanical engineering and electrical engineering were first introduced into the curriculum under the aegis of the United States Naval Academy at Annapolis. As a matter of fact, it was members of the faculty at Annapolis who, in the course of time as they went elsewhere to teach, introduced these subjects directly into the curriculums of other institutions.

The military would prefer to have our American universities provide for as much of the education of our personnel in civilian allied subjects as possible. The Department of Defense does not believe that it should be duplicating those areas in which the universities over the years have proved their indispensable worth to our society. But the fact of the matter is that there are many areas in which civilian educational institutions either do not have the knowhow or are simply not interested in teaching courses which are needed and not a part of the traditional curriculum. A specific example is the collection and analysis of data. The Department is spending huge sums on data, including data about managers, data about people, data about installations, data about material, and even data about data. But the handling of mass data is a new subject for the military as well as for industry, and as a result both are experiencing real difficulties in its management.

In order to establish appropriate management of data, the Department has had to establish a course of its own because this type of course was not to be found in the schools of the land. The same thing is true of management of projects. To be sure, some of our educational institutions are making significant progress in the management of large projects involving technical variables in our scientific capability. But a project manager must know many things. He does not need to be a systems analyst, but he certainly needs to know systems analysis techniques. He must understand relationship of costs in terms of time and costs in terms of money. These new techniques are not sufficiently known in the academic world to send military personnel there. Perforce the Armed Forces have developed a new system of management called PERT—Program Evaluation and Review Techniques—and courses of study to train their personnel on these techniques.

There is no wish here to be critical of colleges and universities; it is apparent, however, that they have not had an adequate job of market research done—the military uses the term "requirements study"—to determine the educational needs and potential of the community.

There is room for optimism when one considers the tremendous progress achieved in the past ten years in the field of adult education. The first breakthrough came when institutions of higher education agreed that a mature adult had learned something valuable through experience and work which could be equated with college subjects. Next came the recognition by institutions of this learning in terms of credit toward a college degree. Now a number of universities have developed or are developing degree programs designed specifically for adults who cannot be present on campus for the traditional semester attendance. The State of New York is a pioneer in measuring educational achievement through the use of proficiency examinations in college subjects for which degree credits may be awarded. Apparently this program has met with success and should encourage other States and institutions to follow suit.

Education must be reoriented to a conception of learning as a lifelong process. Young people should leave formal schooling with an insatiable curiosity, a mastery of the tools of learning, and a commitment to continue learning through the rest of their lives. In the Department of Defense this desire for knowledge permeates every organization and channel. There is an ever-increasing demand for more and better learning opportunities and facilities—not by command fiat, but from within each man and woman in uniform. This demand and similar appeals from other segments of our national society can be answered only if there is a national commitment to provide and support the resources necessary for the development of lifelong learning as an integral part of the American system.

President Johnson recently stated that the next twenty years will demand more of America's military men, America's diplomats, America's political leadership and America's young people, than did the past 200 years of our national existence.

Together we shall continue to face, as we face now, a world in contest—freedom against totalitarianism, the sovereignty of the many against a sovereign few, the rule of law against the rule of men. In this contest, America's objectives will not change.

The world reflects America's strength. The world reacts and responds to America's success. Everywhere that America's military men have been sent in this century the way has been made easier for them by the world's knowledge and the world's understanding of the triumphant record of America's free society. The military man is many persons. He is the leader who commands great fleets and air forces and armies. He is the dedicated professional in school, on patrol, on guard. He is the reservist or the guardsman leaving his home to go to summer training. He is also in a sense the civilian who devotes his mind and his energy to public service. Whoever he is, wherever he serves, the man is a product of our whole society, and he means more to peace today than he ever meant before. Our officers and our enlisted men have no true counterparts in military history. In times of our nation's greatest affluence they and their families willingly and courageously undertake the most spartan sacrifices and hardships for us all.

Around the globe they are, in Emerson's words, the "Brave Men who Work while Others sleep, Who dare while Others shy."

They are fighting men—the best in the world today—but they are also thinking men, men whose mission is peace, men who are devoted to peace, stern in their respect for our democratic values.

The military career today demands a new order of talent and training and imagination and versatility. Our military men have these qualities and they have them in abundance.

In our country's history, the oldest article of faith is the principle that we pursue today. Many others have said it since, but George Washington, our first President, said it first a long, long time ago: "To be prepared for war is one of the most effectual means of preserving peace."

Today America's military men stand vigil for peace and freedom—in

West Berlin and in South Vietnam, at Santo Domingo and in the Seventh Fleet, in nuclear submarines under the sea and in SAC planes high in the skies. Wherever they patrol, our nation's heart is with them. Our nation's life is in their hands. We pray God to keep them and to speed them home in a day of peace that they will have won.

Chapter 21. EDUCATION AND RESPONSIBLE BEHAVIOR IN MODERNIZING SOCIETIES

by Daniel Lerner

I.

MY CONCERN about education and responsible behavior in the world today can be put in the form of an hypothesis: that the gap between education and responsible behavior is wide, and widening, in most modernizing lands. In the pages that follow I want to state, perhaps overstate, the considerations underlying my conviction that this hypothesis is true and important. These considerations are a mixed bag of definitions, valuations, and verifiable propositions. I shall aim only at presenting them in such manner that a reader who does not share my definitions or valuations will, all the same, know what is being asserted. Since verification of propositions is the business of research rather than discussion, I shall aim at clarity and cogency of the assertions rather than documentation and demonstration of their truth.

Education is clearly a word of many dimensions even when defined with precision. In ordinary usage, indeed, it is a multivariate word, since it is made to refer to many different types of behavioral and institutional relationships as well as to different dimensions of a single continuum of behavior. In French, for example, the word *éducation* refers to the training of a child at home by his parents (the words *formation* and *enseignement* being reserved for institutional schooling outside the home). Something of this ambiguity occurs in English if one says that a child's education was "neglected" as well when one means that his institutional schooling was inadequate as when one means that his parents failed to teach him proper manners.

Such confusing usage reflects, of course, the highly intermixed reality of education. It is, in fact, often very difficult to differentiate what a child has learned at school from what he has learned at home. This refers not only to manners and morals, which were traditionally considered to be primarily the responsibility of parents, but also to the substantive content of the school curriculum. For illustration, we need hardly look beyond the fact that Harlem children modally score below State averages in their school subjects while neighboring children on Morningside Heights modally score well above State averages.

Where family and school are mutually-reinforcing, the effects of education are likely to be maximized. Where reciprocity between family and school is absent (or the relationship between them is mutually-subversive), the effects of education are likely to be minimized. It is the latter condition—whether in Harlem or in Turkey—that concerns us here. To take account of these two different, though not unrelated, situations we put forward for discussion two separate propositions:

Prop. 1: Nonreciprocity between school and family occurs most frequently when either school or family, or both, are substandard by the modal educational criteria of their society (the case of Harlem).

Prop. 2: The frequency distribution of nonreciprocity is highest in societies with the largest number of substandard schools and families by the modal education criteria of world society (the case of Turkey).

These propositions inadequately formulate the full range of "considerations" underlying the initial hypothesis above, because they inadequately reduce complex sets of observations by the single criterion of frequency distributions according to the weak test of statistical "modes." However, even an inadequate start is a start—and the function of discussion is to make it more nearly adequate.

Proceeding then to the casual definitions, I pause only for a moment to disclose some of my own *a priori* preferences—philosophical, sociological, and educational. I live in the pluralistic-probabilistic world allusively outlined by William James. In this world there are no eternal verities or immutable tabus. This is a wonderful world to live in, where anything and everything is always open in principle to critical examination or empirical inquiry. But it has its difficult moments, for the constraints of secular knowledge are no less severe than those of revealed knowledge—and the secular canons of evidence-to-inference are, indeed, much more stringent.

Note, then, that these definitions do not attempt to say what the essence of education *is*—because I do not believe that education has a universal essence (*pace* the *Protagoras* of Plato). Nor do they attempt to epitomize the empirical findings of educational research—because I do not believe that education has an empirical epitome (*pace* the valuable comparative studies of Frank Bowles and others). These definitions are an extrapolation from my own personal experience of diverse educational behavior in much of the world—experience which is differentially empirical, relatively unsystematic, and largely ignorant of sub-Saharan Africa and Australia. The definitions are intended, therefore, not for scientific closure (or as close as science ever gets to closure) but for heuristic disclosure—on the chance that disclosure may provoke fruitful discussion of the complex process with which we are concerned. So, without further ado:

Casdef 1: Education is effective in the measure that it maximizes an individual's capacity to enact the values that he shares with his environment;

Casdef 2: Responsible behavior is the most effective enactment of shared values of which an individual is capable.

You will note, to put it more mildly than any member of this conference is obliged to do, that I have neither eliminated ambiguity nor imposed closure by these definitions. On the contrary, what I have done is to shift the problem of meaning and closure from a definitional to an empirical basis. To decide whether these terms of education and responsible behavior are being satisfied we must:

1. Speak only of concrete cases (or sets of cases on a distributive basis):

2. describe these concrete cases only in terms of operational indices of the words measure, maximize, capacity, enact(ment), values, share (d), effective, capable;

3. evaluate the concrete cases only on the basis of their performance on our operational indices.

These are hard lines. We rarely live by them even in our professional work as researchers. The less reason, then, to expect that they will—or should—do more than shape our discussion of these wideranging, deeprooted issues of education and responsible behavior—which I keep thinking of as education *for* responsible behavior.

II. Two Cases: Turkey and Iran

To indicate more concretely what I am thinking aloud about, I shall sketch out two cases bearing on the initial hypothesis, which asserts that the gap between education and responsible behavior is widening in most modernizing lands. I draw these cases from the modernizing lands I know best—those of the Middle East—and leave it to the conference to decide, among other things, whether these cases fairly represent "most" of the modernizing lands in other areas of the world.

The first case is Turkey. Over the forty years since Ataturk took command, the Turks have made heroic and often ingenious efforts to raise their literacy. These efforts began with Ataturk's Village institutes, the first major campaign to introduce coeducational skill-and-value training into a Muslim environment. The Village Institutes produced a "revolutionary" increase of education and responsible behavior as revealed in the subsequent lives of its graduates (notably in their autobiographies).[1] Then under Menderes, shortly after Ataturk died, the Village Institutes were annulled. The coeducational feature, perhaps the most important innovation of all in the "male vanity culture" of Islam, was abolished. The secular value-training feature was sharply downgraded and the skill-training feature was given a monopoly position in Turkish policy toward education and responsible behavior.

The recent, and current, Turkish focus has emphasized literacy-as-skill. It has become the concern of the Turkish Army in dealing with illiterate underskilled rural males—as contrasted with the Village Institutes' concern with undervalued as well as underskilled youth, both male and female. That the Turkish Army has undertaken even this much of the complex task of education is a tribute to its courage. But courage is not enough in these matters. The Turkish Army literacy-training program is failing because it is conceived only as skill-training,

---

[1] See Mahmut Makal, *A Village in Anatolia*, Vallentine, Mitchell, London, 1954; and Resat Nuri Guntekin, *Autobiography of a Turkish Girl*, translated by Sir Wyndham Deedes, G. Allen & Unwin, London, 1949.

without regard to value-training as an essential component of responsible behavior in a developing environment.

The fact is that recent studies have shown this literacy program to be often ineffective—to produce dysfunctional effects—in the existing Turkish environment.[2] Young soldiers lose their tenuous grasp on literacy, when they return to their villages, because they are ignored or ridiculed by their village environment. There is little or nothing to read in the village, and effort to maximize the reading skill is demeaned by the villagers. The reading skill is not, by the tests set forth above (Casdefs 1 and 2), among the values shared by the individual and his environment. Nor will the new literate in Turkey ever be able to maximize his skill until literacy is incorporated among the shared values of rural and illiterate Turks—the significant "environment" of the new literates.

The second case is Iran. Here we illustrate the educational dysfunction not on the lowly level of new literates but on the august level of college graduates. Let me illustrate this by reference to the city of Teheran, where, a decade ago, there were thirty-six registered "film companies." Only one of these companies had actually produced, distributed, and exhibited any films; the other thirty-five had yet to complete production of their first film.

How did this odd situation come about? The sequence of events begins at Teheran University, where the old traditions of Iranian learning and the new demands of Iranian modernization are locked in a deadly struggle, from which there issues annually a horde of distorted and disfigured progeny called "graduates." These are the young men who, under the compulsion to maintain or attain an elevated social status, attended or evaded four years of magistral lectures and passed a final examination. They have acquired certain standard adornments—*i.e.,* acquaintance with Persian history and Shariya law, familiarity with the glories of Persian art and poetry, certified by the ability to quote yards of Firdausi and appropriate stanzas of Saadi.

These young men are all dressed up—but they have no place to go. They are much too numerous to be absorbed into the traditional social

[2] Daniel Lerner and R. D. Robinson, "Swords and Ploughshares," *World Politics,* Volume XIII, number 1, October, 1960.

orders represented by government, army, priesthood. Already the Iranian government periodically discovers itself unable to meet the payroll of its swollen bureaucracy. Nor is Iran developing an adequate supply of new occupations deemed fitting for college graduates. These graduates face only the bleak prospect of unemployment and underemployment. Accordingly they seek to occupy themselves in ways that will be amusing if not rewarding. A half-dozen such graduates organize themselves around a thirty-five millimeter camera and form a "film company." But their outlook is dismal. Most of them will never produce a film; those who do will never be able to market it. It is unlikely that, even if they wish to show it free of charge, their film will ever be seen beyond their circle of friends. There are few cinemas in Teheran, and they are for commercial hire. Frustration and failure thus await most young Iranians who seek to make a career in the mass media.

The key factor in this unhappy situation is the uncertain and inadequate tempo of Iranian modernization. The supply of new life-opportunities does not keep pace with—is indeed steadily outpaced by—the burgeoning demands of the college graduates. In 1958 I summarized the Iranian situation in the following terms, which remain cogent today:

Incorporation of new men is no easy task in a non-growth economy. Iran develops few of those constantly growing and changing occupational roles which embody young men in the elite structure. The clergy, the military, the bureaucracy—all these are charges on the public treasury, already overburdened and scarcely capable of expansion. The teaching corps is pitifully inadequate, but unlikely to multiply opportunities until Iran develops a modernizing economy in which literacy is an essential skill. Without an expanding business sector, there is little room for the lawyer and accountant, for the specialist in industrial management or labor relations, for the insurance broker or the investment manager, for the account executive or the public relations counsel. Advertising is stillborn and the mass media abortive. Where in Iran is "the man in the gray flannel suit"? Whatever his unpopularity among Westerners wearied by opinion brokers, in Iran he would be a more useful stimulus to modernization than the agitational intellectual in a hairshirt of vivid hue.

Given its limited absorptive capacity, Iran suffers from an overproduction of intellectuals. In a society about 90% illiterate, several thousand young persons go through the classical routines of higher education each year. Learning no skills that can be productively employed, these collegians seek outlets in the symbol-manipulating arts toward which their humanistic studies have oriented them. Their effort supplies a poignant instance of usable training rendered useless by its social environment—newspapers without readers that last a week or a month, film companies that never produce a film. The mass media, as distinctive index of the Participant Society, flourish only where the mass has sufficient skill in literacy, sufficient motivation to share "borrowed experience," sufficient cash to consume the mediated product. In Iran the mass media are anemic and with them, annually, die a thousand hopes.[3]

III. The Revolution of Rising Frustrations

These two cases illustrate both extremes of the behavioral continuum —new literates at the lower end and college graduates at the upper end—along which education is producing frustration in the modernizing world today. Our conception of frustration is adapted from an ingenious formula of William James:

$$\text{Self-Esteem} = \frac{\text{Success}}{\text{Pretensions}}$$

James went on to elucidate this equation as follows: "Such a fraction may be increased as well by diminishing the denominator as by increasing the numerator. To give up pretensions is as blessed a relief as to get them gratified, and where disappointment is incessant and the struggle unending, this is what men will always do.[4]

In the vocabulary domesticated by academic psychology since James, this tells us that Satisfaction is a ratio between levels of aspiration and achievement what I call, more simply, the Want:Get ratio. Where the ratio is high, satisfaction is high. Where the ratio is low, satisfaction is low and frustration rises. Our assertion that frustration is rising so

[3] The foregoing material on Iran has been drawn from two of my previous publications: *The Passing of Traditional Society* (Free Press), Macmillan Co., 1958, p. 362; and the essay "Toward a Communication Theory of Modernization," in L. W. Pye, editor, *Communication and Political Development,* Princeton University Press, Princeton, N.J., 1963, pp. 327–328.

[4] Cited from D. Lerner and H. D. Lasswell, *The Policy Sciences,* Hoover Institution on War, Revolution and Peace, Stanford University, Stanford, 1965, p. 30 (paperback).

rapidly as to be called a "revolution," in most of the modernizing world, is based on three additional empirical generalizations:

Empgen 1: that frustration tends to produce irresponsible behavior in its victims;

Empgen 2: that the surplus of education over opportunities (to use one's education in satisfying ways) is a major source of frustration in the world today;

Empgen 3: that the rate of frustration is rising more rapidly in the underdeveloped than the developed countries—hence, as put in our initial hypothesis, that the gap between education and responsible behavior is "widening" in most modernizing lands.

The gap is widening so rapidly, and erratically, we now add, that its effects are "revolutionary." Indeed, I would overstate the case enough, for purposes of discussion, to say that in many modernizing lands today education (along with the mass media) is a major producer of *irresponsible* behavior.

I refer to the fact that since 1950, according to Unesco statistics, the world has been adding over 25,000,000 "new literates" to its population each year—thereby producing, at a modest estimate of acceleration since 1950, nearly 500,000,000 new literates in the *most active cohorts* of the world population as of 1965, and the rate of production of new literates is increasing everywhere in the modernizing world. Hence, Turkey is only an example (and not the worst) of the "new literate" problem.

I refer to the related fact that in many high-aspiration and low-achievement societies now undergoing modernization there are more college students per capita than in England or Italy. Hence, Iran is only an example (and not the worst) of the "college graduate" problem.

IV. *Frustration and Irresponsibility*

That these two sources of an unbalanced Want:Get ratio are producing more—I think logarithmically more—irresponsible behavior follows, on the conceptual level, from psychological studies of frustration over the past forty years. As the Yale and other psychologists have taught us: frustration leads to either aggression or regression. The new literates who "forget" how to read are regressive. The college graduates who "learn" to make personal frustration a rationale for political action are aggressive. Neither regression nor aggression supplies reliable motive power for "responsible behavior." On the contrary, they are promoters of individual and institutional irresponsibility.

Regression is irresponsible behavior because it constitutes withdrawal from the public forum and arena, whereas modernizing societies need increasing participation by individuals to effect the transformation of institutions. When a new literate regresses, in the sense that he allows his rudimentary skill to lapse, it is not enough to say that nothing has been gained. One must perceive that something valuable has been *lost*. In the more obvious sense, an investment of scarce resources has been wasted—namely, the scarce teaching talent and money allocated to raising literacy. With this goes the loss of value that would have been added by regressed literates to the formation of a participant society: in lands that must now run twice as fast to stay in the same place, as the Red Queen put it, every such failure to gain must be computed as a net loss.

Perhaps the deepest and most durable loss to the modernizing society, however, is the loss of hope in the regressed person. When frustration leads to regression, as in lapsed literacy, the individual tends to forfeit all new aspirations. Without aspiration, there is no motive power for achievement. Without individual achievement, there is no institutional transformation or societal modernization. Regression thus initiates a behavioral cycle antithetical to our definition of responsible behavior (in Casdef 2) as "the most effective enactment of shared values of which an individual is capable." In the measure that regression reduces a person to his least effective (infantile) capability, it is rather a source of irresponsible behavior.[5]

A radically different, and even more disruptive, cycle of irresponsible behavior is initiated by the aggressive reaction to frustration. Whereas regression is expressed in a withdrawal from public affairs, hence a net loss to participation by the failure to realize the expected return on an investment (which is wasted), aggression expresses itself by overt

[5] For a fuller discussion of the impact of the regressive cycle upon society, see my essay, "The Transformation of Institutions," in W. B. Hamilton, *The Transfer of Institutions*, Duke University Press, Durham, N.C., 1964.

attack on the existing institutions and processes of public affairs. Aggression manifests an excess, rather than a deficiency, of participation—the metric for "excess" calibrating the quality rather than the quantity of participant behavior. Evaluating this effect requires an effort of empathy by Western observers habituated to the doctrines (and sentiments) of free speech and civil disobedience. Aggression, as a reaction to the frustrations of modernization, should not be confused with the behavioral patterns known to developed democratic societies as "constructive criticism" or "loyal opposition." Such patterns are operational only where rules-of-the-game are widely known and shared, a situation that is conspicuously absent in the modernizing lands. There, in consequence, loyalty to the public order is feeble and aggression tends to be disruptive.

The social formation that exhibits the aggressive reaction is largely composed of frustrated college students, just as the regressive reaction is more characteristic of the frustrated new literates. While this order of psychosociological generalization requires careful qualification, and merits detailed study on a country by country basis, the past decade has produced abundant supportive evidence from every region of the world—from Japan to Santiago de Chile. Our concern here, however, is less to demonstrate the statistical prevalence of aggression among frustrated students than it is to indicate the irresponsible character of this syndrome.

Its major cost to the modernizing societies is that the aggressive students do not study. Instead of acquiring the knowledge provided them at extremely high cost, so that they could in turn repay the societal investment by their improved skills and capabilities, these students tend to displace their frustrations onto political objects. Politization, in this sense, pauperizes education without enriching the polity.

Consider the universities at Damascus and Caracas. Separated from each other by geography, history, religion, culture, they nevertheless have in common the following very contemporary characteristic: they are wasted for a very large part of every academic year. While their professors remain idle and their facilities vacant, the students spend a major portion of their time elsewhere engaged in political activities. The wastage of educational investment in these universities, and the dozens of similar institutions around the world of which these are only somewhat extreme examples, is a huge drain of scarce resources. As in the case of the new literates, and *a fortiori* even more so since the resources here wasted are scarcer and costlier, it must be computed as a net loss both to education and to responsible behavior in the modernizing lands of the world today.

V. Paradox and Predicament

These dour reflections on current events in most of the world gain poignancy from the hypothesis that the situation is worsening—that we face a "revolution of rising frustrations" which is likely to multiply regressive and aggressive reactions over the years ahead.[6] If this hypothesis is correct, no problem of public policy merits deep reconsideration more urgently than the reshaping of environments in which education may be made to produce responsible behavior rather than its opposite.

For the situation today presents a paradox that may be only apparent but a predicament that is certainly real. The paradox, in societies seeking through education to maximize responsible individual participation in the building of appropriate new public institutions and social processes, is that education appears to maximize irresponsible behavior. Our concept of the Want:Get ratio may eliminate the paradoxical element by explaining why frustration rises with education, especially in poor countries. The more a man knows, to simplify the matter exceedingly, the more he wants. Poor countries, on any definition, are least able to enable such people to get all that they have learned to want.

Obviating the paradox, however, does not solve the real predicament. How is education to be made to promote responsible behavior? How is the educated person to be taught to locate his personal wants within the framework of "the values that he shares with his environment"? How is he then to be guided toward "the most effective enactment of shared values of which an individual is capable"? These are the large questions that face public policy in the modernizing most-of-the-world. No worthier purpose could be set for any conference than to help find answers.

[6] See my "Preface to the Paperback Edition," *The Passing of Traditional Society, op. cit.*

Chapter 22. THE SECOND LYMAN BRYSON
LECTURE:
SOME REFLECTIONS ON EDUCATION
AND THE FORMATION OF CHARACTER

by Clarence H. Faust

I MUST CONFESS that I come to you with a mixture of pride and apprehension—pride to be asked to appear in this lecture series which is named for a man whose wisdom and whose skill in guiding group discussion I so much admired; and apprehension because I know from experience how penetrating, forthright, and on occasion devastating the criticisms of my friends and associates of the Conference on Science, Philosophy and Religion can be.

And I have increased my peril by venturing to speak on a subject which has already had a good deal of attention from the participants in the Conference on Science, Philosophy and Religion; though you will not, I am sure, fail to notice that I have tried to give myself a little protection by the modest phrasing of my title. I have timidly entitled my remarks "Some Reflections on Education and the Formation of Character."

Since the Conference has given a good deal of time to the subject of education for character, I wish I could give you a report of resounding success in dealing with it, including a definitive analysis of the problem, a clear appraisal of lines of effort to make education effective in the development of character, and the outlines at least of a promising program of character education. But I think my associates will agree that we have not accomplished these highly desirable tasks. We have had a good many ideas and have pursued a variety of approaches to our problem, but so far as I am aware we have reached no consensus on the subject. I take it up tonight, not to report a triumph for our enterprise, but to present some reflections on the subject of character education for which I can take little credit, since they are at best notions I have probably stolen from my colleagues or results of stimulation I have received from them. And I must at the outset assume full responsibility for the errors I will make since my reflections have not had the benefit of the searching criticism my fellow members of the Conference give to one another's ideas.

Our difficulties with this problem may in part be a consequence of the way in which we have forumlated it. The main terms in our formulation, as in my title tonight, are capable of either very broad or quite narrow reference. The word "education," for example, may refer to formal institutional processes (as it does when we talk about Federal aid to education) or it may be much more broadly used to designate all that complex of forces which mold the young. The term "character," too, may be taken in several ways. To speak of someone as a "character" is to suggest that he is distinctively different, and if not unique, or even odd, at least a clearly marked individual. Or the word "character" may indicate, as in the expression "a man of character," the possession of unwavering good qualities, that is, qualities admirable, praiseworthy, meritorious. Finally, the possible connection of education and character is left wholly open by the conjunction "and" in my title. Let me say then, that for my present purpose I take the term "education" in a broad sense as referring to all those influences which shape the young mind, which mold the outlook and the purposes, as well as the competencies, of the rising generation; and that I take the term "character" in a broad sense also to refer to the possession of well-established habits, attitudes, and principles that are meritorious or good. The term "good" I confess I do not here undertake to define.

I.

Our question, then, is what contribution education so conceived should make to the establishment of character so conceived. Current thinking tends, I find, to take one or more of three lines on this question. One is that what education can do is to instill right principles of conduct, fix in the minds of the young the rules or laws or ideas in the light of which right behavior may be determined. The essence of this approach is the conviction that if people have the right ideas, they will act rightly. Many high school courses in democracy attempt to put this conviction into action. And much, by the way, of the "witch-hunting" in education seems to be based on a corollary of it, namely, that if people, especially young people, are given wrong ideas, they will act wrongly.

A second line of approach stems from the common objection to preoccupation with ideas and principles that people act not from such abstractions, but under the spur of emotion, and that a right state of feeling is therefore the crucial matter. High school courses in democracy which grow out of this conviction try to induce in young people proper feelings of respect for other individuals, proper tolerance of differences of opinion, sympathy for those less privileged, and proper concern for the common good, as essential to the formation of a desirable character in the future citizen of a democracy. This approach has its roots no doubt in those developments in ethics and in religion which, especially in the eighteenth century, stressed the importance of the passions as over against reason. The novel of sensibility in the eighteenth century and the Wesleyan movement in religion illustrate in different ways the strength of this approach two centuries ago.

A third line of approach seems to many people merely simple common sense and to many teachers merely what experience has taught them, although it has an ancient and interesting history. It is, that character depends upon the formation of good habits through appropriate discipline, namely, the wise, consistent, and rigorous application of rewards and punishments, physical or mental, so as to bring the developing personality to disciplined ways, firmly established habits, and in general, behavior that constitutes a desirable character.

I will not attempt to resolve the differences between these three schools of thought, beyond saying that some understanding of reasons or principles seems to me essential as at least a complement of right feelings or good habits. If character is wholly a matter of good passions or habits, if rationality can be disregarded by those who educate and is not viewed as a critical factor in determining feelings or habits, if people are supposed to act from unexamined habit, then education for character is neither truly educative nor is the character formed truly established. The education of reason, the development of powers of thought in relation to moral and ethical issues so that habits and feelings can when situations require be changed, seems to me therefore an essential ingredient in moral education.

II.

Concern about youth and about the relationships of youth to society is not limited to this country. "What is most extraordinary about youth today," writes Edgar Friedenberg in *Coming of Age in America,* "is that adults everywhere should be so worried about it. In American, British, European, Japanese, Australasian, and at least the more privileged Soviet youth, puberty releases emotions that tend toward crisis. Every major industrial society believes that it has a serious youth problem." [1] It may of course be that the problem is simply universal, that in every time and place, the young are to some extent at odds with their elders, that the so-called youth problem is a universal one related to the succession of the generations. Some of us may be inclined to give some support to this view, recalling how in our own childhood and adolescence we developed feelings of alienation as we perceived or felt a difference between our outlook, purposes, and prospects, and those of our parents, teachers, and other representatives of the older society. On the other hand, there is a good deal that seems convincing in the arguments of those who regard the difficulties of contemporary youth as in large part, at least, the effects of modern industrialism, urbanization, and technology, which make it difficult for the young person to determine what his mature role should be, and of change in the family's role, which makes it easy for the young to entertain doubts about the views presented to them at home, and of the modern tensions of ideologies and nationalism. [2]

Whether or not the problems of youth are peculiar to our times, or merely exaggerated by the conditions of our times, one can hardly

[1] Edgar Z. Friedenberg, *Coming of Age in America,* Random House, Inc., New York, 1965, p. 3.

[2] See Erik H. Erikson, *Childhood and Society,* W. W. Norton & Co., New York, 1963; and Marshall McLuhan, *Understanding Media,* McGraw-Hill Book Co., New York, 1963.

avoid concluding, if one observes what is going on about him, attends to the observations of teachers, schoolmen, and churchmen, that there is a serious problem in our day, both for the young and for their elders. The young person today, especially the adolescent youngster, clearly has serious difficulties in his search for identity; in his attempt, in short, to find out who he is. And he has, furthermore, a serious problem in making out for himself what really satisfying role he can look forward to playing in our highly specialized society, with all the serious dilemmas and perils that society so clearly faces. And society has a problem, or a cluster of problems, in trying to induct the young into our society, as is clear from the very considerable increase in discussion, research, and writing about childhood and youth, about the nature and function of schools, and about the opinions of youth and their elders concerning the state of the world and its institutions. I recall an experience in London a few years ago, when I happened to notice an announcement of a meeting of English headmasters in the city. I made my way to the meeting and took a seat near the rear of the hall in which several hundred headmasters were convening. I found that the subject of discussion was the problem of the "teddy boys." As I listened to the papers and the discussion at this session, I was struck by the fact that except for difference of accent and polish in the use of language, I might easily have believed myself to be at a meeting of high school principals in the United States. The same kind of questions were analyzed—the motivation of students and how it could be improved, the adequacy or inadequacy of the current curriculum, the relative functions of the school, the home, and the church in bringing youngsters successfully through adolescence to a useful and satisfying adulthood. It was repeatedly said that youngsters in our day have a peculiarly difficult time in finding themselves and in finding their future place in society; and it was repeatedly pointed out that the schools and other agencies of society were confused and inadequate in dealing with the problem. All of these propositions were of course denied with as much fervor as they were asserted. And, of course, there was no one present to represent youth itself.

Part of my thesis is that to a disturbing extent youth today does not find society and society's agencies for the formation of youth meeting its needs; and that without believing youth to be absolutely right in its judgments, it is, nevertheless, true that youth is often closer both to what it and society really need than its elders realize.

III.

I begin with the proposition for which there is support at least as far back as Aristotle, and for which there is support I think in our own experience and in observations of young people, namely, that youth truly wants to know. It is the natural curiosity of children and their desire to satisfy it that provide the opportunity and the challenge to schools and schooling. Without the curiosity of children, schools and schooling would be futile and even the limited success of the enterprise of education would be impossible. Perhaps an equally natural propensity for boredom is the root of much of youngsters' failures in school. I have often thought that the most fundamental and devastating criticism to be made of our educational system is that it so generally manages to smother the curiosity of the young. Observe children on their first coming into school. For all their restlessness and their limited span of attention, they are eager to find out how to read and to write and to reckon. The Three R's are more than inventions of schoolmen. They are responsive to the interests of children. Children, furthermore, want to know something about the nature of things—what animals are like and how they differ from humans, what makes day and night. They crave, as anyone knows who has been with children much, answers to all sorts of fascinating questions—to know the what, the how, and the why of everything. They want to find out, too, how they should act, to secure the approval of their elders, to satisfy themselves, and above all to win the approval of their peers. But observe these same children five or six years later. School seems much less exciting to them, and what they are asked to do seems much more like drudgery. Observe them again as they enter high school, once more eager-eyed at the prospect of what they may find out about the world, themselves, and society. Then see them at the end of their high school experience. They have become sophisticated, critical of the school, the curriculum, and their teachers; and even granting that a certain amount of this attitude, together with the accompanying expressions of boredom with perhaps all but the social and athletic aspects of high school, is simply a pose of high school student society, or simply a posture assumed to dull the edge of some sense of failure in satisfying the requirements of high school, granting all this, there is still a distressing amount of real apathy and disappointment, as well as a distressing decline of eagerness among high school students.

The process repeats itself with small variations in many college students. As a college dean I was often troubled by the contrast between entering freshmen whom I had met at the beginning of the school year to incite to strenuous academic efforts, and these same freshmen as I saw them when they had become upper classmen. I think they had believed a little at least in the prospect I had held out to them of new worlds of knowledge to master and new heights of maturity to achieve. But as upper classmen, and indeed partly due to the tutelage they had later received from upper classmen, they were in distressing numbers disappointed and blasé when they reached their later college years, or at best grade- and credit-minded. How much of the current unrest among college and university students and how much of their open rebellion may be traced to their having such experiences I do not know, but I suspect that it may be a great deal.

What these impressions add up to is a sense that what the school wants all too often seems to students unimportant or irrelevant. As one critical schoolman has put it, "subjective people (those unusually self-centered and self-conscious) have very little use for the school, and *vice versa*. . . . Particularly in adolescence, they are trying to realize and clarify their identity; the school, acting as a mobility ladder, assumes instead the function of inducing them to change or alter it. They want to discover who they are; the school wants to help them 'make something out of themselves.' They want to know where they are; the school wants to help them to get somewhere. They want to learn how to live with themselves; the school wants to teach them how to get along with others. They want to learn how to tell what is right for them; the school wants to teach them to give responses that will earn them rewards in the classroom and in social situations."[3]

Similar, or at least related, observations might be made with respect to the church and the home. As a human being, the youngster wants to

[3] Friedenberg, *op. cit.,* p. 212.

know about the human condition and about his place in human affairs. Too often he feels that the church merely wants to make him "pious" as defined by its traditions, and he feels that the religious tradition as represented by the church is out of date and irrelevant. Something like this might be said of too many homes. The youngster wants to find himself and to relate himself satisfyingly with others. And he feels that the home is not interested in his real problems and needs, but is concerned only with his adopting the standards of the adult world, which strike him as out of date, or with his causing "no trouble," which strikes him as a low and selfish end, incompatible with his energy and ambitions.

In this situation, despairing of society and the agencies for helping himself and his social role, where should youth turn? What should he believe? Whom should he trust? Where should he look for his models?

In our society, he is faced with a variety of standards. The home sets before him the ideal of "the good boy" who "gives no trouble." (How often the mother of a delinquent son will defend him or perhaps herself on the ground that "he was always a good boy until he fell into bad company," or "he gave me no trouble until some of his companions led him astray.") The school seems to hold up the ideal of "the good student" and former teachers of a delinquent may remark that the boy or girl *was* a "good student" until for some strange reason, perhaps lack of incentive at home or an inexplicable loss of motivation, he ceased to care about classroom achievement. The church seems to hold up the ideal of "the faithful observer"—the "good Catholic," the "good Methodist, or Presbyterian," or "the good Jew"; and his religious mentors, if he falls away from the faith, are puzzled to explain his loss of it except perhaps by reference to the lack of support from the school and the home and to a general decline of society and of social morality.

But the variety of these standards presented to youth by different representatives of the adult world is not its only difficulty. The educational forces or institutions I have mentioned are considerably less clear than the summary description of their aims and hopes that I have given. These guides to the youngster, these claimants for his trust and allegiance, seem often to present confused and confusing standards.

The school talks about the desirability of being a good student, while also praising the "well-rounded," individual and urging the importance of social and physical, as well as mental development. The home seems to want the good boy or the good girl who will make no trouble for it, but at the same time takes pride in the fact that its children are full of life and mischief, in short, healthy, energetic young Americans. And the church may seem as concerned about the development of a good supporter of its institutions as about the development of a true believer and faithful observer.

IV.

It is not surprising that, in this situation, it seems to youth that the best claimant for its attention, its trust, and for being its models is its peer group. The power of the peer group with the young will not need to be proved, to parents, educators, or churchmen. Anyone who has observed young people with any attention must have been impressed by the effectiveness of the peer group in molding youth. Its ideas, its standards, and the models it provides weigh very heavily and are not infrequently decisive in the development of the opinions and behavior of youth. Young people feel that the members of their peer group understand their problems, speak their language, and they have felt how effective, indeed how sometimes cruelly effective, the pressure of the ideas and practices of their age group can be as regards themselves.[4]

Parents, educators, and churchmen are well aware of the power of the peer group. One consequence of this awareness is a conclusion these molders, or would-be molders, of youth may easily reach, namely, that the difficulties of bringing up the young center in a viciousness, or at least rebelliousness, peculiar to modern youth. Many people seem to be relieved to learn that youth are troublesome all around the world. They find the idea comforting. This easy comfort is, I think, blind to two things. It disregards the confusion, or at least pluralism, of aims and standards in modern adult society. It disregards, also, the great and rapid change in our times, which accounts for much of the sense

[4] See James S. Coleman, *The Adolescent Society* (Crowell-Collier), Macmillan Co., New York, 1961.

of irrelevance that many young people have about so much of education.

Since society has always been undergoing change, it may be that this feeling of youth is not a new phenomenon, this sense on the part of youth that their elders are not speaking to them adequately in a time of change. To the extent to which youth has a sense of change in the world and a sense that its elders are not adequately aware of it, we are faced with a more or less universal problem of tension between generations. But at least it must be granted that both the character and the pace of change in our time increases the natural tension between the generations and gives it in our day an especially difficult and urgent quality. We have seen something of this special quality in the experience of immigrant children in American society. To the second generation of immigrants, the first often seemed old-fashioned, out of date, out of touch, and unaware of the demands of a society very different from the foreign one out of which their parents came. A very interesting television show of a few years ago consisted of interviews with Puerto Rican youngsters in New York City. Time and again these youngsters made it clear they felt the need to adjust to a new society which their parents did not understand. There was frequent evidence of a sense on the part of the youngsters of shame for the narrowness of their parents' views and of the disparity between these views of their parents and those generally entertained in a modern American society. The descendants of immigrants can, I think, well understand something of the feelings these youngsters revealed. And we should find it easy to understand the point of view of youth who sense, though they may not be able to analyze nor state their feelings well, that under the impact of technology, of industrialization, of urbanization, and of the variety of ideologies in our time, change is taking place in ways both so momentous and so rapid that the ideas and habits of the older generation are inadequate guides to the younger generation coming onto the scene.

There seems to be a deep chasm between the ideas, ideals, and standards of behavior of the older generation and the ideas, the hopes and aims, and the standards of conduct that strike many of the younger generation as appropriate for their time. One even hears talk of the existence of two cultures—that of youth and that of adults.[5] The

[5] *Ibid.*, pp. 3–58 and 138–142.

development of a youth culture opposed to the one represented by the older members of society would not be an unprecedented phenomenon. In fact, we have had what looked like extreme examples of such developments in our own time. The Hitler *Jugend,* the *Komsomol* of the Soviets are dramatic instances. One thing, however, needs to be observed about these cases. They represent not so much a split between the generations, between youth and their elders, as a division among the elders themselves, some of whom (as in the case of Hitlerism) enlisted some part of youth in their battle with those in their own generation who did not immediately agree with and follow them. If there were two cultures in Nazi Germany, they were not representative of youth on the one hand and adults on the other, but of a split in which some, though not all, of both youth and their elders abandoned the earlier traditions of German culture to take the road Hitler was pointing out to them. German Nazism was not a youth movement in the sense of being conceived by, developed by, and led by young people. The youth who followed the Pied Piper were captivated by him and no doubt influenced by many older people of high station in German society.

I began with the proposition that youth naturally wants to know, though not necessarily what their elders are intent upon their learning. In a pluralistic society and a rapidly changing world, youth is faced in its quest for identity, as indeed are many of their elders, and for a satisfying role in society with the problems of who to believe and who to accept as a model. Faced with the conflicting and often confusing claims of the older representatives of our pluralistic society and conscious of the rapid pace of change so that they know they face a different world from the one their parents faced, and feel sure their children will in turn face a world different from the one now, youth tends to turn to its age mates, its peers, for understanding and guidance.

V.

Having made these propositions about youth, I now go on to make one about its elders and the agencies through which society tries to mold youth. Having said that youth honestly desires to know, it is only fair to say that society honestly wants to help them. Despite the sense that children and youth seem frequently to have that their elders and the institutions these elders have established are not interested in the true needs of youth, or at least in their sharpest desires, the elders know that they have the interets of youth truly at heart. But there is another side to the picture. Edgar Friedenberg, who defends modern youth, asserts that "Adolescents are among the last social groups in the world to be given the full nineteenth-century colonial treatment." He grants that schoolmen mean well, but adds that they are too much like our enlightened colonial administrators who though they decry the punitive expedition, except as an instrument of last resort, are inclined to tolerate a shade more brutality in the actual school or police station than the law allows. They prefer, he says, to study the young with a view to understanding them, not for their own sakes, but in order to learn how to induce them to abandon their barbarism and assimilate the folkways of normal adult life. "The model emissary to the world of the youth is no longer the tough disciplinarian but the trained youth worker, who works like a psychoanalytically oriented anthropologist. . . . Like the best of missionaries, he is sympathetic and understanding toward the people he is sent to work with, and aware and critical of the larger society he represents." And yet, says Friedenberg, he accepts the society he represents, "and often does not really question its basic values or its right to send him to win the young from savagery." [6]

Youth, especially adolescent youth, he goes on, are like colonial society, in being in an ambiguous economic position. They are "a costly drain on the commonwealth and a vested interest of those members of the commonwealth who earn their living and their social role by exploiting it." They are economically dependent and at the same time have a good deal of money in America, "about ten billion dollars a year," so that the "teen-age market is big business."

"Other forms of colonialism are dead or dying,' he says. "Why has the teen-ager remained, so stubbornly, the object of colonial solicitude?" The answer, he thinks, is that society is dependent on him. "Society depends on the succession of the generations, and adults usually assume that this means that their values and life style should be transmitted to the young. Youth cannot be allowed 'to go native' permanently."

[6] Friedenberg, *op. cit.*, p. 4.

There are, I think, several other reasons why the school as an agency of society finds it so difficult to relate itself effectively to youth. It is not merely that the educators have adopted an attitude toward youth which makes it the object of colonial solicitude. For one thing, schooling has by necessity been institutionalized. The problem of youth is intensely individual—finding out about himself or finding himself, and finding his place or function in society. When schools are institutionalized and have to deal with very large numbers of students, the problems of management overshadow those of the individual. In school, learning is packaged (the school term "unit" is itself a symbol of this). Testing of achievement is standardized; the student's interest in making or creating things is carefully organized and regulated (consider school shop or art work); student behavior is patterned and regulated (consider the tyranny of the bell system of schools). Attempts to break the institutionalized and traditional packaging of learning, such as the "new mathematics," are admirable but not really adequate to the situation. Attempts to give students more responsibility for their behavior, such as establishment of student government, are generally too artificial, too much really dominated by teachers and administrators, fully to serve their purpose.

The school obviously desires to be helpful and is obviously willing to adopt new practices, but in general (as has been remarked) "it will not, or can not, change its values, though it may be eager to change its techniques." [7] Yet since what is basically in question when youth is disenchanted with schooling is precisely the value system of the schools, changes in technique can hardly solve the problem with which we are concerned.

Unfortunately, what rare changes in values there are in the school tend simply to reflect new aims of the larger society and are likely to make it more difficult for schools to meet the real needs, as well as the merely felt needs, of youth. One such shift of emphasis in the schools, under pressure from society, has been what might be called the "manpower approach to education." The desire to increase the strength of America in the present international situation and the fear generated by signs of increase of military power and technological ability in nations that we regard as enemies, have led us to charge the schools

[7] *Ibid.,* p. 195.

with meeting the nation's manpower needs. This directive has to some extent replaced and has certainly modified earlier functions of the school represented by such phrases as "the melting pot" and "the ladder of improvement" and "preparation for life." Schools have been pressed to develop vocational guidance and to do so in the light of surveys of the needs in various professions and occupations. They are driven to the use of tests for determining the occupation for which a young person ought to prepare himself; they are driven to set up guidance programs that will press him in the desired direction, and vocational programs that will, it is hoped, develop his competence for the work assigned. The student is dealt with, not as an individual struggling to find himself and his role, but as a manpower resource. He is bound, more or less consciously, to resent this approach, which is in any case most lamentably un-American, for in our society the state exists to serve the need of the individual, not the individual to serve the needs of the state. Parents may resent this new emphasis of the school, as did a mother who objected to the severity of the scientific education her son was getting in a very efficient scientific high school. "I did not raise my boy," she complained, "just to be a manpower resource."

As things are, then, there are disturbing reasons to conclude that schools and educators are failing youth. And are indeed failing society, too. The needs of youth in its search for identity and a satisfying role in the world are not adequately met. The needs of society for new ideas, for effective leadership in adapting itself to the rapid pace of change in our time, its needs for wise followers as well as leaders, and its needs for wise public consensus are also unmet. The response of youth may be apathy or rebellion. Society responds by being excessively, and not always wisely, critical of schools, and by withholding the financial support these institutions need.

VI.

All this seems to come down, not to the emergence of two cultures—one of youth and one of their elders—but to a crisis in our culture itself. The blame is to be placed, not upon youth for being irresponsible and blind to the values of the traditional culture in which they have been born, nor upon the adult sector of society and its agencies, the school, the home, and the church, for being more concerned about their traditional standards and more interested in institutional strength and convenience than in effective response to the needs of youth and society. The problems that society faces—its elders now and its youth soon—are so complex and so extremely difficult that there should be no reason for amazement in discovering that we have not yet established a wholly satisfying tradition in the light of which really effective schooling could be developed and all members of society, from children to what are politely called "senior citizens," could in their appropriate fashion become dedicated, effective, and happy partners in a social enterprise.

Erik Erikson in his book *Childhood and Society* makes an interesting and illuminating analysis of childhood in two primitive societies: a tribe of Sioux Indians on the American plains and the Yurok, a tribe of fishermen along a salmon river in the Northwest. What he has to say bears on the question of childhood's participation in society. He describes how a child in the Arizona Indian tribe is expected and required to perform tasks and to develop skills within his abilities as a child that are useful to, and valued by, his elders. "The essential point of such child training," he says, "is that the child is from infancy continuously conditioned to responsible social participation, while at the same time the tasks that are expected of it are adapted to its capacity. The contrast of our society," he points out, "is very great. A child does not make any contribution of labor to our industrial society except as it competes with adults; his work is not measured against his own strength and skill, but against high-geared industrial requirements. Even when we praise the child's achievements in the home, we are outraged if such praise is interpreted as being of the same order as praise of adults. The child is praised because the parent feels well disposed, regardless of whether the task is well done by adult standards or not, and the child acquired no sensible standard by which to measure its achievement. The gravity of a Cheyenne Indian family is far removed from our behavior. At birth, the little boy is presented with toy bow and arrow, and from the time he could run about, serviceable bows and arrows suited to his stature were especially made for him by the man of the family. Animals and birds were brought to his awareness in a graded series beginning with those most easily taken, and as he brought in his first of each species his family duly made a feast of it, accepting his contribution as gravely as the buffalo his father brought." Erikson goes on to uncover some of the roots of the difference between modern American and the Indian cultures. The Indian cultures are "exclusive." "The image of man begins and ends with the idea of a strong or clean Yurok or Sioux. In our civilization the image of man is expanding. . . . Primitive tribes have a direct relationship with the sources and means of production. . . . Body and environment, childhood and culture, may be full of dangers, but they are all one world. This world may be small, but it is culturally coherent. The expansiveness of our civilization, on the other hand, its stratification and specialization, make it impossible for children to include in their egosynthesis more than the segment of the society which is relevant to their existence." Thus, "childhood, in some classes becomes a separate segment of life, with its own folklore, its own literature." It is no wonder, he thinks, that some of our troubled children break out "into some damaging activity in which they seem to us to 'interfere' with our world; while analysis reveals that they only wish to demonstrate their right to find an identity in it. They refuse to become a speciality called 'child,' who must play at being big because he is not given an opportunity to be a small partner in a big world." [8]

But it is neither possible nor desirable to try to solve the problem of the relationship of the generations and the connected problems of the school, the home, and the church by a return to the outlook and the methods of dealing with childhood and youth in primitive society. We may indeed be sure that such surviving primitive societies as the Yurok and the Sioux will inevitably be troubled by the same problems regarding the preparation of the young for adult life as now trouble us. For they, too, are already confronted and will be increasingly confronted by the powerful tides of change in the modern world and by the pluralism, the diversity of ideas and ideals, which the modern world with its multiple interrelations and its tremendous development of communication presents.

As best, one may take the nature of these primitive societies not as models, but as suggestive (in the way myths are) of some of the requirements for making education more effective for the formation of

[8] Erikson, *op. cit.*, pp. 111–238.

character in the modern world. One of these suggestions may be the indication that we need to develop a world, or at least international culture, clearer, more convincing, amd more potent in commanding the respect and the allegiance of the new members of society. Such a culture must accept change, and rapid change, as not merely inevitable but desirable. It must accept pluralism of beliefs as inescapable and as potentially useful, going beyond the mere tolerance of pluralism to hospitality toward it. It must be sharply self-critical at all points where current practices or institutions are open to questions regarding such principles as justice, as in present race and international relations.

The products of our strength in the modern world—of our interest in and capacity for change and innovation, of our pluralism, of our nationalism—the results of these must be subjected to honest and searching criticism in the light of principles now in general accepted verbally but applied with all too little seriousness to our habits and institutions, such principles as are designated by the words "justice," "respect for the individual," "freedom," and "social responsibility."

VII.

In this endeavor, youth, for all its lack of experience and learning, may become a useful and important, though perhaps always a somewhat difficult, partner. No small part of the problems and dilemmas of education for character rise from the prolonged childhood through which new members of the human race must go. As Waddington has pointed out in *The Ethical Animal,* the prolongation of human childhood gives the human race a kind of double inheritance: a physical inheritance through genes which determines many traits of the human animal; and a cultural inheritance mediated through the processes of education during the long childhood of the human creature.[9] The problems I have been discussing relate of course to this second type of inheritance. As prolonged childhood makes possible such inheritance for the young human being, it also (and this is where many of the difficulties arise) opens the way for children and youth to do more than merely accept their cultural inheritance. They have time to appraise it; and they have the time, and it would seem the inclination, to

[9] C. H. Waddington, *The Ethical Animal,* Atheneum Publishers, New York, 1961, pp. 138 ff. and 201 ff.

become critical of it, to decide whether it is adequate for a rapidly changing society, and whether it does exhibit in practice the ideals it enunciates. The judgments of youth, though ill informed and often distorted by emotions, still deserve the serious attention of its elders. The very freshness of youth's ideas may be useful correctives of the complex, more expediential, and wearier views of older members of society.

I am not suggesting that the views of youth should be taken at face value, any more than those of their elders. They should, I am suggesting, be given careful attention and interpretation in the light of as full an understanding as can be developed through the sciences, such as psychology, anthropology, sociology, and history, as well as through the light thrown on them by the experience their elders have had as once children and youths themselves. Here interdisciplinary methods are called for. The psychiatrist, for example, can be useful but may have a very limited view as a result of his preoccupation with therapy and the treatment of youth showing signs of serious emotional disturbance. The limitations of psychoanalysis have been suggested by a psychoanalyst who has surmounted them remarkably, Erik Erikson, in the story of the very young son of a psychiatrist who "when asked what he wanted to be when he became big and strong said, 'a patient.'"

Erikson has two suggestions. One is to provide for "a continuous interplay between that which we, as students, are gradually learning and that which we believe as people." Another is that provision be made for "mutual enlightenment" through discussions of experts with experts in other fields and with parents and youth. "For," says he, "I fully believe that the new techniques of discussion which are now being developed—and this in industry as well as in education—have a good chance of replacing the reassurances which once emanated from continuity of tradition." [10]

VIII.

What I am urging, I think, comes down to this. In the formation of character we ought to make youth partners in our enterprise, not by turning over leadership to them, but by listening to what they have to say and examining what they express in action, interpreting all this in

[10] Erikson, *op. cit.*, pp. 414 and 421.

the light of what improved understanding we may achieve through serious interdisciplinary efforts of scholars who study childhood and youth. Secondly, and more important, that we give serious and systematic thought to the state of culture in our time of momentous change and to the society for which education is attempting to prepare young people. I am convinced that the main root of our problem is the weakness of our culture, now so evident to childhood and youth as frequently to earn their disrespect and to inhibit their acceptance and allegiance to it.

It is this need, this worldwide need, that has led some of us under the encouragement and leadership of Rabbi Louis Finkelstein to hope for a new institution, which we have often entitled "A World Academy," where leaders of thought in science, philosophy, and religion, together with wisely reflective men of affairs, could engage in systematic and sustained discussion of major problems and issues of our time, could attempt to foresee future development and difficulties, and could reformulate and interpret various religious and philosophical traditions in an effort to bring them to bear upon the human condition of our time. Even partial success of such an endeavor would do more than anything else I can think of to provide a base for new developments in education—education broadly conceived—which might be effective in the formation of character.

Meanwhile, the cluster of activities under the Conference on Science, Philosophy, and Religion, including The Institute on Ethics, and The Institute for Religious and Social Studies, may continue to struggle with the clarification of problems of our culture and its relation to other cultures and may continue to seek what consensus can be reached on major matters of principle and practice.

Meanwhile, too, let us as elders try both from our own experience, and through the help of the relevant sciences to understand the nature and notions of childhood and youth, confident that youth is as serious in desiring to learn as we are; and let us try also to understand the nature, direction, and commitments of modern society as we see it as participants and to some extent formers of it; in the hope that we will then come to a fuller understanding of the problems of the rising generation and to the development of a culture sounder and, consequently, more appealing to the youth than our present confused and confusing one.

APPENDICES

Appendix I. REPORT ON THE CONFERENCE ON SCIENCE, PHILOSOPHY AND RELIGION

"Considerations for an International Conference on the Ethics of Mutual Involvement" was explored with thinkers from Latin America at a seminar held at the Men's Faculty Club, Columbia University, August 29, 30, and 31, 1961 (program on page 427). Other ways to illumine basic philosophical and ethical problems were considered in association with The Institute on Ethics and its parent Institute for Religious and Social Studies of The Jewish Theological Seminary of America. Such discussions took place at Lake Mohonk on January 26–28, 1962, November 30–December 2, 1962, June 14–16, 1963, May 22–24, 1964, December 11–13, 1964, May 7–9, 1965, October 29–31, 1965, and March 25–27, 1966; in New York City on various occasions from late 1962 through spring, 1966, and Washington, D.C., on January 13, 1964. These led to the 1966 Conference on Science, Philosophy and Religion in Chicago which resulted in the present volume.

At the business meeting of August 30, 1966, the following officers were elected:

Louis Finkelstein, The Jewish Theological Seminary of America, *president*

Clarence H. Faust, Fund for the Advancement of Education, The Ford Foundation, *Second Lyman Bryson Lecturer and vice president*

Robert O. Johann, S.J., Fordham University, *Third Lyman Bryson Lecturer*

Harold D. Lasswell, Yale University, *vice president, and chairman of the executive committee*

Jessica Feingold, The Institute for Religious and Social Studies, *executive vice president*

EXECUTIVE COMMITTEE:

R. M. MacIver, Columbia University

Richard P. McKeon, The University of Chicago, First Lyman Bryson Lecturer

Harlow Shapley, Harvard University

Harlan Cleveland (on leave)

Clarence H. Faust

Jessica Feingold
Louis Finkelstein
Daniel A. Greenberg
Charles M. Herzfeld, Advanced Research Projects Agency, Department
of Defense
Hudson Hoagland, Worcester Foundation for Experimental Biology
Robert O. Johann, S.J.
Harold D. Lasswell
Robert W. Lynn, Union Theological Seminary
Samuel D. Proctor, Institute for Services to Education
I. I. Rabi, Columbia University

HONORARY FELLOWS:
William F. Albright, The Johns Hopkins University
William G. Constable, Museum of Fine Arts, Boston
Norman Cousins, "The Saturday Review"
Thurston N. Davis, S.J., "America"
Karl W. Deutsch, Yale University
Lawrence K. Frank
Charles W. Hendel, Yale University
F. Ernest Johnson, Teachers College, Columbia University
Dorothy D. Lee
Jacques Maritain, Princeton University
Robert J. McCracken, The Riverside Church
Margaret Mead, American Museum of Natural History
Henry A. Murray, Harvard University
John C. Murray, S.J., Woodstock College
John U. Nef, The University of Chicago
F. S. C. Northrop, Yale University
Peter H. Odegard *
J. Robert Oppenheimer, Institute for Advanced Study *
Harry A. Overstreet, The City College of The City University of New York
Anton C. Pegis, Pontifical Institute of Medieval Studies, Toronto
Liston Pope, The Divinity School, Yale University
George N. Shuster, Center for the Study of Democratic Institutions
Wendell M. Stanley, University of California at Berkeley
Donald C. Stone, Graduate School of Public and International Affairs,
University of Pittsburgh
Ordway Tead, Harper and Row

* Deceased

M. L. Wilson, The Ford Foundation
Quincy Wright, University of Virginia

FELLOWS
Donald R. Campion, S.J.
Harlan Cleveland
Robert A. Dentler, Center for Urban Education
Clarence H. Faust
Louis Finkelstein
Charles Frankel, Columbia University
Daniel A. Greenberg
Simon Greenberg, The Jewish Theological Seminary of America
Caryl P. Haskins, Carnegie Institution of Washington
Charles M. Herzfeld
Hudson Hoagland
Albert Hofstadter, Columbia University
Robert B. Johnson *
Harold D. Lasswell
Daniel Lerner, Massachusetts Institute of Technology
Robert W. Lynn
R. M. MacIver
Richard P. McKeon
Ernest Nagel, Columbia University
Samuel D. Proctor
I. I. Rabi
Robert Rubenstein, Yale University
Harlow Shapley
Roger L. Shinn, Union Theological Seminary
Seymour Siegel, The Jewish Theological Seminary of America

The Executive Committee on January 27, 1967, appointed a 1968 Program Committee including Daniel A. Greenberg, Chairman, Jessica Feingold, Charles M. Herzfeld, Robert O. Johann, S.J., Robert W. Lynn, and Samuel D.. Proctor. The topic of the Eighteenth Conference on Science, Philosophy and Religion will be "Education, Schooling, and the Future." Drafts of papers commissioned for sections on "Education and Our Changing Way of Life," "The Administrative Order and the School," "The School and the Community," "New Theories of Learning and Their Implications for Education," and "Values and Goals in Education" will each be reviewed in a seminar consisting of the section's other paperwriters and scholars representing the disciplines embraced by the Conference, with special emphasis on transcultural aspects of the issues. The resulting Conference is to take place in New York City on August 26, 27, and 28, 1968. Other proposals for the Conference and criticisms of it generally will be welcome.

May, 1967

Appendix II. CONTRIBUTORS TO "APPROACHES TO EDUCATION FOR CHARACTER" *

Stephen K. Bailey, *Maxwell Graduate School of Citizenship and Public Affairs, Syracuse University,* dean and professor of political science; author, *The New Congress, The Office of Education and the Education Act of 1965, Inter-University Case Program #100;* editor, *American Politics and Government*

Daniel Bell, *Columbia University,* professor of sociology; author, *The End of Ideology, The Reforming of General Education;* editor, *The Radical Right*

Arthur J. Brodbeck, *Center for Urban Education,* senior research psychologist

Louis G. Cowan, *The Graduate School of Journalism, Columbia University,* director of special program in journalism

Peter M. Elkin, *Center for Urban Education,* research assistant

Clarence H. Faust, *Ford Foundation,* vice president; *The Fund for the Advancement of Education,* president (retired)

Arthur W. Foshay, Teachers College, Columbia University, professor of education and associate dean for research and field services; formerly the Association for Supervision and Curriculum Development, president; Ohio State University, Bureau of Educational Research, director; the Horace Mann-Lincoln Institute for School Experimentation, Teachers College, Columbia University, director; editor, *The Achievement of Thirteen Year Olds in Twelve Countries, The Rand McNally Handbook of Education*

Willis W. Harman, *Stanford University,* professor, Joint Engineering-Economic Systems Program; author, *Some Aspects of the Psychedelic Drug Controversy, "Journal Humanistic Psychology,"* volume 3, number 2, *Psychedelic Agents in Creative Problem-Solving: A Pilot Study,* Psychological Reports 19 (with R. H. McKim, R. E. Mogar, J. Fadiman, M. J. Stolaroff), *Old Wine in New Wineskins—in The Challenge of Humanistic Psychology*

* Position generally based on list of August, 1966.

Robert J. Havighurst, *The University of Chicago,* professor of education and human development; author, *The Psychology of Moral Character* (with Robert F. Peck), *The Educational Mission of the Church, Society and Education* (with Bernice L. Neugarten)

Albert Hofstadter, *Columbia University,* professor of philosophy; *Center for Advanced Study in the Behavioral Sciences,* 1966–1967; author, *Truth and Art;* editor (with R. Kuhns), *Philosophies of Art and Beauty*

Robert O. Johann, S.J., *Fordham University,* associate professor of philosophy and adjunct professor of Christian ethics; *Yale University,* visiting associate professor of philosophy, 1963–1964; *Union Theological Seminary,* visiting lecturer, fall, 1966; *Metaphysical Society of America,* counseller, 1962–1966; *Conference on Science, Philosophy and Religion,* executive committee, member; author, *The Meaning of Love, The Pragmatic Meaning of God,* and others

Harold D. Lasswell, *Yale University,* Edward J. Phelps professor of law and political science; visiting professor, various universities in United States of America and abroad; consultant, governmental and private organizations; author, *The Law and Public Order in Space* (with Myres S. McDougal and I. Vlasic), *Power, Corruption and Rectitude* (with A. A. Rogow), *The Future of Political Science, Power Sharing in a Psychiatric Hospital* (with Robert Rubenstein)

Daniel Lerner, *Massachusetts Institute of Technology,* Ford professor of sociology and international communications; author, *The Passing of Traditional Society, The Human Meaning of the Social Sciences, World Revolutionary Elites* (with H. D. Lasswell)

John C. Lilly, *Communication Research Institute,* director; *Man and Dolphin,* co-author *The Dolphin in History,* contributor numerous scientific papers

Robert W. Lynn, *Union Theological Seminary,* dean of Auburn program and professor of religious education; "*Christianity and Crisis,*" member of editorial board; author, *Protestant Strategies in Education, Spiritual Renewal through Personal Groups* and *The Search for Identity;* contributor, *Introduction to Christian Education*

Bernard Mackler, *Center for Urban Education,* senior research psychologist; *Teachers College, Columbia University,* assistant professor of education; author, *Cultural Deprivation: A study in Mythology, "Teachers College Record," A Report on the '600' Schools,* in "*The Urban Review,*" *Creativity: Theoretical and Methodological Considerations* in "*Psychological Record*"

Richard McKeon, *The University of Chicago,* Charles F. Grey distinguished service professor of philosophy and Greek; the *American Philosophical Association, the International Institute of Philosophy, and the Metaphysical Society of America,* former president; *International Society for the History of Ideas,* president; author, *Thought, Action and Passion*

Michael J. Murphy, *City of New York,* police commissioner (retired)

Robert Rubenstein, psychoanalyst; *Yale Psychiatric Institute,* co-director; *Ezra Stiles College, Yale University,* associate clinical professor of psychiatry, and fellow; author, "On the sharing of power in families, hospitals, and schools" in *selections by Fellows of Ezra Stiles College, Occasional Stiles,* February, 1965, "Poitical process in a psychiatric hospital" in *"Political Science Annual,"* volume I (with Harold D. Lasswell), *The Sharing of Power in a Psychiatric Hospital* (with Harold D. Lasswell)

Edgar H. Schein, *Sloan School of Management, Massachusetts Institute of Technology,* professor of organizational psychology and management; author, *Organizational Psychology, Personal and Organizational Change through Group Methods* (with W. G. Bennis), *Interpersonal Dynamics* (W. G. Bennis, D. Berlew and F. I. Steele)

Seymour Siegel, *The Jewish Theological Seminary of America,* associate professor of theology

Wagner P. Thielens, Jr., *Columbia University,* research associate, Bureau of Applied Social Research

Ben M. Zeff, *Office of the Secretary of Defense,* deputy director for education programs

Appendix III. PUBLICATIONS OF THE CONFERENCE ON SCIENCE, PHILOSOPHY AND RELIGION

Science, Philosophy and Religion, A Symposium, 1941. (Prepared for the meetings held in New York City on September 9, 10, and 11, 1940, these 24 papers analyze, in the face of advancing totalitarianism overseas, the interdependence of traditional values and the principles of democracy.) Out of print.

Science, Philosophy and Religion, Second Symposium, 1942. Lyman Bryson and Louis Finkelstein, Editors. (Prepared for the meetings held in New York City on September 8, 9, 10, and 11, 1941, these 31 papers explore the interaction of varied academic fields with the theory and practice of a democratic society.

Science, Philosophy and Religion, Third Symposium, 1943. Lyman Bryson and Louis Finkelstein, Editors. (Prepared for the meetings held in New York City on August 27, 28, 29, 30, and 31, 1942, these 25 papers discuss the need for free interchange between scholars of all fields, as well as men of affairs, to counteract intellectual confusion and isolation.) Out of print.

Approaches to World Peace, Fourth Symposium, 1944. Lyman Bryson, Louis Finkelstein, and R. M. MacIver, Editors. (Prepared for the meetings held in New York City on September 9, 10, 11, 12, and 13, 1943, these 59 papers seek solution to world conflict through closer cooperation among intellectual and spiritual fields previously separated by growing specialization.) Out of print.

Approaches to National Unity, Fifth Symposium, 1945. Lyman Bryson, Louis Finkelstein, and R. M. MacIver, Editors. (Prepared for the meetings held in New York City on September 7, 8, 9, 10, and 11, 1944, these 62 papers consider, as antidote to dangerous intellectual isolation, group relations and intercommunication.) Out of print.

Approaches to Group Understanding, Sixth Symposium, 1947. Lyman Bryson, Louis Finkelstein, and R. M. MacIver, Editors. (Prepared for the meetings held in New York City on August 23, 24, 25, 26, and 27, 1945, these 67 papers focus on understanding across the barriers between nations, disciplines, philosophies, and religions.) Out of print. Cooper Square Publishers, reprint.

Conflicts of Power in Modern Culture, Seventh Symposium, 1947. Lyman Bryson, Louis Finkelstein, and R. M. MacIver, Editors. (Prepared for the meetings held in Chicago on September 9, 10, and 11, 1946, these 62 papers consider problems of aggressiveness or drive for power particularly in the West.) Out of print. Cooper Square Publishers, reprint.

Learning and World Peace, Eighth Symposium, 1948. Lyman Bryson, Louis Finkelstein, and R. M. MacIver, Editors. (Prepared for the meetings held in Philadelphia on September 7, 8, 9, and 10, 1947, these 59 papers evaluate the potential contribution of their particular disciplines to the relief of international tensions.)

Goals for American Education, Ninth Symposium, 1950. Lyman Bryson, Louis Finkelstein, and R. M. MacIver, Editors. (Prepared for the meetings held in New York City on September 7, 8, 9, and 10, 1948, these 22 papers by scholars of various fields assay American education in terms of its values and ends.) Out of print.

Perspectives on a Troubled Decade: Science, Philosophy and Religion, 1939–1949, Tenth Symposium, 1950. Lyman Bryson, Louis Finkelstein, and R. M. MacIver, Editors. (Prepared for the meetings held in New York City on September 6, 7, 8, and 9, 1949, these 52 papers offer an integrated study of major intellectual issues for the period 1939–1949.)

Foundations of World Organization: A Political and Cultural Appraisal, Eleventh Symposium, 1952. Lyman Bryson, Louis Finkelstein, Harold D. Lasswell, and R. M. MacIver, Editors. (Prepared for the meetings held in New York City on September 5, 6, 7, and 8, 1950, these 43 papers study international cooperation through philosophy and religion, social forces, non-governmental and governmental organizations.)

Freedom and Authority in Our Time, Twelfth Symposium, 1953. Lyman Bryson, Louis Finkelstein, R. M. MacIver, and Richard McKeon, Editors. (Prepared for the meetings held in New York City on September 4, 5, 6, and 7, 1951, these 58 papers study contemporary concepts of freedom and authority in philosophy, literature, political science, education, and religion.) Out of print.

Symbols and Values: An Initial Study, Thirteenth Symposium, 1954. Lyman Bryson, Louis Finkelstein, R. M. MacIver, and Richard McKeon, Editors. (Prepared for the meetings held in New York City on September 2, 3, 4, and 5, 1952, these 48 papers center on problems in communication of ideas, beliefs, incentives to action.) Cooper Square Publishers, reprint.

Symbols and Society, Fourteenth Symposium, 1955. Lyman Bryson, Louis Finkelstein, Hudson Hoagland, and R. M. MacIver, Editors. (Prepared for the meetings held at Harvard University on August 30 and 31, September 1 and 2, 1954, these 20 papers center on symbols in their relation to many aspects of society.) Cooper Square Publishers, reprint.

Aspects of Human Equality, Fifteenth Symposium, 1956. Lyman Bryson, Clarence H. Faust, Louis Finkelstein, and R. M. MacIver, Editors. (Prepared for the meetings held in New York City on August 29, 30, and 31, and September 1, 1955, these 19 papers offer analysis of equality, in relation to law, society—local and international, education, and religion.)

The Ethic of Power: The Interplay of Religion, Philosophy and Politics, Sixteenth Symposium, 1962. Harold D. Lasswell and Harlan Cleveland, Editors. (Prepared for the meetings held in New York City on August 29, 30, and 31, and September 1, 1960, these 24 papers investigate the challenge to ethical values posed by an increasingly complex society.)

Ethics and Bigness: Scientific, Academic, Religious, Political, and Military, Seventeenth Symposium, 1962. Harlan Cleveland and Harold D. Lasswell, Editors. (Prepared for the meetings held in New York City on August 29, 30, and 31, and September 1, 1960, these 28 papers examine the responsibility of individual conscience within the large-scale organizations that characterize contemporary life.)

PROGRAMS

PROGRAMS

Programs: SEVENTEENTH CONFERENCE ON
SCIENCE, PHILOSOPHY AND RELIGION
IN THEIR RELATION TO THE
DEMOCRATIC WAY OF LIFE

"Education for Character: Strategies for Change in Higher Education"

Monday, Tuesday, and Wednesday, August 29, 30, 31, 1966

Loyola University Center, 820 North Rush Street (Southwest corner of Rush Street and Pearson Street) Chicago, Illinois

Background Papers (Section I) by [1]
  ALBERT HOFSTADTER
  HAROLD D. LASSWELL
  RICHARD P. MCKEON [3]

As preparation for the entire Conference it is expected that discussion of this material will not be limited to any given session.

All sessions not otherwise indicated will be held in the Georgetown Room, Loyola University Center.

1. For convenient identification the papers in Section I are mimeographed on canary paper, those in Section II on mandarin, Section III on granite, Section IV on green, Section V on gold, and Section VI on pink.
2. Papers available in mimeographed form. All oral discussion off the record.
3. Text not received before program in press.

Monday, August 29

2:00-3:30 p.m. Planning Meeting
Chairmen, Program Committee, and Paper Writers

   HAROLD D. LASSWELL, *Chairman*

4:00-6:00 p.m. General Session
   Harold D. Lasswell, *Chairman*
Discussion of [2]
Special Aspects of Education for Character and Strategies for Change in Educational Institutions (Section II)
based on papers by
   DANIEL BELL [3]
   HORACE R. CAYTON [3]
   ARTHUR W. FOSHAY
   ROBERT J. HAVIGHURST
   BERNARD MACKLER

8:30-10:00 p.m. General Session
   CHARLES M. HERZFELD, *Chairman*
Discussion of [2]
Special Aspects of Education for Character and Strategies for Change in Educational Institutions (Section III)
based on papers by
   STEPHEN K. BAILEY [3]
   ARTHUR J. BRODBECK
   LOUIS G. COWAN [3]
   DANIEL LERNER [3]

Tuesday, August 30

8:30 a.m. Breakfast Business Meeting of the Fellows of the Conference on Science, Philosophy and Religion, to transact necessary business of the corporation, including election of officers.

The President's Room

10:30 a.m.-12:30 p.m. General Session

HUDSON HOAGLAND, *Chairman*

Discussion of [2]

Character Education of Scientists, Engineers, and Practitioners in Medicine, Psychiatry, and Science, with Strategies for Change (Section IV)

based on papers by

DONALD A. BLOCH [3]

DANIEL A. GREENBERG

WILLIS W. HARMAN

JOHN C. LILLY [3]

ROBERT RUBENSTEIN

8:30 p.m. The Second Lyman Bryson Lecture

"Reflections on Education and the Formation of Character"

by CLARENCE H. FAUST

Louis Finkelstein, *Chairman*

Followed by a reception in the Xavier Room

Wednesday, August 31

9:30-11:30 a.m. General Session
  SAMUEL D. PROCTOR, *Chairman*
Discussion of [2]
Moral Education for Law, Security, and Business (Section V)
based on papers by
  JOSHUA M. MORSE, III [3]
  MICHAEL J. MURPHY
  EDGAR H. SCHEIN
  WAGNER P. THIELENS, JR.
  BEN M. ZEFF
2.00-4:00 p.m. General Session
  JAMES E. MCLELLAN, *Chairman*
Discussion of [2]
Education of Theologians and Clergymen (Section VI)
based on papers by
  ROBERT O. JOHANN, S.J.
  ROBERT W. LYNN
  SEYMOUR SIEGEL [3]

Conference on Science, Philosophy and Religion *

* As of August 31, 1960
** Deceased

FELLOWS

Thomas Ritchie Adam, New York University
William F. Albright, The John Hopkins University
Robert Bierstedt, The City College of New York
Harry J. Carman, Columbia University **
Harlan Cleveland
Stewart G. Cole
William G. Constable, Museum of Fine Arts, Boston
Norman Cousins, "The Saturday Review"
Thurston N. Davis, S.J.
Karl W. Deutsch, Yale University
Hoxie N. Fairchild, Hunter College of the City of New York
Clarence H. Faust
Louis Finkelstein
A. Durwood Foster, Pacific School of Religion
Lawrence K. Frank
Philipp G. Frank, Institute for the Unity of Science **
Charles Frankel, Columbia University
Simon Greenberg, The Jewish Theological Seminary
Caryl P. Haskins, Carnegie Institution of Washington
Charles W. Hendel, Yale University
Hudson Hoagland
Albert Hofstadter, Columbia University
F. Ernest Johnson
Robert B. Johnson, National Conference of Christians and Jews
Clyde Kluckhohn, Harvard University **
John LaFarge, S.J.**
Harold D. Lasswell
Dorothy D. Lee, Harvard University
R. M. MacIver
Jacques Maritain, Princeton University
Robert J. McCracken, The Riverside Church
Richard P. McKeon
Margaret Mead, American Museum of Natural History
Henry A. Murray, Harvard University
John Courtney Murray, S.J., Woodstock College
Ernest Nagel, Columbia University
John U. Nef, The University of Chicago
F. S. C. Northrop, Yale University
Peter H. Odegard, University of California at Berkeley

J. Robert Oppenheimer, Institute for Advanced Study
Harry A. Overstreet, The City College of New York
Anton C. Pegis, Pontifical Institute of Mediaeval Studies, Toronto
Gerald B. Phelan, St. Michael's College, Toronto **
Liston Pope, The Divinity School, Yale University
I. I. Rabi
Roy W. Sellars, University of Michigan
Harlow Shapley
George N. Shuster, Center for the Study of Democratic Institutions
Wendell M. Stanley
Donald C. Stone, Graduate School of Public and International Affairs, University of Pittsburgh
Ordway Tead
M. L. Wilson
Quincy Wright, University of Virginia

Office address: 3080 Broadway, New York, New York 10027
Telephone: 212 RIverside 9-8000

Participants in Program

Stephen K. Bailey, Dean, Maxwell Graduate School of Citizenship & Public Affairs, Syracuse University

Robert M. Barry, Associate Professor of Philosophy, Loyola University

Daniel Bell, Professor of Sociology, Columbia University

Felix P. Biestek, S.J., Professor of Social Work, Loyola University

Donald A. Bloch, Associate Director for Research, The Family Institute

Jerald C. Brauer, Dean, The Divinity School, The University of Chicago

Arthur J. Brodbeck, Senior Research Psychologist, Center for Urban Education

John M. Butler, Professor of Psychology and Human Development, The University of Chicago

Donald R. Campion, S.J., Director of Province Research, New York Province of The Society of Jesus

Horace R. Cayton, Professor of Sociology, The University of California at Los Angeles

Eliot D. Chapple, Visiting Professor, School of Industrial and Labor Relations and Department of Anthropology, Cornell University

Seymour J. Cohen, Rabbi, The Anshe Emet Synagogue, Chicago; President, Synagogue Council of America

Louis G. Cowan, Director of Special Program in Journalism, The Graduate School of Journalism, Columbia University

William N. Dember, Professor of Psychology, Department of Psychology, University of Cincinnati

Robert F. Drinan, S.J., Dean, Boston College Law School

Edward D. Eddy, President, Chatham College

Peter M. Elkin, Research Assistant, Center for Urban Education

Moshe Ettenberg, Professor of Electrical Engineering, The City College of The City University of New York

John R. Everett, President, New School for Social Research

Dana L. Farnsworth, Director, University Health Services and The Henry K. Oliver Professor of Hygiene, Harvard University

Clarence H. Faust, Vice-President, The Ford Foundation, President, The Fund for the Advancement of Education (Retired)

Jessica Feingold, Director, The Institute for Religious and Social Studies

Herman Finer, Professor Emeritus of Political Science, The University of Chicago

Louis Finkelstein, Chancellor and Solomon Schechter Professor of Theology, The Jewish Theological Seminary of America

Eugene Fontinell, Associate Professor of Philosophy, Queens College, The City University of New York

Arthur W. Foshay, Associate Dean, Research and Field Services, Teachers College, Columbia University

Robert W. Fuller, Academic Fellow, Center for Advanced Studies, Wesleyan University

Samuel L. Gandy, Dean, School of Religion, Howard University

J. W. Getzels, Professor of Education and Psychology, The University of Chicago

Neil Gillman, Registrar, School of Judaica, Rabbinical Department, The Jewish Theological Seminary of America

Mary F. Gray, Grantee Adviser, The Asia Foundation

Daniel A. Greenberg, Associate Professor of History, Columbia University

Archie J. Hargraves, Director of Mission Development, The Urban Training Center for Christian Mission, Chicago

Willis W. Harman, Professor of Engineering, Stanford Electronics Laboratories, Stanford University

Charles U. Harris, President and Dean, Seabury-Western Theological Seminary

Robert J. Havighurst, Professor of Education, Department of Education, The University of Chicago

Charles M. Herzfeld, Director, Advanced Research Projects Agency, Department of Defense

Hudson Hoagland, Executive Director, The Worcester Foundation for Experimental Biology

Albert Hofstadter, Professor of Philosophy, Columbia University

Bert F. Hoselitz, Professor of the Social Sciences and of Economics, Research Center in Economic Development and Cultural Change, The University of Chicago

Ernest M. Howell, New York Representative, The Asia Foundation

Melvan M. Jacobs, President, Charles Weinfeld Memorial Foundation

Robert O. Johann, S.J., Associate Professor of Philosophy, College of Philosophy and Letters, Fordham University

Howard W. Johnson, President, Massachusetts Institute of Technology

Robert B. Johnson, Chairman, Division of Social Services, Wilberforce University

Solon T. Kimball, Graduate Research Professor, Department of Anthropology, University of Florida

Melvin Kranzberg, Professor of History, Case Institute of Technology

Maynard C. Krueger, Associate Professor of Economics, The University of Chicago

Harold R. Landon, Canon Residentiary, Cathedral Church of St. John the Divine

Harold D. Lasswell, Edward J. Phelps Professor of Law and Political Science, The Law School, Yale University

Daniel Lerner, Ford Professor of Sociology and International Communications, Massachusetts Institute of Technology

Donald N. Levine, Master, The Collegiate Division of Social Sciences, The University of Chicago

Wayne A. R. Leys, Professor of Philosophy, Southern Illinois University

John C. Lilly, Director, Communication Research Institute, St. Thomas, Virgin Islands

Robert W. Lynn, Dean of Auburn Program and Professor of Religious Education, Union Theological Seminary

Bernard Mackler, Assistant Deputy Director, Center for Urban Education

Bernard Mandelbaum, President and Associate Professor of Homiletics, The Jewish Theological Seminary of America

James E. McClellan, Professor of Education, Department of Foundations of Education, Temple University

Richard P. McKeon, Charles F. Grey Distinguished Service Professor of Philosophy and Greek, The University of Chicago

Sterling M. McMurrin, Provost and Ericksen Distinguished Professor of Philosophy, University of Utah

Charles Merrill, Headmaster, Commonwealth School, Boston

Christopher F. Mooney, S.J., Chairman, Department of Theology, Fordham University

Joshua M. Morse, III, Dean, School of Law, The University of Mississippi

Robert W. Mulligan, S.J., Vice-President and Dean of Faculties, Loyola University

Michael J. Murphy, Police Commissioner (Retired), The City of New York

Roger H. Nye, Permanent Associate Professor of Social Sciences, Department of Social Sciences, United States Military Academy, West Point

William V. O'Brien, Chairman, Institute of World Polity, Georgetown University

Philip H. Phenix, Professor of Philosophy and Education, Teachers College, Columbia University

Samuel D. Proctor, President, Institute for Services to Education

James M. Redfield, Master, New Collegiate Division and Associate Professor of Social Thought, The University of Chicago

William J. Richardson, S.J., Associate Professor of Philosophy, Fordham University

George F. Rohrlich, Visiting Professor of Social Policy, School of Social Service Administration, The University of Chicago

Robert Rubenstein, Co-Director, Yale Psychiatric Institute and Associate Clinical Professor of Psychiatry, Yale University

Edgar H. Schein, Professor of Social Psychology and Organization Studies, Sloan School of Management, Massachusetts Institute of Technology

Theodore W. Schultz, Charles L. Hutchinson Distinguished Service Professor, Department of Economics, The University of Chicago

Harlow Shapley, Paine Professor Emeritus of Astronomy, Harvard University

Robert Lewis Shayon, Professor of Communications, The Annenberg School of Communications, University of Pennsylvania

Roger L. Shinn, Dean of Instruction and William E. Dodge, Jr., Professor of Applied Christianity, Union Theological Seminary

Seymour Siegel, Associate Professor of Theology, The Jewish Theological Seminary of America

Ralph Simon, Rabbi, Congregation Rodfei Zedek, Chicago; Vice-President, The Rabbinical Assembly

Malcolm R. Sutherland, President, Meadville Theological School

Jerome Taylor, Associate Professor of English and of the Humanities, Department of English, The University of Chicago

Herbert A. Thelen, Professor of Educational Psychology, Department of Education, The University of Chicago

Wagner P. Thielens, Jr., Research Associate, Bureau of Applied Social Research, Columbia University

John L. Thomas, S.J., Research Associate, Cambridge Center for Social Studies

Preston Valien, Chief, Graduate Academic Program Branch, Division of Graduate Programs, Bureau of Higher Education, United States Office of Education

Warner A. Wick, Professor of Philosophy and Dean of Students, The University of Chicago

Saamuel W. Williams, Professor and Chairman, Department of Philosophy and Religion, Morehouse College

Ben M. Zeff, Deputy Director for Education Programs, Office of the Secretary of Defense

Papers Discussed at Previous Meetings

Science, Philosophy and Religion, A Symposium, 1941. (Prepared for the meetings held in New York City on September 9, 10, and 11, 1940, these 24 papers analyze, in the face of advancing totalitarianism overseas, the interdependence of traditional values and the principles of democracy.) Out of print.

Science, Philosophy and Religion, Second Symposium, 1942. Lyman Bryson and Louis Finkelstein, Editors. (Prepared for the meetings held in New York City on September 8, 9, 10, and 11, 1941, these 31 papers explore the interaction of varied academic fields with the theory and practice of a democratic society.

Science, Philosophy and Religion, Third Symposium, 1943. Lyman Bryson and Louis Finkelstein, Editors. (Prepared for the meetings held in New York City on August 27, 28, 29, 30, and 31, 1942, these 25 papers discuss the need for free interchange between scholars of all fields, as well as men of affairs, to counteract intellectual confusion and isolation.) Out of print.

Approaches to World Peace, Fourth Symposium, 1944. Lyman Bryson, Louis Finkelstein, and R. M. MacIver, Editors. (Prepared for the meetings held in New York City on September 9, 10, 11, 12, and 13, 1943, these 59 papers seek solution to world conflict through closer cooperation among intellectual and spiritual fields previously separated by growing specialization.) Out of print.

Approaches to National Unity, Fifth Symposium, 1945. Lyman Bryson, Louis Finkelstein, and R. M. MacIver, Editors. (Prepared for the meetings held in New York City on September 7, 8, 9, 10, and 11, 1944, these 62 papers consider, as antidote to dangerous intellectual isolation, group relations and intercommunication.) Out of print.

Approaches to Group Understanding, Sixth Symposium, 1947. Lyman Bryson, Louis Finkelstein, and R. M. MacIver, Editors. (Prepared for the meetings held in New York City on August 23, 24, 25, 26, and 27, 1945, these 67 papers focus on understanding across the barriers between nations, disciplines, philosophies, and religions.) Out of print. Cooper Square Publishers, reprint.

Conflicts of Power in Modern Culture, Seventh Symposium, 1947. Lyman Bryson, Louis Finkelstein, and R. M. MacIver, Editors. (Prepared for the meetings held in Chicago on September 9, 10, and 11, 1946, these 62 papers consider problems of aggressiveness or drive for power particularly in the West.) Out of print. Cooper Square Publishers, reprint.

Learning and World Peace, Eighth Symposium, 1948. Lyman Bryson, Louis Finkelstein, and R. M. MacIver, Editors. (Prepared for the meetings held in Philadelphia on September 7, 8, 9, and 10, 1947, these 59 papers evaluate the potential contribution of their particular disciplines to the relief of international tensions.)

Goals for American Education, Ninth Symposium, 1950. Lyman Bryson, Louis Finkelstein, and R. M. MacIver, Editors. (Prepared for the meetings held in New York City on September 7, 8, 9, and 10, 1948, these 22 papers by scholars of various fields assay American education in terms of its values and ends.) Out of print.

Perspectives on a Troubled Decade: Science, Philosophy and Religion, 1939–1949, Tenth Symposium, 1950. Lyman Bryson, Louis Finkelstein, and R. M. MacIver, Editors. (Prepared for the meetings held in New York City on September 6, 7, 8, and 9, 1949, these 52 papers offer an integrated study of major intellectual issues for the period 1939–1949.)

Foundations of World Organization: A Political and Cultural Appraisal, Eleventh Symposium, 1952. Lyman Bryson, Louis Finkelstein, Harold D. Lasswell, and R. M. MacIver, Editors. (Prepared for the meetings held in New York City on September 5, 6, 7, and 8, 1950, these 43 papers study international cooperation through philosophy and religion, social forces, non-governmental and governmental organizations.)

Freedom and Authority in Our Time, Twelfth Symposium, 1953. Lyman Bryson, Louis Finkelstein, R. M. MacIver, and Richard McKeon, Editors. (Prepared for the meetings held in New York City on September 4, 5, 6, and 7, 1951, these 58 papers study contemporary concepts of freedom and authority in philosophy, literature, political science, education, and religion.) Out of print.

Symbols and Values: An Initial Study, Thirteenth Symposium, 1954. Lyman Bryson, Louis Finkelstein, R. M. MacIver, and Richard McKeon, Editors. (Prepared for the meetings held in New York City on September 2, 3, 4, and 5, 1952, these 48 papers center on problems in communication of ideas, beliefs, incentives to action.) Cooper Square Publishers, reprint.

Symbols and Society, Fourteenth Symposium, 1955. Lyman Bryson, Louis Finkelstein, Hudson Hoagland, and R. M. MacIver, Editors. (Prepared for the meetings held at Harvard University on August 30 and 31, September 1 and 2, 1954, these 20 papers center on symbols in their relation to many aspects of society.) Cooper Square Publishers, reprint.

Aspects of Human Equality, Fifteenth Symposium, 1956. Lyman Bryson, Clarence H. Faust, Louis Finkelstein, and R. M. MacIver, Editors. (Prepared for the meetings held in New York City on August 29, 30, and 31, and September 1, 1955, these 19 papers offer analysis of equality, in relation to law, society—local and international, education, and religion.)

The Ethic of Power: The Interplay of Religion, Philosophy and Politics, Sixteenth Symposium, 1962. Harold D. Lasswell and Harlan Cleveland, Editors. (Prepared for the meetings held in New York City on August 29, 30, and 31, and September 1, 1960, these 24 papers investigate the challenge to ethical values posed by an increasingly complex society.)

Ethics and Bigness: Scientific, Academic, Religious, Political, and Military, Seventeenth Symposium, 1962. Harlan Cleveland and Harold D. Lasswell, Editors. (Prepared for the meetings held in New York City on August 29, 30, and 31, and September 1, 1960, these 28 papers examine the responsibility of individual conscience within the large-scale organizations that characterize contemporary life.)

Program: THE INSTITUTE ON ETHICS OF
THE INSTITUTE FOR RELIGIOUS AND SOCIAL
STUDIES, THE JEWISH THEOLOGICAL
SEMINARY OF AMERICA

*"Considerations for an International Conference
on the Ethics of Mutual Involvement"*

HAROLD D. LASSWELL, *Chairman*
CLARENCE H. FAUST, *Co-Chairman*

TUESDAY, WEDNESDAY, and THURSDAY, AUGUST 29, 30, 31,
1961
THE MEN'S FACULTY CLUB, COLUMBIA UNIVERSITY, 400
WEST 117th STREET, NEW YORK CITY
All sessions will be held on the Second Floor of The Men's Faculty Club.
Discussions will center on issues arising from the background paper by
Stuart Gerry Brown, who drew on original material by Harlan Cleveland
and Richard P. McKeon and discussions in January, 1961.

Tuesday, August 29
9:15 a.m. Registration

9:30. Coffee

10:00 Substantive Session
Opening Statement
    CLARENCE H. FAUST

5:30 p.m. Cocktails

6:00. Dinner Meeting
Substantive Session

Wednesday, August 30
10:00 a.m. Substantive Session

5:30 p.m. Cocktails

6:00. Dinner Meeting
Strategic Session

Thursday, August 31
10:00 a.m. through noon luncheon
    CLARENCE H. FAUST, presiding
Session: "Special Problems of the World Academy of Ethics"

Participants In Program *

Stuart Gerry Brown, Maxwell Professor of American Civilization, Maxwell Graduate School of Citizenship and Public Affairs, Syracuse University

Carlos Chagas, Director, Instituto de Biofisica, Universidade do Brasil, Brazil

Harlan Cleveland, Assistant Secretary of State for International Organizations, United States Department of State

H. van B. Cleveland, John Hancock Mutual Life Insurance Company

Gerson D. Cohen, Assistant Professor of Jewish Literature and Institutions, The Jewish Theological Seminary of America

L. A. Costa Pinto, Professor de Sociologia, Faculdades de Economia e Filosofia, Universidade do Brasil, Brazil

Carlos Cueto-Fernandini, Chief of Education, Division of Education, Pan American Union

Orlando Fals Borda, Dean, Facultad De Sociologia, Universidad Nacional De Colombia, Colombia

Clarence H. Faust, Vice President, The Ford Foundation; President, Fund for the Advancement of Education; Director, The Institute on Ethics, 1958

Jessica Feingold, Executive Director, The Institute for Religious and Social Studies, The Jewish Theological Seminary of America

Louis Finkelstein, Chancellor and Solomon Schechter Professor of Theology, The Jewish Theological Seminary of America

Gino Germani, Professor de Sociologia, Universidad de Buenos Aires, Argentina

Simon Greenberg, Vice Chancellor and Professor of Homiletics and Education, The Jewish Theological Seminary of America

Charles M. Herzfeld, Acting Director, Heat Division, National Bureau of Standards

Hudson Hoagland, Executive Director, The Worcester Foundation for Experimental Biology

Alan R. Holmberg, Professor of Sociology and Anthropology, Cornell University

Robert O. Johann, S.J., Assistant Professor of Philosophy, College of Philosophy and Letters, Fordham University

F. Ernest Johnson, Study Consultant for the Department of Church and Economic Life, The National Council of Churches

* Writer of paper and comments and those hoping to attend as of August 10, 1961.

Harry W. Jones, Cardozo Professor of Jurisprudence, Columbia University

John LaFarge, S.J., Associate Editor, "America"

Harold D. Lasswell, Edward J. Phelps Professor of Law and Political Science, Yale University

Daniel Lerner, Ford Professor of Sociology, Massachusetts Institute of Technology

R. M. MacIver, Lieber Professor Emeritus of Political Philosophy and Sociology, Columbia University

Bernard Mandelbaum, Provost and Associate Professor of Homiletics, The Jewish Theological Seminary of America

Richard P. McKeon, Charles F. Grey Distinguished Service Professor of Philosophy and Greek, The University of Chicago

N. A. Nikam, Vice-Chancellor, University of Mysore, India

Roger L. Shinn, William E. Dodge, Jr., Professor of Applied Christianity, Union Theological Seminary

Seymour Siegel, Assistant Professor of Theology, The Jewish Theological Seminary of America

Punya Sloka Ray, Philosophy Lecturer in Residence, Yale University, 1960–1961, from India

Ribert Triffin, Pelatiah Perit Professor of Political and Social Sciences, Yale University

Heinrich A. Wieschhoff, Director, Political and Security Council Affairs, United Nations

The Institute on Ethics of
The Institute for Religious and Social Studies,
The Jewish Theological Seminary of America

The Institute office and that of the Conference on Science, Philosophy and Religion are located at The Jewish Theological Seminary of America, 3080 Broadway, New York 27, New York

The Institute on Ethics

The Institute on Ethics is an effort to study contemporary problems in their moral perspective.

At the first meeting of the Institute in June, 1956, some 20 noted scholars considered the issues raised by the idea of equal opportunity, investigating the implications and the moral principles which might help decide what equal opportunity is, when it applies, and when considerations other than equality should be taken into account. In pursuit of this inquiry, the members of the Institute studied each issue in the light of contemporary knowledge—in science, the social sciences, and general experience—as well as against the background of the wisdom preserved in the humane traditions, religious and philosophic.

This meeting was held at the Lake Mohonk Mountain House, Mohonk, New York, June 4–18, and at The Jewish Theological Seminary of America, June 18–29. At the Seminary, the participants were joined by the group of Fellows. On June 19, at a luncheon meeting of Institute participants and men of affairs at which Mr. Paul G. Hoffman presided, Mr. Henry R. Luce spoke of the need for such a study as the Institute was undertaking.

The six working papers developed by the Institute formed the basis for discussion at the Fifteenth Conference on Science, Philosophy and Religion held at Columbia University, August 27–31, 1956.

During the summer of 1958 the Institute considered problems of ethics illustrated in the population explosion, radiation, and manipulation of personality. Members of the original group were joined by scholars of widely differing background, for the first time including the Middle East and Far East, as well as the Western Hemisphere and Europe. On June 24, 1958, the Institute was host at a luncheon meeting with Dean Badiezaman Foruzanfar, Professor Sheykhol-Eslam, and Professor Seyed Mohammed-Bagher Sabzevari of the University of Tehran. Visitors later in the summer included the Venerable Induruwe Pannatissa of the Buddhist Academy in Colombo, and Doctor Serajul Haque of the University of Dacca.

His Highness, The Maharaja of Mysore, Chancellor of Mysore and Karnatak Universities, addressed a distinguished scholarly audience at a special luncheon meeting of The Institute on Ethics in the Dining Hall of The Jewish Theological Seminary of America, on April 20, 1959.

The Institute continues frequently to be host to distinguished foreign visitors, several returning for additional consultation. Members of the executive committee have met again with the Maharaja of Mysore both in 1960 and 1961.

During the summer of 1959, Scholars and Fellows of the Institute collaborated with Fellows of the Conference on Science, Philosophy and Religion in a four-day seminar on the problem, "One World—One Ethics?" From August 29 through September 1, 1960, the same group and others, including men of affairs and government officials, met at The Jewish Theological Seminary of America to discuss in greater detail "Challenges to Traditional Ethics: Government, Politics, and Administration." The sixty papers are to be published in 1962 in two volumes, edited by Professors Harold D. Lasswell and Harlan Cleveland.

These activities and the discussions between August 29 and 31, 1961, listed in this program, are expected to stimulate conferences in other parts of the world organized in cooperation with The Institute on Ethics.

Speaking recently on behalf of this enterprise, Ambassador Adlai E. Stevenson said: "I am proud and grateful to be identified with such healing scholarship . . . I see a great opportunity here to further the search for those enduring values which transcend the divisive friction between nations. While each country supports its national interests through an ethical rationalization, human progress can only be achieved if a way is found to identify the ethical ideas which are the basis for long range goals helpful to all men."

INDEX